MARKETS, MORALS AND THE LAW

MARKETS, MORALS AND THE LAW

Jules L. Coleman
Yale Law School

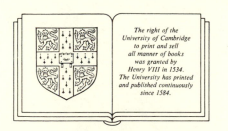

The right of the
University of Cambridge
to print and sell
all manner of books
was granted by
Henry VIII in 1534.
The University has printed
and published continuously
since 1584.

Cambridge University Press

CAMBRIDGE

NEW YORK   NEW ROCHELLE   MELBOURNE   SYDNEY

Published by the Press Syndicate of the University of Cambridge
The Pitt Building, Trumpington Street, Cambridge CB2 1RP
32 East 57th Street, New York, NY 10022, USA
10 Stamford Road, Oakleigh, Melbourne 3166, Australia

© Cambridge University Press 1988

First published 1988

Printed in the United States of America

Library of Congress of Cataloging-in-Publication Data
Coleman, Jules L.
Markets, morals and the law.
1. Law – Philosophy.   2. Law and ethics.   3. Torts –
Economic aspects.   I. Title.
K231.C65   1988   340′.1   88–6139
ISBN 0 521 36305 5 hard covers
ISBN 0 521 36854 5 paperback

British Library Cataloging in Publication applied for

For my father, Herbert Coleman,
and the memory of my mother, Beatrice Coleman

Contents

Preface

This collection brings together essays reflecting various directions my research interests have taken since I was crazy enough in 1971–2 to write a philosophy Ph.D. dissertation on no-fault automobile insurance. All of the chapters in this collection were published previously. All have been revised: some extensively, others nominally. Revisions were motivated by a desire to improve clarity and readability. Although my views have changed – for the better, I hope – I tried to preserve the arguments in their original sense and form. Each essay reflects my thinking at a particular stage of development, and each presents the best arguments I could muster at the time it was written. When it comes to taking responsibility for one's work, I'm a proponent of strict liability.

I have arranged the essays under four headings: "Law and Morality"; "Law and Economics"; "Torts, Crimes and Settlements"; and "Markets, Morals and Politics." Only the essays in Part I address the traditional subject matter of legal philosophy. The first chapter, "Negative and Positive Positivism," presents and defends a version of legal positivism. The essay relies on two distinctions: one between *epistemic* and *ontological* conceptions of the rule of recognition, the other between *negative* and *positive* positivism. The thesis I advance is that positivism is committed to the rule of recognition as a semantic or ontological rule only, and that its essential positive claim is that the authority of law everywhere is a matter of social convention. These points, taken together, make legal positivism both interesting and defensible.

The second chapter, "Rethinking the Theory of Legal Rights," was co-authored with my student Jody Kraus. The problem posed is this: The classical liberal theory of rights holds that rights protect or secure a domain of autonomy. To have a right is to have control or liberty over that to which one is entitled. Calabresi and others working within an economic framework have argued that rights can be secured either by property rules or by liability rules.

Property rules secure rights by entitling people who hold rights both to exclude others from making use of protected property and to transfer protected property on terms agreeable to them. Liability rules secure rights by giving *nonentitled* parties the freedom to take what right owners possess provided they compensate *ex post*. There is an apparent conflict, then, between liability rules and the classical liberal conception of rights. If liability rules confer upon nonentitled parties a liberty to take property without an entitled party's consent, and if rights are a secure domain of autonomy or control, how can liability rules protect rights? Should the conflict be resolved by giving up the claim that liability rules can, even in principle, protect rights, or by giving up the claim that rights are or secure liberties? This chapter offers a way of thinking about legal rights in which both *prima facie* plausible claims must be abandoned.

Chapter 2 introduces the economic analysis of law, but neither explains nor evaluates its central claims. Those tasks are taken up directly in Part II, "Law and Economics." Chapters 3, 4 and 5 address central problems in economic analysis. Economic analysis has both positive and normative dimensions. In both cases, the key concept is efficiency. But what does efficiency mean? Chapter 3, "Efficiency, Auction and Exchange," distinguishes between Pareto optimality, Pareto superiority and Kaldor–Hicks efficiency, and has an extended discussion of the Coase theorem. It was written for the novice, and readers unfamiliar with the basic claims and concepts of economic analysis may find it particularly useful.

One of the central claims in Chapter 3 is that the economic analysis of law relies largely on the Kaldor–Hicks criterion of efficiency, less on Pareto optimality and almost not at all on Pareto superiority. This is important, especially from a normative point of view. What justifies the use of public power, that is, courts, legislatures and administrative agencies, in pursuing efficiency? I like to think (immodestly, perhaps) that prior to the circulation and publication of "Efficiency, Auction and Exchange" the prevailing view was that economic analysis is grounded in utilitarian moral theory: Modern efficiency analysis is a grandchild of classical utilitarianism. In fact, the Pareto criteria, especially Pareto superiority, were first introduced to solve the interpersonal comparability problem of classical utilitarianism. Kaldor–Hicks was then introduced to extend the Pareto rankings. And so it would seem natural that one could justify economic analysis in utilitarian terms. "Efficiency, Auction and Exchange" changed all that, for reasons Richard Posner picked up quickly and which are made more explicit in Chapter 4, "Efficiency, Utility and Wealth Maximization."

Chapter 4 argues first that two states of affairs, S' and S, can be Kaldor–Hicks efficient to each other (the Scitovsky paradox), whereas S' and S cannot each contain more utility than the other. So from the fact that S' is Kaldor–Hicks efficient to S, we cannot infer that S' increases utility over S. If that inference were valid, we could be led to the contradictory conclusion that S and S' increase utility with respect to each other, which is inconceivable. Thus, a utilitarian defense of Kaldor–Hicks is not available.

Next, from the fact that a social state, S, is Pareto optimal, no inference about whether the move to it from a previous social state increases utility can be warranted – at least not without a standard of interpersonal comparability. Recall, however, that the Pareto criteria were introduced precisely because interpersonal comparisons were thought to be impossible. If interpersonal comparisons were possible, we could discover which moves to Pareto-optimal states increase utility and which do not. However, were interpersonal comparisons possible, there would be no need for the Pareto criteria!

The chapter goes on to show that only Pareto superiority bears the desired relationship to utilitarianism; that is, if S' is Pareto superior to S, then S' increases utility with respect to S. Unfortunately, by everyone's admission, Pareto superiority, for reasons the chapter details, is rarely, if ever, used in economic analysis. The rest of the chapter discusses at length various lines of defense for normative economic analysis.

James Buchanan, the 1986 Nobel laureate in economics, has always been something of a renegade among economists. Few philosophers, however, are familiar with Buchanan's work. That is unfortunate, for several reasons. First, he is one of the few economists openly to advocate economics as a normative social science. Second, he is a founding father of Public Choice as a field of study, an area of which philosophers, to their detriment, are largely ignorant. Third, John Rawls's book *A Theory of Justice* is openly indebted to Buchanan and Gordon Tullock's landmark work in social contract theory, *The Calculus of Consent*.[1]

Chapter 5, "The Foundations of Constitutional Economics," discusses the differences between Buchanan's "constitutional economics" and traditional efficiency analysis. Consider an argument for efficiency that I believe originated with Kaldor. Because a Pareto improvement makes no one worse off and at least one person better off, one could argue that everyone would *consent* to making

Pareto improvements. Thus, Paretianism can be defended on consensual grounds. In an effort to avoid the pitfalls of the utilitarian defense of Paretianism, lawyer economists like Posner have in fact turned to this sort of consent-based defense of efficiency. Buchanan stands this argument on its head. What makes a state of affairs efficient, he claims, is that everyone agrees or consents to it. *S* is efficient because it is consented to, rather than the other way round, as Kaldor's argument suggests. Both lines of argument seek to provide a foundational connection between efficiency and autonomy. In traditional Paretianism the link is justificatory; in Buchanan's work it is analytic.

The essays in Part III reflect my interests in law proper, that is, in criminal law, torts and civil procedure. For example, Chapter 6, "Crimes, Kickers and Transaction Structures," asks: Why have a criminal law at all? – a question philosophers of law have largely ignored.

Critics are quick to dismiss forms of strict liability as morally objectionable, as departures from the requirements of justice that are justifiable only in certain narrowly defined areas of law in which strict liability has strikingly positive effects on reducing the level of harmful activity. The prevailing view has it that strict liability is normally indefensible because justice prohibits us from penalizing people who cause harm through no fault of their own. I hold a contrary view. In Chapter 7, "The Morality of Strict Tort Liability," I argue that strict liability in *torts* is both defensible and central to all forms of tort liability. For example, the rule that injurers can be penalized only when they are at fault can be thought of as a form of strict *victim* liability. Under this rule, a victim bears a loss when an injurer's conduct is faultless, even though the victim may also have acted appropriately. In torts, then, the question is often which of two blameless parties ought to bear the costs of an accident; and so issues of strict liability, rather than being peripheral to tort law, are at its very core.

Chapter 8, "Corrective Justice and Wrongful Gain," summarizes the rest of my theory of torts, responds to objections from critics, especially Richard Posner, and previews the central argument of my forthcoming book *Accidents*.[2] Central to my account is a distinction between two questions: (1) What grounds a victim's claim to recovery? and (2) What justifies holding an injurer liable for the harms his conduct occasions? That these two questions are distinct, I argue, can be seen from the fact that a society could permit all victims to seek compensation for all injuries (other than injuries that are self-imposed) while providing that injurers can be held liable only when their conduct is faulty or negligent. Such an arrangement might be undesirable, but that would be a normative matter, not an analytic one. In other words, it is *not* analytic that compensation flows from an injurer to a victim. That is our tort practice; and, in my view, it is a practice that needs a defense. By distinguishing between the *grounds* and *modes* of rectification, I try to show how a scheme of no-fault liability can be made consistent with the demands of justice in liability.

Chapter 9, "Justice in Settlements," was co-authored with Charles Silver. Charlie was then studying with me at Yale, and he is now teaching law at the University of Texas. The chapter falls into two sections. In the first, we discuss the practice of settling disputes instead of fully litigating them. Since settlements often depart from the requirements of individual desert, the practice of encouraging settlements requires a defense. We argue that even though settlements are voluntarily agreed upon and are often made in the light of the parties' rational expectations of the outcome at trial, they may have several objectionable features. In the end, we do not deny that a policy of encouraging settlements may be desirable. We claim only that many questions that bear on the desirability of the policy remain unanswered.

We also point out that further questions of justice can arise after disputes settle, especially in certain categories of cases. The second half of "Justice in Settlements" discusses the most important of these categories: the class action. In it we ask whether compensatory or corrective justice demands that monies paid in settlement of class actions be distributed among class members, as the law currently requires. Our view is that in certain class actions which we call paradigm class actions justice does not require this result. Instead, the principle that people should be compensated for wrongfully inflicted losses leaves open the possibility that monies paid in settlement of paradigm class actions could be used in other ways, including ways that deprive class members of benefits entirely.

When we wrote the original essay, we thought the second part would prove controversial. So we wrote the first section as a general introduction to the debate and as a way of saying a few useful, noncontroversial but interesting things about the practice of encouraging settlements. As it happens, the entire paper has proved extremely controversial. Even prior to its publication, objections to it were published by Judge Frank Easterbrook.[3] The paper's arguments, even the ones we found least controversial, were met with resistance at workshops at the Chicago, Yale and North-western law schools. In fact, the arguments met with resistance whenever they were presented to lawyers. Because the essay raised doubts about a practice that conserves resources and enables parties to agree voluntarily, it rankled many lawyer economists who saw settlement agreements as mutually beneficial contracts. And because it challenged the priority of peace over justice, it bothered communitarians who viewed settlements as desirable means of reducing the damage disputes do to social relationships. Although our claims were heavily criticized by both the new Right and the new Left, we remain convinced that our arguments have merit, even if we have not yet succeeded in making their merit clear. Our commitment to the project is so strong that we have decided to discuss the moral issues settlements pose at greater length in what we hope will be a useful, and more widely accepted, book on the subject.[4] When we stand behind our arguments in the future, we hope not to stand alone.

Part IV contains four essays that reflect my continuing interest in the applicability of economic models to the analysis of nonmarket institutions. I am currently working on a book, *The Market Paradigm*,[5] that explores the extent to which nonmarket institutions can be explained and justified as responses to problems of market failure. These chapters reflect my interest in the problem of market failure in the political and moral domains.

Chapter 10, "Market Contractarianism," discusses two theories about legitimate political authority. The first is that political institutions are justified because they emerge as the outcome of a rational bargain among individuals who recognize the state of nature as a prisoners' dilemma. The state of nature thus constitutes a form of market failure, and coercive political institutions are justified as solutions to the problem of market failure. I call this thin market contractarianism. In contrast, thick market contractarianism is the view that political authority is justified not only to rectify market failure, but to make possible the conditions of market success – in the classical economic sense. This essay introduces in my work a move from classical economic models to more general rational choice models, especially bargaining theory. In the past five or six years, I have come to be impressed by the usefulness of modeling contractual relations, agreements and social choices as forms of rational bargaining. In "Market Contractarianism" I try to integrate formal bargaining theory into general concerns about political legitimacy – not always successfully. What I once saw largely as market failure problems, I now see as bargaining problems embedded in prisoners' dilemmas. This chapter is, perhaps, the least tightly argued and the most rambling and insecure of the collection. For that reason, it is the essay I find least satisfactory. But, my reservations notwithstanding, I also think the chapter contains some interesting points about the relationship between politics and economics, and I decided to include it for that reason. I'm certain that I've not yet figured out the best way to integrate game theory and bargaining theory into traditional political philosophy. I'll know more, I hope, before my book on the subject is completed.

Just about the same time that I began learning bargaining theory, I started reading in the area of formal social choice theory. It seemed to me that if we thought about legitimate political authority as the outcome of a rational social contract (rational bargaining in a state of nature), then legitimate institutions would be those chosen by rational bargainers. Our rational bargainers would have to choose a voting rule by which collective decisions would be made. But a rational choice *ex ante* would require an analysis of the likely consequences of various voting rules. Thus, the interest in social choice theory.

Chapters 11 and 12 take up, respectively, unanimity and majority rule, two different kinds of voting rules. Chapter 11 discusses the view that on both economic and moral grounds unanimity is the preferable voting rule. Unanimity captures the essential Paretian and consensual features of market exchange, and is thus uniquely defensible on both market and moral grounds. Departures from unanimity are unavoidable but must be seen as necessary evils. The usual criticism of unanimity is that it unjustifiably favors the status quo. In this chapter I ask whether unanimity actually bears the relationship to market exchange that its proponents take to justify it uniquely, a question I find more interesting.

If in most contexts we are required to accept less than unanimity, what voting rule is best? To answer this question we need to know something about the fairness and the mapping properties of various voting schemes. That is, we need to know whether the relationship between outcomes and individual preferences or judgments is, in a suitable sense, rational. This is the domain of social choice theory. What precisely does social choice theory tell us about the rationality of voting rules? What interpretations should we give to those results? Chapter 12, "Democracy and Social Choice," written with John Ferejohn, the mathematical political scientist, begins to answer that question. It is cast as a response to the work of William Riker, who has argued that social choice theory undermines the coherence of populist democratic theory and makes plausible only a very weak form of Madisonian liberalism. In Riker's view, voting is legitimate and desirable only because it enables us to remove officials, thereby constraining their ability arbitrarily to constrain our liberty over time.

Chapter 13, "Morality and the Theory of Rational Choice," written with Jody Kraus, considers the possibility of analyzing morality as a solution to the problem of market failure. Given what I have already said, this entails viewing morality as the outcome of a rational bargain nested in a prisoners' dilemma. Can morality be the outcome of a rational bargain? David Gauthier thinks so. This chapter, which was written as part of a symposium devoted to Gauthier's wonderful book *Morals by Agreement,* takes up the possibility of deriving morality from rationality. Whatever the specific shortcomings of Gauthier's argument, its great power is in seeing the deeply instrumental nature of morality. Morality is a social construct devised to solve problems that arise from the logical structure of human interaction. Like much of our normative life, a defensible morality is tied up with mutual advantage in ways the market failure–prisoners' dilemma paradigm enables us to see – to which other ways of modeling the problem blind us.

My education did not end when I received my Ph.D., or when I received my M.S.L. either. Indeed, because I went to Rockefeller University, I received a Ph.D. degree without the benefit of a traditional education. What I learned at Rockefeller was how to learn from one's peers and colleagues, a lesson I like to think I learned fairly well. In this regard, I'd like to thank Brian Barry, Michael Bayles, Lea Brilmayer, Ronald Coase, Robert Cooter, Donald Davidson, Ronald Dworkin, Jon Elster, Richard Epstein, Owen Fiss, David Gauthier, Allan Gibbard, Henry Hansmann, Russell Hardin, Alvin Klevorick, John Koethe, Tony Kronman, Keith Lehrer, David Lyons, Ned McClennen, David Malament, Steve Maser, Steve Munzer, Jeffrie Murphy, Jim Nickel, Robert Prichard, George Priest, John Rawls, Joseph Raz, William Riker, Roberta Romano, Alan Schwartz, Julius Sensat, Judith J. Thomson, Michael Trebilcock, Richard Wasserstrom and Ernie Weinrib.

I am especially indebted, in ways I cannot fully or adequately articulate, to James Buchanan, John Ferejohn, Sandy Kadish, A. Mitchell Polinsky, Richard Posner and Norman Schofield, all of whom – no doubt unbeknownst to them – have had in me an eager, earnest and grateful postgraduate student. Joel Feinberg directed my dissertation at Rockefeller and was my colleague at the

University of Arizona. Guido Calabresi, my mentor while I was a student at Yale Law School, is my colleague at Yale. These two giants in their fields remain the two most influential people in my academic life. I would like to make special mention, however, of Paul W. Taylor. Paul was my first philosophy teacher at Brooklyn College. He was a subtle and quietly inspirational teacher. He taught me not only how to do philosophy, but to respect the doing of it.

I have had the benefit of several talented students. So great has been their contribution to my own thinking that two of them, Jody Kraus and Charles Silver, forced me to rethink the meaning of the teacher–student relationship. I have come to regard them not just as my peers, but as part of my family.

In the preparation of this manuscript I am especially indebted to Charles Silver. Charlie standardized more than a dozen manuscripts that originally appeared in a variety of different formats, edited and proofread the drafts, suggested improvements, and did everything thoughtfully, quickly and professionally.

The support staff at Yale has been wonderful. I am especially grateful to Carmelita Morales for her help in preparing the manuscript for publication, and to Dean Stephen Yandle for making other Yale resources available to me.

There aren't many people who could put up with my highly strung, obsessive personality, my peculiar and suspicious tastes and my passions for rock 'n' roll, TV and golf. I like to joke, following the line from the film *Morgan,* that my wife, Mimsie, married me to achieve insecurity. That much I'm sure I've given her. What Mimsie has given me cannot be expressed here, except to say that what is in this book, and indeed in everything else I've written, is at the deepest level her doing.

I had hoped to complete this book in time for publication prior to my mother's death. Unfortunately, my mother passed away recently after suffering through a long, gruesome illness that ravaged her body. It never, however, ravaged her spirit or her soul. Though lacking any advanced formal education, she was my most inspiring teacher. From her I learned the value of hard work, perseverance, grace under pressure and self-effacing good humor. Most of all I learned the importance of family, friendship and commitment. I shall miss her.

Yale Law School   Jules L. Coleman
New Haven, Connecticut

Acknowledgments

"Negative and Positive Positivism" is reprinted from *Journal of Legal Studies* 11 (1982): 139 by permission of the University of Chicago Press.

"Rethinking the Theory of Legal Rights" is reprinted from *Yale Law Journal* 95 (1986): 1335 by permission of The Yale Law Journal Company and Fred B. Rothman & Company.

"Efficiency, Auction and Exchange" is reprinted from *California Law Review* 68 (1980) 221 by permission of The Regents of the University of California. Copyright 1980 by The Regents of the University of California.

"Efficiency, Utility and Wealth Maximization" is reprinted from *Hofstra Law Review* 8 (1980) 509–551 by permission of *Hofstra Law Review*.

"The Foundations of Constitutional Economics" is reprinted from *Constitutional Economics: Containing the Economic Powers of Government,* ed. Richard B. McKenzie (1984), p. 141, by permission of D. C. Heath & Company. Copyright 1984 by D. C. Heath & Company.

"Crimes, Kickers and Transaction Structures" is reprinted from *Criminal Justice: Nomos XXVII,* ed. J. Roland Pennock and John W. Chapman (1985), p. 313, by permission of New York University Press. Copyright 1985 by New York University.

"The Morality of Strict Tort Liability" is reprinted from *William and Mary Law Review* 18 (1976) 259 by permission of *William and Mary Law Review*.

"Corrective Justice and Wrongful Gain" is reprinted from *Journal of Legal Studies* 11 (1982) 421 by permission of the University of Chicago Press.

"Justice in Settlements" is reprinted from *Social Philosophy and Policy* 4 (1986) 102 by permission of the Social Philosophy & Policy Center.

"Market Contractarianism" and "Unanimity" are reprinted from *Social Philosophy and Policy* 2 (1985) 69 by permission of the Social Philosophy & Policy Center.

"Democracy and Social Choice" is reprinted from *Ethics* 97 (1986) 6–25 by permission of the University of Chicago Press.

"Morality and the Theory of Rational Choice" is reprinted from *Ethics* 97 (July 1987) 715 by permission of the University of Chicago Press.

PART I

Law and morality

1. Negative and positive positivism

1. INTRODUCTION

Every theory about the nature or essence of law purports to provide a standard, usually in the form of a statement of necessary and sufficient conditions, for determining which of a community's norms constitute its law. For example, the naive version of legal realism maintains that the law of a community is constituted by the official pronouncements of judges. For the early positivists like Austin, law consists in the commands of a sovereign, properly so called. For substantive natural law theory, in every conceivable legal system, being a true principle of morality is a necessary condition of legality for at least some norms. Legal positivism of the sort associated with H. L. A. Hart maintains that, in every community where law exists, there exists a standard that determines which of the community's norms are legal ones. Following Hart, this standard is usually referred to as a rule of recognition. If all that positivism meant by a rule of recognition were "the standard in every community by which a community's legal norms were made determinate," every theory of law would be reducible to one or another version of positivism. Which form of positivism each would take would depend on the particular substantive conditions of legality that each theory set out. Legal positivism would be true analytically, since it would be impossible to conceive of a theory of law that did not satisfy the minimal condition for a rule of recognition. Unfortunately, the sort of truth legal positivism would then reveal would be an uninteresting one.

In order to distinguish a rule of recognition in the positivist sense from other statements of the conditions of legality, and therefore to distinguish positivism from alternative jurisprudential theses, additional constraints must be placed on the rule of recognition. Candidates for these constraints fall into two categories: (1) restrictions on the conditions of legality set out in a rule of recognition and (2) constraints on the possible sources of authority (or normativity) of the rule of recognition.

An example of the first sort of constraint is expressed by the requirement that in every community the conditions of legality must be ones of pedigree or form, not substance or content. Accordingly, for a rule specifying the conditions of legality in any society to constitute a rule of recognition in the positivist sense, legal normativity under it must be determined, for example, by a norm's being enacted in the requisite fashion by a proper authority.

The claim that the authority of the rule of recognition is a matter of its acceptance by officials rather than its truth as a normative principle, and the related claim that judicial duty under a rule of recognition is one of conventional practice rather than critical morality, express constraints of the second sort.

Ronald Dworkin expresses this second constraint as the claim that a rule of recognition in the positivist sense must be a social, rather than a normative, rule. A social rule is one whose authority is a matter of convention; the nature and scope of the duty it imposes are specified or constituted by an existing, convergent social practice. In contrast, a normative rule may impose an obligation or confer a right in the absence of the relevant practice or in the face of a contrary one. If a normative rule imposes an obligation, it does so because it is a correct principle of morality, not, *ex hypothesi,* because it corresponds to an accepted practice.

Dworkin, for one, conceives of the rule of recognition as subject to constraints of both sorts. His view is that only pedigree standards of legality can constitute rules of recognition, and that a rule of recognition must be a social rule.[1] Is legal positivism committed to either or both of these constraints on the rule of recognition?

2. NEGATIVE POSITIVISM

Candidates for constraints on the rule of recognition are motivated by the need to distinguish legal positivism from other jurisprudential theses: in particular, natural law theory. Positivism denies what natural law theory asserts, namely, a necessary connection between law and morality. I refer to the denial of a necessary or constitutive relationship between law and morality as the separability thesis. One way of asking whether positivism is committed to any particular kind of constraint on the rule of recognition is simply to ask whether any constraints on the rule are required by commitment to the separability thesis.

To answer this question we have to make some preliminary remarks concerning how we are to understand both the rule of recognition and the separability thesis. The notion of a rule of recognition is ambiguous; it has both an epistemic and a semantic sense. In one sense, the rule of recognition is a standard that one can use to identify, validate or discover a community's law. In another sense, the rule of recognition specifies the conditions a norm must satisfy to constitute part of a community's law. The same rule may or may not be a rule of recognition in both senses, since the rule one employs to determine the law need not be the same rule as the one that makes law determinate. This ambiguity between the epistemic and semantic interpretations of the rule of recognition pervades the literature and is responsible for a good deal of confusion about the essential claims of legal positivism. In my view, legal positivism is committed to the rule of recognition in the semantic sense at least; whether it is committed to the rule of recognition as a standard for identifying law (epistemic sense) is a question to which we shall return later.[2]

In the language that is fashionable in formal semantics, to say that the rule of recognition is a semantic rule is to say that it specifies the truth conditions for singular propositions of law of the form "It is the law in C that P," where C is a particular community and P a putative statement of law. The question whether the separability thesis imposes substantive constraints on the rule of recognition is just the question whether the separability thesis restricts the conditions of legality for norms or the truth conditions for propositions of law.

The separability thesis is the claim that there exists at least one conceivable rule of recognition (and therefore one possible legal system) that does not specify truth as a moral principle among the truth conditions for any proposition of law.[3] Consequently, a particular rule of recognition may specify truth as a moral principle as a truth condition for some or all propositions of law without violating the separability thesis, since it does not follow from the fact that in one community in order to be law a norm must be a principle of morality that being a true principle of morality is a necessary condition of legality in all possible legal systems.

It is tempting to confuse the separability thesis with the very different claim that the law of a community is one thing and its morality another. This last claim is seriously ambiguous. In one sense, the claim that the law of a community is one thing and its morality another may amount to the very strong assertion that there exists no convergence between the norms that constitute a community's law and those that constitute its morality. Put this way, the thesis is an empirical one whose inadequacies are demonstrated by the shared legal and moral prohibitions against murder, theft, battery and the like.

Instead, the claim may be that one can identify or discover a community's law without having recourse to discovering its morality. This is an epistemic claim about how, in a particular community, one might go about learning the law. It may well be that in some communities – even those in which every legal norm is a moral principle as well – one can learn which norms are law without regard to their status as principles of morality. Whether in every community this is the case depends on the available sources of legal knowledge, not on the existence of a conceptual relationship, if any, between law and morality.

A third interpretation of the thesis that a community's law is one thing and its morality another, the one Dworkin is anxious to ascribe to positivism, is that being a moral principle is not a truth condition for any proposition of law (in any community). Put this way the claim would be false, just in case "It is the law in C that P" (for any community, C, and any proposition of law, P) were true only if P stated a (true) principle of morality. Were the separability thesis understood this way, it would require particular substantive constraints on each rule of recognition; that is, no rule of recognition could specify truth as a moral principle among its conditions of legality. Were legal positivism committed to both the rule of recognition and to this interpretation of the claim that the law and morality of a community are distinct, Dworkin's arguments in Model of Rules I (MOR-I) would suffice to put it to rest.

However, were the claim that the law of a community is one thing and its morality another understood, not as the claim that in every community law and morality are distinct, but as the assertion that they are conceptually distinguishable, it would be reducible to the separability thesis, for it would assert no more than the denial of a constitutive relationship between law and morality.

In sum, the phrase "the law of a community is one thing and its morality another" makes either a false factual claim or an epistemic claim about the sources of legal knowledge, or else it is reducible to the separability thesis. In no case does it warrant substantive constraints on particular rules of recognition.

Properly understood and adequately distinguished from the claim that the law and morality of a community are distinct, the separability thesis does not warrant substantive constraints on any particular rule of recognition. It does not follow, however, that the separability thesis imposes no constraints at all on any rule of recognition. The separability thesis commits positivism to the proposition that there exists at least one conceivable legal system in which the rule of recognition does not specify being a principle of morality among the truth conditions for any proposition of law. Positivism is true, then, just in case we can imagine a legal system in which being a principle of morality is not a condition of legality for any norm: that is, just as long as the idea of a legal system in which moral truth is not a necessary condition of legal validity is not self-contradictory.

The form of positivism generated by commitment to the rule of recognition as constrained by the separability thesis I call negative positivism to draw attention to both the character and the weakness of the claim it makes.[4] Because negative positivism is essentially a negative thesis, it cannot be undermined by counterexamples, any one of which would show only that, in some community or other, morality is a condition of legality at least for some norms.

3. POSITIVE POSITIVISM: LAW AS HARD FACTS

In MOR-I, Dworkin persuasively argues that in some communities moral principles have the force of law, though what makes them law is their truth or their acceptance as appropriate to the resolution of controversial disputes rather than their having been enacted in the appropriate way by the relevant authorities. These arguments would suffice to undermine positivism were it committed to the claim that truth as a moral principle could never constitute a truth condition for a proposition of law under any rule of recognition. The arguments are inadequate to undermine the separability thesis, however, because the separability thesis makes no claim about the truth conditions of any particular proposition of law in any particular community. The arguments in MOR-I, therefore, are inadequate to undermine negative positivism.

However, Dworkin's target in MOR-I is not really negative positivism; it is that version of positivism one would get by conjoining the rule of recognition with the requirement that the truth conditions for any proposition of law could not include reference to the morality of a norm. Moreover, in fairness to Dworkin, one has to evaluate his arguments in a broader context. In MOR-I Dworkin is anxious to demonstrate not only the inadequacy of the

separability thesis, but that of other essential tenets of positivism
– or at least what Dworkin takes to be essential features of positivism – as well.

The fact that moral principles have the force of law, because
they are appropriate, true or accepted even though they are not
formally enacted, establishes for Dworkin that (1) the positivist's
conception of law as rules must be abandoned; as must (2) the
claim that judges exercise discretion – the authority to extend beyond the law to appeal to moral principles – to resolve controversial cases; and (3) the view that the law of every community can
be identified by use of a noncontroversial or pedigree test of legality.

The first claim of positivism must be abandoned because principles, as well as rules, constitute legal norms; the second because,
while positivists conceive of judges as exercising discretion by appealing to moral principles, Dworkin rightly characterizes them
as appealing to moral principles, which, though they are not rules,
nevertheless may be binding legal standards. The third tenet of
positivism must be abandoned because the rule of recognition in
Dworkin's view must be one of pedigree, that is, it cannot make
reference to the content or truth of a norm as a condition of its
legality; and any legal system that includes moral principles among
its legal standards cannot have as its standard of authority a pedigree criterion.[5]

The question, of course, is whether positivism is committed to
judicial discretion, to the model of rules or to a pedigree or uncontroversial standard of legality. We know at least that it is committed to the separability thesis, from which only negative positivism
appears to follow. Negative positivism is committed to none of
these claims. Is there another form of positivism that is so committed?

Much of the debate between the positivists and Dworkin appears rather foolish, unless there is a version of positivism that
makes Dworkin's criticism, if not compelling, at least relevant.
That version of positivism, whatever it is, cannot be motivated by
the separability thesis alone. The question, then, is what other than
its denial of the central tenet of natural law theory motivates positivism?

One easy, but ultimately unsatisfying, response is to maintain
that Dworkin's objections are to Hart's version of positivism. While
this is no doubt true, such a remark gives no indication of what it
is in Hart's version of positivism that is essential to positivism
generally. Dworkin, after all, takes his criticisms of Hart to be

criticisms of positivism generally, and the question remains whether positivism is committed to the essentials of Hart's version of it.

A more promising line of argument is the following. No doubt positivism is committed to the separability thesis. Still, one can ask whether commitment to the separability thesis is basic or derivative of some other, perhaps programmatic, commitments of legal positivism. That is, one can look at the separability thesis in isolation or as a component, perhaps even a derivative element, of a network of commitments of legal positivism.[6] We are led to negative positivism when we pursue the former route. Perhaps there is a more interesting form of positivism in the cards if we pursue the latter.

Certainly one reason some positivists have insisted upon the distinction between law and morality is the following: While both law and morality provide standards by which the affairs of people are to be regulated, morality is inherently controversial. People disagree about what morality prescribes, and uncertainty exists concerning the limits of permissible conduct and the nature and scope of one's moral obligations to others. In contrast, for these positivists at least, law is apparently concrete and uncontroversial. Moreover, when a dispute arises over whether or not something is law, there exists a decision procedure that, in the bulk of cases, settles the issue. Law is knowable and ascertainable; so that, while a person may not know the range of his moral obligations, he is aware of (or can find out) what the law expects of him. Commitment to the traditional legal values associated with the rule of law requires that law consist in knowable, largely uncontroversial fact; and it is this feature of law that positivism draws attention to and that underlies it.

One can reach the same characterization of law as consisting in uncontroversial, hard facts by ascribing to legal positivism the epistemological and semantic constraints of logical positivism on legal facts. For the logical positivists, moral judgments were meaningless, because they could not be verified by a reliable and essentially uncontroversial test. In order for statements of law to be meaningful, they must be verifiable by such a test (the epistemic conception of the rule of recognition). To be meaningful, therefore, law cannot be essentially controversial.

Once positivism is characterized as the view of law as consisting in hard facts, Dworkin's ascription of certain basic tenets to it is plausible, and his objections to them are compelling. First, law for positivism consists in rules rather than principles, because the legality of a rule depends on its formal characteristics – the manner

and form of its enactment – whereas the legality of a moral principle will depend on its content. The legality of rules, therefore,
will be essentially uncontroversial; the legal normativity of principles will be essentially controversial. Second, adjudication takes
place in both hard and simple cases. Paradigm or simple cases are
uncontroversial. The answer to them as a matter of law is clear,
and the judge is obligated to provide it. Cases falling within the
penumbra of a general rule, however, are uncertain. There is no
uncontroversial answer as a matter of law to them, and judges
must go beyond the law to exercise their discretion in order to
resolve them. Controversy implies the absence of legal duty, and
to the extent to which legal rules have controversial instances,
positivism is committed to a theory of discretion in the resolution
of disputes involving them. Third, positivism must be committed
to a rule of recognition in both the epistemic and the semantic
senses, for the rule of recognition not only sets out the conditions
of legality, it provides the mechanism by which one settles disputes about what, on a particular matter, the law is. The rule of
recognition for the positivist is the principle by which particular
propositions of law are verified. Relatedly, the condition of legality set forth in the rule of recognition must be ones of pedigree or
form; otherwise the norm will fail to provide a reliable principle
for verifying and adjudicating competing claims about the law.
Finally, law and morality are distinct (the separability thesis) because law consists in hard facts, while morality does not.

Unfortunately for positivism, if the distinction between law and
morality is motivated by commitment to law as uncontroversial,
hard facts, it must be abandoned because, as Dworkin rightly argues, law is controversial, and even where controversial may involve matters of obligation and right rather than discretion.

There is no more plausible way of understanding Dworkin's
conception of positivism and of rendering his arguments against it
(at least those in MOR-I) persuasive. The result is a form of positive positivism that makes an interesting claim about the essence
of law – that by and large law consists in hard, concrete facts – a
claim that Dworkin neatly shows is mistaken. The entire line of
argument rests, however, on ascribing to legal positivism either a
programmatic or a metaphysical thesis about law. It is the thesis
of law as hard facts – whether motivated by semantic, epistemic
or normative arguments – that explains not only positivism's
commitment to the separability thesis, but its adherence to other
claims about law, that is, discretion, the model of rules and the
noncontentful standard of legality.

The argument for law as hard facts that relies on the positivist program of knowable, ascertainable law is straightforwardly problematic. Legal positivism makes a conceptual or analytic claim about law, and that claim should not be confused with programmatic or normative interests certain positivists, especially Bentham, might have had. Ironically, to hold otherwise is to build into the conceptual account of law a particular normative theory of law; it is to infuse morality – the way law ought to be – into the concept of law – or the account of the way law is. In other words, the argument for ascribing certain tenets to positivism in virtue of the positivist's normative ideal of law is to commit the very mistake positivism is so intent on drawing attention to and rectifying.

The argument for law as hard facts that relies not on the programmatic interest of some positivists but on the semantics and epistemology of logical positivism is both more plausible and more interesting. Hart's characterization of his inquiry as an analysis both of the concept of law and of how one determines if a norm constitutes valid law as if these were one and the same thing suggests a conflation of semantic and epistemic inquiries of the sort one associates with logical positivism. Recall, in this regard, Hart's discussion of the move from the "prelegal" to the "legal." The move from the prelegal to the legal is accomplished by the addition of secondary rules to the set of primary social rules of obligation: in particular, by the addition of a rule of recognition that solves the problem of uncertainty, that is, the epistemic problem of determining which norms are law. Moreover, Hart's discussion of judicial discretion – that is, the absence of legal duty – as arising whenever the application of a general term in a rule of law is controversial further suggests the identification, for Hart at least, of law with fact ascertainable by the use of the reliable method of verification. Still, in order to justify the ascription to positivism of the view that law consists in hard facts, we need an argument to the effect that part of what it means to be a legal positivist is to be committed to some form of verificationism.

The problem with any such argument is that the separability thesis can stand on its own as a fundamental tenet of positivism without further motivation. After all, verificationism may be wrong and the separability thesis right; without fear of contradiction one can assert both a (metaphysical) realist position about legal facts and the separability thesis. (As an aside, this fact alone should suffice to warrant caution in ascribing logical positivism to legal positivism on the ground that they are both forms of positivism; otherwise one might be tempted to ascribe metaphysical or scientific realism to legal realism on similar grounds, which, to say the least, would be preposterous.)[7] In short, one alleging to be a positivist can abandon the metaphysics of verificationism, hang on to the separability thesis and advance the rather plausible position that the motive for the separability thesis – if indeed there is one – is simply that the distinction it insists on between law and morality is a valid one; and, just in case that is not enough, the positivist can point out that there is a school of jurisprudence that denies the existence of the distinction. In effect, the positivist can retreat to negative positivism and justify his doing so by pointing out that the separability thesis needs no further motivation, certainly none that winds up committing the advocate of a sound jurisprudential thesis to a series of dubious metaphysical ones.

While I am sympathetic to this response, it is not going to satisfy Dworkin. There is something unsatisfactory about a theory of law that does not make an affirmative claim about law. Indeed, one might propose as an adequacy condition that any theory of law must have a point about law. Negative positivism fails to satisfy this adequacy condition. Natural law theory satisfies it by asserting that in every conceivable legal system moral truth is a necessary condition of legality – at least for some norms. Since negative positivism consists in the denial of this claim, it makes no assertion about what is true of law in every conceivable legal system. The view Dworkin rightly ascribes to Hart, but wrongly to legal positivists generally, that the point of positivism is that law consists in hard facts, meets the adequacy condition and makes the kind of claim, mistaken though it may be, that one can sink one's teeth into.

I want to offer an alternative version of positivism that, like the law-as-hard-facts conception, is a form of positive positivism. The form of positive positivism I want to characterize and defend has, as its point, not that law is largely uncontroversial – it need not be – but that law is ultimately conventional: that the authority of law is a matter of its acceptance by officials.

4. POSITIVE POSITIVISM: LAW AS SOCIAL CONVENTION

It is well known that one can meet the objections to positivism Dworkin advances in MOR-I by constructing a rule of recognition (in the semantic sense) that permits moral principles as well as rules to be binding legal standards.[8] Briefly, the argument is this: Even if some moral principles are legally binding, not every moral principle is a legal one. Therefore, a test must exist for distinguishing moral principles that are legally binding from those that are not. The characteristic of legally binding moral principles that distinguishes them from nonbinding moral principles can be captured in a clause in the relevant rule of recognition. In other words, a rule is a legal rule if it possesses characteristic C; and a moral principle is a legal principle if it possesses characteristic C_1. The rule of recognition then states that a norm is a legal one if and only if it possesses either C or C_1. Once this rule of recognition is formulated, everything Dworkin ascribes to positivism, other than the model of rules, survives. The (semantic) rule of recognition survives, since whether a norm is a legal one does not depend on whether it is a rule or a principle but on whether it satisfies the conditions of legality set forth in a rule of recognition. The separability thesis survives just so long as not every conceivable legal system has in its rule of recognition a C_1 clause – that is, a clause that sets out conditions of legality for some moral principles – or if it has such a clause, there exists at least one conceivable legal system in which no principle satisfies that clause. Finally, one argument for judicial discretion – the one that relies not on controversy but on the exhaustibility of legal standards – survives. That is, only a determinate number of standards possess either C or C_1, so that a case may arise in which no legal standard under the rule of recognition is suitable or adequate to its resolution. In such cases, judges must appeal to nonlegal standards to resolve disputes.[9]

Given Dworkin's view of positivism as law consisting in hard facts, he might simply object to this line of defense by noting that the "rule of recognition" formed by the conjunction of the conditions of legality for both principles and rules could not be a rule of recognition in the positivist sense, because its reference to morality would make it inherently controversial. Put another way, a controversial rule of recognition could not be a rule of recognition in the epistemic sense; it could not provide a reliable verification principle. For that reason, it could not be a rule of recognition in the positivist sense. Interestingly, that is not quite the argument Dworkin advances. To be sure, he argues that a rule of recognition of this sort could not constitute a rule of recognition in the positivist sense. Moreover, he argues that such a rule would be inherently controversial. But the argument does not end with the allegation that such a rule would be controversial. The controversial character of the rule is important for Dworkin, not because it is incompatible with law as hard fact or because a controversial

rule cannot be a reliable verification principle, but because a controversial rule of recognition cannot be a social rule. A controversial rule of recognition cannot be a conventional one, or one whose
authority depends on its acceptance.

At the outset of the essay I distinguished between two kinds of
constraints that might be imposed on the rule of recognition: those
having to do with substantive conditions of legality and those having to do with the authority of the rule of recognition itself. The
difference between Dworkin's arguments against positivism in
MOR-I and Model of Rules II (MOR-II) is that, in the former
essay, the version of positivism he objects to is constrained in the
first way – legality must be determined by a noncontentful (or
pedigree) test – whereas the version of positivism he objects to in
MOR-II is constrained in the second way – the rule of recognition's authority must be a matter of convention.

Against the law-as-convention version of positivism, Dworkin
actually advances four related arguments, none of which, I want
to argue, is ultimately convincing. These are what I shall refer to
as (1) the social rule argument; (2) the pedigree argument; (3) the
controversy argument; and (4) the moral argument.[10]

4.1. The social rule argument

Legal obligations are imposed by valid legal norms. A rule or
principle is a valid one provided it satisfies the conditions of legality set forth in the rule of recognition. The question Dworkin raises
in MOR-II concerns the nature of duties under the rule of recognition itself. Does the rule of recognition impose duties on judges
because they accept it or because the rule is defensible within a
more comprehensive moral theory of law? For Dworkin this is
the question of whether the rule of recognition is a social or a
normative rule.

Dworkin's first argument in MOR-II against law-as-convention
positivism is that the social rule theory provides an inadequate
general theory of duty. The argument is this: According to the
social rule theory, an individual has an obligation to act in a particular way only if (1) there is a general practice of acting in that
way and (2) the rule that is constructed or built up from the practice is accepted from an internal point of view. To accept a rule
from an internal point of view is to use it normatively as providing
reasons both for acting in accordance with it and for criticizing
departures from it. But as Dworkin rightly notes, there may be
duties even where no social practice exists, or where a contrary

practice prevails. This is just another way of saying that not every duty is one of conventional morality.

If the positivist's thesis is that the social rule theory provides an adequate account of the source of all noninstitutional duties or of the meaning of all claims about such duties, it is surely mistaken. Not all duties imposed by rules are imposed by conventional rules. Fortunately, the law-as-convention version of positivism makes no such claim. The question is not whether the social rule theory is adequate to account for duties generally; it is whether the theory accounts for the duty of judges under a rule of recognition. An inadequate general theory of obligation may be an adequate theory of judicial duty. Were one to take the social rule argument seriously, it would amount to the odd claim that the rule of recognition could not be a social rule and, therefore, that obligations under it could not be ones of conventional morality, simply because not every duty-imposing rule is a social rule.

4.2. The pedigree argument

The first serious argument Dworkin makes against the social rule theory of judicial obligation relies, in part, on the argument in MOR-I. In meeting the objection to MOR-I, I constructed a rule of recognition that set out distinct conditions of legality for both rules *(C)* and moral principles C_1*).* Let us abbreviate this rule as "*C* and C_1." Dworkin's claim is that such a rule cannot be a social rule.

The argument is this: The truth conditions in "*C* and C_1" make reference to moral principles as well as to legal rules. Unlike legal rules, moral principles cannot be identified by their pedigree. Because determining which of a community's moral principles are legal ones requires reliance upon the content of principles, controversy over legality will naturally arise. But if there is substantial controversy, then there cannot be convergence of behavior sufficient to specify a social rule. The social rule theory requires convergence of behavior, that is, a social practice. A nonpedigree standard implies controversy; controversy implies the absence of a social practice; the absence of the requisite social practice means that the rule cannot be a social rule. A rule of recognition that made reference to morality – the kind of rule of recognition we constructed to overcome Dworkin's objections in MOR-I – could not be a social rule and, therefore, could not be a rule of recognition in the positivist sense.

The argument moves too quickly. Not every reference that a

rule of recognition might make to morality would be inherently controversial. It does not follow from the fact that "C and C_1" refers to moral principles that this rule cannot determine legality in virtue of some noncontentful characteristic of moral principles. For example, C_1 could be an "entrenchment" requirement of the sort Rolf Sartorius has proposed, so that whether a moral principle is a legal principle will depend on whether it is mentioned in preambles to legislation and in other authoritative documents: the more mentions, the more weight the principle receives.[11] Or C_1 could state that a moral principle is a legal principle only if it is widely shared by members of the community. In short, the legality of a moral principle could be determined by some of its noncontentful characteristics. In such cases, to determine which moral principles are legally binding would be no more troublesome or controversial than to determine which rules are legal ones.

Though not every reference to morality will render a rule of recognition controversial, some ways of identifying which of a community's moral principles are law will. Suppose C_1 makes moral truth a condition of legality, so that a moral principle could not be part of a community's law unless it were true. Whereas its entrenchment is not a controversial characteristic of a moral principle, its truth is. Any rule of recognition that made moral truth a condition of legality would be controversial. A controversial rule of recognition results in divergence of behavior sufficient to undermine its claim to being a social rule. If a rule of recognition is not a social rule, it cannot be a rule of recognition in the positivist sense.

Not every possible rule of recognition, therefore, would be a social rule. For example, the rule "the law is whatever is morally right" could never be a rule of recognition in the positivist sense. Because positivism of the sort I want to defend holds that law is everywhere conventional – that (in the language of this discussion) the rule of recognition in every community is a social rule – it must be mistaken.

4.3. The controversy argument

Dworkin's view is that the rule of recognition in any jurisdiction is either a social rule or a normative rule; it imposes a duty, in other words, either because it is accepted or because it is true. Law-as-convention positivism is the view that, in every community, the rule of recognition is a social rule. At this level, negative positivism is the view that, in at least one conceivable community, the rule of recognition is a social rule. Natural law theory would then be the view that, in every conceivable legal system, the rule of recognition is a normative rule. Dworkin's claim is that the rule of recognition is a normative rule, and therein lies the justification for placing him within the natural law tradition.

The argument of the previous section is compatible with some rules of recognition being normative rules and others being social rules. For example, a rule of recognition that made no reference to morality or, if it did, referred only to noncontentful features of moral principles, might, for all that the previous argument shows, still be a social rule. If it were, Dworkin's arguments, based on the controversial nature of rules of recognition that refer to morality, would be inadequate to establish the normative theory of law.

What Dworkin needs is an argument that no rule of recognition can be a social rule: that regardless of the conditions of legality it sets forth, no rule of recognition can account for certain features of law unless it is a normative rule. Dworkin has such an argument and it appears to be this: Regardless of the specific conditions of legality it sets forth, every rule of recognition will give rise to controversy at some point. For example, a rule that made no reference to morality could still give rise to controversy concerning either the weight to be given to precedent or the question of whether – and if so, to what extent – the present legislature could bind a future one. Though the rule itself would not be controversial, particular instances of it would be. Were the rule of recognition a social rule, it could not impose duties on judges in such controversial applications. In those controversial cases, the social rule interpretation of the rule of recognition could not account for the rule's imposing an obligation on judges. That is because, in the social rule theory, obligations derive from convergent practice; and in both the controversial and the as yet unresolved cases there exists no convergent practice or opinion from which an obligation might derive.

The rule of recognition is either a social rule or a normative rule. If it imposes obligations in controversial cases, it cannot be a social rule. Therefore, if the rule of recognition imposes a duty upon judges in controversial cases, it must be a normative rule. Because the rule of recognition in every community is a normative rule, the obligations of judges under it are ones of critical rather than conventional morality; and the ultimate authority of law is a matter of morality, not convention.

The argument from controversy presupposes that judges are

bound by duty, even in controversial cases, under the rule of recognition. Positivism, it appears, is committed to judicial discretion in such cases and is, therefore, unable to explain either the
source or nature of the duty. Because the social rule theory of
judicial obligation is unable to explain the fact of judicial obligation in controversial cases, it must be false and, therefore, its alternative, the normative rule theory, must be true.

One response a positivist might make to Dworkin's argument
is to deny that in such cases judges are bound by duty, in which
case the failure of the social rule theory to account for judicial duty
would not be troublesome. Dworkin quickly dismisses the plausibility of this response with the offhand remark that such a view
likens law to a game in which the participants agree in advance
that there are no right answers and no duties where sufficient controversy or doubt exists regarding the requirements of a rule. The
analogy to a game is supposed to embarrass positivism, but it need
not. Anyone even superficially familiar with Hart's work knows
that the bulk of examples he draws upon to illustrate his claims
about rules, law and the nature of adjudication are drawn from
games like baseball and chess. So the positivist might welcome,
rather than eschew, the analogy to games.

Whether it is advanced to support or to criticize positivism, the
alleged analogy to games is unsatisfying. The more interesting tack
is to suppose along with Dworkin that judges may be obligated
by a rule of recognition, even in its controversial applications, and
then ask whether, in spite of Dworkin's arguments to the contrary, the social rule theory can explain this feature of law.

4.4. The moral argument

That Dworkin takes judicial obligations in cases involving controversial applications of the rule of recognition to be ones of critical
morality rather than conventional practice is illustrated by the moral
argument. Unlike the previous arguments I have outlined, the moral
argument is direct and affirmative in the sense that, instead of trying
to establish the inadequacies of the social rule theory, its purpose
is to provide direct support for the normative interpretation of the
rule of recognition. The argument is simply this: In resolving hard
or controversial cases that arise under the rule of recognition, judges
do not typically cite the practice or opinions of other judges. Because these cases are controversial, there exists no convergent
practice among judges to cite. Instead, in order to resolve these
disputes, judges typically appeal to principles of political morality.

For example, in determining how much weight to give precedent, judges may apply alternative conceptions of fairness. If, as the social rule theory claims, the source of a judge's duty depends on the rule or principle he cites as its basis, the sources of judicial obligation in these controversial cases are the principles of political morality judges cite as essential to the resolution of the dispute. The duty of judges in controversial cases can only be explained if the rule of recognition is a normative one whose authority depends on its moral merits; whose normativity, in other words, depends on moral argument of precisely the sort judges appear to engage in.

4.5. Summary

Dworkin has three distinct, powerful arguments against law-as-convention positivism. Each argument has a slightly different character and force. The point of the pedigree argument is that a rule of recognition that makes reference to the content of moral principles as a condition of their legality will spur controversy and, because it will, it cannot be a social rule, or, therefore, a rule of recognition in the positivist sense. The argument is weak in the sense that, even if sound, it would be inadequate to establish the normative account of the rule of recognition. Only controversial rules of recognition fail to be social rules; for all the argument shows, uncontroversial rules of recognition may be social rules.

The more general argument from controversy appears to fill the gap left by the pedigree argument. Here the argument is not that every rule of recognition will be systematically controversial. Instead, the argument relies on the plain fact that even basically uncontroversial rules of recognition will have controversial instances. The social rule theory cannot account for judicial obligation in the face of controversy. If the rule of recognition imposes an obligation on judges in controversial cases, as Dworkin presumes it does, the obligation can be accounted for only if the rule is a normative one whose capacity to impose a duty does not depend on widespread convergence of conduct or opinion. The point of the argument can be put in weaker or stronger terms. One can say simply that obligations in controversial cases exist and positivism cannot account for them; or one can put the point in terms of natural law theory as the claim that the duties that exist are ones of critical morality rather than conventional practice.

The point of the moral argument is that, in resolving hard cases, judges appear to rely on principles of political morality rather than

on convergent social practice. Judges apparently believe that they
are bound to resolve these controversies and, more important, that
their duty to resolve them in one way rather than another depends
on the principles of morality to which they appeal.

5. CONVENTION AND CONTROVERSY

Each of the objections to the social rule theory can be met.[12] Consider the pedigree argument first; that is, the claim that a rule of
recognition which refers to morality – which has a C_1 clause satisfied by some norm – will be controversial and, therefore, cannot
be a social rule of recognition. Suppose the clause in the rule of
recognition states, "The law is whatever is morally correct." The
controversy among judges does not arise over the content of the
rule of recognition itself. It arises over which norms satisfy the
standards set forth in it. The divergence in behavior among officials as exemplified in their identifying difference standards as legal ones does not establish their failure to accept the same rule of
recognition. On the contrary, judges accept the same truth conditions for propositions of law; that is, that law consists in moral
truth. They disagree about which propositions satisfy those conditions. While there may be no agreement whatsoever regarding
which standards are legal ones – since there is no agreed-upon
standard for determining the truth of a moral principle – there is
complete agreement among judges concerning the standard of legality. That judges reach different conclusions regarding the law
of a community does not mean that they are employing different
standards of legality. Since disagreement concerning which principles satisfy the rule of recognition presupposes that judges accept
the same rule of recognition, the sort of controversy envisaged by
the pedigree argument is compatible with the conventionalist account of the authority of the rule of recognition.

Notice, however, that were we to understand the rule of recognition epistemically, as providing a reliable test for identifying
law, rather than as specifying truth conditions for statements of
law, the sort of controversy generated by a rule of recognition like
the rule "the law is whatever is morally correct" would be problematic, since the proposed rule of recognition would be incapable
of providing a reliable test for identifying legal norms. This just
draws our attention once again both to the importance of distinguishing between the epistemic and semantic interpretations of the
rule of recognition, and to the necessity of insisting upon the semantic interpretation of it.

Even on the semantic interpretation, the phrase "controversy in the rule of recognition" is ambiguous. Controversy may arise, as it did in the previous case, over which norms satisfy the conditions of legality set forth in the rule of recognition; or it can arise over the conditions of legality set out in the rule of recognition. Cases of the first sort are the ones Dworkin envisions arising from a rule of recognition that includes a clause specifying legality conditions for moral principles. These cases are not problematic, because controversy presupposes agreement about and acceptance of the rule of recognition. In contrast, the claim that every rule of recognition will be controversial in some of its details is precisely the claim that, in some cases, controversy will arise over the content or proper formulation of the rule of recognition itself. The question that these cases pose is not whether judges agree about which norms satisfy the same rule of recognition; rather, it is whether judges can be said to be applying the same rule. Since the social rule theory requires of the rule of recognition that its formulation be specified by convergence of behavior or belief, the controversy concerning the proper formulation of the rule means that the rule cannot be a social rule and, therefore, that it cannot be a rule of recognition in the positivist sense.

One way of interpreting Dworkin's claim is that, wherever controversy exists in the proper formulation of a rule, the rule cannot be a conventional or social rule. This is counterintuitive, since all rules – those of conventional as well as critical morality – are vague at points and, therefore, their application in some context will be controversial. If we take Dworkin to be making the argument that the existence of controversy is straightforwardly incompatible with the idea of a social rule, then no rule could be a social rule. Certainly, in spite of the controversial nature of all rules governing behavior, we are able to distinguish (at least in broad terms) the conventional rules from those whose authority depends on their truth.

A more sympathetic and plausible reading of Dworkin is that he does not mean to contest the existence of social rules. Instead his claim is that social rules cannot account for duties beyond the range of convergent practice. Social rules cannot explain duties in controversial cases. With respect to the rule of recognition, the social rule theory cannot account for the obligation of judges to give the correct formulation of the rule of recognition in its controversial instances. On the assumption that judges have such an obligation, the social rule theory fails. Only a normative interpretation of the rule of recognition can explain the duty in cases of divergent opinions or conduct, since the duty, according to the normative theory, does not derive from convergent practice but from sound moral argument.

Schematically, Dworkin's argument is as follows:

(1)   Every rule of recognition will be controversial with respect to its scope and, therefore, with respect to the nature and scope of the obligations it imposes.
(2)   Nevertheless, in resolving disputes involving controversial aspects of the rule, judges are under an obligation, as they are in the uncontroversial cases, to give the right answer.
(3)   The social rule theory which requires convergence of behavior as a condition of an obligation cannot account for the obligation of judges in (2).
(4)   Therefore, positivism cannot account for judicial obligation in (2).
(5)   Therefore, only a normative theory of law in which the duty of judges depends on moral argument rather than convergent practice can account for judicial duty in (2).

As I suggested earlier, a positivist might respond by denying the truth of (2), that is, by denying that judges are obligated in controversial cases in which behavior and opinion diverge. Hart, for one, denies (2), and he appears to do so because he accepts (3). That he denies (2) is made evident by his characterizing these kinds of cases as involving "uncertainty in the rule of recognition" in which "all that succeeds is success." If a positivist were to deny (2) to meet Dworkin's objections on the ground that he (the positivist) accepts (3), it would be fair to accuse him of begging the question. He would be denying the existence of judicial obligation simply because his theory cannot account for it. Moreover, from a strategic point of view, it would be better to leave open the question whether such duties exist, rather than to preclude the very possibility of their existence as a consequence of the theory; otherwise, any argument that made the existence of such duties conceivable would have the effect of completely undermining the theory. Notice, however, that Dworkin is led to an analogous position, since his argument for the normative theory of law – i.e., (5) – requires that judges are under obligations in every conceivable case – i.e., (2). The social rule theory logically precludes judicial obligation in such cases; the normative theory requires it. Both theories of law will fail, just in case the existence of judicial duty in controversial cases involving the rule of recognition is a contingent feature of law. In other words, if it turns out that in some legal systems judges have an obligation to provide a particular formulation of the rule of recognition when controversy arises over its proper formulation, whereas in other legal systems no such duty exists and judges are free to exercise discretion – at least until one or another formulation takes hold – both the theory that logically precludes judicial duties in all controversial cases and the one that logically entails such duties will fail.

Denying the existence of the duties to which Dworkin draws attention is a strategy that will not serve the positivist well. One alternative would be to admit the existence of the duty in some cases, but to give up the social rule theory according to which the nature and scope of a duty are completely specified by convergent practice in favor of some other theory concerning the way in which conventional or social rules give rise to duties. There is a promising line of argument I am not prepared to discuss here. However, it seems to me that the discussion of conventions in David Lewis's brilliant book *Convention*[13] might provide the theoretical foundations for an alternative to the standard social rule theory. Briefly, the idea is that the duties imposed by social rules or conventions are the results of expectations that arise from efforts to coordinate behavior. Vested, warranted expectations may extend beyond the area of convergent practice, in which case the obligations to which a social rule gives rise might cover controversial, as well as uncontroversial, cases.[14]

Another alternative strategy, the one I have been trying to develop, follows the social rule theory in restricting the duty imposed by a conventional rule to the area of convergent practice. In this view, if controversy arises in the rule of recognition itself, it does not follow that the judges are free to exercise discretion in providing a formulation of the rule. What counts is not whether controversy exists, but whether there exists a practice among judges of resolving the controversy in a particular way. And to answer the question of whether such a practice exists, we do not look to the rule of recognition – whose conditions of legality are presumably in dispute – but to the social rule constituted by the behavior of judges in applying the rule of recognition. Whether a duty exists will depend, in part, on whether the judges have developed an accepted social practice of resolving these controversies in a particular way.

Suppose that, in applying the rule of recognition, judges have developed a practice of resolving controversial instances of it. Suppose further that in some jurisdictions, for example, the United States and England, judges, by and large, resolve such disputes, as

Dworkin believes they do, by providing arguments of principle; so that in determining, for example, whether and to what extent the Supreme Court can review the constitutionality of federal legislation, judges argue from principles of political morality, for example the separation of powers and so on. According to Dworkin, we should have a controversy in the rule of recognition itself that judges would be required to resolve in the appropriate way; and the obligation of judges would derive from principles of morality that constitute the best argument. This is the essence of what I referred to as the "moral argument," and it shows that the rule of recognition is a normative, not a social, rule.

For the traditional positivist, we should have a case in which no obligation existed, where all that succeeded was success: a case in which the judges' recourse to the principles of political morality necessarily involved an exercise of discretion.

Both of these positions are mistaken. If, as Dworkin supposes, judges as a general rule look to moral principles in resolving controversial features of the rule of recognition, then there exists a practice among them of resolving controversial aspects of the rule of recognition in that way; that is, as the moral argument suggests judges in the United States and England do. If this is, in fact, the practice of judges in constitutional democracies like ours – as it must be if Dworkin's arguments are to be taken seriously – and if the practice is critically accepted by judges, then there is a legal duty even in controversial cases: a duty that does not derive from the principles judges cite (as in Dworkin) but from their acceptance of the practice of resolving these disputes by offering substantive moral arguments. All that Dworkin's arguments really show is that judges have adopted critically the practice that the best moral argument wins, which explains both their appeal to substantive moral principles and, contrary to the traditional positivist, their duty to make the appeal.

What, in Dworkin's view, is evidence for the normative theory of the rule of recognition – that is, general and widespread appeal to moral principle to resolve controversies in it – is, in my view, evidence of the existence of a social practice among judges of resolving such disputes in a particular way; a practice that specifies part of the social rule regarding judicial behavior. The appeal of substantive moral argument is, then, perfectly compatible with the conventionalist account of law.

To argue that the appeal to moral argument is compatible with the conventionalist account is not to establish that account, since the appeal to moral argument as a vehicle of dispute resolution is also consistent with the normative theory of law. One could argue that, at most, my argument shows only that Dworkin's arguments, which rely on both the controversial nature of law and the appeal to moral principle to resolve controversy, are inadequate to undermine positivism. We need some further reason to choose between the normative and conventional theories of law.

For the normative theory of law to be correct, judges must be under a legal obligation to resolve controversies arising in every conceivable rule of recognition by reliance on substantive moral argument. That is because Dworkin's version of the normative theory entails the existence of judicial duty in all cases, and because the resolution of the dispute must involve moral argument. After all, if the rule of recognition is, as Dworkin claims, a normative rule, then its authority rests on sound moral argument, and the resolution of disputes concerning its scope must call for moral argument. Were judges to rely on anything else, the authority of the rule of recognition would not be a matter of its moral merits; or if they appeal to nothing at all, then in such jurisdictions we would have reason to believe that judges are under no particular obligation to resolve a controversy in the rule of recognition.

The real acid test seems to be not whether positivism of the sort I am developing can account for judicial obligations in the kinds of cases we are discussing, but whether these obligations constitute a necessary feature of law which, in every jurisdiction, is imposed by moral principle. As long as the existence of such duties is a contingent feature of law, as is the duty to resolve disputes by appealing to moral argument, the normative theory of law is a less plausible account than is the conventionalist theory. Indeed, it seems straightforwardly false, since we can imagine immature legal systems (which are legal systems nonetheless) in which no practice for resolving disputes in the rule of recognition has yet developed – where all that succeeds is success. Or we could imagine the development of considerably less attractive practices for resolving such disputes, for example, the flip of a coin: heads, defendant wins; tails, plaintiff does. In the first sort of legal system, it would seem odd to say judges were legally bound to resolve such disputes (though they might always be morally bound to do so), since no practice had as yet developed. Eventually, such a practice is likely to develop, and the range of judicial discretion will narrow as the practice becomes widespread and critically accepted. As the second example shows, the practice that finally develops need not conform to judicial practice in the United States and England. Though judicial discretion narrows as the range of judicial obligation expands, it may do so in a way that is considerably less attractive than the moral argument envisions; in a way that is, in fact, less attractive than a system in which all that succeeds is success.

Unlike traditional positivism, which has trouble explaining judicial behavior in mature legal systems, and the normative theory of law, which has difficulty explaining developing and immature legal systems (for reasons that the first precludes obligations in controversial cases, while the second requires them), law-as-convention positivism understands such duties to be a contingent feature of law that can be explained as arising from the critical acceptance of a practice of dispute resolution, rather than from the principles of morality which judges under one kind of practice might cite.

6. CONCLUSION

Dworkin makes three correct observations about the controversial nature of some legal standards:

1. A legal system can (and does in the United States and Britain) recognize certain standards as part of the law even though they are "essentially controversial" in the sense that there may be disagreements among judges as to which these are, and there is no decision procedure which, even in principle, can demonstrate what they are, and so settle disagreements.

2. Among such essential controversial legal standards are moral principles owing their status as law to their being "true" moral principles, though their "truth" cannot be demonstrated by any agreed-upon test.

3. The availability of such controversial principles fills the "gaps" left by ordinary sources of law, which may be partially undetermined, vague or conflicting, so that, at least with respect to the resolution of disputes involving standards subordinate to the rule of recognition, a judge never has to exercise lawmaking power or "discretion" to fill the gaps or remove the indeterminacy if such moral principles are a part of the law.

In this essay, I have drawn distinctions among three versions of positivism and have discussed their relationship to Dworkin's claims: (1) "negative positivism," the view that the legal system need not recognize as law "controversial" moral standards; (2) "positive, hard-facts positivism," the view that controversial standards cannot be regarded as law and, hence, rejects Dworkin's three points; and (3) "positive, social rule positivism," which insists only on the conventional status of the rule of recognition but accepts Dworkin's three points.

Since the inclusion of controversial moral principles is not a necessary feature of the concept of law, Dworkin's arguments to the effect that such principles figure in judicial practice in the United States and England are inadequate to undermine the very weak claim of negative positivism. On the other hand, if Dworkin is right – and I am inclined to think that he is – in thinking that controversial moral principles sometimes figure in legal argument, then any form of positivism that is committed to the essential noncontroversial nature of law is mistaken. Finally, what I have tried to do is to develop a form of positivism which accepts the controversial nature of some legal reasoning, while denying that this is incompatible with the essential, affirmative claim of the theory that law is everywhere conventional in nature. If I am correct, there is a form of positivism which can do justice to Dworkin's insights while rendering his objections harmless.[15]

2. Rethinking the theory of legal rights

1. INTRODUCTION

In the economic approach to law, legal rights are designed, in part, to overcome the conditions under which markets fail. In correcting for market failure, economic analysis endorses two rules for assigning legal rights.

The first specifies the allocation of rights under conditions of rational cooperation, full information and zero transaction costs. Provided that exchange is available and that obstacles to exercising it are insignificant, rational cooperators will negotiate around inefficiencies. Under these conditions, legal rights are not assigned in order to establish optimal levels of resource deployment directly; rather, they establish well-defined entitlements or negotiation points which create a framework in which mutually advantageous bargains leading to optimal outcomes can be realized. This role of legal rights in securing optimal outcomes is suggested by the Coase theorem.[1]

The second rule for assigning legal rights specifies the procedures to be followed in the event the conditions of full information, rational cooperation and zero transaction costs are inadequately satisfied. Where impediments to successful negotiations are substantial, inefficiencies in the initial allocation may not be overcome through mutually advantageous exchange. Unable to rely upon the exchange process to overcome inefficiencies, a court must allocate entitlements efficiently from the outset. In doing so, the court continues to rely upon the exchange process, though in a different manner. Instead of relying upon exchange to *rectify* inefficiencies, including inefficient judicial decisions, the court relies upon the market paradigm to help it *identify* the efficient outcome it seeks to replicate.

Let us refer to an exchange market in which the conditions of the Coase theorem are met or approximated as a Coasean market.

When a court cannot avail itself of the Coasean market, it is left to imagine what the parties would have agreed to in a *hypothetical* Coasean market. In this market, the right to use a resource would have been secured ultimately by that party who would have paid the most for it. The court then mimics the outcome of the idealized but unrealized Coasean market by "auctioning" entitlements to those who value them most – as judged by each litigant's willingness to pay.[2]

Once assigned, entitlements need to be secured. In their seminal piece that sets out the accepted framework for securing legal entitlements, Calabresi and Melamed distinguish among three ways of protecting entitlements: (1) property rules, (2) liability rules and (3) inalienability rules.[3] In their view, a property rule protects an entitlement by enabling a right bearer to enjoin others from reducing the level of protection the entitlement affords him, except as he may be willing to forgo it at a mutually acceptable price. If a right is protected by a liability rule, a nonentitled party may reduce the value of the entitlement without regard to the right holder's desires, provided he compensates *ex post* for the reduction in value. The value of the reduction, that is, damages, is set by a collective body, usually a court; it need not coincide with what the entitled party would have been willing to accept for a reduction in the value of his entitlement.

If transaction costs are high, a property rule is likely to prove inefficient, because transfer to more valued use requires negotiations. Consequently, property rules may lead to entitlements being held by individuals who value them less. Under a liability rule, individuals who value entitlements more than those on whom the rights are initially conferred can secure the entitlements without *ex ante* negotiations: They can compel transfers to themselves and pay damages. In such cases, the entitlement is secured by the party who values it most, thus duplicating the outcome of the Coasean market exchange process. When transaction costs are high, therefore, efficiency considerations may necessitate the forgoing of property rules in favor of liability rules.

If damages under a liability rule set by a court are equal to the reduction in the value of the entitlement to the injured party, the optimal outcome is secured through a Pareto-superior, or mutually beneficial, *forced transfer*. If damages are set below the value of the entitlement to the injured party, the forced transfer is not Pareto superior, even if it is Pareto optimal. Property rules, therefore, induce optimal transfers through Pareto improvements, whereas whether liability rules involve Pareto improvements depends on the level of compensation and on the transaction costs of administering them.

When a right is protected by an inalienability rule, transfers of any sort are prohibited. The right to one's freedom from servitude and the right to vote are examples of rights protected by inalienability rules. On first blush, protecting a right by an inalienability rule appears to be a decision forgoing efficiency in favor of promoting some other social good. After all, some people might well wish to exchange their rights, and their doing so might be efficient; blocking such transfers might then seem inefficient. However, a willingness to exchange a right, like freedom from servitude, for money may indicate a lack either of full information or of rationality. Presumably such transfers would not occur in a costless market populated by fully informed, rational persons. Inalienability rules, therefore, may also be explained (justified) in efficiency terms.

In encouraging the efficient distribution of resources, a court actually has four options. Suppose a polluter, *A*, claims an entitlement to continue polluting; and the victim–plaintiff, *B*, seeks an injunction to prohibit *A* from polluting further. The court's options are presented in Figure 2.1.

The court can, as it does in cells (2) and (4), decide in favor of the polluter; or it can, as it does in cells (1) and (3), decide in favor of the plaintiff. In the usual jargon, this constitutes the court's "entitlement decision." The court's decision in favor of the plaintiff, represented in (1) and (3), can differ in the nature of the protection it affords the plaintiff. If the entitlement is protected by a property rule, then *A* is enjoined from polluting *B* unless *A* can reach an accord with *B* that would permit it to pollute at a price *B* finds acceptable. In contrast, if the court opts to protect *B*'s entitlement by the use of a liability rule, as in cell (3), then *A* may pollute *B* and pay damages at a price set *ex post*.

Similarly, if the court decides in favor of the pollutor, it may protect its right to pollute by a property rule, as it does in (2), which enjoins *B* from reducing *A*'s pollution without first securing *A*'s consent. The court may alternatively protect *A*'s right to pollute by a liability rule, as it does in (4), which grants *B* the liberty to reduce the level of *A*'s output provided he compensates *A ex post*.

Each of these four options has in fact been employed by courts in establishing and securing legal entitlements. The celebrated *Spur Industries* case was resolved by use of the last, and least obvious, option.[4] The Calabresi–Melamed framework and the *Spur* case are

HOW TO PROTECT

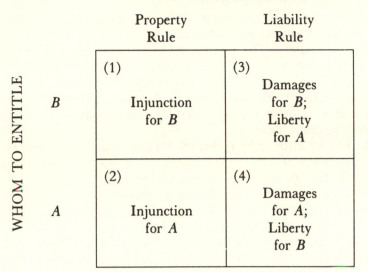

	Property Rule	Liability Rule
B	(1) Injunction for *B*	(3) Damages for *B*; Liberty for *A*
A	(2) Injunction for *A*	(4) Damages for *A*; Liberty for *B*

WHOM TO ENTITLE

Figure 2.1

widely viewed as mutually supportive. The theoretical framework locates and legitimates the decision – one that might otherwise have seemed to lack a foundation. At the same time, the decision suggests the usefulness of the framework.

This is not to say that the decision itself cannot be or has not been criticized.[5] Still, whatever objections to the decision have been made, it remains true that no commentator has thought to criticize it on the grounds that the decision is deeply paradoxical. This is surprising. The *Spur* case, and the Calabresi–Melamed framework that encompasses it, suggests that it is possible to protect a person's right by giving *others* the liberty to invade it provided they compensate for the invasion. *Ex post* compensation can sometimes be adequate both to legitimate forced transfer and to secure or protect a legal right. It is surely odd to claim that an individual's right is protected when another individual is permitted to force a transfer at a price set by third parties. Isn't the very idea of a forced transfer contrary to the autonomy or liberty thought constitutive of rights?

A perfectly natural way of characterizing what it means to have a right to a resource or to property is in terms of autonomy or control. Rights, in this view, demarcate a realm of liberty or control. Rights are secured or protected liberties.[6] But how can my liberty or control over a resource or over a set of choices be protected by denying me autonomy or control, and instead by conferring control on others, even on the condition that they compensate me for whatever *diminution in the value* of my resources their conduct occasions? The point of conferring an entitlement arguably is to secure a domain of control, not to guarantee a particular level of welfare or utility. One who conceives of rights as securing a sphere of liberty does not believe that the concept of a right is reducible to or otherwise identifiable with a point on a right bearer's indifference curve.

The liberty implied by rights ownership is not equivalent to any particular level of welfare: certainly, not if one wants to maintain the distinction between autonomy and utility.[7]

If rights entail or secure liberties, then it is hard to see how liability rules protect them. Let us refer to the thesis that part of what it means to have a (legal) right to a resource is to have a secured domain of autonomy as the classical liberal theory of legal rights.[8] Faced with a conflict between his understanding of rights and the property–liability rule framework, the classical liberal may simply give up the latter, that is, deny that liability rules *protect* entitlements.

It is important that we not misunderstand this response. Someone who denies that liability rules protect rights does not deny either that liability rules play a role in reducing the incidence of "taking" or that they protect something. Of course liability rules can deter, and for an obvious reason. Rendering compensation *ex post* imposes a cost on potential "takers," adequate, one hopes, to reduce the level of forced transfers. Moreover, liability rules protect something. Compensation under a liability rule is for harm done and loss suffered. The loss is the diminution in value of one's resources or, loosely speaking, one's property. In this sense the "objective" value of one's holdings is protected by liability rules; the value of the interest is left intact. But a liability rule confers no liberty or autonomy on an entitled party, and therefore secures no such liberty. Quite the contrary. In the classical liberal view, the right is the liberty, not the value (i.e., utility) to anyone of having or exercising that liberty. Thus, in the view that rights entail liberties, the most liability rules can secure is a level of welfare equal to the value of the right bearer's interest, including even his interest in his autonomy. However, because utility is not autonomy, and because liability rules neither confer nor respect a domain of lawful control, liability rules cannot, in this view, protect rights. The "cannot" here is a conceptual one. The very idea of a "liability rule entitlement," that is, of a right secured by a liability rule, is inconceivable.

We have, then, at least two possible conceptual frameworks for thinking about the relationship between rights and the property–liability rule scheme. The discussion to this point suggests that in the framework within which economic analysis operates, rights can be secured by liability rules if rights are not thought of as entailing autonomy or liberty. Rights secure a level of well-being or utility. Liability rules protect rights by compensating for diminutions in the level of well-being owing to the conduct of others. In the classical liberal framework, rights entail a realm of control which cannot be secured by liability rules. Rights secure a domain of autonomy. Liability rules permit others to act without regard to the right holder's autonomy over his holdings. The tension between the two frameworks appears to require that we give up one or another plausible claim: either that a right is a domain of protected control or that liability rules protect rights. Both claims are plausible, but apparently incompatible. Which ought we abandon?

Answering this question, I believe, requires a theory of legal rights, meaning an account of what it means to have a legal right, as well as an account of the role of property and liability rules within any such theory. In what follows, I take up the challenge of providing a conceptual theory of legal rights whose point of departure is a reinterpretation of the Calabresi–Melamed framework. One consequence of my analysis is that once the concept of right is properly understood, it is necessary to give up both the claim that rights entail liberties and the claim that liability rules protect rights. The correct theory of legal rights, in other words, demonstrates the inadequacies of both the economic and classical liberal theories of rights.

2. A THEORETICAL FRAMEWORK FOR INSTITUTIONAL RIGHTS

2.1. The basic questions

An adequate theory of institutional (e.g., legal) entitlements must address three different sorts of questions:

(1) What is the *foundation* of rights? What goals or aims are institutions which create rights designed to promote? A foundational theory of institutional rights provides their *normative* basis. Among the possible foundational views are those which are liberty-based and those which are, in some sense, welfare-based. In these

views, institutions which create rights are designed either to promote individual liberty or to promote welfare (individual, average or general). Justificatory questions – for example, why confer upon individuals a right to freedom of speech, to a speedy and fair trial, or to private property? – are answered by reference to the "foundational" theory.

(2) What is the correct *analysis* of rights? Theories of the correct analysis of rights typically assert that rights are or entail, for example, interests, liberties or claims. But these theories conflate two distinct questions concerning the proper analysis of rights. A correct analysis of rights distinguishes between the *logical form* and the *content* of rights.

A theory of the logical form of rights seeks to specify the necessary features or properties of rights. These properties hold of rights analytically; that is, all institutional rights possess them necessarily. Further, these properties, whatever they are, remain constant across foundational theories. In contrast, the content of rights may vary depending on the foundational or normative theory of rights advanced. A theory of the content of rights is a theory of their *constitutive elements*. And these elements are not constitutive of rights as a matter of logical form, but rather as a matter of contingent fact. In any overall theory of institutional rights, the constitutive elements of rights are a function of the foundational theory.

The difference between the logical form and the content of rights is analogous to the distinction between syntax and semantics.[9] We might say, then, that a proper analysis of rights addresses both the syntax and the semantics of rights. By separating the logical form from the content of rights, we seek to draw attention to an important point: Different views of the purpose of institutional rights may require different theories of their content, while maintaining that certain features of rights may be necessary features of them which obtain irrespective of the range of various foundational theories.[10]

(3) How might or ought a system of institutional rights be *enforced?* How should the claims given by rights be vindicated? What institutions are available to enforce rights, and which are appropriate to use and why? This is the question of institutional enforcement. At this level, we want to know, for example, whether we ought to enforce or vindicate a particular set of claims by providing injunctive relief, tort liability or some combination of the two, or, perhaps, by imposing criminal sanctions.

2.2. The basic answers

In keeping with the distinction I draw between the logical form and the content of rights, I shall argue first that, regarding their logical form, rights are best understood as "conceptual markers," or "place holders," used to designate a subset of legitimate interests or liberties to be accorded special protection by law.[11] Once chosen, the relevant interest or liberty enjoys a privileged status by being labeled a right or entitlement. Second, property, liability and inalienability rules are best understood as devices for generating or specifying the *content* or *meaning* of such rights. Because property and liability rules specify the meaning of rights, they enter into the overall theory of institutional rights at the level of providing an analysis of them. This is the point at which my conception of the property, liability and inalienability framework departs from previous work which, following Calabresi–Melamed, locates the transaction structure squarely within what I am calling the domain of institutions for securing or protecting entitlements.

Finally, because the property–liability–inalienability rule framework concerns only transactional aspects of institutional entitlements, I conclude that part of the content of a right is a claim specifying the conditions of legitimate transfer. These claims must be respected in order for transfers governed by rights to be legitimate.

Putting these points together, my thesis is as follows: (1) All institutional rights are *necessarily* conceptual markers designating certain legitimate interests or liberties as warranting a privileged status. (2) The privileged status is to be spelled out as follows: Each legitimate interest, for example, that is marked as a right is necessarily associated with, and in fact entails, some legitimate claims.[12] In contrast, whether or not a legitimate interest that is not marked as a right generates enforceable claims is a contingent matter.[13] Rights, however, entail legitimate claims. (3) The specific content of these claims is a function of the rule – property, liability or inalienability – applied to them. Therefore, I say that property and liability rules specify the content of rights by generating specific legitimate claims from them. (4) The claims property and liability rules generate specify conditions of legitimate transfer. Thus, I refer to them, following Alvin Klevorick, as constituting a "transaction structure."[14] Though the claims given rise to by rights within the domain of transactions are a function of the transaction rules applied to them, (5) the choice of which rule or rules to apply depends on the foundational theory. That is, we cannot say whether a right's content should be given by a property or by a liability rule or by some combination of the two until we know what general purpose we want institutional rights to serve. (6) Finally, besides providing the basis for determining the content of rights, the foundational theory specifies the appropriate institutions for enforcing the claims these rights create. In this way, the foundation theory fuels the complete theory of institutional rights. A commitment at the foundational level will suggest, though it will not strictly entail, certain views about the content and enforcement of rights. We should, therefore, expect that different foundational or normative theories will endorse different institutional arrangements, confer somewhat different institutional rights and suggest different mechanisms for their enforcement.

2.3. Rights and the transaction framework

The goal of every theory of institutional rights is to specify a set of rights which will create claims which, when respected, will best promote the goals set forth by the foundational theory. We can understand the process of designing a system of institutional rights by imagining a temporal progression beginning with the endorsement of a foundational theory. For ease of exposition, let us assume that the purpose of a system of institutional rights is to maximize net welfare. In seeking to promote this goal, we might begin by designing a set of legitimate interests as rights, which at this level of analysis just means "conceptually marking" them. In choosing among the set of legitimate interests for demarcation, we should select those that, if protected, would maximize overall welfare. Of course, whether elevating these interests to the level of legal rights would in fact maximize net welfare depends on the specific content or meaning given to them; that is, the claims they give rise to, as well as the mechanisms by which those claims are to be vindicated or enforced.

The next order of business is to specify more completely the content of the rights, which means associating particular legitimate claims over various domains with them. Prior to specifying the content or meaning of a right, we know only that the entitled party has a legitimate claim or set of such claims, but we have no idea of the precise nature of the claims. Property, liability and inalienability rules enter at this juncture as devices for generating particular, fully specified, legitimate claims from rights or entitlements.

The general point is really rather straightforward. We begin by supposing that a community has chosen to design its legal institutions to maximize welfare. (Our choice to focus on welfare maximization is, in this context, based purely on expository considerations.) In order to maximize welfare, some interests, but not others, are accorded the status of rights. At this point in the analysis, rights are just place holders: Each right has yet to be filled in, given specific content. The content of rights is then given in terms of claims. The claims entailed by rights range over several domains, including the domain of transfer or transaction.

The specific claims given rise to by rights are in turn derived from norms or rules governing the terms of legitimate transfer. Again, the idea is simple enough. Once a community settles on a set of legitimate holdings (or entitlements), it needs to specify the uses to which these holdings might be lawfully or otherwise legitimately put. Among the uses to which right holders may wish to put their entitlements are those which involve or require transactions. Consequently, a community requires a set of norms specifying the conditions of lawful or legitimate transfer. These rules constitute a community's transaction framework. The transaction framework is a normative one specifying legitimacy conditions.

We can imagine a wide range of norms that make up a transaction framework, from those conferring liberties in setting the conditions of transfer to those imposing duties on the bearers of rights. Consider some examples. One possible rule would give right holders complete autonomy to alienate their claims; another might prohibit alienation altogether. Still others would impose a duty to give up part or all of that to which one is lawfully entitled, either at one's discretion – as in the duty to be charitable – or at the command of the state – as in the obligation to pay taxes. The terms of transfer can vary widely and in many respects. Different communities, pursuing different social goals through their legal institutions, facing different socioeconomic and other conditions, will employ and emphasize different rules from the general category of transaction norms. The point we are anxious to emphasize is that property, liability and inalienability rules are best thought of as constituting a subset of the set of norms governing the transfer of lawful holdings. They are transaction norms. By generating claims entailed by right ownership, property, liability and inalienability rules (as well as combinations of them) specify the *content* of rights over the domain of transfer.

A useful way to think about the role played by property, liability and inalienability rules in our theory is to view them as mathematical functions whose domains are the set of institutional rights specified, and whose ranges are a subset of legitimate claims. Thus, these rules act like functions which take rights or entitlements as their *arguments* and generate particular legitimate claims as their values. These claims in turn specify the content of an entitlement *over a certain domain:* the domain of transfer. Property, liability and inalienability rules constitute a transaction structure specifying the range of legitimate claims individuals have with respect to the transfer of the objects of their entitlements, such as resources or property.

The particular claims associated with property, liability and inalienability rules are as follows:

(1)   If the content of an entitlement is given by a property rule, then the entitled party has a legitimate claim to *ex ante* agreement as both *necessary* and *sufficient* to the justifiable transfer of that to which he is entitled.

(2)   If the content of an entitlement is given by a liability rule, then the entitled party has a legitimate claim to *ex post compensation,* as both *necessary* and sufficient to the justifiable transfer of that to which he is entitled.

(3)   If the content of entitlement is given by an inalienability rule, then the entitled party has a *nonrelinquishable* or nontransferable legitimate claim to that to which he is entitled.[15]

Two points need to be emphasized. First, whether legitimate transfer is governed by property or liability rules only, or by some combination of the two, depends entirely upon the foundational theory *and* the facts of the world: that is, by a theory of what is desirable as constrained by what is feasible (and at what cost). There is absolutely nothing in the meaning of rights that entails or requires that the conditions of transfer be set by any one rule or other, or by any combination of them. This is important, for it means that someone's liberty to dispose of his property as he sees fit, far from being a logical implication of what it means to have a right, is a contestable normative assertion connecting a particular normative theory about the point of legal rights with a particular conception of the constitutive elements of rights. The rule of liberty of transfer is thus a *normative, not an analytic,* one supportable, if at all, by substantive argument, not linguistic convention.[16]

Second, there is an important difference between conceiving of property and liability rules as partially specifying the terms of legitimate transfer and conceiving of them as entitlement-securing devices. In the latter view, entitlements come to the property–

liability rule or transaction structure fully specified, their content somehow otherwise given. But how? Either the claims of rights ownership follow analytically from the very concept of a right or they derive from normative rules. If we say that Jones has a right to his watch which we "protect" by a liability rule, what does the expression "right to his watch" mean? What is the right's content? That is, just what is it that the liability rule is protecting? What are the claims that liability rules enforce or vindicate? What does the claim that Jones has a right to his watch tell us about the scope of his entitlement; in particular, about the conditions under which he might transfer it to others, or the conditions under which the interests of others in the use of Jones's watch will be recognized? Marking a legitimate interest as a right does not, by itself, give content to the right. It does not specify in any detail the claims entailed by rights ownership. Put another way, if liability and property rules *protect* rights by enforcing or vindicating the claims entailed by rights, as traditionally thought, then what rules give rise to the claims enforceable by them? Once one recognizes that the content of rights is not given *a priori,* then it is clear that the specific content of any right is a function of a set of norms. If liability and property rules are not among these norms, what are?

Giving the meaning to rights, at least over the domain of transfer, is the task of property, liability and inalienability rules. That is all the transaction rules do. That is why it is unhelpful to think of them as tools or instruments for protecting entitlements. Thus, we insist upon a distinction between the rules by which claims are generated and the rules that create the institutions for enforcing those claims: a distinction all too often blurred in previous work on the property–liability rule distinction. Conflating this distinction between right and remedy is commonplace within the Realist tradition that so dominates American jurisprudence. However commonplace the conflation, it is a mistake, and in conceiving of property and liability rules as we do, we mean to be taking issue with Legal Realist strands within the accepted interpretation of the Calabresi–Melamed framework.[17]

2.4. Deepening the property–liability rule distinction

So far we have a skeletal version of the property–liability–inalienability rule distinction, and an account of the role it is to play in the larger theory of institutional rights. I also have presented some reasons for thinking that mine is an appropriate way of thinking about the distinction. Having come this far, I shall now turn my attention to developing the distinctions among property, liability and inalienability rules more fully.

2.4.1. Two versions of the liability rule. We can distinguish between two understandings of liability rules. In our view, if the content of someone's entitlement is specified by a liability rule only, then he is not at liberty to seek a voluntary exchange with others. In a plausible alternative view, if the content of someone's entitlement is given by a liability rule, he is at liberty to negotiate the transfer of his entitlement, but others are also free to circumvent negotiations and to impose transfers at their discretion.[18]

In the language of claims, rather than liberties, I distinguish between our understanding of property and liability rules and the alternative view as follows.

In my view:

(1)   If the content of *B*'s entitlement is specified by a *property rule only,* then he has a legitimate claim against *A* that any transfer of his resources from *B* to *A* must proceed according to terms established by *ex ante* agreement. Agreement is necessary and sufficient for legitimate transfer.

(2)   If the content of *B*'s entitlement is specified by a *liability rule only,* then *B* has a legitimate claim to compensation against *A* in the event *A* takes what *B* is entitled to. But *A* has a legitimate claim that *B* not prevent him from securing that to which *B* is entitled, provided *A* is prepared to render adequate compensation.[19]

(3)   If the content of *B*'s entitlement is given by *both a property and a liability rule,* then *B* has two claims: One is to the liberty to seek a transfer through *ex ante* agreement with *A;* the other is to recompense in the event *A* imposes a transfer upon him.

In the alternative view:

(1′)   If the content of *B*'s entitlement is given by a *property rule only,* then *B* has a legitimate claim against *A* that any transfer of *B*'s resources to *A* must proceed according to terms established by *ex ante* agreement. Agreement is necessary and sufficient for legitimate transfer.

(2′)   If the content of *B*'s entitlement is specified by a *liability rule only,* then *B* has two claims: One is to the liberty to seek a transfer through *ex ante* agreement with *A;* the other is to recompense in the event *A* forgoes negotiations and imposes a transfer upon him.

Both views characterize property rules in the same way: (1) and (1′) are identical. What we refer to as a combination of property and liability rules – (3) – is equivalent in the alternative view to liability rules – (2′). The alternative framework provides no place for what we think of as liability rules. Is the difference important?

Yes, and there are reasons for preferring my account of liability rules. Any account that distinguishes among property and liability rules and the combination of the two provides more options for giving content to entitlements. This would not be a genuine virtue of my approach if occasions did not arise when we might want to avail ourselves of the additional options. But in fact such occasions do arise. Suppose *B* has a right against *A;* the exact content is given by a liability rule only. This means that *A* can seek to secure what *B* is entitled to provided he pays damages. *A* might want to negotiate around his potential liability to *B*. One reason we might choose to give content to *B*'s entitlement with a liability rule is to rule out the possibility of *A*'s reducing or eliminating entirely his potential tort liability.[20]

2.4.2. Two ways of combining property and liability rules. I think it is important, then, to give a narrow characterization of the kinds of claims to which liability rules give rise, especially to avoid conflating them in any way with property rules. Part of the reason for doing so has to do with potential combinations of property and liability rules. One way of combining them has been characterized above:

(3) If the content of *B*'s entitlement is given by both a property and a liability rule, then *B* has two claims: One is to the liberty to seek a transfer through *ex ante* agreement with *A;* the other is to compensation in the event negotiations fail or if *A* forgoes them and imposes a transfer upon him.

In this view, it is sufficient to legitimate a transfer that *A* and *B* settle on terms *ex ante*. It is not necessary, however. *A* may legitimately compel a transfer provided he renders compensation *ex post*. Such action does not constitute a violation of *B*'s right, the content of which is to be spelled out in terms of two claims: the claim to (i) freedom to negotiate *ex ante* and (ii) compensation *ex post* should a transfer be forced upon him. In (3), *B* does not have a legitimate claim to *ex ante* negotiation as a *necessary* condition for legitimate transfer.

The point of specifying the content of an entitlement by this sort of arrangement is that in doing so we enable *B* to pursue a jointly favorable voluntary agreement, but we do not limit legitimate transfers to all and only those cases in which he succeeds. Obstacles to successful negotiations which, for example, were not known or did not exist at the onset of negotiations might emerge. And while we might not want to foreclose *B*'s seeking a transfer on terms acceptable to him, we might also not want to preclude transfer in the event satisfying those terms should prove infeasible, or if obstacles to negotiating should make voluntary transfer too costly or impractical. Moreover, compensation may be set too high, so that inefficiently few transactions will take place if voluntary transactions are forbidden. The key feature of this combination of liability with property rules is that once the nonentitled party (in this case *A*) has either negotiated *ex ante* to effect a transfer or forced a transfer and compensated the entitled party (in this case *B*) *ex post,* the entitled party's claims have been exhausted.

Compare this way of combining property and liability rules with the following alternative:

(3′)   If the content of *B*'s entitlement is given by a combination of property and liability rules, then *B* has two legitimate claims: One is to *ex ante* agreement as both *necessary and sufficient* for legitimate transfer; the other is to recompense in the event *A* imposes a transfer on him after either negotiations fail or *A* forgoes them.

According to this way of combining property with liability rules, *A* is never at liberty to impose a transfer upon *B*. The only legitimate form of transfer is *ex ante* agreement. Should *A* fail to seek agreement with *B* and take what *B* is entitled to, *B* has a claim to repair against *A*. Even when *A* renders compensation to *B,* the forced transfer remains illegitimate, and *B* retains a claim against *A*. *B's* claim to *ex ante* negotiation as a necessary condition for legitimate transfer has been violated rather than exhausted. *A*'s rendering compensation does not satisfy *B*'s claim against him. The liability rule aspect of this combination affords the nonentitled party no liberties in setting the terms of legitimate transfer.

We might characterize the difference between (3) and (3′) as follows: If the content of an entitlement is specified by the property–liability rule scheme represented by (3), then both voluntary exchange and full compensation after forced transfer are sufficient to legitimate transfer. If, however, the content of an entitlement is given by a combination of property and liability rules as represented by (3′), only voluntary exchange is a legitimate basis for transfer. Under (3′) compensation does not legitimate transfer, but functions instead to secure more firmly the integrity of the property rule as stating both the necessary and sufficient conditions of legitimate transfer.

Integrating the discussion in this and the preceding section provides a fuller characterization of liability rules. If the content of an entitlement is given by a liability rule only, then it cannot be part of the meaning of the entitlement that its holder is free to set the terms of legitimate transfer. A liability rule may, however, be used in conjunction with a property rule. Sometimes when it is so conjoined, the liability rule is intended to enable nonentitled parties to effect legitimate transfers; on other occasions the point of the liability rule is to strengthen the integrity of the property rule as specifying the only terms under which transfer is legitimate.

One way to see how liability rules might strengthen the integrity of the property rule is to imagine that we wanted to establish *ex ante* agreement as both necessary and sufficient for legitimate transfer, and that in order to do so we specified the content of an entitlement by a property rule only. In that case, the nonentitled party would not be at liberty to set the terms of legitimate transfer. Suppose, however, that the nonentitled party acted beyond the range of his liberty and took what he had no right to. If we had not also conferred a liability rule on the entitled party, the "victim" would have no claim to repair against a nonentitled party. In the absence of a liability rule, *A*'s failing to abide by the terms of transfer governed by a property rule, *B* would be left without a claim to compensatory relief, where such relief is either necessary or otherwise desirable. But then the presence of a liability rule cannot be understood to signify the legitimacy of forced transfer.

All this suggests that liability rules are employed sometimes to generate a claim to repair in the event the conduct of a nonentitled party is wrongful, that is, in the event it fails to respect the conditions of transfer under a property rule; whereas, on other occasions, liability rules are employed to generate a claim to repair as part of the conditions of legitimate transfer.

It is odd even to think of functions like (3′) as combinations of property and liability rules. Combinations of rules are better thought of as specifying jointly or individually sufficient conditions of legitimate transfer, whereas the liability rule in (3′) does not specify terms of legitimate transfer. Instead, the liability rule in (3′) provides a layer of potential "enforcement" for entitlements whose conditions of transfer are otherwise fully specified by a property rule. It does so by creating a legitimate claim to repair in the event a nonentitled party fails to respect the terms of legitimate transfer

set forth under the property rule. Whether liability rules themselves are employed to set out a sufficient condition of legitimate
transfer or to create claims to repair in the event the terms set out
elsewhere (e.g., by a property rule) are disregarded will depend,
in part, on the foundational theory.

3. IMPLICATIONS OF THE THEORY

3.1. Appreciating the importance of the difference between (3) and (3′)

The distinction between (3) and (3′) has implications for tort theory both with respect to explaining and justifying claims to repair,
and to the debate over whether liability rules serve to justify "private takings" or to buttress property rules and thereby discourage
and penalize private takings.

3.1.1. Compensation and rights. Following Joel Feinberg[21] and Judith
Jarvis Thomson,[22] it has become commonplace in classical rights
discourse to distinguish between two ways in which nonentitled
parties might invade or act contrary to the rights of others. In one
case, A wrongfully or unjustifiably invades B's right; in the other,
A permissibly invades B's right. Consider two cases. In the first,
A happens upon B's cabin in the mountains and wantonly destroys
it. In the second, A, caught in a blizzard, takes shelter in B's cabin,
burns the furniture to stay warm and avails herself of whatever
food is stored in the cupboards. We can suppose that in neither
case does A seek to secure B's permission to enter, use or destroy
his property. In the first case, A's conduct is invasive and imper-
missible. In the second case, A's conduct is invasive though permissible. Feinberg and Thomson agree that B is owed compensation in both cases. The problem is to locate the foundation or source
of B's claim to repair.

Suppose we begin by following Feinberg and Thomson in holding that in both cases B has a valid claim to repair. One possible
explanation of B's claim to repair is that A's conduct in both cases
is invasive of or contrary to B's right. This is the Rights or Infringement Thesis, according to which compensation is justified if
and only if it is to repair loss resulting from an invasion of a right.

There are at least two arguments to support the contention that
the basis of a legitimate claim to repair is conduct infringing upon
a right. According to the first, when A harms B's right, there are
two normative dimensions of the event: A's conduct and B's right.

A's conduct, as the preceding example illustrates, can be either wrongful or not. If A's action is both wrongful and invasive, then we might be inclined to hold that B's right to repair could be supported by either the wrongfulness of A's conduct, for example, her recklessness in harming B, or by the fact that in harming B she invaded a right of B's. No help here in sorting out the source of B's claim. Let us consider, then, the case in which A acts justifiably. If wrongfulness is a necessary condition of a legitimate claim to repair, then B ought not recover whenever A acts reasonably. In this case, we are assuming that B ought to recover. If B ought to recover, his claim cannot rest on the wrongfulness of A's conduct, because in this case A acted reasonably. If B has a claim to repair, it is because A invaded a right of his, even if, under the circumstances, her doing so was reasonable. Then, if compensation is B's due whenever a right of his is invaded, the moral character of A's conduct is not the source of the claim to repair. Instead the right to repair rests on a victim's suffering loss due to a right of his being injured. Therefore, compensation requires rights.

Alternatively, one could argue that the invasion of a right is necessary (and sufficient) for compensation to be warranted by deriving that claim from a particular conception of corrective justice. This argument proceeds by claiming first that the point of institutional or legal rights is to do justice. Because compensation falls within the domain of corrective justice, those legal institutions, like torts, concerned to make available compensatory relief are best understood as pursuing the ideal of corrective justice. Precisely what does corrective justice require? One conception of corrective justice requires that all and only losses owing to the invasion or infringement of a right deserve to be repaired: that a wrongful or compensable loss is one occasioned by the infringement of a right. The gist of the argument is that only rights can create other rights. How, after all, could someone have a right in justice to recompense for harm done to him if, in causing him harm, no right of his had been invaded, that is, if he had no right not to be harmed in the first place?

At best, the first argument for the Infringement Thesis establishes only that action contrary to a right is sufficient as the basis of a claim to recompense. To establish the general thesis or a claim that rights invasions are necessary and sufficient for compensation to be justified, one needs to argue that losses occasioned by wrongs that invade no rights ought not to be compensated – or, at least, that justice does not require that they be compensated. The argument from corrective justice we just sketched provides the missing premise. It holds that all and only wrongful losses deserve to be annulled, and that in order to be wrongful a loss must result from the invasion of a right. Other losses, even those resulting from negligence or recklessness, are simply not compensable as a matter of corrective justice. It makes sense, then, to treat the two arguments for the Infringement Thesis sketched above as a complementary pair.

If it turned out that corrective justice required that losses other than those occasioned by action contrary to a right be annulled, the Infringement Thesis would fail. As it happens, one of us has argued for precisely such a conception of corrective justice.[23] In that view, a claim to repair exists for losses occasioned by the *wrongful harming of interests,* as well as for losses resulting from the invasion of rights. Not every interest, not even every legitimate interest, is a right. To harm is to invade an interest. So I can harm you without invading a right of yours. And if I harm you *wrongfully,* say through fraud, deceit or simple negligence, then my conduct, though it invades no right of yours (*ex hypothesi*), causes you a wrongful loss. Wrongful losses, so conceived, require rectification as a matter of justice.

One way of trying to save the Infringement Thesis from this objection is by arguing that your right to repair derives from my violating your right that I-not-harm-you-wrongfully. The argument is this: Whenever I harm you though my wrongful behavior, that is, my negligence or recklessness, I violate the general right of yours (and others) not-to-be-harmed-wrongfully. Thus, the right to repair rests on the invasion of another right: the right not to be harmed wrongfully.

But this is not a very persuasive way of reintroducing the concept of a right as essential to the claim to repair. The right grounding your claim to repair would be the right not to be *harmed wrongfully*. This "right" has no content independent of the category of "wrongful harmings." The right here does no work. What does the work is the concept of a wrongful harming. Moreover, the point of the Infringement Thesis is that it distinguishes between justified and unjustified invasions of rights. (Recall the example with which this section began, in which the victim's claim to repair is assumed to be justified quite apart from the reasonableness of the injurer's conduct.) But if your right against me *is* the right that I not harm you *wrongfully,* then that is not a right that can be invaded justifiably.

The debate at this level is a *normative* one between two conceptions of corrective justice. Although we are confident that the broader conception of corrective justice, in which justified claims to repair do not require the invasion of preexisting entitlements, is the correct one, we may be wrong. It may turn out that every legitimate claim to repair requires reference to a preexisting right. Even then, it would not follow that the legitimacy of the claim to repair depended on a right's having been *invaded*. To see this, simply return to the analysis of liability and property rules introduced above. This analysis, which emphasizes a distinction between two ways in which liability rules generate claims to repair, allows us to explain the legitimacy of someone's claim to repair without necessarily relying on the characterization of others' conduct as invasive of a right.

Assume that B is legally entitled to his property. This just means that B's interest in his property is being marked or identified as special. But the precise nature of the claims attending B's entitlement are fully determined only after some rule or combination of rules from the transaction structure has been applied to it. Whether A's harming of B's interest, for example, by taking what B has a right to, constitutes in *invasion* of B's right depends on the exact nature of the claims afforded B by his entitlement, and that, in turn, depends on the transaction rule applied.

If we imagine that the content of B's right includes the claim to voluntary agreement as a *necessary condition* for the legitimate transfer of his property *in all cases,* then A's conduct, whether or not it is morally permissible, constitutes an invasion of B's right. That is because the content of B's entitlement is given by a combination of property and liability rules like (3') above. Under this combination, agreement *ex ante* is both necessary and sufficient for legitimate transfer; and in taking from B, A did not secure, indeed might not even have sought, B's consent. If the content of B's entitlement is given by (3'), then in taking without first securing B's consent, A acted without regard to B's legitimate claims against her. She invaded B's right whether or not, on balance, she would be justified in having done so. B's claim to repair is justified because his right so defined was invaded. Moreover, A's rendering compensation to B does not exhaust B's claims regarding the terms of transfer. B maintains his claim against all such imposed transfers. The Infringement Thesis can now be seen to rely upon a particular analysis of what it means to have a right, namely what we have called the classical liberal account.

B's entitlement could, of course, generate quite different claims, such as those set out in (3) above. Under these circumstances, B may be free to seek *ex ante* agreement with A, and should they reach an accord, the ensuing transfer would be legitimate. Should negotiations fail, or should *A* choose to circumvent them from the outset, she is free to impose a transfer upon *B*. In doing so, *A*'s rendering *B* compensation is a condition of her doing so legitimately. If compensation is full and otherwise adequate, *B*'s claims against *A* are fully exhausted.

In this case, *B*'s claim to repair does not rest on his right having been invaded. On the contrary, compensation for *A*'s taking is all that *B* is entitled to. A claim to repair that arises from a liability rule as in (3) does not rest on a right's having been involved but is, instead, a condition of a right's having been fully respected – of its claims having been fully exhausted.

In sum, legitimate claims to repair need not presuppose action contrary to a preexisting right, for two reasons. First, wrongful harming of an interest can give rise to a right to repair for subsequent damages even if the interest itself does not rise to the level of a right. Second, even in those cases in which compensation presupposes a right, it need not presuppose action contrary to the right; in some cases rendering recompense is all that is required to respect the right and to exhaust the claims it entails. This is another way of saying that if a person's entitlements in the domain of transfer happen to be specified by a combination of property and liability rules like (3), in which case *ex post* compensation specifies a condition of legitimate transfer, then recompense is what is required to respect a right; it is not someone's due in virtue of his right's having been in some sense disrespected.[24]

Let us stay with this distinction between (3) and (3′) for a moment. If, by connecting compensation with the invasion of a right, philosophers have taken inadequate notice of transaction rules like (3), rules that treat *ex post* compensation as satisfying the claims entailed by a right, economists have been guilty of precisely the opposite mistake: that is, of failing to appreciate the extent to which compensation *ex post* does not legitimate transfers. Economists, in other words, inadequately appreciate rules like (3′). Let us see where they go wrong.

3.2. Compensation, rights and utility

At one end of the tort-theoretic spectrum, recompense is conceived of as a device for respecting prior entitlements and for reinforcing the claims to which those rights give rise. This is the view of torts that certainly emerges within the libertarian and perhaps within other rights-based traditions. It is a view of torts suggested by the Infringement Thesis and exemplified by the role liability rules play in (3').

At the other end of the spectrum are theorists who view compensation rendered *ex post* as a kind of licensing fee one has to pay in order to take things to which others in fact are entitled. In this view, tortious actions are conceived of as private takings in which the role compensation plays between private parties is analogous to the role it plays under the takings clause of the Fifth Amendment to the U.S. Constitution. In that context, compensation is understood as legitimating transfers of private resources to public uses. Making one's victims whole is viewed as the price one pays to make justifiable or legitimate use of another's resources for one's private purposes.

While the rectificatory conception of liability rules emerges from the "justice" or "rights" traditions, the "takings" view of them falls out of the larger economic framework. To see this, suppose that the norms governing legitimate transfer were derived from the principle of efficiency. What turns out to be efficient depends of course on contingent features of the world. If the parties are rational and transaction costs are low, governing their relationship by property rules in jointly wealth maximizing. When transactions are costly, however, wealth maximization requires forgoing property for liability rules. Liability rules, then, define a realm of takings which may be rendered legitimate (because efficient) by *ex post* compensation. In a well-formulated, efficient tort law, injurers do not have a duty to refrain from harming others, but to compensate for the harm they cause. Compensation, in this view, is not redress for wrong done. Indeed, it cannot be; liability rules exist to specify the terms of legitimate transfer when the costs of setting those terms in a market are too great. Instead, it is instrumental in ensuring the movement of resources to more highly valued uses, an end, given the overall goal of efficiency, that renders the "forced exchange" legitimate.

In contrast, if liability rules in torts function as they do in (3'), compensation serves not to legitimate forced transfer, but to redress wrongs done. Compensation for loss owing to a wrong is not equivalent to righting the wrong. It does not serve as a way of righting what would, in its absence, constitute a wrong. The difference between (3) and (3') is just the difference between the claim that conduct is conditionally wrong, depending upon the payment of compensation, and the claim that some conduct is wrong, whether or not compensation is paid. Compensation is due in the latter case to redress losses resulting from failure to

comply with the conditions of legitimate transfer, not to legitimate it. Compensation can legitimate transfer, as it does in (3),
only if both the liability and the property rule specify sufficient
conditions of legitimate transfer. Once the distinction between (3)
and (3') is clarified, it is obvious that the key, but inadequately
examined, issue in tort theory is whether liability rules ought to
be thought of as they are in (3), as justifying forced transfer, or in
(3'), as denying the legitimacy of forced transfer. The difference
between the takings or conditional liability view of torts and the
rights view of torts is just the difference between the interpretation
liability rules are given in (3) and (3') respectively – and that is all
the difference in the world.

This discussion suggests two questions: one normative, the other
positive. In an ideal world, what sort of tort system ought we
have: one in which compensation legitimates forced transfers only
– as in (3) – or one in which compensation is paid because all
forced transfers are wrongful – as in (3') – or some combination
of the two? The answer to this question ultimately depends on
one's foundational view. The second question is positive. It asks
whether the best explanation of current tort law is an economic or
a justice one: one that emphasizes the legitimating (3) or the rectificatory (3') dimensions of tort liability. Both accounts of current
tort law have been enthusiastically endorsed. Neither strikes us as
completely compelling.[25]

When Lake Erie Corporation is required to pay the damages
caused by its ship's ramming into Vincent's dock, its liability payment can be interpreted plausibly as a condition of legitimating its
use or taking of the dock.[26] Similarly, when the Perini Corporation is required to make good garage owner Spano's losses resulting from Perini's nonnegligent blasting, it is plausible to interpret
Perini's liability as constituting a condition of its legitimately
blasting.[27] Nonnegligent blasting is permissible provided compensation is paid; otherwise not. On the other hand, when drunken
Jones recklessly rams his car into someone, it is not plausible to
interpret his liability rule as specifying terms of legitimate transfer.
This becomes even more obvious once we note that certain intentional torts warrant punitive damages or even criminal sanctions,
which can only make sense if we deny that rendering compensation is always sufficient to legitimate transfer.[28]

The claim that liability rules invariably constitute forms of legitimate transfer is ludicrous, but this has not prevented intelligent
people from embracing it explicitly or being otherwise committed
to it. Of all economic analysts of torts, Richard Posner seems to

be most obviously committed to precisely this position. (He is committed to this claim, we will show, by the internal logic of his argument, not by any explicit assertion.) In arguing in another context for the claim that adopting Pareto-improving policies is morally justified, Posner claims that because a Pareto improvement makes at least one person better off and no one worse off, it secures the consent of each affected party. Thus, Pareto improvements are justified on consensual grounds; that is, they are justified because all the affected parties consent to them. It is this line of argument that creates the problem for Posner's tort theory. Let us see why.

If we suppose that Pareto improvements are consented to, then it must also follow that an individual gives his consent by accepting compensation *ex post*. That is because some Pareto improvements are made by imposing losses and then rendering compensation. And if all Pareto improvements are consented to by the relevant parties, the initially injured party must be presumed to give his consent by accepting compensation *ex post*. Under a liability rule, therefore, full compensation turns an illegitimate act, that is, a forced transfer, into a legitimate one, that is, an *"ex post consensual exchange."* In this view, the legitimating force of liability rules comes from the fact that in accepting full compensation injured parties give their consent. When conjoined with the presumption that injurers act voluntarily (consensually), the net result is a consensualist defense of liability rules. Liability rules set up "forced but consented-to exchanges." Because the exchanges are consented to, they are legitimate. Liability rules, therefore, always specify terms of legitimate transfer.[29]

An argument like Posner's treats liability rules as normatively equivalent to property rules. In both cases consent turns out to be the necessary and sufficient condition of legitimate transfer. Under property rules, consent is given *ex ante;* under liability rules, it is given *ex post* – through the acceptance of compensation. The difference between them is temporal, that is, when consent is given. And that is a function of relevant facts or conditions of the world, for example the presence or absence of significant transaction costs. In the standard economic account, liability rules substitute for property rules when transaction costs are significant.

If Posner is right, one kind of economic response to our puzzle about *Spur,* namely how liability rules can protect rights if they turn control or autonomy over to others, is that on a deeper level, liability rules return autonomy or control to entitled parties by requiring their consent to "forced transfers": that consent being given by their acceptance of compensation *ex post*. Because Pareto improvements through liability rules are consented to (by definition), there is no real incompatibility between the economic and classical liberal conceptions of rights. A Posnerian account of liability rules simply eliminates the tension between liability rules and the classical liberal conception of rights, a tension that motivates our analysis in the first place. Posner pulls the rug from under us by arguing, in effect, that efficiency is just another way of talking about autonomy.

Fortunately for us, the Posnerian reduction of efficiency to autonomy rests on the deeply confused claim that accepting compensation entails giving one's consent.[30] If Posner were right, the only way in which a victim of another's wrongdoing could refuse to give his consent to being wronged would be to refuse compensation. If however he demands and receives compensation as his due because he has been wronged, then he consents to his being wronged. Surely this is a perverse enough consequence of the compensation-as-consent claim to dismiss it as implausible, if not incoherent.

Nonconsensual economists – those who argue for liability rules on straightforward efficiency grounds – do not face this objection. Of course, they face the problem of defending efficiency on normative grounds other than consent. Interestingly, like Posner, these economists treat liability and property rules on a normative par. Both are defensible because, used properly, both can be efficient. Liability rules can be efficient, but an efficient transfer can nevertheless be an illegitimate transfer, if, for example, it violates someone's rights. The problem is how a transfer imposed under a liability rule can be legitimate if it involves taking that to which another is entitled. The problem, once again, is to square the efficiency of liability rules with the concept of right. Liability rules can be efficient, but are they compatible with rights? Can they protect or secure rights?

One approach the economist could take would be to assert that efficiency, not compatibility with or respect for rights, is the criterion of legitimacy. Alternatively, he could stipulate a definition of efficiency such that action in violation of a right is necessarily inefficient. A more intriguing solution to what we take to be a genuine, serious problem would try to render efficiency and rights compatible by providing an efficiency theory or analysis of rights. The trick is to analyze a right to something as giving someone a guarantee of a stream of welfare or utility, and no more. Facts of the world will then dictate how this stream of welfare or utility is to be realized. When transaction costs are low, the stream of utility is secured by exchange; when exchange is sufficiently costly, it may be secured by liability rules. In neither case does having a right entail any control or liberty, but in every case having a right guarantees a stream of utility.

Here, as in the compensation-as-consent view, property and liability rules are treated as normative equivalents: not because liability rules are really property rules with a temporally delayed consent element, but because both liability and property rules are ways, in differing circumstances, of giving right holders what they are entitled to, namely, a particular level of welfare or utility.

The Posnerian account of the relationship among liability, property rules and rights analyzes rights in terms of a realm of autonomy or control and then argues that, contrary to what we might otherwise have thought, liability rules, in virtue of their compensatory element, specify a realm of autonomy. The traditional economic approach analyzes rights entirely in terms of individual utilities,[31] in which case property and liability rules are simply instruments; and the choice between them is entirely a function of pertinent facts of the world, such as transaction costs. In both accounts, liability rules legitimate forced transfers in spite of the fact that the transfer is a taking of what another is entitled to. Both accounts achieve this result by offering distinct conceptions of what it means to have a right. The Posnerian opts for the classical or autonomy theory of rights, and argues that by accepting compensation an individual fully exercises his autonomy over his holdings. In contrast, the traditional economist opts for a welfare or utility conception of rights, and argues that, provided the compensation is adequate, paying compensation fully exhausts one's claims within the scope of one's rights.

Both theories, in addition to justifying liability rules as legitimating transfers (rather than as compensating for wrongs), solve as well the conflict between liability rules and the classical liberal conception of rights. The Posnerian manages this feat by accepting the classical theory and reconstructing liability rules as instruments of autonomy. The traditional economist solves the riddle the easy way; he dumps the classical liberal theory of rights in favor of a more convenient economic one.

The argument to this point is a bit misleading. I have argued at length that liability rules do not always serve a legitimating function. Yet I have just taken pains to show how on two different economic theories of them, liability rules seem invariably to legitimate. This last discussion, in particular, would appear to suggest that economic analysis is unable to contemplate liability rules other than as setting conditions of legitimate transfer. But economic analysis can in fact comprehend alternative uses of liability rules, though only at the expense of abandoning the economic analysis of rights. Because I have argued for a theory of rights in which rights are neither necessarily utilities nor liberties, this is a price well worth paying. The first task is to show that it is a price that must be paid.

I have taken some care in distinguishing two forms of economic analysis comprehending two different economic theories of rights. In the traditional theory, acts, rules or institutions are justified if and only if they are efficient, while in consensualist theory they are justified if and only if they are (or would have been) consented to. In Posner's view, for example, the consent or autonomy theory is the deeper one, because only it provides an independent, non-question-begging reason for pursuing efficiency. Moreover, only it renders efficiency and the classical theory of rights compatible. Happily, the two forms of argument, efficiency and autonomy, converge on outcomes, or so he believes. Now let us see how these two conceptions of rights fit with the role of liability in torts.

Consider the case of the reckless driver, whose unjustifiably risky conduct injures a pedestrian. Under the classical liberal view, the victim's right not to be injured or harmed entails that others are not free to "injure" or "take" without securing his consent. In this analysis his right not to be harmed is intended to secure a realm of autonomous control over what happens to him. Under the compensation-as-consent thesis, if the reckless motorist fully compensates his victim, he secures the injured party's consent, and thereby rights what otherwise might have been a wrong. Compensation under a liability rule gives consent and thereby satisfies the autonomy condition imposed by rights ownership. The reckless driver did no wrong and in the end violated no one's rights; or, alternatively, the victim consented to the wrong.

This is the merger of classical liberalism and economic efficiency achieved by the compensation-as-consent trick. The merger, if it worked, would have one desirable property, but one fatal flaw as well. It is the same property in both cases. The problem is that the same argument that legitimates forced but efficient transfers legitimates forced but inefficient transfers as well. The elements of consent are present whenever the victim accepts compensation and the injurer acts voluntarily (which is distinguishable from whether he acted rationally or efficiently). Neither actor need have acted efficiently. The consensual form of economic analysis is compatible with the liberal conception of rights as secured liberties, but it is overbroad; if the compensation-as-consent account justifies anything, it justifies too much, at least from an efficiency point of view. Presumably, the economist wants to justify liability rules only if they are efficient; but they can be consented to (in the Posnerian sense) even when they are inefficient.

The traditional form of economic analysis can avoid the problem of having to hold that the "forced exchange" between the reckless driver and the pedestrian is legitimate, but not without cost. The traditional efficiency economist almost certainly will begin by noting that reckless conduct is, by definition, inefficient. Negligence is, following the Hand formula, inefficient: The costs of accident avoidance are less than the expected value of the harm. Recklessness is just gross negligence. Therefore, the reckless motorist who makes repair under the liability rules does not legitimate his "taking." So the economist wants to deny – with good reason – that such a transfer is legitimate, even if consented to. But can he? There is a problem in his doing so, and here it is.

In the standard form of economic analysis, rights are defined in terms of guaranteed streams of utility or welfare. This is the move that makes it possible for liability rules to legitimate transfers in the first place. By compensating someone an amount equal to the level of utility secured by his right, a "taker" ensures that his "victim's" right is fully respected, its claims against the taker fully exhausted. But look what happens when this analysis of rights is transposed to the context of a reckless motorist. If the "forced transfer" is not legitimate, it cannot be because in taking without the pedestrian's permission the injurer violated the pedestrian's right. By rendering full compensation under the liability rule, he gave the pedestrian all that his right entitled him to – given the economic account of rights. If the transfer is illegitimate, it cannot be because it violates the pedestrian's right. So considerations of efficiency lead the economist to deny the legitimacy of the transfer, but his analysis of rights prevents him from doing so.

The culprit is the economic conception of rights and the corollary conception of liability rules either as legitimating transfer or as exhausting the claims of rights. One way of avoiding the conclusion that, by compensating the pedestrian, the reckless motorist violates no right of his is to deny that a pedestrian's right is to a level of welfare or utility only. The pedestrian's right against the motorist is not a right to compensation only. It is not a right, in other words, whose content can be given by a liability rule as in

(3). Instead, the pedestrian's right must be specified by a liability rule such as in (3′). As between (3) and (3′), only in (3′) does the payment of compensation fail to legitimate. The failure is because, according to (3′), only voluntary agreement legitimates transfer. So if the economist wants to deny that the reckless motorist's conduct is legitimate – which he rightly wants to do – then he has to claim that by paying compensation the motorist does not give the pedestrian what he is entitled to, does not respect his rights. What we need is a transaction rule like (3′) in which compensation fails to legitimate or, alternatively and more naturally in this context, an inalienability–liability rule combination. This discussion leads to two important conclusions.

First, the economist has to give up what we called the economic conception of rights in which rights are merely secured levels of welfare. For the example of the reckless motorist shows that the only way to deny the legitimacy of inefficient forced but fully compensated transfers is to claim that some rights are more than guarantees of utility alone. Second, and perhaps more important, sometimes the foundation goal of efficiency is best secured by having rights secure liberties rather than interests. Sometimes, autonomy-preserving rules like (3′) can be utility maximizing. A domain of rights as secured liberties may be required on utilitarian or efficiency grounds. So even if the goal of the law is to promote overall welfare or utility, it does not follow that the legal rights created for that end are themselves conceptually no more than guarantees of welfare or utility. As a matter of logic or necessity, legal rights are neither protected domains of autonomy nor levels of protected welfare. Their content is a contingent matter depending on the foundational theory. Moreover, as this discussion shows, even a broad utilitarian foundational theory will not, indeed cannot, always specify the content of rights in terms of utilities or interests only.

Standard economic analysis emphasizes the role of liability rules in legitimating transfer under conditions of high transaction costs. This emphasis leads the economist to think of legal rights in largely utilitarian terms, as protected levels of welfare, and to ignore at the same time the role of liability rules in redressing for wrong done. Focusing on illegitimate forced transfers, however, enables us to broaden the economist's understanding of legal rights while allowing us to demonstrate once again our central claim, namely that it is a mistake to analyze rights as necessarily specifying either a realm of autonomy or a level of welfare. Rights are just conceptual markers. The extent to which rights turn out to secure a realm of control or to guarantee a level of welfare will depend on the foundational theory and the structure of human interaction. It will rest on normative argument, in the light of pertinent facts of the world, not on conceptual analysis.

More important, whether liability rules in particular contexts turn out to specify terms of legitimate transfer will depend on whether particular rights secure a realm of control or a level of utility. Consequently, it is a mistake to treat liability rules as if they always specified terms of legitimate transfer: no greater a mistake, however, than to treat them as if they never did. The simple truth is that liability rules in torts play both roles. Distinguishing between them in a principled manner is the task of tort theory.[32]

4. THE TRANSACTION STRUCTURE AND THE CRIMINAL LAW

One purported advantage of the property–liability–inalienability rule framework is that it suggests a plausible explanation of the existence of the criminal law. In the Calabresi–Melamed view, the criminal law exists to discourage individuals from turning property rules into liability rules. Richard Posner advances roughly the same position. The criminal law exists to encourage market forms of transfer (property rules) when individuals might otherwise prefer to impose nonconsensual transfers.[33] In both the Calabresi–Melamed and Posner views, the basic idea is simple. Circumstances are likely to arise in which the costs to nonentitled parties of respecting property rules exceed the costs of imposed transfer. Absent adequate incentives, nonentitled parties will naturally opt for the less costly (to them) means of transfer. The criminal law provides the incentive necessary to induce respect for property rules. In this sense, it prevents nonentitled parties from converting property rules into liability rules.

In an excellent article, Alvin Klevorick expands upon the Calabresi–Melamed–Posner explanation.[34] Klevorick argues that in addition to discouraging individuals from turning property into liability rules, the criminal law discourages individuals from turning both inalienability and liability rules into property rules. In short, Klevorick's view is that the criminal law attempts to induce compliance with the entirety of the transaction structure.

In my view, the transaction framework partially specifies the content of rights by setting forth conditions of legitimate transfer. The property–liability rule framework does not in general protect rights. One question we might ask then is whether the economic argument for a criminal category is affected by our understanding of the role of transaction rules in the analysis of entitlements. This is the question I want to raise and answer in this section; but before we reach it, I want to consider whether the familiar economic explanation outlined above is persuasive.

Before I evaluate the economic argument, a bit of clarification is in order. Despite having a system of injunctions and tort-like remedies to enforce certain claims, an enjoined party might refuse to comply with an injunction, or a party liable in torts might refuse to pay damages. A criminal law might then be necessary to enforce compliance. In this sense the criminal law is always in the background of the transaction structure, supporting it as a whole. The criminal law, or some institutional arrangement very much like it, is therefore necessary to enforce the primary means of institutional relief. Notice that this is by no means a purely economic argument for the criminal law. Nor is it a very robust one, for the essential crimes are easily enumerated: (1) failure to abide by an injunction, (2) failure to pay tort damages, (3) failure to pay damages awarded for breach of contract and so forth. All "crimes" would be contingent upon other forms of remedial relief. And the criminal law would itself enforce no standards of behavior other than those imposing the duty to comply with injunctions, damage awards and the like.

Those who have attempted to explain the existence of a criminal category by reference to the transaction framework have invariably had something else in mind. In their view, the criminal law is necessary not just because a person who is enjoined may seek to ignore the injunction, but because individuals may seek to convert transaction rules of one sort into rules of another sort. The claim is that for every transaction they face, individuals will decide whether to seek *ex ante* agreement or to pay compensation *ex post* entirely on grounds of maximizing utility. The transaction structure is intended to make this decision nonoptional, but in the absence of a criminal law, rational individuals will consider themselves free to conduct transactions on terms dictated by expediency rather than on terms specified by the transaction structure. But this analysis of the necessity of the criminal law is inconsistent with the standard economic interpretation of the transaction structure.

In the Calabresi–Melamed view, property rules provide for injunctive relief. The post–Calabresi–Melamed literature also treats the availability of injunction relief as entailed by property rules. That is why the prevailing wisdom is that a rational person would prefer to have his entitlements "protected" by property rules rather than by liability rules. At best, liability rules guarantee compensation set by a third party. A rational person should expect to do at least as well negotiating on his own behalf – especially if the property rights are well defined and if his entitlement is secured by injunction.

But if injunctions are part of the meaning of property rules – as standard economic analysis assumes – then the criminal law cannot be necessary to induce compliance with property rules. A person who is enjoined from taking is prevented from taking. Because he is prevented from taking, he is not in a position to treat the property rule as if it were a liability rule. If injunctions can be sufficient to prevent individuals from converting property rules to liability rules, the criminal law cannot be necessary.[35]

A better argument for the criminal category, consistent with he argument advanced by Calabresi–Melamed, Posner and Klevorick, relies on a distinction between known and unknown injurers. Not everyone who might invade *B*'s rights will be known to him. Against those individuals, an injunction affords *B* no relief. The reason is obvious; *B* doesn't know whose conduct to enjoin. In these cases, injunctive relief is not available. A taking contrary to the property rule will call for compensation only, and strangers who cannot be enjoined will thus be free to treat property rules as if they were liability rules. Here is a place for the criminal law, not as an enforcer of injunctions, but as a "kicker" which, when conjoined with potential damage awards, may suffice to induce compliance with property rules among strangers. The combined costs to a stranger of liability (discounted by the probability of its being imposed) and the criminal sanction (similarly discounted) can be designed to exceed whatever gain he expects by forgoing voluntary agreement in favor of forced exchange. Properly set, the combined costs may be sufficient to induce compliance with property rules. This is the right sort of economic argument for the criminal category because it explains the role that criminal law plays in inducing compliance with property rules when, in the absence of a criminal law, individuals (in this case, strangers) would in fact have reason to ignore them in favor of liability rules.

Unfortunately, this argument for the criminal law explains a good deal less than the traditional economic argument purports to. It applies only to strangers, because only against strangers are injunctions infeasible. The standard argument is more robust, but unsound.

I now want to consider whether the economic argument for the criminal law is more robust if, instead of treating property and liability rules as ways of protecting rights, we treat them, as I suggest they ought to be treated, as normative rules specifying the content of rights within the transactional domain. It is not.

Transaction rules themselves entail no institutions of enforcement. They merely specify terms or conditions of transfer. Consequently, in the absence of enforcement mechanisms of any sort, nonentitled parties may be encouraged to disregard entirely the legitimacy of the claims of entitled parties, whether to *ex ante* agreement or to *ex post* compensation. Suppose B is entitled to be free of A's pollution, and that we specify in part the content of that right by a property rule. A cannot pollute B other than on terms agreeable to B. If no enforcement mechanism of any sort is available to vindicate B's claim, A may be encouraged simply to bypass it. It is not as if he will treat B's claim differently, as a claim to repair under a liability rule, as if he had any intention of paying damages. Absent means of enforcement, nonentitled parties do not turn or convert one sort of rule into another so much as they may be disposed to ignore the lot of them.

A criminal law which penalizes individuals for failing to respect property, liability and inalienability rules may be adequate to induce compliance with the conditions set forth in each, provided that both the absolute level of the penalty and the probability of its being administered quickly are sufficiently high. But this argument for a criminal law is not that in its absence nonentitled parties will substitute one sort of transaction rule for another. Instead, this argument for the criminal law is that in its absence nonentitled parties may be inclined to treat the entitlements of others as if they imposed no constraints on them at all.

However sound, this reinterpretation of the economic argument for the criminal law establishes only that the criminal law may be sufficient to induce compliance with the transaction structure, not that it is necessary. Nor does this argument suggest that the point of the criminal category is to prevent individuals from substituting transaction rules for one another.[36]

5. INTERESTS, LIBERTIES AND TRANSACTION STRUCTURE

Calabresi and Melamed do not address the question of whether the transaction structure is compatible with all possible analyses of rights. In contrast, our account of the property–liability rule distinction is motivated in part by a desire to respond to the tension between liability rules and the classical liberal conception of rights. The tension is expressed in the questions raised in the *Spur* case: How can liability rules protect entitlements if a liability rule provides nonentitled parties a liberty to impose transfers on terms set by third parties? How can forced transfer be made compatible with the liberal conception of rights?

I said earlier that a correct analysis of rights would require giving up both the classical liberal conception of rights and the economic conception of the proper role of property and liability rules. The time has come to see if I have made good on my promise. In the economic conception of them, property and liability rules protect rights. I have argued that they do not; that instead they specify the content of rights over the transactional domain. The classical liberal conception holds that rights necessarily specify a domain of autonomy or control. We have shown that the claims to which rights give rise depend on the transaction rules applied to them, and that the choice of transaction rule depends on the foundational theory. Sometimes one's rights require others to seek agreement as a condition of transfer; other times not. This is one consequence of the distinction, much emphasized here, between (3) and (3′). In either case, moreover, the choice between (3) and (3′) depends on the purposes for which institutions are designed; and so whether rights provide autonomy or are designed purely to guarantee a level of welfare is a contingent feature of them, resolved not by appeal to meanings but by appeal to justifications. To the extent the classical liberal conception of rights is taken as providing an account of the meaning of the concept, it too fails.

Having made good on my basic claim, I want to close by exploring briefly some other connections between rights and liability rules. The alleged incompatibility of the economic framework and the liberal conception of rights presupposes not just that rights secure a domain of autonomy but that liability rules necessarily place nonentitled parties at liberty. In fact, there are at least two kinds of cases in which liability rules fail to confer a liberty to compel transfer. The first is by now very familiar. If the content of an entitlement is given by a combination of property and liability rules – in which case *ex ante* agreement is both necessary and sufficient for legitimate transfer, and a taking creates a claim to recompense but does not legitimate, as in (3′) – the liability rule does not warrant forced transfer.

Second, suppose I have a right against you that you not do x, and that the content of my right over the domain of transfer is given by a liability rule only. If you do x, I have a claim against

you to repair, no more. It does not follow that you are at liberty
to do *x,* even if you compensate me – even if my claim against
you has been exhausted – because doing *x* may be wrong on other
grounds. And if it is wrong to do *x* (e.g., to torture me), then you
are not at liberty to do *x* even if I am no longer entitled or empow-
ered to prevent you. It is not, therefore, part of the meaning of
liability rules that they place nonentitled parties at liberty to compel transfer. Another way, therefore, in which the tension between liability rules and classical liberalism can be eased is simply
to emphasize that liability rules do not always function as economic analysis suggests they do: as setting terms of forced transfer.

I have argued against both the economic conception of liability
rules and the classical liberal theory of rights. Given my analysis
of liability rules, it is possible, even within classical liberal theory,
to convey a sense in which liability rules protect rights. That is,
even if rights necessarily secure a domain of autonomy or control,
liability rules could sometimes be construed as protecting them.
Here is how. Once again, the key is (3'). Under (3'), property
rules specify fully the conditions of legitimate transfer, so that the
liability rule component plays no role in legitimating transfers imposed against a right holder's will. The liability rule simply provides the right holder with a claim to relief grounded on the injurer's conduct violating the conditions of transfer set out by the
property rule, that is, its invasion of the relevant right. The right
to relief is grounded not just in the harming of an interest, but in
the transfer's occurring without the right holder's's *ex ante* consent. Where property rules specify fully the content of a right over
the transactional domain, as they must if rights mark liberties, and
as they can even if rights mark interests, then a liability rule can
serve to protect the relevant liberty or interest, not by specifying
an alternative mode of legitimate transfer, but by increasing the
costs to injurers of their invasive conduct. This is not to say that
liability rules are sufficient to secure liberty of control and transfer,
only that there is a limited sense even within the liberal–libertarian
conception of entitlements in which liability rules protect rights.

Ultimately what sets apart the classical liberal and economic
conceptions of rights and liability rules is the case in which liability
rules are thought sufficient to justify a transfer, not the case in
which liability is imposed because the injurer failed to respect a
victim's rights. For it can never be any part of the classical liberal
account that by compensating someone for taking what is his
without his consent, an injurer respects the victim's rights; whereas

the core of economic analysis is the possibility that by compensating a victim, an injurer (at least sometimes) gives his victim all that he is entitled to, thereby legitimating the taking. And it is precisely this sort of role for liability rules that emerges within the economic account in which liability rules are introduced because transaction costs preclude voluntary movement of resources to higher-valued uses.

It is not surprising, then, that although I have shown that the transaction structure is not restricted to economic analysis, it was first developed and, to this point, has been fully appreciated only within the overall economic framework. I hope that by more accurately and fully analyzing the transaction structure, especially its role within an overall theory of institutional entitlements, I have helped to widen its applications while locating and strengthening its foundations.

PART II

Law and economics

3. Efficiency, auction and exchange

1. INTRODUCTION

Conversational literacy in neoclassical welfare economics is an apparent prerequisite to gainful employment in American law schools. Loose talk of efficiency, cost minimization and the liability rule–property rule distinction punctuates faculty lounge discussions. There is simply no denying that the new law-and-economics has arrived. So it is a fond (if only temporary) farewell to Rawls and Nozick, and a warm welcome to Coase, Pigou, Calabresi and Posner.

The new law-and-economics is not without critics, however. There is a growing literature which represents the view that law-and-economics ought to be relegated to a suitable place in the history of intellectual fads – the sooner, the better. Much of what has been written against law-and-economics, however, is based on unsympathetic, insensitive and largely superficial understandings of the central works in the field. Unfortunately, much of what is written in the name of law-and-economics is equally insensitive to the limits within which economic analysis might prove fruitful. As unsound criticisms and unwarranted extensions of the economic approach to law mount, the time appears ripe for an examination of its analytic framework.

Three distinct but related activities fall within the domain of law-and-economics: Two of these are conceptual in nature; one is normative. Analytic law-and-economics may be either descriptive or positive. Descriptive law-and-economics is concerned with the principle of economic efficiency as an explanatory tool by which existing legal rules and decisions may be rationalized or comprehended. Richard Posner's "Theory of Negligence"[1] is characteristic of this approach. In his essay, Posner attempts to show that a large number of negligence cases were decided along lines of economic efficiency. His view is not that judges articulated and invariably applied an economic standard of adjudication. Instead, he claims that these cases may be rationalized or reconstructed in light of an economic theory of adjudication.

Positive law-and-economics is concerned less with the actual explanatory power of economic efficiency than it is with the capacity of market models to provide a conceptual apparatus within which traditional legal problems may be conceived. Typical is Isaac Ehrlich's work on crime.[2] Ehrlich presents the interplay between the criminal, viewed as engaged in an economic activity – namely, committing crimes – and the criminal law and the rules and strategies governing its enforcement as the medium through which consumers – namely, possible victims of crime – express their decisions about how much crime they are willing to accept at various prevention prices.

Normative law-and-economics is the home of reformers. Existing legal rules are evaluated and new ones fashioned in terms of their economic efficiency. Guido Calabresi's *The Costs of Accidents*[3] is an exemplary text in normative law-and-economics. It sets out and evaluates various systems of accident law according to the capacity of each to minimize the sum of the costs of accidents and the costs of avoiding them.

Whether the new law-and-economics is restricted to model theoretic applications or whether instead it is advanced as an explanatory or normative discipline, its central organizing idea is that of economic efficiency. The concept of economic efficiency, however, is complex and widely misunderstood. There are three or perhaps four notions of efficiency it comprehends – allocative efficiency, Pareto optimality, Pareto superiority and Kaldor–Hicks efficiency.[4] Inadequate understanding of the diversity of these concepts surfaces in both inapt applications and unfounded criticisms of the economic approach to law. Distinguishing the good from the bad in law-and-economics requires a deeper appreciation of the relationships among these notions of efficiency than has marked the literature to this point. The purpose of this essay is to provide at least the beginnings of such an understanding. Section 2 discusses Coase's theorem and the concept of allocative efficiency. Section 3 defines Pareto optimality and superiority and considers an argument that Coase's theorem is not about efficiency in the Paretian sense. Section 4 briefly discusses Coasian and Pigouvian approaches to externalities. Section 5 discusses Richard Posner's "auction rule" for assigning entitlements where bargains cannot be struck and explores its relationship to Paretian and Kaldor–Hicks notions of efficiency. Section 6 raises doubts about the adequacy of Posner's property right assignment rule as a duplication of the essential aspects of Coase's theorem. The essay concludes with some brief remarks about the force of efficiency arguments in matters of public policy.

2. COASE'S THEOREM AND ALLOCATIVE EFFICIENCY

One way of stating Coase's theorem[5] – the one that is thought to have the most relevance to law–and–economics – is: Given traditional assumptions of substantial knowledge,[6] perfect rationality and the absence of both transaction costs and income effects,[7] the assignment of legal entitlements in cases of two-party incompatible land uses will be neutral as to the goal of allocative efficiency. A simple example best develops this insight.

Suppose that a rancher and a farmer own adjacent plots of land. The rancher raises cattle on his land, while the farmer plants corn on his. Suppose as well that at the present time the rancher raises only one cow. He wants to raise a second cow. The farmer is opposed to this, however, because a roaming second cow will cause additional crop damage. Coase demonstrates that provided the rights are divisible and transferable the initial assignment of relevant property rights does not determine whether the second (or additional) cow is actually raised.

To see this, let us suppose that the value of the second cow to the rancher is $50. This figure represents his gain (profit) from raising a second cow. The cost imposed on the farmer by the second cow is the market value of the crop damage caused by the cow. The crop damage may be greater than, equal to or less than the value of the second cow. Consider two cases. In one, the value of the expected crop damage is, say, $25; in the other, it is $75.

The rancher will raise an additional cow in the first case; he will not in the second. These results are independent of the initial assignment of entitlements. In the first case, if the state assigns the farmer the right to prohibit a second cow, the parties will reach an agreement whereby the farmer will permit the rancher to raise a second cow, in return for which the rancher will compensate the farmer for any crop damage the second cow causes (plus whatever surplus the farmer's negotiation skills bring him). Provided they are able to negotiate with each other, the farmer is willing to sell his right to prohibit a second cow for at least $25 and the rancher is willing to purchase it for as much as $50. Under these conditions, rational persons will reach an accord that will entitle the rancher to a second cow. If, in the first case, however, the state

assigns the entitlement to the rancher straightaway, no transaction
will occur. The farmer will be unwilling to purchase the right to
prohibit the second cow for any more than the value of the crop
damage, that is, $25. The rancher, on the other hand, will be un-
willing to part with his entitlement for less than the value of the
second cow to him, that is, $50. When the marginal value of the
second cow exceeds the marginal value of the expected corn-crop
damage, the rancher will raise a second cow. This result occurs
regardless of the initial assignment of entitlements.

In the second case – in which the marginal value of the expected
crop damage exceeds the marginal value of the second cow – the
additional cow will not be raised. If the state assigns to the rancher
the right to raise a second cow, the farmer and the rancher will
reach an accord in which the farmer, in exchange for the right to
prohibit a second cow, will pay the rancher an amount greater
than or equal to the value of the cow to the rancher, that is, $50,
and less than or equal to the value of the farmer's expected crop
damage, that is, $75. If, however, the state assigns to the farmer
the right to prohibit a second cow, no transaction will occur. The
rancher will be unwilling to offer more than $50; the farmer will
be unwilling to accept less than $75. Thus, regardless of the initial
assignment of entitlements, the rancher will not raise a second cow
in this case.

The primary lesson of Coase's example is that whether or not
there will be a second, third, fourth or nth cow does not depend
on the initial assignment of property rights. Instead, the number
of cows raised and amount of corn grown are determined by the
intersection of the relevant marginal profit (of ranching cows) and
marginal damage (to corn) curves. The particular marginal profit
and damage curves depend in turn on the relative market values
of cows and corn. The farmer and the rancher will negotiate and
trade until it is no longer beneficial (profitable) for either (or both)
to trade further. The point at which bargaining ceases represents
an efficient allocation of cows and corn. There the resources are
put to their most productive use. This point is represented by the
intersection of the marginal profit and damage curves.[8]

Coase's theorem is not an empirical claim but is instead an analytic truth about what it means, under certain conditions, to act
rationally. In the circumstances suggested by the rancher–farmer
example, to act rationally is to maximize productive use of resources. Rationality requires of the incompatible land users that
they behave "as a firm" with two productive interests. The question before the "firm" is how to use the land to maximize its productive output or profit. The answer to that question, above all

else, depends on the market values of resources, not on the assignment of property rights. To act rationally, then, is to promote allocative efficiency, which, in cases of this sort, is to put resources to their profit-maximizing use. Although the assignment of entitlements is neutral as to the pursuit of optimal resource use, it is not neutral with respect to the distribution of wealth between competing land users. If the value of the second cow exceeds the value of expected crop damage, then the assignment of the property right to either party will have no impact on the rancher's raising a second cow. If the state assigns the entitlement to the farmer, however, he will sell it to the rancher for at least $25, thus increasing his wealth by that sum. If the state assigns the right to the rancher, his wealth will increase by the right's market value. Similarly, the assignment of entitlements will affect the parties' relative wealth in the case in which the value of the expected crop damage exceeds the value of the second cow.

The traditional understanding of Coase's theorem might be summarized as follows: Allocative efficiency, or the maximum productive use of resources, does not depend on the initial assignment of entitlements. The initial assignment is only the starting point for negotiations. The point at which negotiations cease represents the efficient allocation of resources. The initial assignment of entitlements, however, does affect the relative wealth of the competing parties simply because the assignment determines which party has to do the purchasing (or what economists misleadingly call bribing).

Economists differ about whether Coase's theorem can be extended to cover more complex cases involving multiparty transactions,[9] and about whether it holds in the short run only, that is, whether the efficient result is unique.[10] This essay will ignore those complications and focus instead on related matters pertaining to the limits within which the theorem may be legitimately extended. The first question concerns the relationship between the concept of allocational efficiency explored by Coase and the Paretian standards of efficiency employed in recent works about law-and-economics.

3. MIMICKING MARKETS: PARETO OPTIMALITY AND ALLOCATIVE EFFICIENCY

Any discussion of Pareto efficiency must begin with definitions of Pareto optimality, Pareto superiority and Pareto inferiority. To claim that resources or goods are allocated in a Pareto–optimal fashion is to maintain that any further reallocation of resources will benefit one person only at the expense of another. An allocation of resources is Pareto superior to an alternative allocation if and only if no person is disadvantaged by it and the lot of at least one person is improved. An allocation of resources is Pareto inferior to another if there is a distribution Pareto superior to it. The concepts of Pareto superiority and optimality are analytically connected in the following way: A Pareto-optimal distribution has no distributions Pareto superior to it.

Robert Nozick draws an important and useful distinction between "patterned" and "historical" allocation principles.[11] The distinguishing feature of patterned principles of allocation is that they evaluate existing distributions of wealth – what people have at any given moment in history – without considering the manner and history of acquisition. In contrast, a historical standard of evaluation emphasizes the manner in which people come to have what they have, and thereby rejects the plausibility of evaluating allocations purely against a history-neutral standard. Historical standards for evaluating allocations require that a story be told. Certain story lines are defensible; others are not. In any event, the given end state is normatively unimportant independent of the manner in which it was reached.

Nozick's distinction may be transposed to discussions of Pareto efficiency.[12] The patterned aspect of Pareto efficiency is captured by the idea of Pareto optimality. The historical aspect of Pareto efficiency is loosely captured by the idea of Pareto superiority. This distinction is easily understood. A Pareto-optimal distribution can be reached either by Pareto-superior steps or "moves," by Pareto-inferior moves or by a combination of the two. Saying that a distribution is Pareto efficient, therefore, may call attention to the efficiency of the existing distribution regardless of the efficiency of the steps along the way to it. In contrast, however, labeling a distribution Pareto efficient might mean not only that the existing distribution is Pareto optimal, but also that it is the result only of Pareto-superior (and efficient in that sense) moves. In "The Problem of Social Cost," Coase never explicitly uses Paretian notions of efficiency. He talks only about allocative and allocational efficiency. One argument recently proposed by George Fletcher denies that there is an analytic relationship between Paretian and allocative efficiency. Fletcher's argument is interesting for the following reason. The new law-and-economics is wedded to the Paretian standard and at the same time identifies its roots in Coase (as well as in Pigou). If Fletcher is right, then, much of the new law-and-economics derives from an unwarranted extension of Coase's theorem. In short, if Fletcher is right, the new law-and-economics may simply rest on a mistake. He writes that the leap of faith by the new school of law-and-economics is that bargains, say, between smokers and nonsmokers, are just like the problem of allocative efficiency between the rancher and the farmer. But there are two critical reasons that render this leap of faith but an embrace of the unknown.[13]

The crucial difference, according to Fletcher, is that in the rancher–farmer case, the rancher and the farmer bid against each other on the basis of established prices. This is significant for Fletcher because "it implies that the Coasian standard of allocative efficiency is immune to the distribution of income between farmer and rancher."[14] In contrast, the bargains struck between smokers and nonsmokers express their subjective preferences and are a function of their relative wealth. So the efficiency that results in the allocation of resources between crops and cows is different from the efficiency that results in the resource allocation between smokers and nonsmokers.

It is more fruitful to put this observation in a more technical fashion before considering its force. Suppose that the rancher–farmer and smoker–nonsmoker examples are understood to be providing definitions of rationality. The definition of rationality expressed in Coase's theorem apparently is: To act rationally is to maximize profits through optimal use of productive resources. The definition of rationality the smoker–nonsmoker example generates is this: To act rationally is to maximize utility or welfare through the satisfaction of one's preferences.

For Fletcher's argument to count against the new law-and-economics, the definition of rationality comprehended by cases of the smoker–nonsmoker variety would have to be an inappropriate extension of the definition of rationality comprehended by the rancher–farmer example. But it is not. Both Coase's example and the smoker–nonsmoker example express the general principle that to act rationally is to maximize individual utility. In Coase's rancher–farmer example, the relevant preference is profit maximization, and pursuing it obviously depends on market prices; the rancher's and the farmer's utility functions depend on the market prices of beef, grain and the like as well as on their wealth. Notably, nothing Coase says hangs on the fact that what the farmer and the rancher are willing to bid is a function of their interest in maximizing profit. The argument will work just as well if the farmer, for example, were willing to pay an additional $10 beyond the market cost of the expected corn damage just to avoid having another "ugly" cow in the neighborhood. In such a case his utility is a function both of his desire to profit and to live in an aesthetically pleasing environment.

Coase's example, then, is simply a special case of the general utility argument in which maximizing utility is extensionally equivalent to maximizing profit. It is a peculiar feature of Coase's example – which admittedly is not present in cases involving, for example, aesthetic preferences – that in seeking to maximize their respective welfare, both the farmer and the rancher ensure that the resources are put to their profit-maximizing use.

The argument against extending Coase's theorem to cases involving subjective preferences is based on an inadequate understanding of an important dimension of Coase's essay. Coase was trying to argue not only that the assignment of entitlements between, say, ranchers and farmers would be irrelevant to the efficiency of the ultimate allocation of cows and corn, but also that the resulting efficient allocation would be unique; and that its uniqueness could not be upset over the long run. Indeed, it is the uniqueness claim that is particularly novel and controversial. To argue for the uniqueness of the efficient allocation of cows and corn, Coase's proof assumes that the economy is perfectly competitive, that the prices of goods are set outside the context of the externality problem and, as it were, given to the rancher and the farmer (the partial equilibrium model), and that the bargains struck between the rancher and the farmer are not affected by their relative incomes; that is, their exchanges do not exhibit "income effects." That the farmer and the rancher bid against one another on the basis of established prices, then, is merely a constraint imposed on the argument in order to generate the uniqueness result. It is not relevant to the claim that the result of their exchanges will be efficient in either the allocational or Paretian sense. Whether the absence of constraint from income effects in conjunction with other assumptions of the argument suffices to establish uniqueness remains a matter of some controversy.[15]

Fletcher advances another intriguing argument against a Paretian interpretation of Coase's theorem. This argument requires reconsidering the rancher–farmer example. Consider the case in which the marginal value of the second cow exceeds the marginal value of the expected damage to the corn. In this case, the rancher will raise a second cow. Is his doing so, however, Pareto efficient? Fletcher is not convinced that it is. He argues quite simply that if the rancher raises a second cow, the farmer will be disadvantaged by an amount equal to the damage the cow will cause him. The rancher's raising a second cow, then, is Pareto efficient, in Fletcher's view, only if the rancher compensates the farmer for the damage the second cow causes. In the absence of compensation, raising the second cow is not Pareto efficient, because the farmer is made worse off. So a distribution of resources which is allocatively efficient need not be Pareto efficient.

This argument is illuminating but mistaken. To see this, let us first depict the rancher–farmer example systematically:

(1) Let S_1 be the situation in which one cow is ranched.
(2) Let S_2 be the situation in which the state assigns to the farmer an entitlement to prohibit the second cow.
(3) Let S_3 be the situation in which the state assigns to the rancher an entitlement to raise the second cow.
(4) Let S_4 be the situation in which the rancher purchases the right to raise the second cow from the farmer.

Both S_3 and S_4 represent the allocatively efficient distribution of cows and corn. Fletcher contends that they are not both Pareto efficient. But they are. If the state assigns the entitlement to the farmer (S_2), the situation is not Pareto optimal, because there exists a redistribution Pareto superior to it (S_4). That is, in S_4 the farmer is made no worse off, because he is compensated for his loss, and the rancher's lot is improved. S_4 is Pareto optimal; once it is reached, no rearrangement of the resources can enhance the farmer's position without harming the rancher. For similar reasons, S_3 is also Pareto optimal; it is impossible to imagine a redistribution that would improve the farmer's position that would not also disadvantage the rancher. It follows, then, contrary to Fletcher, that Coase's theorem is about Pareto efficiency – because it is about Pareto optimality.

Although both S_3 and S_4 are Pareto optimal, they differ in an important respect. S_2 is Pareto superior to S_1, and S_4 is Pareto superior to both. In contrast, S_3 is not Pareto superior to S_1. That is because in S_3 the farmer is worse off than he was in S_1. He is going to lose whatever crops the second cow destroys without being compensated. Thus, society achieves a Pareto-optimal outcome either in S_3 or S_4 but makes a Pareto-inferior move in going from S_1 to S_3. In reaching S_4 through the intermediate step of S_2, on the other hand, each move to the optimal result is itself Pareto superior to the previous one.

Fletcher's claim that Coase's theorem is unrelated to Pareto efficiency because cases like S_3 make one party worse off than before thus rests on a confusion. Coase's theorem shows that regardless of the initial assignment of entitlements, either S_3 or S_4 will result, both of which are Pareto optimal. S_3 and S_4 differ, however, with respect to S_1, in particular with respect to the relative well-being of the farmer.[16]

Coase's theorem and Fletcher's misunderstanding of it provide the perfect opportunity to emphasize the distinction I have drawn between Paretian efficiency in its historical and end-state aspects. Coase's theorem is about Pareto efficiency in its end-state or patterned dimension; it is about Pareto optimality. It is not necessarily about Pareto efficiency in its historical aspect; it is not about Pareto superiority. Coase's theorem implies that from the point of view of optimality society should be indifferent between S_3 and S_4. Economists sometimes argue that the reasons for preferring, for example, S_4 to S_3 have nothing to do with efficiency but with considerations of wealth distribution. This argument suggests that one relevant distinction between S_3 and S_4 has to do with Paretian notions of efficiency. S_4, but not S_3, involves only Pareto-superior moves from S_1. Only S_4 is the result of "mutual gain through trade."

Coase's claim that, under conditions of rationality, substantial knowledge and zero transaction costs, the outcomes of trades will be efficient holds in cases of both the farmer–rancher and smoker–nonsmoker variety.

4. CAUSATION AND EXTERNALITIES[17]

The efficiency problem of concern to Coase arises from the existence of externalities. Externalities are a category of external effects. External effects are byproducts of an activity that influence the production of other goods or the welfare (or utility) of other individuals. External effects therefore may be either beneficial or harmful. Externalities are inefficient external effects – social costs or benefits that result in inefficient production or nonoptimal distributions of welfare.[18] To internalize an externality is to eliminate the inefficiency in production or exchange it generates. Internalization need not, and often does not, require that the external effect itself be eliminated.

The argument Coase develops in "The Problem of Social Cost" is primarily a response to the Pigouvian approach to externalities. Where Pigou argues that externalities ought to be controlled by taxes to internalize their social costs, Coase demonstrates that under certain conditions the externality can be internalized by private

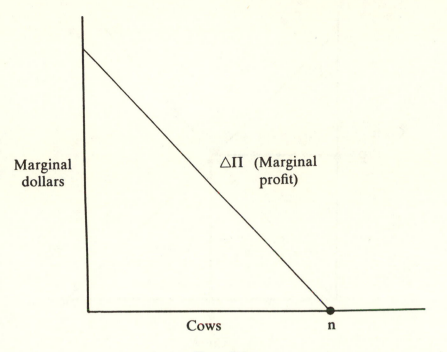

Figure 3.1

exchanges between the individuals engaged in the externality-causing activity and those harmed by it.

The differences between the Pigouvian and Coasian approaches to externalities, as well as the important and widely misunderstood distinction between external effects and externalities, are illustrated by Figures 3.1 and 3.2.

Figure 3.1 represents the marginal profit of raising cows as a function of the number of cows raised. Raising cows continues, though marginal profit diminishes, until that point represented by *n*, at which marginal profit equals marginal cost.

Figure 3.2 represents the marginal damage to corn as a function of the number of cows ranched. Again, *n* represents the number of cows that, in the absence of farming, the rancher would raise. The intersection of the marginal profit and damage curves represents the efficient allocation of corn and cows. At that point, *o* cows are ranched and *p* corn is grown. When *o* cows are ranched and *p* corn is grown the distribution of resources is efficient in the sense discussed earlier: that is, there is allocational efficiency.

Figure 3.2 also illustrates the distinction between an external

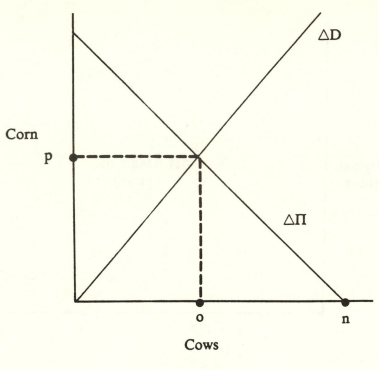

Figure 3.2

effect and an externality. Every point to the right of the vertex represents an external effect of ranching on farming. Only points to the right of the intersection of the marginal profit and marginal damage curves, however, represent externalities of ranching on farming. All points to the left of the vertex constructed at *n* constitute external effects of farming on ranching. This follows from the fact that in the absence of fencing, an increase in the corn crop requires a corresponding reduction in ranching. Put another way, a reduction in damage to the corn crop requires a reduction in cows ranched, which in turn means a reduction in the rancher's marginal profit (a forgone benefit). Every point to the left of the intersection of the marginal profit and damage curves represents an externality of farming on ranching.

To distinguish Pigou from Coase, suppose that the rancher is raising *n* cows where *o* would be optimal. The question is, how should society reduce the number of cows from *n* to *o*? According to Pigou, imposing a tax on ranching equal to the marginal damage associated with each additional cow beyond *o* would eliminate

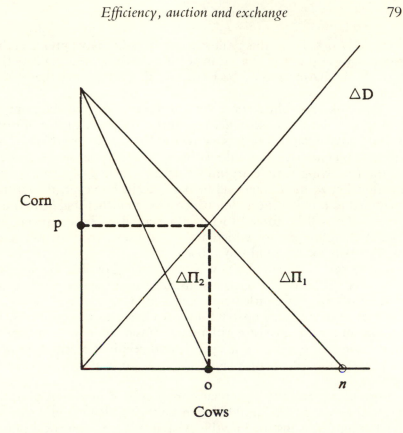

Figure 3.3

the marginal profit of ranching any more than *o* cows. The rancher would then behave as if his marginal profit curve intersected the axis at *o* rather than at *n*. That is because he will ranch up to that point at which marginal profit equals marginal cost. The Pigouvian tax shifts that point from *n* to *o*. This is illustrated in Figure 3.3.

Coase rejects the Pigouvian approach to externalities. His attack is threefold. First, Coase takes issue with the causal basis of the Pigouvian analysis. Secondly, he argues (as section 1 illustrated) that the optimal allocation may be secured through private exchange. Finally, he claims that as long as the parties are free to negotiate, the Pigouvian tax may lead to an inefficient allocation of resources.

The Pigouvian approach to externalities begins with the plausible initial premise that the rancher's cows cause the farmer measurable damage: that, in general, certain activities cause harm to other activities. From this philosophically indubitable premise, the Pigouvians argue that as a means of internalizing externalities the costs of the harms should be borne by those activities that cause them.

Coase, like his followers in contemporary law and economics, is skeptical about the existence of natural, in-the-world, nonreciprocal causal relations necessary to the Pigouvian approach. The ultimate reciprocity of causal relations, for Coase, is demonstrated by the following simple argument: If the rancher is permitted an additional cow, the farmer will be harmed. If, however, the farmer is entitled to prohibit the additional cow, the rancher will be harmed (that is, he will be forced to forgo a benefit). The question, for Coase, therefore, is not which activity causes harm; instead, it is which harm society ought to allow.

The general Coasian position is that it is impossible to conceive of nonreciprocal causal relations in the absence of, or outside the context of, a set of entitlements. Only after we know who is entitled to what can we know who causes harm to whom. Further, because in the absence of entitlements causal language is inappropriate, we cannot employ alleged causal relations as the basis for assigning entitlements or as a justification for imposing a tax burden.

Both Coase and the Pigouvians are confused in philosophically interesting ways: the Pigouvians in believing that the imposition of a tax burden is justified by the existence of nonreciprocal causal relations; Coase in believing that the Pigouvian conclusion is not warranted because the premise from which it follows is false. In fact, Pigou is right in believing that such causal relations exist but wrong in assessing their justificatory import. Coase is right in questioning their normative significance but wrong in denying their existence. Coase's arguments against the very existence of nonreciprocal causal relations is based on an obvious conceptual mistake. One does not have to know the assignment of property rights between ranchers and farmers or between polluters and pollutees to know that roaming cattle destroy (cause harm to) corn crops or that pollution harms its victims. The harm cattle cause crops is not offset by any reciprocal harm corn causes cattle – provided, of course, the corn is not poisonous. It may be true that in prohibiting an additional cow or in restricting the polluter society causes each a certain harm; or that in permitting an additional cow society causes the farmer harm. But the harms society causes by making one rather than another entitlement decision are conceptually different from the harms two competing activities may or may not cause each other.

Like Pigou, certain critics of the economic approach to law, for example Richard Epstein, have made too much of the fact that nonreciprocal, in-the-world causal relations exist.[19] It does not follow from the existence of such relations that liability or tax burdens may be justified on the basis of them. The justification for such burdens requires further controversial normative premises. Proponents of law and economics are surely wrong in denying the existence of nonreciprocal causal relations. Still, this error does not necessarily undermine their deeper claims – at least not in this case. For we could understand Coase (and perhaps other proponents of law-and-economics) not as denying the existence of causal relations but as denying the relevance of such relations to securing economic efficiency. Put this way, the point of Coase's theorem is that if rationality, substantial knowledge and zero transaction costs exist, identifying an activity as externality causing is irrelevant to securing efficiency. For in a market through trade, a point of optimal satisfaction will be reached, regardless of both the original assignment of entitlements and the depth of our ignorance of the metaphysics of causal relations.

Coase's other important point is that as long as the parties are free to negotiate, a Pigouvian tax may lead to an inefficient result. This is illustrated in Figure 3.4.

The Pigouvian tax reduces the number of cows to o from n and increases the amount of corn to p. The new marginal profit curve through o, however, intersects the marginal cost curve at s. Consequently, both the rancher and the farmer can gain through trade by negotiation with each other until s is reached, thus reducing both corn and cow production. The result of their negotiations will be q cows and r corn, which by hypothesis is inefficient.

5. PARETO EFFICIENCY, KALDOR–HICKS EFFICIENCY AND POSNER'S PROPERTY RIGHT ASSIGNMENT RULE

Coase's theorem holds only where transaction costs are sufficiently insignificant to allow the market to work its way to the efficient result through the process of mutual gain through trade. In many cases, however, the existence of transaction costs may make it impossible for the relevant parties to reach an accord that will promote their respective utilities. Consider, for example, the case in which the farmer is initially assigned the right to prohibit

Law and economics

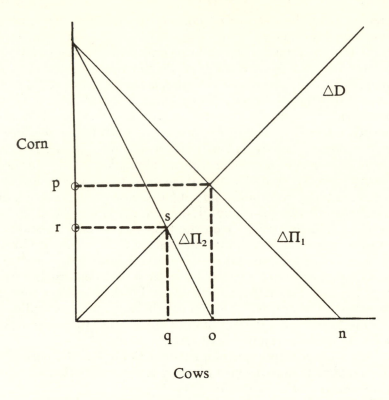

Figure 3.4

a second cow. If the cost of the transaction exceeds the difference
between the value to the rancher of the second cow and the value
to the farmer of the corn destroyed by that cow, the rancher will
not purchase the right to a second cow from the farmer. For if it
will cost the rancher $30 in transaction costs to purchase the right
from the farmer, he will be required to pay $55 for what he values
at $50. Because no transaction occurs, the farmer maintains the
entitlement though his doing so is inefficient; that is, there exists
a redistribution Pareto superior to it. Failures of this sort are termed
market failures.

Where transaction costs create market failures, the initial assignment of entitlements makes a difference from the point of view of
efficiency. Consequently, the critical question concerns how externalities are to be internalized (or controlled) when transaction
or other costs threaten the adequacy of the market to promote
efficiency through private exchange.

The recent literature indicates three approaches to the problem of controlling externalities when markets are inadequate to the task: taxes or subsidies, property rules and liability rules. Each approach involves some sort of intervention in the market by a central (public) authority. The tax approach was discussed earlier. The fundamental idea is to tax on a unit basis the inefficient output of the externality-generating activity. The tax is set equal to the marginal damage associated with each nonefficient unit of output, thus promoting an efficient output by aggregating marginal social cost and marginal private cost. (The tax approach is often thought to be equivalent economically to a subsidy in which the firm is subsidized an appropriate amount for each unit of reduced inefficient output.)[20]

The Pigouvian tax or subsidy may be contrasted with both the liability and property rule approaches. The latter approaches both involve two components for controlling externalities. Common to both is the initial assignment of entitlements. The approaches differ, however, with respect to the instruments employed to protect the entitlement once assigned. Property rules protect entitlements by enabling the right bearer to enjoin others from reducing the level of protection the entitlement affords him except as he may be willing to forego it at a mutually acceptable "price." According to the liability rule, a nonentitled party may reduce the value of the entitlement without regard to the right holder's desires provided damages are paid. The amount of damages is set by a collective body, usually a court, and need not reflect what the entitled party would have been willing to accept for a reduction in the value of his entitlement. Liability rules give nonentitled parties the right to purchase at an objectively set price part or all of an entitlement that is held by another. Property rules prohibit such takings in the absence of agreement between the relevant parties.[21]

In this essay I want to consider what is common to the property rule and liability rule approaches, namely, the assignment of entitlements.[22] The problem of assigning entitlements arises because costs (usually transaction and information costs) make it impossible to internalize externalities through private exchange. Consequently the initial assignment of entitlements will affect the efficiency of the ultimate outcomes. The question then is by what principle ought entitlements to be assigned.

To resolve this question Richard Posner offers the following assignment principle (AP): Confer the entitlement on that party who would have purchased it had the transaction costs not made it irrational for him to do so. Simply put, AP confers entitlements on efficient uses. Another way to express this is that where markets cannot be used to secure efficiency, entitlements should be assigned to stimulate or mimic the market by producing the results the market would have produced. The general principle is to assign entitlements to mimic the market.[23]

This and the following section explore the relationship between the property right assignment rule and both Coase's theorem and the concept of Kaldor–Hicks efficiency. My primary purpose is not to evaluate the property right assignment rule's success or failure but to develop its relationship to the work from which it allegedly derives.

A redistribution of resources is Kaldor–Hicks efficient if and only if under the redistribution the winners win enough so that they could compensate the losers. The notion of Kaldor–Hicks efficiency does not require that the winners actually compensate the losers. In effect, a redistribution is Kaldor–Hicks efficient if and only if it is a "possible" Pareto-superior redistribution.

Kaldor–Hicks efficient distributions do not in general map onto Pareto-superior distributions. The failure to require compensation may have the effect of producing losers; the requirements of Pareto superiority are thus not satisfied. In general, a distribution that is Kaldor–Hicks efficient need not be Pareto optimal either. If a distribution is Kaldor–Hicks efficient, then the position of the winners has been improved more than the position of the losers has been worsened. It does not follow that from their new relative positions the winners and losers are incapable of further mutual improvement through trade. Thus, a Kaldor–Hicks–efficient allocation need be neither Pareto superior nor Pareto optimal, though it may be either or both. In addition, Kaldor–Hicks efficiency has the property that if the parties are already at a Pareto-optimal point, applying Kaldor–Hicks efficiency will not produce a non–Pareto-optimal distribution. The formal way of putting this point is: Kaldor–Hicks efficiency will not lead away from the "contract curve." If the parties are not already on the contract curve, however, applying the Kaldor–Hicks formula will not ensure that they will find it. The differences between the concepts of Pareto optimality, Pareto superiority and Kaldor–Hicks efficiency are usefully illustrated by Figure 3.5, which depicts an Edgeworth–Bowley box.

Let *a* equal initial distribution of all records between Jones and Smith.

(1) The line drawn through *a, b* and *d* represents Jones's indifference curve with respect to records and books.
(2) The line drawn through *a, c* and *d* represents Smith's indif-

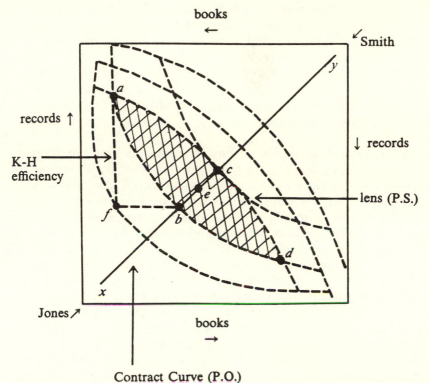

books
←

Smith

records ↑

↓ **records**

K-H efficiency

c

e

lens (P.S.)

f

a

b

d

x

y

Jones ↗

books
→

Contract Curve (P.O.)

Figure 3.5

ference curve with respect to the same resources. (The slope of the respective indifference curves is given by the respective marginal rates of substitution of books and records.)

(3) A move from *a* to *b* is Pareto superior because Jones is no worse off (*b* is on his indifference curve) while Smith is better off (*b* is farther out from his origin).

(4) A move from *a* to *c* is also Pareto superior, this time because it makes Jones better off while Smith is no worse off.

(5) A move from *a* to *e* is Pareto superior by making both Smith and Jones better off.

(6) The shaded area formed by the intersection of indifference curves drawn through *a* is the lens; it represents all possible Pareto-superior moves from *a*.

(7) The tangents of indifference curves each represent Pareto-optimal distributions.

(8) The line *x, y* drawn through these points is the contract

curve. (Not every Pareto-optimal distribution, however, corresponds to a point on the contract curve.)[24]

(9)   Point *c* represents a Pareto-optimal allocation that is also Pareto superior to *a*.

(10) The move from *a* to *f* is Kaldor–Hicks efficient, since at *f* Smith could compensate Jones so that Jones would be no worse off than at *b* and Smith would still be better off (farther from the origin).

There is a close and important relationship between Kaldor–Hicks efficiency and Posner's assignment rule. By assigning the appropriate entitlement to the party who would have purchased it had it not been for transaction costs, Posner's principle ensures that the entitlement will be secured by a party who would have been able to compensate the loser and still gain by the assignment. So assignments of entitlements according to Posner's "high-bidder" rule or "auction rule"[25] are Kaldor–Hicks efficient. A Kaldor–Hicks–efficient reallocation need not be Pareto efficient; it certainly need not be Pareto superior. Because Posner's rule does not require that the losing bidder be compensated, it does not guarantee that after the entitlement has been assigned the resulting allocation is Pareto superior. Because the rule is designed to mimic or simulate an efficient market outcome, applying it will theoretically produce a Pareto-optimal assignment. Posner's rule then generates outcomes that are both Kaldor–Hicks efficient and Pareto optimal.[26]

Coase's markets, Pigou's taxes and Posner's property right assignment rule are all means of controlling externalities. Strictly speaking, externality problems cannot be represented in an Edgeworth box. That is because Edgeworth theory assumes both perfect competition and the absence of externalities. Representing an externality problem in an Edgeworth box would therefore violate a basic assumption necessary for constructing such a box. Still, it might be useful to refer back to the Edgeworth box to understand the relationship between Posner's assignment rule and the various notions of efficiency that the box illustrates. Taking some liberties with Edgeworth analysis, then, it might be said that Posner's rule in effect holds that we should assign entitlements so that the resulting allocation of resources is Kaldor–Hicks efficient as constrained by the requirement that it fall on the contract curve. By not requiring that the party assigned the entitlement compensate the loser of the auction, the rule does not guarantee that the redistribution takes place within the lens.

6. AUCTION AND EXCHANGE

Posner's assignment rule does not require that the losing bidders be compensated. Why not? The answer given – that is, the justification offered for denying that interventions in the market of voluntary exchanges require compensation – depends on whether Posner's principle is seen as more closely allied to Coase (Pareto) or to Kaldor–Hicks. The Coasian and Kaldor–Hicks arguments apply to different sorts of economic problems – a fact few proponents of law-and-economics seem cognizant of – and provide, therefore, very different justifications for not requiring compensation. In exploring both Coasian and Kaldor–Hicks arguments for denying compensation, this section attempts to raise doubts about both the justification for doing so and the claim that Posner's assignment rule mimics the market in the Coasian sense.

Let us begin by placing the burden of the argument on those who would require compensation. What is the case for compensating losers? Consider a standard auction. Suppose *A* and *B* both bid for a Frank Stella painting. *A*'s bid is higher than *B*'s and he is awarded the painting. Should *A*, the winner, be forced to compensate *B*, the loser? Surely not. By the same token, why should the winner of Posner's auction be compelled to compensate the loser(s)?

The answer to this question is complex. Its complexity will unfold as we go along. For now, it is enough to note at least two differences between auctioning a work of art and auctioning entitlements along the lines Posner suggests. First, when *A* wins the auction for a work of art, he still has to fork over the money. He does not simply receive the art work gratis in return for submitting a high and flattering bid. The winners of Posner's auctions do not pay for their prizes. They win merely by bidding. (This presents a difficult problem regarding the reliability of information bids provide.) Second, in standard auctions individuals who lose the bidding are not disadvantaged (if we ignore envy or jealousy) by the winner's winning. The art collector's "consuming" the Stella does not disadvantage his rival. The winner wins, but the loser does not really lose. He loses the auction but is not harmed by the result. This is not to suggest that a loser is no worse off than he would have been had he won. Because the loser is forced to accept his second-best alternative, he is clearly worse off than he would have been had he won the auction. Still, he need be no worse off than he was prior to the auction. In the language of efficiency, this characteristic of auctions might be put as follows: Auctions of private goods are Kaldor–Hicks efficient and Pareto superior. They are both Kaldor–Hicks efficient and Pareto superior because they produce no real losers. In contrast, if we auction property rights between polluters and their neighbors, or between smokers and nonsmokers, then if the smokers or polluters win the auction, the losers really do lose. When smoke gets in one's eyes it burns. So auctioning property rights to pollute or to smoke on a high-bid basis may have the result of worsening the lot of the auction's losers. Moreover, it follows from the fact that Posner's rule is Kaldor–Hicks efficient that the high bidder could have compensated the loser and still gained by the assignment. Why advance a rule that disadvantages some individuals when not even efficiency requires it? The burden is shifted. Why not compensate?

As suggested above, the justification advanced for denying compensation to losers will ultimately depend on whether one adheres to a Kaldor–Hicks or Coasian reading of the auction rule. The prevailing view is that Posner's auction rule derives from Coase's theorem. Against Pigou, Coase argues for the success of private exchange as a vehicle for securing efficiency. But exchange markets sometimes are unavailable or too costly to be efficient. Posner's rule is: Where markets fail, mimic them. In other words, where transaction costs create market failures, Posner's rule assigns entitlements to produce the result the market, under ideal conditions, would have produced. Since the market, as Coase demonstrates, eventually would have worked to move the entitlement to the party who would have been willing to pay more for it, where markets are too expensive or otherwise unworkable why not simply assign the entitlement to the high bidder straightaway? This Coasian interpretation of Posner's auction rule raises two closely related questions. First, in what ways and to what extent does the auction rule mimic the market in the Coasian sense? Second, if the auction rule derives from Coase's argument, what are the Coasian-related considerations for failing to compensate losers?

Coase's argument relies on exchange rather than auction markets. The point of Coase's argument is that regardless of the assignment of entitlements, market mechanisms will provide the opportunities for mutual gain through trade, and that this process will result in an efficient allocation of resources. Coase's argument therefore emphasizes not only the efficiency of the result – which admittedly could be secured in any number of nonmarket ways – but also the unique capacity of the market to secure an optimal result by individuals' exercising autonomy in an effort to maximize utility through exchanges.

There are significant differences between auction and exchange markets. Exchanges (by rational, well-informed persons) are made only when they are to the advantage of all parties to them. Auctions are not trades; they do not guarantee that all parties to the bidding gain or are at least not disadvantaged by the result. Some auctions – for example, those involving works of art – have the effect of improving the lot of some individuals without worsening the lot of others. Other auctions – for example, those involving pollution rights – provide no such guarantees. The phrase "mimic the market" is ambiguous therefore between auction and exchange markets. Coase's market is an exchange market; Posner's is an auction. The question is, to what extent and in what respects do Posner's auctions simulate the outcomes of exchange markets? To answer this question, let us reconsider the rancher–farmer example. In this example we distinguish four states of affairs: S_1, in which no entitlements have as yet been conferred; S_2, in which the farmer is assigned the entitlement to prohibit the second cow; S_3, in which the rancher is assigned the entitlement to raise the second cow; and S_4, in which the rancher purchases from the farmer the entitlement to raise the second cow. (This is the story one would reconstruct in that case in which the value of the second cow exceeds the expected crop damage.)

Coase's theorem is that under ideal conditions S_3 or S_4 would result, either of which would be Pareto optimal. From the point of view of Pareto optimality, we ought to be indifferent with respect to the two. Posner's principle states simply that where there are high transaction costs, choose S_3. But S_3 and S_4 are not morally equivalent from the point of view of Pareto superiority; S_4 but not S_3 is Pareto superior to S_1.

Posner's rule implores us to choose S_3 cases even though there may be Paretian-related reasons for preferring S_4 cases. To mimic the outcome of the market as the notion is employed in Coase's argument, at the very least Posner's assignment principle should read as AP': (a) Assign the entitlement to the party who would have purchased it (S_3 cases), or (b) assign the entitlement to the party who would have produced it and require that the winner compensate the loser (S_4 cases).

Only indifference between these two disjuncts of AP' comes close to mimicking the exchange market. Put another way, Posner's rule comes into play only where exchange markets cannot be

established. The best that can be done is an assignment rule that
mimics the market. An exchange market can, as Coase shows,
reach a Pareto-optimal result in one of two ways. If Posner's rule
is supposed to mimic the market, it should include reconstructed
mappings of these two paths.

A defender of Posner's assignment rule might object that while
this is all well and good, the costs of rendering compensation might
be too great to apply the second disjunct. The costs of compensation, in other words, like the costs of making the transaction in
the first place, may exceed the difference between the value the
higher and lower bidders place on the entitlement. Requiring
compensation may defeat the purpose of the rule by producing a
result that is not Pareto optimal. If an assignment rule is to mimic
the market at all, it can duplicate only the efficiency of the outcome. To ensure at least an efficient outcome, the compensation
requirement must be abandoned. The auction rule then is simply
the best compromise. But is it?

When conjoined with the cost of making compensation, a full
compensation rule may generate an inefficient allocation. Something less than full compensation, however, need not. That is,
requiring compensation up to that amount which, when added to
the cost of compensation, is still less than or equal to the price the
higher bidder is willing to pay would be a second-best option. The
result would be a Pareto-optimal allocation that involved a close
approximation of a Pareto-superior move. Being a little disadvantaged is preferable to being significantly disadvantaged. Alternatively, the difference between the total cost of compensation and
the point at which it becomes inefficient for the high bidder to
compensate might be paid by the government. After all, why should
the loser be forced to suffer any loss whatsoever in the name of
efficiency?

Arguments against the compensation requirement based on the
costs of rendering compensation are inconclusive at best. Moreover, some sort of commitment to compensation is required if
Posner's auction rule is to duplicate Coase's exchange market. Still,
a defender of Posner's rule might argue that the information costs
of alternative assignment rules, such as the near–Pareto-superior
one, are so great as to render them useless. That is, the costs of
ascertaining the relevant information to determine when compensation is adequate and efficient would be overwhelming, thus
making such a rule impractical. The problem of information costs
is more general. Indeed, criticisms based on information costs may
be forcefully pressed against Posner's own rule. Posner's rule is to

assign the entitlement to the highest bidder, or, more precisely, to the individual who, transaction costs aside, would have purchased it in an exchange market. The information problem is this: How do we gather information regarding the relative willingness of individuals to pay for a particular entitlement? In the absence of a market in which a person's willingness to pay is expressed through trades and bids, the cost of ascertaining willingness to pay would be enormous and the reliability of that information suspect. If, however, a market exists or may be established to determine willingness to pay, Posner's rule is simply otiose. If a market can be established to reveal relative willingness to pay among interested parties, everything necessary for an exchange market exists and there is no need whatsoever to make an assignment of entitlements along the lines of Posner's or anyone else's assignment principle.

6.1. Auctions and Kaldor–Hicks

As noted earlier, the phrase "mimicking the market" is ambiguous between auction and exchange markets. The previous section considered what the difference amounted to. In addition, there is the question of which aspect of the market Posner's rule is intended to mimic or simulate. Under one interpretation, Posner's concept of mimicking the market could only mean producing the efficient outcome the market would have produced. Alternatively, in denying compensation by mimicking the market, Posner's rule may be drawing upon aspects of its Kaldor–Hicks heritage. In particular, the denial of compensation in Posner's rule may be justified on the same grounds that Kaldor–Hicks advances for failing to do so. There are in general two kinds of cases in which applying Kaldor–Hicks standards of efficiency rather than Paretian ones are thought to be justified: The first involves entry into, and exit from, markets; the second involves removal of impediments to competition.

If *A* enters *B*'s market and drives him from business, *A* is not required to compensate *B,* even though in a perfectly competitive economy *A* could do so and be in a better position than before. This is the principle of costless entry into the market, and it involves the Kaldor–Hicks rather than the Pareto-superior standard of efficiency. The justification for this principle is that it encourages weeding out inefficiency. Because Posner's assignment rule is not restricted to cases of entry into markets, the application of Kaldor–Hicks and the consequent failure to provide compensation are generally unwarranted.

Kaldor–Hicks is more often used where impediments to competition are removed and the losers are those who have previously
been advantaged by the absence of competition. The justification
for applying Kaldor–Hicks is that those monopolists who have
benefited from impediments to competition are not entitled to or
do not deserve compensation. The farmer and the nonsmoker who
lose out in Posner's auctions, however, are not inefficient monopolists; they have not been advantaged by impediments to competition the removal of which would bring them warranted losses.
Nor are the farmer and nonsmoker like unsuccessful, that is, inefficient, competitors in a market. Not compensating losers on
Kaldor–Hicks grounds therefore seems inappropriate, at least in a
wide range of cases in which Posner's auction rule applies.

6.2. The case against always compensating

Posner's auction rule does not require that losers be compensated.
Coasian and Kaldor–Hicks considerations might be brought to
bear to justify the auction to the exclusion of the bargain. None of
these arguments are sufficiently persuasive to justify an auction
rule like Posner's. The question that remains is whether an auction
rule that requires compensation would always be preferable to the
Posner rule that never does. Does it follow, in other words, from
the arguments that seem decisive against Posner that full compensation or its nearest efficient approximation ought in every case to
be required? This question is very closely related to, but slightly
different from, the question whether it is always preferable to pursue a Pareto-superior path to a Pareto-optimal outcome.

This leads inevitably to considering the question economists and
lawyers enamored of the economic approach to law seem to shy
away from. And that is: Even where it is possible to secure a Pareto-optimal outcome via a Pareto-superior path, is it always preferable to do so? Consider a case in which doubt about doing so
exists.

Suppose the neighboring residents of a polluting manufacturer
outbid a polluter seeking the right to continue polluting at his current rate. The neighbor's right to a cutback in pollution forces the
manufacturer to reduce output, and in the end it suffers an economic loss. In a Coasian world, the neighbors would have bought
away some of the pollution from the manufacturer, and so through
mutual gain via trade an efficient result would have been reached.
The manufacturer, in this example, is disadvantaged by the auction. The loss it suffers could be reduced or eliminated by requir-

ing its neighbors to compensate it. There is, however, a legitimate question here about whether the Pareto-superior path to the Pareto-optimal outcome is preferable to the Pareto-inferior path that application of Posner's rule would bring about. There are numerous other cases of this sort, some in which our intuitions would be firmer, others in which they would be less firm. For example, would compensation be preferable if the polluting manufacturer were a monopolist? This is just the sort of case that the Kaldor–Hicks formula was meant to cover. What could make the Pareto-superior path more defensible than the Kaldor–Hicks path in such cases?

These examples suggest that while the Posner rule simply lumps together all sorts of cases in which the justifiability of failing to render compensation differs enormously, the alternative rule of always requiring compensation – thereby ensuring the Pareto-superior path to the Pareto-optimal outcome – also lumps together all sorts of cases about which our intuitions regarding the propriety of compensation may differ drastically. The simple point is that no assignment rule or principle for intervening in the market can be defended *a priori* as abstracted from the kinds of cases it is intended to cover.

Moreover, these examples demonstrate the related point that every economic notion of efficiency is of derivative and limited use in the public policy arena. Consider the various notions of efficiency and their relation to social choice. First, there can never be *a priori* arguments for choosing a Pareto-optimal distribution of resources to a non–Pareto-optimal one. Second, the notion of Kaldor–Hicks efficiency derives from some deeper noneconomic theory of desert and entitlement. Its application is thought justified, after all, precisely in those cases in which parties who have gained, but did not deserve to gain, from impediments to competition are denied compensation when the impediments are removed. Finally, even the notion of Pareto superiority – everyone's golden boy – is useless as a basis of policy independent of a noneconomic justification of the initial distribution with which the reallocations are to be compared. Whether a person should never be made worse off by a redistribution of resources will ultimately depend on his deserts and his rights. Unless we know what a person deserves or is entitled to on grounds other than efficiency, we should remain agnostic about the virtues of reallocations that leave him no worse off than before.

One final point about mimicking the market. The state is sometimes asked to allocate resources through the political process, not because the market will be unable to do so efficiently, but because, on other grounds, the market is viewed as inappropriate. The allocation of scarce life-saving medical resources, for example, may be best left to nonmarket allocative devices. One problem, then, with unreflective commitment to the principle of mimicking the market is that in certain cases it may require the state to step into an area in order to allocate resources as the market (under ideal circumstances) would have, when the state is really being asked to allocate resources precisely because the market is viewed as inappropriate.

7. CONCLUSION

The purpose of this essay has not been to find fault with Posner's assignment rule in the hope that doing so might lead to insights about the construction of a more satisfying property right assignment principle. In the end, I am not sufficiently sympathetic to the economic vision of human affairs and social institutions to engage in such a task. Instead, my goal has been to look at aspects and examples of the economic approach to law from the inside, not as a critic of the entire enterprise but as someone trying to work his way through it. This essay does not attempt to rebut all of law-and-economics. For even if efficiency does not carry the day in matters of social policy, arguments from efficiency must be taken seriously. I hope, however, that this essay has contributed to a deeper appreciation of the limits of the economists' contribution to the design of social and legal institutions.

4. Efficiency, utility and wealth maximization

1. INTRODUCTION

A fully adequate inquiry into the foundations of the economic approach to law[1] would address at least the following four related questions:

(1) What is economic efficiency; that is, what does it mean to say that resources are allocated in an economically efficient manner or that a body of law is efficient?

(2) Does the principle of efficiency have explanatory merit; that is, can the rules and principles of any or all of the law be rationalized or subsumed under an economic theory of legislation or adjudication?

(3) How should law be formulated to promote efficiency; that is, in what ways must legal rights and duties be assigned and enforced so that the rules that assign and enforce them are efficient?

(4) Ought the law pursue economic efficiency; that is, to what extent is efficiency a desirable legal value in particular, and a normatively attractive principle in general?

The first question concerns the analytic framework of law-and-economics, what one might call the philosophic foundations of the economic approach to law. The second question concerns the capacity of certain principles of welfare economics to bring together in a coherent fashion a diverse body of existing law. The third problem is technical in nature. The fourth concerns welfare economics as a normative discipline.

Until recently, proponents of economic analysis have traded on the initial plausibility of utilitarianism in order to provide a normative basis for the various efficiency criteria. Utilitarianism, however, has been the target of powerful and, in the minds of many philosophers, decisive objections. These objections fall into two categories: those which do not question the consequentialist character of utilitarianism and those which do. Objections of the first sort include: (1) boundary problems – whose utilities or preferences should count and which of a person's preferences should count; (2) the total or average utility problem – whether utilitarianism is committed to promoting total utility without regard to its distribution; and (3) the interpersonal utility comparison problem – how to determine if a course of conduct or policy that makes some individuals better off and others worse off increases total utility, and if it does, by how much.

Substantive criticisms of classical utilitarianism boil down to the claim that utilitarianism is an impoverished moral theory, incapable of accounting for the full range of moral obligation and right action. Because utilitarianism is a consequentialist or outcome morality, it may require an individual to violate an important moral principle simply because doing so increases total utility. Further, the utilitarian principle might obligate one to act for the benefit of others and is therefore incompatible with a deeper commitment to personal liberty. Finally, utilitarianism can neither provide a theory of *moral* rights nor take either moral or legal rights seriously.[2]

In responding to these objections, economic analysis has confined itself to coping with utilitarianism's technical deficiencies, in particular, the problem of interpersonal utility comparisons. The failure of economic analysis to address the substantive criticisms combined with the alleged connection between efficiency criteria and utilitarianism has led critics of utilitarianism to dismiss economic analysis outright.

In a controversial essay, Richard Posner attempts to fill this void in the literature by addressing many of the textbook objections to utilitarianism.[3] "Address" may be the wrong word, since Posner accepts most of the substantive as well as technical objections to utilitarianism. Because Posner also accepts the identification of traditional efficiency criteria with utilitarian moral theory, he concludes that utility-based efficiency criteria are subject to the same decisive objections.[4] The problem, as Posner sees it, is to extricate economic efficiency from this unholy alliance with utilitarianism, an association once cherished but now to be eschewed. To free economic efficiency from the grip of a normatively unattractive moral theory, Posner introduces what he takes to be an efficiency criterion that is immune to the substantial criticisms of utilitarianism: the criterion of "wealth maximization."[5]

In contrast to the prevailing view, I argue that the familiar efficiency-related standards do not have the connection to classical utilitarianism necessary for the criticisms of utilitarianism to undermine the normative use of efficiency criteria. Therefore, even if utilitarianism is wrongheaded – as I think it is – it may be possible to construct alternative normative bases for economic efficiency criteria. Section 2 analyzes various familiar efficiency notions and explores their relationship to classical utilitarianism, arguing that while some relationships between efficiency criteria and utilitarianism exist, these relationships are not necessarily justificatory in nature. Section 3 turns to the system of wealth maximization, first to consider whether it is an efficiency standard at all and then to explore the conceptual foundations of the theory and some of its consequences as a guide to individual conduct and institutional choice. Section 4 discusses and rejects three arguments for wealth maximization. Section 5 discusses nonutilitarian strategies for defending the traditional Pareto efficiency criteria, arguing that none of these is ultimately satisfactory.

2. EFFICIENCY AND UTILITY

Economists as well as proponents of the economic analysis of law employ at least four efficiency-related notions, including: (1) productive efficiency, (2) Pareto optimality, (3) Pareto superiority and (4) Kaldor–Hicks efficiency. If it constitutes a suitable efficiency criterion, Posner's wealth maximization would increase the total to at least five. In this section of the paper, I want to focus on the analytic and normative relationships between Pareto and Kaldor–Hicks notions of efficiency.[6]

2.1. The Pareto criteria

Resources are allocated in a Pareto-optimal fashion if and only if any further reallocation of them can enhance the welfare of one person only at the expense of another. An allocation of resources is Pareto superior to an alternative allocation if and only if no one is made worse off by the distribution and the welfare of at least one person is improved. These two conceptions of efficiency are analytically related in that a Pareto-optimal distribution has no distributions Pareto superior to it.

Both Pareto concepts express standards for ranking or describing states of affairs. The Pareto-superior criterion relates two states of affairs and says that one is an improvement over the other if at least one person's welfare improves while no one else's welfare is diminished. The optimality standard relates one distribution to all

possible distributions and says in effect that no Pareto improvements can be made from any Pareto-optimal state. In addition,
Pareto-optimal distributions are Pareto noncomparable; the Pareto-
superior standard cannot be employed to choose among them.
Another way of putting this last point is to say that the social
choice between Pareto-optimal distributions must be made on
nonefficiency grounds.

2.2. Kaldor–Hicks

Like Pareto superiority, Kaldor–Hicks efficiency is a relational
property of states of affairs. One state of affairs (E') is Kaldor–
Hicks efficient to another (E) if and only if those whose welfare
increases in the move from E to E' could fully compensate those
whose welfare diminishes with a net gain in welfare. Under Kaldor–
Hicks, compensation to losers is not in fact paid. Were the payment transaction costless and full compensation given to the
losers, Kaldor–Hicks distributions would be transformed into
Pareto-superior ones. This characteristic of Kaldor–Hicks has led
some to refer to it as a "potential Pareto-superior" standard.[7]

Kaldor–Hicks–efficient distributions do not necessarily map onto
Pareto-superior distributions. The failure to require compensation
has the effect of making some individuals worse off and thus fails
to satisfy the requirements of Pareto superiority.

In general, a distribution that is Kaldor–Hicks efficient need not
be Pareto optimal either. If a distribution is Kaldor–Hicks efficient, then some individual has been made sufficiently better off
so that he could – hypothetically at least – fully compensate those
who have been made worse off. It does not follow, however, that
from their new relative positions the winners and losers are incapable of further mutual improvement through trade. Thus a Kaldor–
Hicks–efficient allocation need be neither Pareto superior nor
Pareto optimal, although it may be either or both.

The differences among the concepts of Pareto optimality,
Pareto superiority and Kaldor–Hicks efficiency are usefully illustrated by the Edgeworth–Bowley box shown in Figure 4.1. Let *a*
equal the initial distribution of all records and books between Jones
and Smith.

(1)   The line drawn through *a*, *b*, *d* represents Jones's indiffer-
      ence curve with respect to records and books.
(2)   The line drawn through *a*, *c*, *d* represents Smith's indiffer-
      ence curve with respect to the same resources. (The slope of

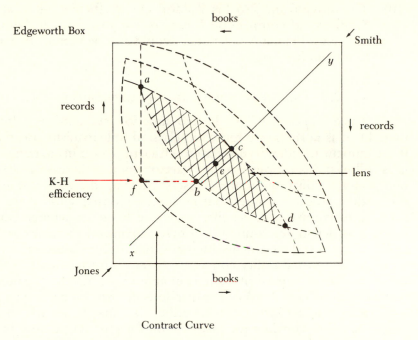

Figure 4.1

the respective indifference curves is given by the respective marginal rates of substitution of books and records.)

(3)   A move from *a* to *b* is Pareto superior, because Jones is no worse off (*b* is on his indifference curve), while Smith is better off (*b* is farther out from her origin).

(4)   A move from *a* to *c* is also Pareto superior, because it makes Jones better off while Smith is no worse off.

(5)   A move from *a* to *e* is Pareto superior by making both Smith and Jones better off.

(6)   The shaded area formed by the intersection of indifference curves drawn through *a* is the lens, and it represents all possible Pareto-superior moves from *a*.

(7)   The points of common tangency of Smith's and Jones's curves represent Pareto–optimal distributions.

(8)   The line *x, y* drawn through these points is the contract curve. (Not every Pareto–optimal distribution, however, corresponds to a point on the contract curve.)

(9)   Point *c* (as does point *b*) represents a Pareto–optimal allocation that is also Pareto superior to *a*.

(10)   The move from *a* to *f* is Kaldor–Hicks efficient, since at *f*
        Smith could compensate Jones so that Jones would be no
        worse off than at *b* and Smith would still be better off (far-
        ther from her origin).

2.3. The Pareto standards and utilitarianism

2.3.1. Pareto superiority. The Pareto-superior standard is often
thought of as normatively rooted in classical utilitarianism. Briefly,
the argument for identifying Pareto efficiency with utilitarianism
is as follows: Allocations that are Pareto superior increase at least
one person's utility without adversely affecting the utility of another; they produce winners but no losers. Consequently there is
no need to compare the relative gains and losses of winners and
losers in order to determine if a course of conduct increases total
utility. Pareto improvements increase total utility, although not
all increases in total utility constitute Pareto improvements.[8] Because the Pareto-superiority criterion appears to obviate the need
to make interpersonal utility comparisons in order to determine if
a course of conduct increases total utility, it is easy to see why one
might be led to consider the justification for pursuing Pareto improvements to be utilitarian.

Aspects of this argument are misleading, others mistaken. First,
the Pareto-superior criterion does not eliminate the need for a
standard of utility comparison. If the Pareto-superior standard is
to be an index of total utility, interpersonal utility comparisons are
necessary, since the concept of total utility presupposes the capacity to aggregate individual utility functions, which in turn requires
a standard of comparison. Provided such a standard exists, Pareto
improvements increase total utility; and because they do, one could
argue that the justification for pursuing Pareto improvements relies on its connection to utilitarianism. That would be a mistake.

We presume that the concept of total utility is meaningful, and
because we do, we must believe that some standard of interpersonal comparability exists. From this it follows that Pareto improvements increase total utility. Suppose, however, that the very
idea of total utility were meaningless. In that case, we should be
unable to make sense of claims concerning increases or decreases
in total utility. We should, however, still be capable of talking
meaningfully about Pareto improvements.

There is an important distinction among individual preference
theories, total utility theories and social welfare theories.[9] Pareto
judgments are expressed in terms of orderings of individual pref-

erences rather than in terms of total utility. To say that an action is Pareto superior is to say only that at least one person is higher along his or her preference ranking, while no one else is any worse off with respect to his or hers. The existence of a standard of comparison enables us to bring these distinct judgments about the relative standings of individuals with respect to their preference orderings into a single judgment about total utility. As we have just seen, however, the Pareto judgment has empirical significance independent of its connection to utility.

At bottom is the distinction between the claim that Pareto judgments may warrant claims about utility and the claim that utility justifies the pursuit of Pareto improvements. Those committed to utilitarianism will no doubt embrace the Pareto standard, since they are committed to a conception of the right and the good from which Pareto superiority follows as a particular instance, that is, as one way of promoting utility. But because Pareto judgments have empirical significance apart from their connection to utility, it is possible to conceive of alternative justifications for the pursuit of actions and policies that satisfy the Pareto-superior criterion.

For example, one could plausibly argue that the Pareto-superior standard is normatively defensible not because applying it gives an index of total utility, but because rational self-interested persons would consent to its use. That is, few would object to policies that made at least one person better off if doing so never required anyone else to suffer. This line of defense does not rest on the utility of the Pareto standard, but on the fact that rational, self-interested persons would consent to its use.

Alternatively, one might advance a normative defense of Pareto superiority that relies on a libertarian rather than a contractarian or utilitarian political morality: Exchanges among knowledgeable, rational persons in a free market are generally Pareto superior; rational individuals do not strike bargains with one another unless each perceives it to be in his or her own interest to do so. A successful exchange between such parties is, therefore, one in which the value to each of what he or she relinquishes is perceived as less than the value of what each receives in return. Such exchanges make no individual worse off; often they improve the lot of all concerned. Pareto superiority is connected in this way to the ideal of a free-exchange market.

We can imagine, then, at least three distinct normative defenses for the Pareto-superior standard, only one of which is utilitarian. These are the utilitarian argument, the contractarian or consent argument and the libertarian argument. The important point for our present purposes is that one can remain unpersuaded by the utilitarian conception of the good and the right, yet stand prepared to endorse certain institutional arrangements that work to at least some person's benefit and to no one's detriment, on the ground either that rational self-interested persons would consent to such arrangements or that certain of these arrangements respect or are required by a deeper commitment to individual liberty or autonomy. Whether the use of the Pareto-superiority standard can be adequately defended on either contractarian or libertarian grounds is a question to which we shall return.[10] In any event, it simply does not follow that the normative use of the Pareto-superior criterion must be abandoned even if utilitarianism is wrongheaded.

2.3.2. Pareto optimality. Let us now turn to Pareto optimality in order to develop its relationship to utilitarianism. To say that resources are distributed in Pareto-optimal fashion is to say that no further distributions are capable of enhancing anyone's welfare without making someone else worse off. Pareto-optimal distributions have no distributions Pareto superior to them.

The set of all possible Pareto-optimal distributions of resources that an economy in general equilibrium can generate is represented as points on the "contract curve." The points on the contract curve may be further represented as points on the grand utility–possibility frontier. The fact that all Pareto-optimal allocations may be represented as points on a utility–possibility frontier suggests a relationship of Pareto optimality to utilitarianism. That is, all points on the utility–possibility frontier are Pareto improvements over all points to their southwest. With respect to every other point, a point on the frontier is Pareto noncomparable. This is illustrated in Figure 4.2. (1) c is Pareto superior to x, but Pareto noncomparable to y. (2) f is Pareto superior to y but Pareto noncomparable to x. (3) c and f are Pareto noncomparable. (4) c and f are Pareto superior to z. This is not to say, of course, that there are no distributions that contain more total utility than a Pareto-optimal distribution. Rather, given the constraints of the theory, we cannot determine, short of making actual interpersonal comparisons, which distributions they are.

From the fact that a distribution of resources is Pareto optimal two utility judgments follow: First, every Pareto-optimal distribution contains more total utility than some set of distributions represented by points within the utility–possibility frontier, because every distribution represented by a point on the utility–

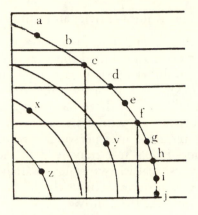

Figure 4.2

possibility frontier is Pareto superior to *some* distributions[11] represented by points within the frontier, those to the southwest.
Second, the overall utility of a Pareto-optimal distribution cannot
be increased by a Pareto-superior move, because a Pareto-optimal
distribution has no distributions Pareto superior to it.

From the fact that a distribution of resources is Pareto optimal
it does not follow that the move to it increases utility, because not
every move to a Pareto-optimal distribution involves a Pareto improvement. Pareto-optimal distributions may result from Kaldor–
Hicks–efficient or non–Pareto–superior moves as well as from
Pareto-superior ones. Moreover, no judgments about the relative
utility content of the various members of the set of Pareto-optimal
distributions is warranted. This is because the set of Pareto-optimal
distributions cannot be compared by the Pareto-superiority standard.

Every utility judgment warranted by the optimality standard is
a logical consequence of its definitional relationship to Pareto superiority. It follows, therefore, that whether Pareto optimality is
rooted in utilitarianism will depend on whether Pareto superiority
is. Moreover, the same consent and libertarian defenses for Pareto
superiority may be brought to bear on Pareto optimality. First,
the ultimate outcome of voluntary exchanges will be Pareto optimal: Rational, knowledgeable persons all contract to a Pareto-
optimal point, never away from it. Second, because rational, self-
interested persons would presumably consent to Pareto-superior
moves, they would theoretically consent to the ultimate consequence of such moves, Pareto-optimal distributions.

2.4. Kaldor–Hicks and utility

Both Pareto-superiority and Pareto-optimality judgments entail certain total utility claims provided the very weak condition that a standard of comparability exists is satisfied. The same cannot be said for Kaldor–Hicks. First, in order to infer from the satisfaction of the Kaldor–Hicks test that there has been a net gain in utility, we need to know whether winners have won more than losers have lost, which requires interpersonal-cardinal comparability. Second, the Kaldor–Hicks test may lead to inconsistent preferences over social states; that is, two states of affairs may be Kaldor–Hicks efficient to one another. This is the Scitovsky paradox.[12] A demonstration of the paradox follows.

Suppose there are two persons, A and B, and two commodities, X and Y. Figure 4.3 gives the outputs in two states of the economy: E and E'.

In E, Mr. A has two units of X and no units of Y; Ms. B has no units of X and one unit of Y. In E', A has one unit of X and none of Y. Suppose now that A and B have the following preferences for X and Y: Mr. A prefers one unit of X and one unit of Y to two units of X and no units of Y, which is itself preferred to one unit of X and no units of Y. Ms. B prefers one unit of X and one unit of Y to no units of X and two of Y, which is itself preferred to no units of X and one of Y. E is Kaldor–Hicks efficient to E', and E' is Kaldor–Hicks efficient to E. In E Mr. A has two units of X and none of Y; were he to give one unit of X to Ms. B, he would be exactly as well off as he was in E'; Ms. B would be better off. She would then have one unit of X and one of Y, which she prefers to both E' and E. Compensation would make her better off and Mr. A no worse off. So E is Kaldor–Hicks efficient to E'.

As it stands, Kaldor–Hicks does not provide an adequate efficiency basis for preferring one state of the economy to another. The Kaldor–Hicks criterion may be reformulated so that one state of affairs is Kaldor–Hicks preferable to another if and only if the winners could compensate the losers in going from E to E' but the winners could not compensate the losers in going from E' to E. This eliminates the paradox, but then Kaldor–Hicks will not be transitive.[13]

Consequently, from the satisfaction of the Kaldor–Hicks test it does not follow that there has been a net gain in utility, since (1) one can determine whether Kaldor–Hicks has been satisfied without appealing to any *particular* standard of interpersonal comparison, but, in cases in which there are both winners and losers, one

	E		E'	
	X	Y	X	Y
A	2	0	1	0
B	0	1	0	2

Figure 4.3

cannot tell whether total utility has been increased by a Kaldor–Hicks improvement without appealing to such a standard; and (2) E can be Kaldor–Hicks superior to E' and E' to E, whereas E cannot have more utility than E' while E' has more utility than E.[14]

Of the three efficiency-related criteria, only Pareto superiority may be transformed into an index of utility. Utility judgments warranted by Pareto optimality are a consequence of its analytic relationship to Pareto superiority. Kaldor–Hicks efficiency is paradoxical as a standard of utility and therefore cannot be transformed into an index of utility even if interpersonal utility comparisons were possible.

Further, it does not follow from the fact that utilitarianism is mistaken that the normative use of the Pareto standards must be abandoned. Even though Pareto superiority can be employed as a standard of utility, it has content aside from this connection, and its application in social and legal policy matters may be justified on nonutilitarian grounds, in particular on the basis of consent or liberty. If utilitarianism is wrong, a proponent of economic analysis has a choice: He or she can either abandon the normative use of the Pareto criteria in favor of a nonutility-based efficiency criterion or try to construct nonutilitarian normative arguments for the Pareto criteria.

3. THE CONCEPTUAL BASIS OF WEALTH MAXIMIZATION

The discussion in the preceding section suggests that Posner may have been too hasty in abandoning utilitarian in favor of wealth-maximizing conceptions of efficiency. Nevertheless, Richard Posner offers the system of wealth maximization as an alternative both to utilitarian moral theory and to Pareto efficiency.[15] Wealth max-

imization is supposed to be a more attractive moral principle than
utilitarianism, and wealth maximization is supposed to replace the
Pareto criteria, which, in Posner's view at least, are rooted in utilitarian moral theory. Wealth maximization, however, is no more
defensible than utilitarianism, nor is it an alternative efficiency criterion. Indeed, it is not an efficiency criterion at all.

3.1. Wealth and efficiency

A distinction must be drawn between tests for ordering or ranking
states of affairs and the characteristic(s) in virtue of which the states
of affairs are to be ranked. The Pareto standards rank social states;
they do not provide the characteristic in virtue of which one state
may be compared with another. On the other hand, both wealth
and utility maximization express characteristics of states of affairs
that enable them to be compared by use of the Pareto standards.
For example, we might say that S_1 is a Pareto improvement over
S and mean that in S_1 no one's *utility* decreases, whereas at least
one person's utility increases; or we could mean that in S_1 no one
is less *wealthy* than in S, while at least one person is wealthier. The
traditional Pareto standards are not abandoned under a system of
wealth maximization: They are employed to rank or describe social states in terms of the wealth, rather than the utility, relationship among them.[16]

The concrete example I shall use to illustrate the relationships
between wealth maximization and the Pareto criteria comes from
Coase.[17] Suppose that a rancher and farmer own land adjacent to
one another. Each seeks to maximize his or her revenue from the
relevant activity. In the absence of the other activity, the rancher
would raise cows until the marginal benefit of his doing so equaled
his marginal cost; the farmer would grow corn until her marginal
benefit equaled her marginal private cost. Where marginal revenue
equals marginal private cost, revenue is maximized; any additional
ranching or farming will be more costly than profitable.

Where the two activities affect one another, more cows will mean
less corn and vice versa. This is the essence of an externality problem. In the efficient resolution of this externality problem, marginal revenue again is equal to marginal cost, but marginal cost
(for the rancher) is equal to the sum of his marginal cost in raising
cows plus the marginal damage each cow causes the farmer's corn
crop. The problem is illustrated by Figure 4.4.

In the absence of farming, the rancher will ranch to A; with
farming, he will ranch to B. B represents the wealth-maximizing

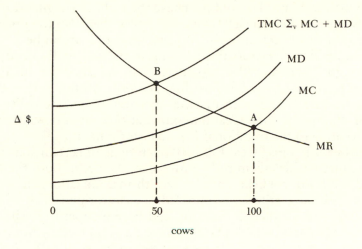

Figure 4.4

solution to the externality problem – on the assumption that the rancher and farmer are interested in their land and its productive uses for the purposes of profit only. If either had preferences other than increasing his or her respective wealth, *B* would not necessarily reflect the optimal solution to the externality problem.

It is easy to show, moreover, that *B* is not only wealth maximizing but Pareto optimal as well. To see this, consider two possible alternative starting points. In one, the rancher has the right to raise as many cows as he wishes. He is free to act as if there were no corn crop that would be damaged by his cattle; in the other, the farmer has an absolute right to prohibit cattle. In the first case, the rancher starts out ranching one hundred cows (the number of cows represented by *A*); in the other case, he starts out with no cattle. Consider the last case first. Because the loss the rancher incurs by not being able to ranch the first cow is far greater than the damage the cow will cause the corn crop, the rancher will buy the right to the first cow from the farmer by compensating her for the damage the cow will cause. This move will be Pareto superior to the starting point. For every cow up to the fiftieth one, a similar Pareto-superior move can be made whereby the rancher raises an additional cow and reimburses the farmer for the associated crop damage, thus making the farmer no worse off than before each additional cow is added. No Pareto-superior moves from *B* can be made, however, since in order to add a fifty-first cow, the rancher must pay more in damages to the farmer than the cow is worth to him. He could purchase the right to the fifty-first cow only by making himself worse off. *B* is then Pareto superior to any point to its left or right. A similar argument can be advanced to show that if negotiations begin at *A,* they will end up at *B* through a series of Pareto-superior moves and that no Pareto-superior move from *B* is possible. *B* represents not only a wealth-maximizing but a Pareto-optimal solution to the externality problem. Because it does, wealth maximization cannot be viewed as an alternative to the traditional Pareto criterion.

Instead, because wealth is a characteristic of certain states of affairs that enables them to be ranked by the use of both the Pareto and the Kaldor–Hicks criteria, wealth maximization, in conjunction with these criteria, can provide a basis for preferring one state of affairs to another. For example, a Pareto-superior exchange is, in the system of wealth maximization, a good thing – not because it increases welfare, but because it increases wealth. Wealth maximization is not an efficiency criterion; it is an alternative to the utilitarian basis for justifying the pursuit of efficiency.

3.2. Consequences of the reliance of wealth on prices

3.2.1. Exchange. Exchanges between rational, self-interested, well-informed individuals usually increase welfare or utility. Individuals do not in general engage in transactions that are not in their interest. It is not clear, however, that such exchanges are wealth maximizing. That is because, in the absence of either market prices or quasi-prices, exchange has no effect on wealth. In the absence of prices, *A*'s exchange of his last orange for *B*'s last two apples is neither wealth maximizing nor wealth reducing. While we can infer from the exchange that *A* prefers *B*'s last two apples to his last orange – that *A*'s utility increases when he has the two apples – and that *B* prefers *A*'s last orange to her last two apples – that her utility increases when she has that one orange – we cannot say anything at all about whether the transaction has increased wealth – *A*'s, *B*'s or society's – in the absence of prices. Therefore, free exchange need not be wealth maximizing; indeed, exchange *simpliciter* is not wealth maximizing at all. Only exchanges that involve prices can be wealth maximizing.

Because wealth maximization relies on the existence of prices, utilitarianism, but not wealth maximization, can provide the outline of a consequentialist argument for free exchange. Very roughly, the utilitarian argument would be that free exchange under the constraints of, among others, substantial knowledge and rationality increases utility and is desirable for that reason. In contrast, the system of wealth maximization can support free exchange only where exchanges involve prices. It is hard to see why free exchange is a good thing when it involves prices, but morally neutral, as it would be on wealth-maximizing grounds, otherwise.

3.2.2. Scarcity. Because the principle of wealth maximization necessarily involves the existence of prices, a proponent of wealth maximization would have to condemn as wealth reducing any recommendation to eliminate scarcity. Prices, after all, are necessary only in so far as scarce goods must be allocated. The elimination of scarcity eliminates the need for prices. The elimination of scarcity eliminates prices and, therefore, wealth.[18] I do not mean to suggest that the elimination of scarcity is *necessarily* a good thing. The point is that for the proponent of wealth maximization, the elimination of scarcity is necessarily a bad thing. In fact, whether abundance is good or bad, it is *contingently* so.

3.2.3. Theoretical incompleteness. The reliance on prices reveals the fundamental incompleteness of wealth maximization as a moral maxim. The principle of wealth maximization purports to provide a general invocation to action: Actions are right or obligatory to the extent that they promote wealth. Unfortunately, wealth maximization can tell us nothing of our rights and liberties, nor of our duties and responsibilities in the absence of a system of fixed relative prices. Surely some things are right and others wrong, even in the absence of prices.

3.2.4. Assigning basic entitlements. The problem of relying on prices arises once again when we reach the question whether one could employ wealth maximization to assign basic entitlements. Wealth maximization requires a fixed set of relative prices. The prices of goods depend, among other things, on the relative demand for them. The demand for goods depends in turn on the distribution of wealth. And the distribution of wealth is of course a function of what individuals are entitled to. Therefore, the system of wealth maximization must presuppose a set of initial entitlements in order to get started; and these initial entitlements cannot, by hypothesis, be accounted for on wealth-maximizing grounds. The system of wealth maximization therefore cannot provide a basis for an initial assignment of entitlements.

3.2.5. Circularity of preferences. The questions that arise in virtue of the role the *existence* of prices plays in the system of wealth maximization are different from those we might have concerning the role price *changes* play in wealth maximization. One way in which price changes may have an adverse effect on the system of wealth maximization surfaces in connection with an analogue of the Scitovsky paradox.

Before the publication of "Utilitarianism, Economics, and Legal Theory," Posner professed to employ utility-based notions of economic efficiency. In a previous article, I argued that Posner justified market interventions as well as particular assignments of rights on the basis of the Kaldor–Hicks criterion.[19] Posner acknowledges and accepts my argument that he applies the Kaldor–Hicks test.[20] He acknowledges using Kaldor–Hicks, but Kaldor–Hicks is subject to the Scitovsky paradox, and for that reason alone cannot constitute a utilitarian efficiency criterion. The Scitovsky paradox arises when the Kaldor–Hicks test is employed to rank social states in terms of their utility. Wealth maximization ranks social states in terms of dollar equivalents, not utilities. Unlike utilities, dollars are comparable. Therefore, whatever its deficiencies may be, the system of wealth maximization – even to the extent that it employs the Kaldor–Hicks test – is not subject to the Scitovsky paradox.

Although wealth maximization avoids the Scitovsky paradox, it is subject to an informal circularity-of-preference problem that results from its reliance on prices. The system of wealth maximization assumes at any given time a set of fixed prices for all commodities. On the basis of the prices at t_1, imagine that the principle recommends a shift in legal rules from strict liability to negligence. At t_2 the negligence rule is therefore instituted. The changeover in liability rules causes a change in relative prices. At t_3, suppose we reevaluate from the wealth-maximization point of view the efficiency of strict liability and negligence. It is perfectly plausible to suppose that, in at least some cases, the principle of wealth maximization, given the prices of goods at t_3, will recommend a change from negligence to strict liability. The problem is straightforward. Wealth maximization requires and affects prices. Prices must be fixed to employ the principle, but employing the principle to recommend structural changes in the law affects prices.

To meet this objection, one can restrict the use of the principle to those cases in which applying it will not affect prices, except perhaps minimally. But then the principle would have been stripped of its power in helping to frame or shape the common law. For it is precisely the landmark cases effecting structural changes in the law that are supposed to be explained and warranted by the principle of wealth maximization.

In sum: Contrary to Posner, the system of wealth maximization is not an alternative efficiency criterion. It is not a means of ranking social states, but is instead a characteristic of social states that enables them to be ranked by both the Pareto and Kaldor–Hicks criteria. Because it avoids the Scitovsky paradox, wealth maximization, unlike utilitarianism, can be employed in conjunction with the Kaldor–Hicks test. Therein lies one reason other than the ones Posner advances for preferring wealth maximization to utilitarianism.

Unfortunately the system of wealth maximization has its fair share of drawbacks – many of which arise because of the conceptual or logical connection of wealth maximization to the existence of prices. First, because the reliance on prices is necessary and not merely contingent, the system of wealth maximization cannot tell us anything about right conduct where no prices exist. Second, prices are in part the result of demand, demand the result of prior entitlements. Consequently, wealth maximization cannot generate an initial set of entitlements. Rearrangement of entitlements, once assigned, may be further restricted by the feature of wealth maximization that applying it both requires and affects prices – and, therefore, value.

4. THE ETHICAL BASIS OF WEALTH MAXIMIZATION

Suppose we could overlook the serious conceptual problems that reliance on prices creates for the system of wealth maximization. We should still have to ask whether wealth maximization constitutes an attractive moral maxim, one the law in particular ought to promote. There are two kinds of questions we could ask about the normative appeal of wealth maximization: one narrow, one general. The narrower question concerns the relative attractiveness of wealth maximization vis-à-vis utilitarianism. The point of the choice is this: If one is committed to pursuing efficiency as a fundamental social goal, are one's arguments for doing so enhanced if efficiency is understood as maximizing wealth or maximizing utility?

The more general question concerns the attractiveness of wealth maximization vis-à-vis the full range of alternative moral theories, including other consequentialist theories as well as nonconsequentialist ones such as libertarianism or Rawlsian justice. This question does not focus on alternative reasons for pursuing efficiency, but on the issue of whether the pursuit of efficiency, rooted either in utility or wealth maximization, is preferable to some other conception of right action or justice. This is the question of whether and to what extent social institutions should be arranged to pursue efficiency.

Because there are two kinds of questions involving wealth maximization, there are two ways of reading Posner's arguments on its behalf: narrowly, to the effect that wealth maximization is more attractive than utility; or generally, to the effect that wealth maximization is a correct first principle. I think it is fair to say that Posner's arguments are to be taken both ways: narrowly, because he believes wealth maximization is a more desirable basis for efficiency than utility; generally, because of the overall importance he accords efficiency in the determination of the institutional basis of society.

Unlike happiness or well-being, wealth is not something of intrinsic value. If the pursuit of wealth is a good, it must be because pursuing wealth promotes other things of value. So one kind of argument for the attractiveness of wealth as a normative system is instrumentalist. This is the argument Posner advocates in "Utilitarianism, Economics, and Legal Theory."

Another line of argument one might take on behalf of wealth maximization relies on a different methodology. In this view, a set of normative principles is justified if individuals under certain constraints would have consented to or chosen them. This is a familiar line of moral justification, especially fashionable since publication of John Rawls's *Theory of Justice*.[21] One would then have to argue that under a set of constraints, individuals conceived of in a certain way would have consented to or chosen the principle of wealth maximization as the fundamental moral maxim. This is the consent or contractarian argument.

A final, more limited argument is based on the premise that individuals exercising their liberty through market behavior act in a wealth-maximizing way. Because voluntary exchange is wealth maximizing, wealth maximization may be defended by its connection to liberty. This is the libertarian argument. Posner seems to advance both contractarian and libertarian arguments to support the system of wealth maximization.[22]

4.1. The instrumentalist argument

Because wealth is not something of intrinsic value, its claim to moral worth depends on its extrinsic value, that is, on its capacity to secure other things of value. Posner's view is that a society that aims at maximizing wealth will "produce an ethically attractive combination of happiness, of rights (to liberty and property), and of sharing with the less fortunate members of society."[23] If individuals value liberty, equality, security and happiness, as well as wealth, why will they achieve a more attractive package of these goods if they act as if they prefer only wealth than they will if they act as if they prefer one or another particular mixture of liberty, equality, security and happiness?

I do not mean to deny that people value wealth: They obviously do. But since any instrumentalist defense of wealth maximization must presuppose that individuals value things other than wealth, there is no basis for the belief that individuals, by acting as if they were interested only in wealth, would achieve a more attractive mix of preference satisfaction than they will if they act on the basis of the complex set of preferences they have. Moreover, it is at least plausible that individuals who act as if they desire only wealth might secure more wealth and less of other things than they will secure if they act as if they prefer all the things they in fact do.

Posner contends not only that a system predicated on the wealth principle would secure desirable levels of liberty, equality and security but also that it would confer moral rights and impose moral obligations. This claim is ambiguous. Does Posner mean that in order to maximize wealth, certain rights will be conferred and obligations imposed; or does he mean to advance the very different claim that people acting to maximize wealth will invariably respect those rights that other individuals have – rights which can be derived from principles other than wealth maximization? In other words, are the rights to which Posner refers "instruments" in the pursuit of wealth, or are they independent of the pursuit of wealth?[24]

If the rights Posner refers to are *not* mere instruments of the pursuit of wealth, the claim that pursuing wealth would not interfere with them is implausible. For example, it is easy to imagine that pursuing wealth may require violating the right to a minimal level of economic security. One might counter, on Posner's behalf, that there is no right to economic security of this sort. No doubt any particular theory of rights will be controversial. But it begs the question to assert that a putative right is no right at all if it does not coincide in every case with the pursuit of wealth.

The *instrumentalist* conception of rights is troublesome for a number of reasons. I shall discuss only two problems. By treating all rights as instruments of wealth maximization, it suggests that

wealth maximization is the only good in society; rights are conferred and duties imposed in order to secure that good. Such a
view is incompatible with the claim that wealth is valued instru-
mentally as a means to other social ends. This is in sharp contrast
to a utilitarian theory of rights in that, unlike wealth, utility is
valued in itself, and therefore rights and duties are established precisely to secure that end. But if there are ends other than wealth –
for example, welfare, security, autonomy – why should the only
rights individuals have be means to the end of wealth maximization? Why not confer rights to a certain level of welfare, security,
freedom and so on? If there are such rights, then they exist apart
from the principle of wealth. If such rights exist independent of
the pursuit of wealth, then the pursuit of wealth may at times
require disrespecting them. If it does, either we pursue wealth or
respect the relevant right.

If, in the event of conflict, the right is respected though doing
so is not wealth maximizing, then there exist values more important than wealth – which apparently are best pursued not by pursuing wealth but by failing to do so. In addition, these rights could
not be mere instruments in the pursuit of social wealth. On the
other hand, failure to respect the right in favor of an incremental
advantage in the pursuit of wealth implies that the principle of
wealth maximization is unable to account for fundamental features
of what it means to have a right. For at the very least, a right
provides its holder with authority to foreclose policies or actions
that could otherwise be justified in the name of the common good.
Rights need not be trumps in order for them to alter the normative
status of both individuals who possess them and others affected
by them. But if a right is a mere instrument of some conception
of the common good, then whenever pursuing the common good
would require disrespecting or ignoring a right, so much the worse
for rights and right holders. A mere instrument can never be a
right, in that part of what it means to have a right is that incremental arguments on behalf of the common good – or wealth – need
not be decisive against a valid right claim.

All instrumentalist defenses of wealth maximization are doomed
to failure. The very idea of an instrumentalist defense of wealth
maximization is paradoxical. According to wealth maximization,
wealth is *the* good, and maximizing it the right. Yet in order to
defend the normative use of wealth maximization, the instrumentalist argument presupposes that there are other goods, that wealth
is not the ultimate social good. Next, all instrumentalist defenses
of wealth maximization rely on the very implausible claim that a

society will achieve a more attractive combination of wealth and other social goods by pursuing wealth only than it would were it to pursue this or that combination of social goals. Moreover, the system of wealth maximization cannot give rise to a full moral theory, one that includes both moral rights and duties, since a mere instrument in the pursuit of some conception of the good can never be a right. Finally, the rights and obligations that would constitute instruments of wealth maximization would not prove particularly attractive.[25]

4.2. The consent argument

4.2.1. Wealth and freedom. In "The Ethical and Political Basis of the Efficiency Norm in Common Law Adjudication," Posner augments the instrumentalist defense of wealth maximization with arguments based on his understanding of the principles of liberty and consent.[26] The argument begins by drawing a distinction between alternative normative arguments for the traditional Pareto criteria. After arguing that Pareto superiority is rooted in utilitarianism, Posner notes:

> It is also possible to locate Pareto ethics in a different philosophical tradition from the utilitarian, in the tradition, broadly Kantian, which attaches a value over and above the utilitarian to individual autonomy. One ethical criterion of change that is highly congenial to the Kantian emphasis on autonomy is consent. And consent is the operational basis of the concept of Pareto superiority.[27]

In this view, actions that are freely consented to by the relevant parties are normatively justifiable not because the transactions increase utility or wealth but because they involve the exercise of liberty. Transactions that are wealth maximizing are justified because in exercising their liberty individuals consent to them. Thus, the system of wealth maximization is justified on consensual grounds.

The argument seems headed for trouble from the outset. If consenting to a transaction is what justifies it, then actions that are *not* wealth maximizing may be normatively justified – if they are consented to. It follows that consent is too weak a principle to justify the system of wealth maximization, that is, the theory of the good as the maximization of wealth.

Posner does not specifically address what appears to be the obvious problem of non–wealth-maximizing market transactions, in part because he seems to believe that no such cases exist: "In the setting of a market free from third-party effects, it is clear that forbidding transactions would reduce both the wealth of society and personal autonomy, so that the goals of maximizing wealth and of protecting autonomy coincide."[28] In Posner's view, then, voluntary market exchange is invariably wealth maximizing; otherwise forbidding exchange would not necessarily reduce wealth. This view is mistaken, since transactions in the absence of prices are not wealth maximizing in his sense.[29] If I trade you one apple for one orange, social wealth is not increased.[30] Moreover, actual consent is an inappropriate justification for wealth maximization insofar as the principle of wealth is supposed to guide institutional design, that is, the development of alternative, as yet *unrealized,* wealth-maximizing institutions. The principle of actual consent justifies too much and is of the wrong sort to justify the system of wealth maximization.

4.2.2. Kaldor–Hicks, Pareto and wealth. The problem Posner faces goes even deeper. Not only can we distinguish wealth-maximizing institutions from other institutions, we can also differentiate those wealth-maximizing institutions that increase wealth through Pareto improvements – such as, in Posner's view, the free market[31] – from those that maximize wealth through Kaldor–Hicks moves – such as, again in Posner's view, the negligence system in torts.[32] The distinction between Pareto-superior and Kaldor–Hicks wealth maximization is even more complex, since we can further distinguish between two cases of Pareto-superior wealth improvements.
     Consider the following three cases:

(1) *A* and *B* exchange with one another. This is the paradigm of mutual gain through trade.
(2) Because of a market failure, *A* and *B* do not exchange with one another. A good is awarded to *A* that had it been awarded to *B* would have been inefficient in that *B* would have sold it to *A,* as in (1) above. *A,* however, compensates *B* so that he (*B*) is indifferent between his current state and where he would have been had he been awarded the good originally.
(3) Again because of a market failure, *A* and *B* do not actually exchange with one another. A good is awarded to *A* which had it been awarded to *B* would have been inefficient. *B,* however, is not compensated by *A* or anyone else, and is therefore worse off than he was prior to the assignment.

The first case involves a Pareto-superior move that is the result of individuals exercising their liberty. The second case involves a Pareto-superior move that is not the result of the exercise of liberty, because the individuals do not consummate a mutually advantageous exchange. The third case involves a Kaldor–Hicks move. In terms of consent: In the first case individuals express their consent to the transaction through their market behavior; in the second case, individuals consent by accepting compensation *ex post*.[33] In the third case, however, individuals do not appear to consent to particular transactions through the exercise of their liberty or through their acceptance of compensation. In what sense can we say losing parties in Kaldor–Hicks wealth improvements, individuals like *B* in the third case, consent to institutions that make them less well off but are wealth maximizing?

The remarkably bold claim Posner advances is not just that wealth maximization is justified because it is consented to; it is that wealth maximization of the Kaldor–Hicks variety – as in case (3) – is justified because it is consented to. Posner puts the task as follows: "I want to defend the Kaldor–Hicks or wealth-maximization approach not by reference to Pareto superiority as such or its utilitarian premise, but by reference to the idea of *consent* that I have said provides an alternative basis to utilitarianism for the Pareto criterion."[34] The principle of consent is supposed to justify not simply the pursuit of wealth over other goals, but its advancement through a series of Kaldor–Hicks interventions. The obvious problem is that Kaldor–Hicks interventions produce losers; and why would a possible loser consent to a system that made him worse off – especially when he could be assured of being made no worse off by opting for Pareto-superior wealth-maximizing intervention?

The claim that rational individuals would consent to Kaldor–Hicks wealth-maximizing institutions over Pareto-superior ones must be modified. After all, rational persons would likely choose to leave a wide range of social choices to the market. A free market involves Pareto-superior rather than Kaldor–Hicks improvements. Posner's claim therefore cannot be that individuals would generally choose to forgo the market. Suppose we understand Posner to be arguing not that Kaldor–Hicks institutions are preferred to the market, but that where the market breaks down or where structural changes in it are required rational individuals would choose to follow a Kaldor–Hicks path to wealth maximization.

4.2.3. Consent and ex ante *compensation.* For Posner, the question
of whether Kaldor–Hicks wealth maximization is justified is the
question of whether it is appropriate to say of the losers in Kaldor–
Hicks interventions or institutions that they have consented to
their losses.[35] By way of an introduction to his argument, Posner
notes that he proposes to defend wealth maximization by appealing to a notion of consent, according to which, "if you buy a
lottery ticket and lose the lottery, then, so long as there is no question of fraud or duress, you have consented to the loss."[36]

This introduction is a warning of the confusions to follow. If I
buy the lottery ticket and lose, my loss may be a fair or legitimate
one, one that it may be appropriate to pin on me. It would be fair
because I had willingly taken a risk by consenting to or voluntarily
joining an enterprise that was risky in the relevant way. But it
would hardly follow that I had consented to the loss. Consenting
to or taking the risk is not equivalent to consenting to or taking
the loss, irrespective of the fairness of the loss.

Posner argues not only that individuals who lose in Kaldor–
Hicks institutions consent to their losses, but that their consent is
given by their accepting *ex ante* compensation.[37] The argument
appears to be this: Wealth-maximizing institutions by hypothesis
are less costly than non–wealth-maximizing ones. A system in
which compensation is paid and accepted *ex post* – that which is
Pareto superior – is more costly than one in which compensation
is not paid. The initial costs of wealth-maximizing, Kaldor–Hicks–
based institutions are, therefore, lower. The difference in initial
entrance costs constitutes a kind of *ex ante* compensation. So possible losers who engage in such activities consent by their acceptance of the lower entrance fee. They give their consent by accepting *ex ante* compensation in the form of lower costs.

The general argument can be illustrated by example. Suppose,
as Posner does,[38] that the negligence system is less costly than a
system of strict liability. One way in which strict liability and negligence differ concerns the likelihood of a victim's recovering
damages. In strict liability a victim is more likely to recover than
in negligence, where the conditions of liability are more demanding. For example, victims can recover in strict liability in cases in
which the injurer is not at fault, whereas in negligence liability the
victim will not recover unless the injurer is at fault.

Posner apparently believes that in strict liability a victim's acceptance of compensation *ex post* constitutes consent to the activity that caused the harm.[39] In negligence liability, the lower costs
of the system, as exemplified in insurance premiums, constitute a

form of *ex ante* compensation, the acceptance of which constitutes for each victim consent to an uncompensated loss.[40]

Even if it made sense to say that everyone under the fault system accepted the lower costs, it would hardly follow that by accepting the reduced costs the actual victims had consented to the loss, any more than it would follow that by accepting *ex post* compensation for a loss, one had consented to the activity that caused the loss. I may never approve of, let alone consent to, reckless driving, but I would certainly accept, indeed demand, compensation were I the victim of another's carelessness. My acceptance of compensation *ex post* would not signify my consent to being injured. Instead, it would signify that I had been wronged by another's misdeeds. Compensation enforces my right to security; it is not the instrument through which I express my consent to having the level of my security reduced.

In Posner's view, accepting full compensation for a loss amounts to giving one's consent to the activity that caused the loss. If accepting compensation constitutes consent, then it does not matter from a moral point of view whether compensation is accepted *ex post* or *ex ante;* the temporal dimension carries no moral weight. The problem with Posner's argument does not concern the difficult epistemic questions of how to determine if an individual has accepted *ex ante* compensation. The real question is whether accepting compensation constitutes consent.

Were we to follow Posner, it would be impossible to accept full compensation and not thereby give one's consent. So the only way traffic victims, for example, could refuse to consent to being run over would be to refuse to accept compensation. If they demand, are offered and then accept compensation because their right to freedom from unnecessary risk has been violated, they have, in Posner's view at least, consented to being harmed. They have in effect waived their right to security from undue risk. Surely the victims do not see it that way. If they tell us that they refuse either to give consent or to waive their right, then we must tell them, following Posner, that they must refuse compensation. But if they refuse compensation for an injury – when compensation is ordinarily due them – would we not be likely to take *that* as a sign that in fact they had, unknown to us, waived their right, that they had given their consent to being injured, or, at the least, that they had willingly assumed the risk? Something is deeply wrong in Posner's account of the relationship between consent and compensation.[41]

The mistake arises because Posner is misled by his own paradigm of justification via consent. In the paradigm case, *A* and *B* consummate a free exchange. By accepting one another's offerings, each gives consent to the transaction and to the resulting redistribution, thereby justifying both. In the first sort of derivative case, *A* and *B* do not exchange. *A* benefits at *B*'s expense; *A* however compensates *B* *ex post*. For Posner, *B*'s acceptance of *ex post* compensation constitutes his consent to the activity and to the resulting redistribution. In the third case, the one that particularly interests Posner, *A* again benefits at *B*'s expense. The risks of being a loser however were accounted for in the initial costs of the game, so that even though neither *A* nor anyone else compensates *B* *ex post*, *B* is compensated *ex ante* by accepting lower costs. Therefore, he consents to the activity that caused the loss and to the loss itself.

The derivative cases however are not illuminated by the paradigm. If *A* gains at *B*'s expense, *B*'s acceptance of compensation need not constitute his consent to *A*'s gaining at his expense, any more than a traffic victim's acceptance of compensation constitutes his or her consent to being a traffic victim. The same individual therefore does not consent to being a traffic victim by supporting the wealth-maximizing negligence system. Compensation, whether *ex post* or *ex ante,* neither constitutes nor is a surrogate for consent. Once this is made clear, it is also easy to see why Posner's claim[42] that the system of wealth maximization can be rooted in the libertarian political morality of Nozick and to a lesser extent Epstein is mistaken.[43]

The prevailing view is that economic analysis falls on the other end of the political spectrum from libertarianism. Libertarianism, as Nozick defends it, opposes market interventions for whatever reasons – egalitarian, paternalistic or utilitarian. It would hardly favor market intervention for the purpose of promoting efficiency.[44] One interesting claim Posner makes is that the consent justification of wealth maximization forges a merger of libertarianism and economic analysis. The argument is that economic analysis requires promoting wealth through Kaldor–Hicks moves. Individuals would give their consent to this endeavor; winners do so by accepting their gains, and losers consent by accepting *ex ante* compensation. Giving consent is an exercise of one's liberty. Therefore the pursuit of wealth (economic efficiency) is justified on libertarian grounds. Unfortunately, compensation, whether offered and accepted *ex post* or *ex ante,* does not constitute consent. Freely accepting *ex ante* compensation does not amount to consenting to either a loss, should it arise, or the activity or institution that gives rise to the loss. All this is quite apart from the question whether the loss is justifiably imposed on someone; the only point is that even if it is justified it is not because the loser consents to her loss through the exercise of her liberty.

Posner's effort to forgo an alliance with the libertarians is interesting because, once we abandon the hopeless effort to justify Kaldor–Hicks wealth-maximizing institutions on the ground that the losers consent to their losses by accepting *ex ante* compensation, we are left with the much more sensible argument that such institutions are justified because rational persons in a position of uncertainty would have chosen them. We are left defending wealth maximization by the use of a Rawlsian argument from the principles of rational choice under conditions of uncertainty.

Posner is confused both about what he has to argue for and how to go about arguing for it. Since compensation does not constitute consent, by accepting compensation losers do not consent to their losses or to the activities that cause them. To defend wealth maximization through the principle of consent, Posner does not have to show that each individual loser consents to the loss; he has to show only that each individual would choose to take the risk of losing. Individuals do not have to consent to the loss for the losses they suffer to be fairly imposed upon them or for the institutions that give rise to the losses to be justified. The institutions themselves may be justified because they are agreed upon, and the losses they give rise to justified accordingly – even if each particular loss is not consented to.

Instead of the argument Posner advances we should ascribe to him a more plausible one: Risk-neutral, rational persons facing economic choice under uncertainty would choose to pursue wealth through Kaldor–Hicks institutions. The argument for this claim would then rely on *ex ante* compensation not as constituting consent but as a reason for preferring Kaldor–Hicks to Pareto-superior wealth improvements. If individuals had chosen to pursue wealth through Kaldor–Hicks moves, then their losses would be justified because they freely risked them, not because they consented to them. The question then is whether the argument from rational choice can be sustained.

4.2.4. Choice under uncertainty and wealth maximization. There are really two distinct but related claims here: first, that individuals under uncertainty[45] would choose the pursuit of wealth over other social goals; second, that in pursuing wealth they would opt for Kaldor–Hicks rather than other institutional arrangements. The striking feature of Posner's argument is that he ignores entirely the first claim. His entire argument, especially its reliance on the idea of *ex ante* compensation, is directed at demonstrating that principles of rational choice would favor *ex ante* compensation, that in order to maximize wealth and minimize cost, rational, risk-neutral people would choose Kaldor–Hicks over Pareto superiority.

I leave it up to the economists to worry about the validity of Posner's argument on this score, though it seems to me interesting, if ultimately implausible.[46] The real problem, however, is the one Posner fails to confront: whether rational choice under uncertainty would dictate the pursuit of wealth as opposed to, say, Rawls's two principles of justice or some variant of utilitarianism. After all, the claim Posner has to make is that wealth maximization is a normatively defensible first principle; not the weaker and less interesting claim that Kaldor–Hicks wealth maximization is more morally defensible than are all other means of promoting wealth. The latter claim may be true and the former false.

The fact is that Posner does not argue that rational individuals under uncertainty would prefer wealth maximization *simpliciter* to the pursuit of any or all other goals. More significantly, because wealth is not something of intrinsic value, any argument that rational persons facing uncertain choice would prefer to pursue wealth to anything else would have to be instrumentalist in nature: Rational people facing uncertainty would choose to pursue wealth maximization because in doing so they would secure a desirable combination of wealth, freedom, security, happiness and so on. The instrumentalist argument therefore cannot be circumvented by the argument from consent. Moreover, if the instrumentalist argument is a good one, there is a sense in which the argument from rational choice is excess baggage. However, for precisely the reasons already discussed, the instrumentalist argument fails.[47] Because it does, any argument that relies on it, such as the putative argument from consent or rational choice, must fail as well.

5. NONUTILITARIAN ARGUMENTS FOR PARETIANISM

I concluded section 2 of this essay by noting that the weaknesses of utilitarianism as a theory of right action and obligation left the proponent of economic analysis with a choice. Either he could abandon the efficiency criteria he views as normatively unjustifiable because of their connection to utilitarianism in favor of non-utility-based efficiency criteria, or he could try to construct nonutilitarian defenses for those efficiency criteria otherwise conceived of as utilitarian. In sections 3 and 4 I explored and evaluated one instance of the former strategy, Richard Posner's effort to introduce and defend a nonutilitarian efficiency criterion: wealth maximization. In this section I want to pursue the search for other nonutility-based justifications for the traditional Pareto criteria.

5.1. The Pareto criteria and liberty

One set of arguments for the normative use of the Pareto criteria relies on the fact that exchanges in free markets are generally Pareto superior. Individuals transact when it is in their interest to do so; when each views the transaction as liable to make him or her better off. Moreover, the ultimate outcome of Pareto-superior market behavior is Pareto optimality. Individuals will engage in transactions until it is no longer in the interest of at least one of them to do so. At that point negotiations cease because there are no further mutual gains through trades to be had. In the ideal world of noncoercive markets free from transaction costs and third-party effects, in which individuals are both rational and knowledgeable, the exercise of liberty leads to Pareto-optimal states of affairs through a series of Pareto-superior exchanges.

These considerations provide the bases for a number of related arguments for pursuing Pareto improvements. One argument, analogous to the one Posner briefly discusses in connection with wealth maximization, emphasizes that in exercising their liberty individuals promote efficiency. Consequently, the pursuit of Pareto efficiency is justified not because of its relationship to net utility but because noncoercive market behavior is efficient. The moral value we attach to individual autonomy is transferred to the pursuit of efficiency.

This line of argument fails for a number of reasons. First, not all markets are Pareto efficient. For example, lack of adequate information may transform free choice into something less than Pareto-superior action. Further, it is at least plausible that some individuals acting freely make themselves worse off; freedom does not necessarily ensure increased happiness. This much we know.

One could respond by saying that choices based on insufficient information are not totally free.[48] To the extent that market failures or inefficiencies result from inadequately informed choice, they are less than fully free. Consequently, an action that is not Pareto superior must be the result of a choice that is less than fully free.

One has to be careful not to build too much into the conditions for free rational choice, thereby making contradictory the claim that a rational person could act freely to his detriment. As long as it is logically possible to act freely to one's detriment, it is possible that at least some market exchanges will not be Pareto superior.

A second, more telling objection to the autonomy argument is that pursuing Pareto superiority or optimality may require intervention in the exchange market – at both the individual and institutional levels. Where the conditions of competitive equilibrium are not satisfied, a market will not secure an efficient outcome. To secure the efficient outcome, the political order must intervene in the market. In sum, not every free exchange is Pareto superior, and pursuing efficiency may sometimes require abandoning non-coercive markets. Consequently, the argument from autonomy is both too weak and too strong to justify adequately the pursuit of Pareto improvements.

This discussion suggests a simple but important distinction between the market and economic approaches to social policy problems. According to one form of economic analysis, the fundamental goal of social policy is efficiency. When the initial conditions of the Coase theorem, for example, are satisfied, efficiency may be secured through noncoercive markets. When the conditions for equilibrium are not met, however, markets will not necessarily be efficient. Consequently, pursuing efficiency often requires coercive intervention in the market.

The breakdown in symmetry between markets and efficiency suggests a tension in the underlying political morality of economic analysis. Does the proponent of economic analysis support the market because of its connection to personal autonomy in spite of its inefficiency; or does the defender of the economic approach to law advocate pursuing efficiency, even if this means abandoning the free market? In other words, is the underlying political morality of economic analysis libertarian or utilitarian?[49]

Posner's principle for justified market intervention, the principle of "mimicking or simulating the market,"[50] appears to exacerbate the problem, since it is unclear which aspect of the market – autonomous free exchange or efficient outcomes – the legal order is supposed to mimic.[51] Following Posner, proponents of economic analysis seem to hold the view that where markets fail and coercive intervention is required, legal rules should be formulated to produce the result the market would have produced had it been capable of exchanges that lead to efficient outcomes.[52] They opt, in other words, for the efficient outcome aspect of markets rather than their autonomous exchange component.

As I have argued here and in more detail elsewhere, entitlement assignments according to the principle of mimicking markets involve the Kaldor–Hicks–efficiency standard.[53] This assignment rule is meant to *replace* free, but inefficient, market exchanges; therefore, the rule cannot be justified as involving the exercise of liberty.[54] Second, since the assignment rule involves the Kaldor–Hicks rather than the Pareto-superior efficiency criteria, no particular assignment based on it can be justified on utilitarian grounds simply because Kaldor–Hicks is not an index of utility.

This is paradoxical. Market failures reveal the tension that exists between the apparently competing moralities of libertarianism and utilitarianism in economic analysis. In responding to market failure by the use of Kaldor–Hicks interventions, however, one's policies do not receive support from principles of either liberty or utility. Intervention by its very nature is coercive and therefore incompatible with the free-exchange ideal of libertarianism; and an intervention that is Kaldor–Hicks efficient may or may not increase utility. Certainly in the absence of a *known* standard of interpersonal utility comparison we have no reason to think that any particular assignment of legal rights increases utility.

One way out of this paradox is to argue as follows: Suppose market interventions and subsequent assignments of entitlements are restricted to cases in which the result in Pareto optimal. Those interventions would be both Kaldor–Hicks efficient and Pareto optimal. We could argue that the interventions are justified not because they are Kaldor–Hicks efficient but because they are Pareto optimal. Yet that will not take us very far if what we are seeking is some normative justification for the intervention. Once again, the mere fact of intervention precludes the possibility of the libertarian defense. The fact that the result of the intervention is Pareto optimal will not suffice to tell us anything about whether the intervention increases total utility. In short, intervening in the market to secure a Pareto-optimal result may not be justifiable on either libertarian or utilitarian grounds.

The claim that a market intervention is justified because it is Pareto optimal, not because it is Kaldor–Hicks efficient, is problematic in a much deeper way. Indeed, the entire enterprise of normative law-and-economics, which would have us justify intervening in inefficient markets to promote or secure efficiency, involves a deep theoretical error. The error is in thinking that any

Pareto-optimal point or distribution is better from the point of view of economic efficiency than any non–Pareto-optimal, inefficient distribution. That this is a mistake is easy enough to show. The claim that intervention to promote efficiency is justified whenever the market is inefficient presupposes that efficiency (Pareto optimality) is preferable to inefficiency. As everyone familiar with economic theory knows, however, not every Pareto-optimal distribution is preferable to every non–Pareto-optimal one. Pareto-optimal distributions are preferable on economic grounds only to distributions represented by points to their southwest. All other points are Pareto noncomparable.

The only way out of this problem is to require compensation of losers in all interventions. Then, if the result is Pareto optimal, it is secured via a Pareto-superior path, one that increases utility and may be justifiable at least on utilitarian grounds. Unfortunately, an assignment rule that required compensation would be inefficient whenever the costs of compensation were nontrivial, that is, most of the time.[55]

This point can be made in the following manner. You are a proponent of normative economic analysis of law. You believe that the law should keep its hands clear of free exchanges between individuals, provided their exchanges are efficient. When markets fail to promote efficiency you contend that the law ought to intervene and rearrange affairs among the relevant parties to produce the efficient result the market would have had it not failed.

I ignore the enormous information problems involved in trying to determine which outcomes the market would have reached. Instead, I ask you this question: Why do you think intervening in the market is justified?

You respond first that the intervention increases utility. (You are too smart to claim that the economic intervention is justified on *libertarian* grounds.)

I respond that the intervention most likely involves a Kaldor–Hicks improvement. Because of both the interpersonal comparability problem and the Scitovsky paradox, a Kaldor–Hicks improvement, I point out, need not increase utility. Certainly, from the fact that the intervention is Kaldor–Hicks efficient, we have no reason to suppose that it does.

Then you point out that the intervention does not only involve a Kaldor–Hicks improvement, but – information-cost problems again set aside – the result is a Pareto-optimal arrangement of resources. You tell me that because the resulting distribution is Pareto optimal, not because it is Kaldor–Hicks efficient, there is a net increase in utility. I point out that it does not follow from the fact that a distribution of resources is Pareto optimal that the move to it increases total utility.

You agree, but then you say that the justification for the intervention has really little to do with utilitarianism anyway. Rather, while the conditions of free exchange have led to inefficiency, the legal order has secured efficiency. Efficiency is preferable to inefficiency.

But you are wrong. In economic theory, not every efficient distribution is preferable to every nonefficient one. Only points to the southwest of a point on the utility–possibility frontier represent less preferable distributions. About the relationships between the points representing the remainder of possible distributions of resources, economics has precious little to say. So I ask, rhetorically this time: What is the economic efficiency-related justification for the intervention?

The overall point is not just that a tension exists in the underlying political morality of economic analysis between libertarianism and utilitarianism. It is that once one uses economic analysis to recommend market interventions, one may be doing so without the support of either libertarianism or utilitarianism or, for that matter, simple economics.

5.2. Paretianism and consent

An adequate nonutilitarian defense of Paretianism cannot rely entirely on the efficiency of free choice as revealed in noncoercive market behavior, for it is possible to envision efficient institutions other than the market. The free-market argument for Paretianism is at best a tie breaker – whenever a Pareto-efficient state of affairs may be secured through market and nonmarket means, choose the market because of its reliance on individual free choice.

Suppose one could argue, as Posner does, that an action is justified if it is consented to. An individual might consent to an action that is Pareto superior either by freely engaging in a transaction or by accepting full and adequate compensation for a loss resulting from some institutional arrangement or policy. In both cases the move is Pareto superior; in both cases the relevant parties give their consent to the course of action or policy that promotes efficiency. In both cases the action is justified because it is consented to. The only difference between these cases is the action that constitutes or specifies consent. In the first case, consent is given by free exchange; in the second, it is given by the relevant parties' accepting compensation, ex post.[56]

Suppose then we try to construct an argument for both Pareto superiority and Pareto optimality from consent.[57] On its behalf, we can note that the argument from consent is more general than the argument from liberty. Indeed, the argument from liberty is just a particular instance of the argument from consent; in some cases consent is given by free and rational exchange. Moreover, the consent argument will justify Pareto superiority in cases in which Pareto improvements are not secured through free and rational exchanges.

Unfortunately, this argument is of the wrong sort to justify Paretianism. It justifies only a given set of Pareto-superior states of affairs, namely those that are consented to. It does not provide a moral reason for pursuing Pareto improvements. This argument says that there are Pareto improvements that are consented to and that are justified on that basis. The argument is of the wrong sort to show that every Pareto-superior move would be consented to or that it would be consented to because it would be Pareto superior.[58]

An adequate defense of the normative use of the Pareto criteria requires an argument from hypothetical, not actual, consent. One would have to argue that individuals under certain constraints would choose Paretianism as a moral maxim. The argument would go as follows: An action is Pareto superior if it makes no one worse off and at least one person better off; rational, self-interested individuals would offer no objection to such policies; therefore, such policies are justified, and because they are justified in the abstract, it is no wonder that in particular cases individuals give their consent to them either by exchange or through their acceptance of compensation.

This argument is of the right sort, but it is not persuasive. Whether an individual would consent to all policies and institutional arrangements that worked to the advantage of some and that were harmless to the interests of others would depend on his theory of rights and deserts. For example, monopolies are sometimes inefficient. In breaking up a monopoly in the name of efficiency, we can either compensate the monopolist or fail to. If we compensate her, the policy is Pareto superior; if not, it is Kaldor–Hicks efficient. What moral argument could one advance in favor of pursuing the Pareto-superior rather than the Kaldor–Hicks-efficient policy? Generally, a policy that makes A better off and no one worse off would be Pareto superior, even if A had no right to be made better off, or if he deserved to be made worse off, or even if *B*, not *A*, should have been better off. Until we know something about the rights and deserts of individuals affected by alternative courses of conduct, we should remain agnostic about the moral value of those policies that would otherwise be recommended to us as Pareto superior. In the absence of a prior non-efficiency-based theory of rights and moral deserts, it would be irrational to consent to Pareto superiority as a moral maxim.[59]

Can a similar but more successful argument be made for Pareto optimality? The set of Pareto-optimal states of affairs that can be generated by an economy in general competitive equilibrium is represented by points on the "contract curve." The contract curve gets its name from the fact that it connects points in an Edgeworth box that represent states of affairs to which producers and consumers would freely exchange (or contract).[60] Because Pareto optimality may be represented as the outcome of free exchanges, one could argue that rational persons would consent to institutional arrangements and courses of conduct that are efficient. In other words, what objection would an individual have to pursuing an efficient allocation of resources if such an allocation resulted from one's free action?

This argument will not work. One can secure Pareto-optimal outcomes through Pareto-superior, non–Pareto-superior, or Kaldor–Hicks–efficient steps. In other words, we can reach a Pareto-optimal result in a particular case by making no individuals worse off or by making some individuals worse off. It is unlikely that a rational individual would have no objection to pursuing optimal outcomes without regard to the path used to reach them. Once the question of path arises, however, the question of whether in every case to prefer Pareto superior to Kaldor–Hicks follows, and as we have just seen, a resolution of that matter requires a nonefficiency-based theory of rights and moral desert.

6. CONCLUSION

I want to close with two related remarks. One concerns the limits of economic analysis; the other concerns the economic theory of adjudication.

6.1. Positive and normative economics

One can do economic analysis of law in two seemingly related but really quite distinct ways. The first way, which I call positive eco-

nomic analysis, involves evaluating, for example, a set of possible
tort rules to determine which, if any, would be efficient in the
sense of securing the optimal number of accidents. John Brown
and William Holahan's article "Taxes and Legal Rules for the
Control of Externalities When There Are Strategic Responses"[61]
is a good example of this sort of economic analysis, as is the majority of work by A. Mitchell Polinsky and Steven Shavell.[62] In
all of this work, the authors are committed to the existence of a
Samuelson-like social welfare function,[63] of which Pareto optimality is a necessary but not a sufficient condition. As economists
they seek to determine which sort of rules or policies would be
efficient in the abstract. At its purest, this sort of economic analysis says nothing about the types of policies governments should
impose at the present time or the kinds of judicial opinions judges
should reach.

The second sort of economic analysis views economic efficiency
as a goal both of current social policy and judicial behavior and
argues that governments should intervene in human affairs or
rearrange sociopolitical and legal institutions to promote efficiency. This sort of economic analysis is exemplified by much,
though not all, of Posner's work, and it is economic analysis of
this sort that is subject to the kinds of criticisms I have been advancing. That is, once one advocates a change in the existing order, the question of the justification for doing so arises. With that
question follow others about the dislocation effects of the change
– who will be made worse off, who better and by how much.
Then the issue of Kaldor–Hicks versus Pareto superiority comes
to the fore, and with it all the questions regarding their alleged
utilitarian or libertarian normative bases. The point is that when
proponents of economic analysis do what most of them normally
do, that is, propose social policy, they get into trouble of the sort
I have been drawing attention to. In the more restrained quarters,
economists avoid many, but not all, of these problems.[64]

6.2. Economics and adjudication

Suppose that none of my objections to the various normative
strategies for defending the pursuit of Pareto efficiency are persuasive and that Paretianism constitutes an adequate moral theory.
Suppose even that wealth maximization does so as well. It still
would not follow that judges in particular cases had the authority
to resolve disputes on the basis of efficiency criteria. It does not
follow from the fact that in general we ought to pursue efficiency

that every actor or agent, regardless of his or her institutional role and circumstance, has the obligation or authority to promote efficiency. An argument that judicial behavior should be structured by efficiency considerations requires a further theory of institutional competence. The question is whether judges have the authority to seize upon a private dispute framed by and in terms of the litigants' interests as an opportunity to promote desirable social policies, for example, efficiency and distributional justice.

The alternative and I believe commonsense view is that the responsibility of a judge is to determine which of the litigants in a dispute has the relevant legal right.[65] It may be that in determining which party is entitled to a decision in its favor the judge must take account of efficiency considerations. He or she might hold that an individual who suffers harm caused by the unreasonably risky conduct of another is entitled to compensation. Following Learned Hand,[66] he or she might then go so far as to provide an economic analysis of fault or negligence. The fact that an economic argument is relevant to determining fault, for example, does not show that liability based on fault is justified on efficiency grounds, or that in awarding compensation to the plaintiff in a particular negligence case the judge is following an economic theory of adjudication. It is perfectly possible to describe the judicial behavior as follows: The judge is trying to determine which party has a right to the decision; the theory of legal rights he or she believes is correct has as a consequence that individuals who suffer from the economically inefficient conduct of others are entitled to compensation. Consequently, determining whether a particular plaintiff is entitled to recompense would require some sort of economic argument.

The difference between proponents of economic analysis and critics such as Dworkin and myself – on this question at least – is that we have different theories of institutional competence generally, and of adjudication in particular. The advantage of our way of looking at the problem is this: We draw a distinction between what, on balance, it is morally right or defensible to do and what a particular person, occupying an institutional role, has authority to do. Even were we to agree that pursuing efficiency would be morally defensible, we should argue that it is a further question whether judges have the authority to do so. In addition, we argue that adjudication primarily – or always – concerns rights rather than the promotion of some useful social policy while at the same time it provides a substantial and meaningful role for economic argument. The economic theory of adjudication, however, be-

cause it views private disputes in terms of global interests and social goals, explains the reference to economic argument in adjudication at the expense of the commonsense view of law as concerned
with rights and obligations – rights and obligations it is the court's
duty to enforce rather than create.[67]

5. The foundations of constitutional economics

1. INTRODUCTION

Philosophers distinguish between arguments advanced to justify undertaking a particular action or policy and those offered in support of adopting institutions. Because institutions are generally thought of in terms of the set of rules that defines them, the distinction philosophers draw is usually put in terms of the difference between justifying rules and the actions that fall under them. Philosophers emphasize as well a further distinction, that between two kinds of justifications advanced on behalf of pursuing either a goal, action or policy or an institutional arrangement. This is the distinction between teleological (or consequentialist) modes of justification and consensual ones.[1] Roughly, a justification is consensual if the grounds for arguing on behalf of the decision to promote a goal, pursue a policy or frame an institution is that the affected individuals have given their consent, that is, have agreed voluntarily to act in a certain way, to abide by certain rules, or the like. Goals, policies or institutions are justified on teleological grounds when the argument on their behalf is that pursuing, promoting or following them will have a net desirable effect on, for example, the well-being or utility of those affected by them. When the two distinctions are taken together, they give rise to four categories of justification. These are: (1) teleological arguments for pursuing individual actions, policies or goals; (2) teleological arguments for implementing a set of rules or for adopting an institutional arrangement; (3) consensual arguments on behalf of individual actions; and (4) consensual arguments on behalf of institutions.

Act utilitarianism – the view that a particular course of conduct is justified if and only if it, among the set of feasible alternative actions, maximizes net expected utility or welfare – is a form of teleological justification of individual states of affairs. *Rule utilitar-*

ianism – the application of the utilitarian calculus to choices among
institutions or the rules that form them – is an instance of the
teleological mode of justification applied at the level of social or
institutional choice. So we can distinguish between the claim that
a particular market transaction or trade is justified because it promotes the welfare of the parties involved and the claim that markets for the distribution of certain kinds of resources are preferable
to nonmarket allocation devices on the ground that markets generally are more efficient.

It is not difficult to find instances of particular actions justified
because they are agreed to. Any typical, noncoerced market transaction will suffice. No one, to my knowledge, has held the view
that voluntary agreement is a necessary condition for the justification of each particular course of conduct. That view creates
problems whenever implementing a policy or action produces losers as well as gainers. In such a case, the proponent of the view
that only voluntary agreement or consent justifies would have to
hold either that because losers have not agreed to their losses, the
policy that creates them is not justified; or that the policy is justified because, in spite of the common wisdom that rational people
do not normally agree to make themselves worse off, losers in fact
consent to their losses.

The proposition that policies imposing losses cannot be justified
simply by virtue of the fact that losers have not consented to their
losses is obviously implausible. There are, after all, perfectly good
reasons for imposing unwelcome burdens and losses. Punishing
the guilty is an obvious example.

The view that losers in particular cases in fact consent to their
losses is more interesting. Richard Posner has come closest to ad-
vocating such a position, namely, that losers consent to their losses,
and for that reason policies that impose losses in order to promote
the general welfare or to maximize social wealth are justified. I
shall discuss aspect of Posner's view in more detail later. For now,
it is enough to note that even Posner restricts the application of his
argument to certain market and legal contexts.

While few have seriously advanced the claim that only consent
can justify individual actions, several economists, philosophers and
social theorists have claimed that arguments from consent form
the justificatory foundation of political institutions or constitutions. Here the claim is not that any event which occurs within an
institutional framework is justified because it is consented to. It is
rather that the network of rules constituting the institution are
justified because they are freely consented to; and that particular

institutional events – actions, policies or decisions – are justified because they are required by rules that are consented to. In one sense, constitutional economics is the application of the principles of economics to decisions regarding the choice of institutions.

These distinctions suggest that the general characterization of the difference between constitutional and traditional modes of economic analysis as that between an emphasis on the long term (in the former case) and the short term (in the latter) is grossly inadequate. Instead the difference is this: Traditional economic analysis is consequentialist or teleological, not consensual, in its mode of justification. Moreover, it believes that what is to be justified are particular events or rules, in isolation – as if these could be treated independently of any particular institutional framework. Constitutionalists, in contrast, believe that individual events – policies, market transactions, political decisions or the like – can be given content or meaning only within an institutional framework. In the constitutionalist view, the proper object of justification is not an event or rule in isolation but the network of rules that gives it life and substance. Moreover, these institutions are to be measured not by their effect on the pursuit of some socially desirable end state, for example, their capacity to increase social wealth; rather, their measure is the acceptance they secure within a given population or community. This is not to say that considerations of social wealth, utility or welfare do not figure in the evaluation of institutions. Surely they do, but indirectly, and only to the extent that such factors figure in any individual's decision regarding which set of rules to adopt. What we have called consequentialist factors can, though they need not, figure as reasons in an individual's choice regarding institutions. It is the voluntary choice, unanimous agreement in most cases, that carries a justificatory weight, not those factors that may ground a particular individual's choice.

2. EFFICIENCY AND AGREEMENT

I have emphasized a distinction between justificatory arguments of self-interest and those from consent. This distinction is crucial to moral argument, but there has been a tendency – especially among economists – to miss it. The source of this confusion is the axiom of rational choice that rational, fully informed individuals naturally agree to pursue goals, promote policies and support institutions that maximize their expected utility. Thus, to argue that a goal, policy or institutional arrangement is efficient or welfare

maximizing is equivalent to saying that rational persons would
agree to it. In this view, to show that there has been voluntary
agreement to some course of conduct by the parties involved is
tantamount to demonstrating that each individual views the decision as likely to promote his or her welfare. One consents to what
is in one's interest; what is in one's interest, one consents to. Thus,
consent and self-interest cannot be two distinct sources of justification. Both the traditional economist and the constitutionalist blur
this distinction in ways that rob their respective enterprises of normative grounding. The traditional economist does so by building
an individual's consent into an ordering of his preferences. The
constitutionalist does so by building efficiency into an individual's
expression of consent. It is instructive to uncover the flaws involved in both arguments.

2.1. Agreement and traditional economics

Economists distinguish among three efficiency-related concepts:
Pareto superiority, Pareto optimality, and Kaldor–Hicks efficiency. S_2 is Pareto superior to S_1 if, and only if, no one prefers S_1
to S_2 and at least one person prefers S_2 to S_1. S_2 is Pareto optimal
just in case there exists no state S_n such that S_n is Pareto superior
to S_2. S_2 is Kaldor–Hicks efficient to S_1 just in case in going from
S_1 to S_2 the winners gain sufficiently so that they could compensate the losers with a net gain in welfare: that is, resources could
be redistributed (at S_2) so that no one would prefer S_1 to S_2 and at
least one person would prefer S_2 to S_1. Thus, the Kaldor–Hicks
test is sometimes called the potential–Pareto-superiority criterion.

One argument in favor of pursuing Pareto improvements is that
doing so promotes self-interest or net welfare. If going from S_1 to
S_2 makes party A and party B better off and no one worse off,
then S_2 contains more total utility than does S_1. This is an argument for Pareto superiority from welfare or utility.

Recently, advocates of law and economics have rediscovered an
argument for efficiency from consent that was first put forth by
Kaldor. Suppose you want to engage in a risky activity that is
certain to cause me damage. Assume that the value of the activity
is \$100 to you, the damage to me is \$50 and the probability of its
occurrence is 1.0. We can specify the following state descriptions.

(S_1)   You do not engage in the activity.
(S_2)   You engage in the activity without compensating me for the
        damage I suffer.

(S_3) You engage in the activity and gain \$100 but compensate me \$51 for the damage I suffer.

Very likely you order these states as follows: S_2, S_3, S_1. I order them S_3, S_1, S_2. Clearly, we both prefer S_3 to S_1. But to say that you and I prefer S_3 to S_1 is just to say that (were we in a position to do so) we should have chosen S_3; we should have agreed to move to S_3. S_3 then is Pareto superior to S_1: that is, neither of us prefers S_1 to S_3 and at least one of us – indeed both of us – prefer(s) S_3 to S_1. In the economist's view, S_3, the Pareto-superior state, would be justified on a consensual ground, namely, the ground that we would have agreed to it. The justification of efficiency is consent.

The problem with this argument is that it builds consent analytically into the ordering of a person's preferences; if you prefer S_3 to S_1, that just *means* that you would choose S_3 over S_1. In that case, the argument from consent adds absolutely nothing to what is already contained in the claim that you prefer S_3 to S_1. There is nothing in consent so conceived that is not already in a statement of what you prefer. We might just as well say S_3 is justifiably brought about because it increases our welfare (yours and mine). Indeed, that is precisely what the claim that you and I would consent to S_3 means – nothing more.

In order to make good the distinction we recognize between autonomy and utility, we must admit that it does not follow logically that people would consent to what they prefer. This sounds odd at first, but it need not. The root idea, I think, is that efficiency or utility is a property of social states themselves. Autonomy speaks to the concern for the process by which one moves from one social state to another. Put another way, an ordering of one's preferences over social states is path independent, whereas which social states one consents to or agrees to is path dependent. Thus, I always prefer the state of affairs in which I have the gold and you do not, although I would not agree to the world in which I have the gold and you do not if the manner by which I secure it involves fraud or theft.

All this is by way of emphasizing the importance of the distinction between what a person prefers and what that person is prepared to consent to, and the different role these facts about an individual play in the theory of political justification. In trying to meet this objection one could, of course, build the path taken to it into the complete description of a social state. My having the gold and your not is thus an incomplete description of a social state.

More complete ones are: my having the gold and your not in virtue of, say, my earning it or my purchasing it from you; and my having the gold and your not in virtue of my defrauding or robbing you of it. I prefer having the gold to not having it when I secure it legitimately, but not when I come to it through illegitimate means.

This kind of response greatly reduces the scope of arguments from hypothetical consent, since in many cases I prefer those states of affairs that when fully described include my having attained them through actual consent, not through other means. So to reconsider the original example: It turns out that I do not most prefer S_3 where you engage in your risky activity and then compensate me for the damage I suffer unless this is the arrangement we explicitly have made *ex ante*. It therefore will not suffice for you, say, to damage my interests and then leave a check at my doorstep to cover my costs – even if the check you leave more than covers my costs. I simply don't prefer S_3 unless the move to S_3 follows the conditions of an explicit *ex ante* arrangement. The fact that we may very well have reached such an accord *ex ante* – if true – simply does not prevail. The fact is we did not.

You may respond that I do not prefer S_3, as originally described, to S_1, because although the compensation you give me exceeds the damage I suffer, it does not cover the costs to me of S_3's coming about in the absence of an actual agreement. The problem is that when you compensate me, say, $51 for the $50 in damage I suffer, I am not better off, because $51 does not cover the costs to me of the damaging my property without my consent. The check does not cover the harm to my interests in autonomy. Surely there is some dollar figure that represents the value to me of forgoing explicit agreement. In this example, if that figure is less than $50, then we can describe a Pareto-superior move which I should have consented to even though the path to the preferred social state did not include my agreeing to it. I do not doubt that we can imagine many cases in which individuals are prepared to place a value on the exercise of their autonomy. Nevertheless, for this general line of argument to succeed, it must at a minimum always be possible in principle for individuals to place a dollar value or utility on their autonomy, even if the value they put on exercising their liberty is infinite, thereby in effect making it impossible to impose forced exchanges upon them.

More important, notice that by giving a utilitarian value to autonomy (reducing, in other words, consensualism to utilitarianism) we are no longer in a position to treat arguments from consent as normatively distinct from arguments of interests, desires or preferences. Our doing so is an instance of the general problem of treating all the standard deontological categories – rights, justice, fairness, equality and so on – exclusively as objects of preference or as reducible to preferences or as arguments in utility functions and no more. No doubt some people may prefer a just world to an unjust one; freedom to coercion; equality to inequality. But the moral value of these goods can be specified independently of anyone's preference for them. What is worse, if arguments from consent *could* be reduced to those from utility, the former could hardly be asked to serve as independent justification of the latter. If autonomy or consent is reducible to utility or preference satisfaction, it is impossible to defend policies that maximize preference satisfaction on autonomy grounds. Such a move simply bases the pursuit of utility on the pursuit of utility. Yet it was the desire to defend Paretianism on nonefficiency grounds that motivated the argument in the first place.

The traditional economist, because of his reliance upon preference rankings as the basis of consent arguments, fails to appreciate the difference between teleological and consensual modes of justification. The constitutionalist makes the same mistake in reverse. To see this, let us examine the work of the leading constitutional economist, James Buchanan.

2.2. Agreement and constitutional economics

The core of Buchanan's thesis is the claim that the only test for efficiency is unanimous agreement. There are two ways of understanding Buchanan's claim. One of these is *epistemic;* the other *semantic*. These correspond to two ways of understanding the concept of a test. In the epistemic interpretation, agreement is the best evidence for the claim that a trade or decision is efficient. In the semantic interpretation, to say that a decision, trade or rule is efficient just means that it has secured unanimous agreement. In the second sense, agreement is both logically necessary and sufficient for efficiency.

The constitutionalist economist is, as a constitutionalist, a contractarian; as an economist, she is committed to efficiency as a normative criteria. The central question concerns how she sees the relationship between these two normative principles: consent and efficiency. In the epistemic view, the link is not an analytic or conceptual one. In the semantic view, the connection is a conceptual one.

If we understand Buchanan's claim epistemically, he does not commit the fallacy of building efficiency into consent. If agreement is only evidence of efficiency, then we can specify what it is for something to be efficient without recourse to showing that people agree to it, since it is not agreement that *makes* social states efficient. Presumably, what makes a rule or policy efficient is that it promotes welfare or minimizes costs, or some such traditional rendition of the maximand or minimand. But it may be hard in practice for us to determine whether a change in rules or policy will have the desired effect on welfare or cost reduction. If we have evidence that people by and large agree to the policy, then we can be confident that the policy is efficient. That is because rational individuals aim to promote their expected welfare. If they do, then they are likely to agree to things that make them better off. If everyone agrees to abide by a rule, then each person believes that adhering to that rule will be to his advantage. When everyone is made better off by a rule, it is efficient.

In the epistemic theory of the relationship between agreement and efficiency, efficiency is characterized *objectively* in terms of the effect of a rule or decision on net welfare. Agreement, then, is not equivalent to efficiency, but is instead evidence of it. Agreement is evidence of efficiency only because of a rule of rational behavior that connects a person's behavior to his desire to promote his well-being. This rule need not be axiomatic. It may admit of exceptions it may even be as weak as a rule of thumb about human behavior. After all, we need only know that people by and large act to promote their welfare to infer from the fact of unanimous agreement that the rule agreed upon is efficient.

Buchanan, however, views the connection between consent and autonomy as semantic (in part for reasons I shall explore later regarding the subjective character of "costs"). There are two serious problems with seeing the connection as an analytic one. The first is that the vocabulary of efficiency is a "maximizing" one. The Pareto rankings state ordering relations – they order social states with respect to some property or characteristic, usually utility or welfare. So we say S_2 is Pareto superior to S_1 because S_2 has more utility than S_1. I have argued, however, that we need not restrict the Pareto rankings to utility or welfare characteristics of social states. Posner, for one, does not. In his system of wealth maximization, to say that S_2 is Pareto superior to S_1 is to say that no one is any less wealthy in S_2 than in S_1 and at least one person is wealthier in S_2 than in S_1. Perhaps we could even use the Pareto rankings to compare social states in terms of the extent to which rights are distributed in them. Thus, to say that S_2 is Pareto superior to S_1 would mean that no one has more rights in S_1 than in S_2 and at least one person has more rights in S_2 than in S_1. Regardless of the characteristic of social states involved, the efficiency criteria linearly order them along a maximizing scale. S_3 is Pareto superior to S_2, which is Pareto superior to S_1, just in case S_3 has more than S_2, which has more than S_1 of whatever it is the Pareto criteria range over.

When analyzed in terms of agreement, efficiency loses its maximization dimension. There is often not any one good that is maximized when people secure agreement among themselves. Jones may agree to a rule for one reason; Smith for another; Brown for yet another. The rule is agreed to unanimously, yet no one thing is maximized by their decision.

One could try the following counterargument: Neither Jones nor Smith nor Brown would have agreed to a rule unless each viewed it as in his or her interest to do so. To say a rule is in one's interest is to say it promotes one's welfare. Agreement entails welfare maximization and efficiency in that sense; therefore agreement maximizes welfare.

According to this response, the agreement among Jones, Smith and Brown is efficient because it is welfare maximizing, not because it is the outcome of their bargain or choice. In that case, efficiency is specified independently of their agreement. The relationship between agreement and efficiency is evidentiary and causal. What causes each to give his consent is the fact that the agreement promotes the self-interest of each. But the fact of unanimous agreement all by itself does not entail the maximization of anything, since there may be any number of reasons for reaching an agreement. If agreement is the semantic criterion of efficiency, efficiency is not a maximization concept. Then what sort of concept is it? What, in this view, is added to an argument in favor of a policy or a rule unanimously agreed upon by the assertion that it is efficient? Nothing. And for the simple reason that in saying that it is efficient we are merely repeating the fact that it has secured each affected party's consent. We have again reduced what appeared to be two distinct kinds of arguments in favor of policies, rules and institutions – those from consequences and those from consent – to one: in this case, to arguments from consent. If the traditional economist can be justly accused of conflating the distinction by reducing consent to efficiency, the constitutionalist can be rightly accused of making the same kind of mistake by reducing efficiency to consent.

3. SUBJECTIVISM AND REALISM IN CONSTITUTIONALISM

I want to begin this section by presenting two arguments about the limits of economic analysis in policy matters. The punchline of the first argument is that the way resources are distributed is at any given time Pareto optimal. How can that be? Well, if the distribution were not Pareto optimal, there exists a redistribution Pareto superior to it. If a redistribution of resources Pareto superior to the current one exists, society would move to it. People would act to make themselves better off. Because we are where we are, where we are is Pareto optimal. If the status quo is Pareto optimal, how could we ever appeal to the criterion of optimality to justify change?

The second connected argument is based on the Coase theorem; that is, when transaction costs are zero, the assignment of legal rights is irrelevant to the goal of efficiency. The basic idea is that legal rights are in general designed to overcome market failures resulting from externalities; when transaction costs are trivial (or zero), externalities can be internalized by exchange (trade). Legal rights then are necessary only to establish the background for trade; they specify who must "bribe" whom, not whether or not the result of trade will be efficient. It will be regardless of the initial allocation decision.

This line of argument breaks down when transaction costs are not trivial. That is because transaction costs sometimes make efficient trading impossible. In economic analysis the law must, therefore, reproduce the efficient outcome the market would have; the law must mimic the market. But which market? The costless market of the Coase theorem, of course. But how do we know what result would have been reached in that market, since that is not the market in which actual trading has ceased? In addition, economists generally accept the view that the most (perhaps the only) reliable evidence regarding an individual's preferences is that which is revealed by his behavior in actual markets. We simply cannot replicate the result of the costless Coasian market. What about requiring the law to mimic the result the actual market produces? That result is the inefficient one that we want the law to redress. Perhaps we should have said that the law ought to bring about the result that the existing market would have, given the existing transaction costs. Given the existing transaction costs, however, assigning a right to either of the parties to litigation is likely to be efficient; after all, the existence of nontrivial transaction costs is what blocks further exchanges in the first place. So, given that no further trades are imaginable, either result is efficient. Efficiency, then, does not seem to be of much help to judges in determining who should be awarded legal rights.

The point of both of these arguments is that the economist's criterion of efficiency or Pareto optimality is virtually useless as a guide to public policy generally, and to law specifically. In the first case that is because, assuming voluntariness and rationality in transactions, all existing states of affairs are optimal. If an existing state of the world were not optimal, rational autonomous agents would make a Pareto-superior move. If every existing state of affairs is optimal, it is unlikely that the criterion of optimality can serve as a guide to change.

The line of argument in the second case is a bit more complex and introduces a distinction between two notions of efficiency. The gist of the argument is this: Coase finds there is a need for law only when markets fail to redistribute resources to their most valued uses. This occurs most often when transaction costs block efficient trades. Following Coase, Posner holds that the law should mimic Coase's market: that is, produce the outcome that would have been secured in a market of costless exchange. The problem is twofold. We cannot replicate *that* result, since we do not have the information that only a market can reveal to us regarding the preferences of traders within that particular environment for trade. We do, however, have the actual market bogged down in transaction costs. But there is no need for the law to intervene to mimic that market, since it would simply reassert the result which that market has already secured – and at great cost. Where transaction costs are not nontrivial, any assignment of right will be efficient, since no further trades, given the costs, are likely to occur.

Both arguments invite us to explore what it means to call a state of affairs Pareto optimal. Do we mean to say that a state of affairs is Pareto optimal if and only if no further gains from trade can be had *given existing transaction costs;* or do we mean to say that a state of affairs is Pareto optimal only if we can imagine no further gains through trade *in the absence of transaction costs?* The first argument suggests the problem of identifying optimality with free trade given existing transaction costs. The second argument, however, presupposes that free trade in the absence of transaction costs is the useful notion. The distinction is crucial for obvious reasons and for less obvious ones as well. I shall explore both in the context of the foundations of constitutionalism.

The distinction is, I suggest, a distinction between a *counterfactual* conception of optimality and a *realist* conception of it. Thus, in the counterfactual view, S_1 is Pareto optimal if and only if in the absence of transaction costs parties would trade to, and not away from, S_1. It is the fact that there were transaction costs that makes this criterion of efficiency counterfactual. In the realist conception of efficiency, S_1 is Pareto optimal just because under the *given* constraints the relevant parties fail to move from it.

The kind of constitutionalism James Buchanan advances rests on a *realist* conception of optimality. All realist conceptions of efficiency involve the claim that in determining which policies, trades or rules are efficient, we are restricted to the framework defined by existing transaction costs. Among the realists, we can distinguish the *objectivists* from the *subjectivists*. The objectivists believe that what is efficient (given the existing transaction costs) can be specified independently of individual voluntary market behavior. They may adhere to the epistemic claim that voluntary agreement or behavior is the criterion of efficiency. In contrast, the *subjectivist* claims that what is optimal *cannot* be characterized other than as the outcome of voluntary transactions. It is easy to see that there are four possible positions to hold regarding the concept of efficiency. These are:

(1)   Realist–subjectivist
(2)   Realist–objectivist
(3)   Counterfactualist–subjectivist
(4)   Counterfactualist–objectivist

All realists believe that the existing transaction costs define the framework within which the notion of optimality may be usefully characterized. Countefactualists believe that we can make sense of the optimality criteria in terms of costless market behavior. Objectivists believe that what is efficient can be specified independent of agreement; subjectivists deny that it can be. Most proponents of the economic analysis of law, like Posner, are (in my terms) counterfactualist–objectivist about optimality. Buchanan and other constitutional economists are realist–subjectivists. All of these people are economists, but that is where the similarity ends. For there is a real difference between the claim that only actual agreement within a given framework of trade can specify what is optimal and the claim that what is optimal may be specified in terms of the properties of social states we can imagine under conditions of reduced transaction costs and independent of actual trades. My guess is that a good deal of confusion in the literature is owed to a failure to appreciate just how different various economic theories (all resting on the desirability of promoting efficiency) can be.

Because Buchanan is a realist–subjectivist about efficiency, he seems vulnerable to the charge that, in his view, as long as force and fraud are absent, inefficiency is logically impossible. That is the source of the first argument in this section. Any existing state of the world, provided it does not result from force or fraud, is efficient. In other words, given the constraints of an existing institutional framework, including transaction costs and the criterion of efficiency as the outcome of free choice within that framework, it is impossible that there be an inefficient actual state of the world. This may or may not be an objectionable consequence of the theory – at least for the constitutionalist, Buchanan. If it is an objection to the theory, he can meet it by shifting focus from the efficiency of individual states of affairs to the efficiency of institutions: thus, constitutionalism. Consider the trades made under a set of rules, R, and those made under another set of rules, R'. The constitutionalist may be committed to claiming that from the perspective of R, the outcomes generated by free trade are efficient. He is not committed, however, to saying that *only* those trades are efficient, because the outcomes of free trade under R' are efficient relative to R'. The constitutionalist need not stop there, however; R and R' can be compared as well. In case the populace chooses R' over R, the institution defined by R' can be said to be more efficient than that defined by R. Thus, there is a two-tier account of efficiency as shown in Figure 5.1.

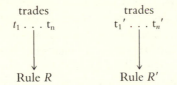

Figure 5.1. Two-tier account of efficiency

Particular trades can be evaluated as efficient or not *only* within institutional settings. Thus, we can talk meaningfully of efficient trades only in relation to a given framework. The efficiency of particular exchanges is necessarily relative to institutional settings. However, institutional settings can themselves be compared for their relative efficiency by the test of agreement. Thus we can say that R' is more efficient than R if people agree to move from R to R'. We can never state, even after such a move, that some particular trade in R', say, t_1', is more efficient than some trade in R, say, t_1. Outcomes of trade can be compared for their efficiency only within postulated frameworks for trade.

What is it that defines an institutional setting? Why, for example, should everything that counts as a transaction cost fall under the umbrella of a given institutional setting? For Buchanan, the phrase "efficient given existing transaction costs" is part of the meaning of "efficient within a given institutional setting." That, after all, is part of what makes so plausible the move from the realist's perspective on efficiency to the elevation of efficiency as a criterion of evaluation from particular trades to institutional frameworks. When we compare two trade settings with different transaction costs for trade, we are necessarily, in this view, comparing two distinct institutional settings. We are not imagining possible or hypothetical trades within the same framework. We cannot, therefore, compare the trades, but we can compare the frameworks: thus, the easy move from transaction costs to institutional settings to efficiency as a criterion of evaluation among institutions.

My view is that some of the things which count as transaction costs should be considered part of an institutional setting; others not. The fact that in certain circumstances trades require lawyers may well result from a rule of contract and thus fall within the institutional structure. There may also be institutional rules that make gathering information costly. These information and transaction costs may legitimately be included within the institutional setting. But there may be scientific, natural or technological reasons why some information is hard or expensive to come by. It is hard for me to imagine that all transaction costs would count as part of an institutional setting – unless we stretch the concept of an institution to the point where it ceases to be a useful one. Surely all transaction costs broadly characterized are part of the background of choice. But no one can seriously mean to include everything in the background of decision as part of the institutional setting within which decisions are to be made. If every change in transaction costs entailed a change in institutions, the constitutionalists, rather than enriching the role of institutions in economic analyses, would be trivializing the concept of an institution. Because transaction costs are part of the background of trade, but not necessarily part of the institutional setting, one is not forced to go as quickly as the constitutionalist would from the efficiency of trades within institutions to the efficiency of institutions.

The constitutionalist takes *voluntary* agreement to be the criterion of efficiency. An agreement is not voluntary if it results from force or fraud. He thus needs *force* and *fraud* as constraints on agreements within all possible institutional frameworks. But is this emphasis on voluntary trade warranted? There is nothing about either the logic of the term "agreement" or the idea of an institutional framework, however, that requires that efficiency in trades within frameworks be determined by *voluntary* choice. Why isn't simple agreement – voluntary or not – constitutive of efficiency? Why not go the constitutionalist one further and distinguish between alternative institutional frameworks – those that require that trades be voluntary and those that do not? We should then have to talk about efficient trades relative to *those* frameworks. Thus, S_1 is efficient under the rule of *voluntary* agreement, whereas S_2 is efficient under the rule of simple assent. S_1 and S_2 are simply non-comparable. It may be that there is little to commend in trades agreed to involuntarily, but such trades could be efficient by the criterion of agreement specified at the institutional level, that is, one that permits coerced exchange. That there may be little to commend in trades that are efficient in this sense suggests both that it is the *voluntariness* of the transaction that carries the bulk of the moral weight and that the two key notions – consent and efficiency – are crucially different. Moreover, if we think of force and fraud as conditions of agreement within particular institutional settings, the constitutionalist must abandon the general characterization of efficiency as the outcome of *free* or *voluntary* choice.

In the two-tier analysis of efficiency, we do not compare outcomes within different institutional settings. Instead we compare different institutional settings for their efficiency, employing the test of agreement. Buchanan sees this as fully analogous to the market situation of trades under postulated rules: rules that define the form, scope and content of possible trades. The choice of rules or institutions is to be viewed on the market model. But if we press the market analogy between choices within rules and choices of rules, we must specify a set of meta-rules or decision rules that define the scope and nature of the choice of institutional rules. Just as we can imagine different institutional frameworks within which particular trading takes place, we can also conceive of competing criteria or rules for institutional decision making. Because there is, *a priori*, no reason to believe that only one such set of rules for institutional decision making exists, the two-tier analysis of efficiency expands to include at least a third tier, as shown in Figure 5.2.

Figure 5.2 can be complicated further by adding possible candidates for rules of institutional decision making. It need not be further complicated, however, to make the point that an institu-

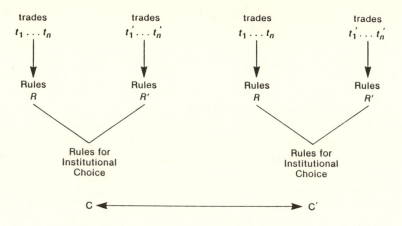

Figure 5.2. Three-tier account of efficiency

tional arrangement can no longer be viewed as efficient by itself. Trades are efficient relative to institutional frameworks; institutional frameworks are efficient relative to rules of institutional decision making. Everything is further relative to choice among decision procedures – for example, voluntary agreement with full information as opposed to simple assent behind a veil of ignorance. Of course, there is no reason to stop even at this level of abstraction. If the market analogy is to hold, then the constitutionalist's insistence upon understanding market behavior only within the context of a set of rules will lead him to postulate ever more levels of abstraction in decision making. The paradox unfolds. Either the constitutionalist must give up the claim that market behavior makes sense only within an existing market structure or institutional setting, or he must be able to specify in some objective way criteria for the choice of institutions independent of actual choice – that is, he must abandon his subjectivism. Either he must give up, in other words, his understanding of market behavior or he must abandon the market as the paradigm of social choice.

Buchanan stands on fundamentally sound ground in objecting to Coase's followers for lumping all costs under the transaction-costs umbrella, ignoring therefore the relationship between certain transaction costs and institutional features that create them. Buchanan's response to this mistake is to deny that it is possible to conceive of efficient trades within a given institutional framework other than those actually made. I shall provide an example to illustrate just how strong a claim this is. Suppose I own a painting worth $10,000 to me, less than that to nearly everyone else and presumably more than that to you, say, $10,499. Suppose it is very costly to transport the painting from where I have it to where you would like it to be. Transaction costs block our exchange. In the *realist*–constitutionalist view, the current state of affairs is efficient because it is the best each of us can do, restrained as we are by the transaction costs of this particular institutional setting for trade. In the *subjectivist*–constitutionalist view, it is efficient just because it is the outcome of free trade. If we can imagine that both of us are better off by a transfer (my painting for your money), the subjectivist believes that the state of affairs would be efficient only if it were brought about by actual agreement between the parties. The realist objects that the trade entails a different institutional framework and thus cannot be compared with the current allocation of resources for their efficiency. This response requires the conceptual link between x's being a transaction cost and x's being part of an institutional setting, which we have already dismissed.

There is, however, another kind of argument for Buchanan's point: Even if we admit that not every hypothetically possible trade involves a shift in institutional frameworks, determining which hypothetical trades would be made within a given institutional framework requires that we determine the truth of certain counterfactual conditionals; for example, if it did not cost $500 to ship the painting from me to you, you would have bought it from me. This proposition is counterfactual just because it does cost $500 to ship the painting – the antecedent of the conditional is counter to actual fact. And there is no way of confidently asserting knowledge of such claims.

There are then two possible sources of the realism in constitutionalism: One is the view that efficiency is relative to institutional frameworks and a change in the level of transaction costs entails a change in institutional frameworks; the second is a radical skepticism about our knowledge of the truth of counterfactual conditionals. The first view is mistaken, and radical skepticism regarding the second is unwarranted. Surely there are any number of counterfactuals we know to be true. Only radical skepticism about the nature of empirical knowledge generally could warrant the sort of skepticism about counterfactuals that underwrites the realist component of constitutionalism. Undifferentiated skepticism about empirical knowledge of the sorts of trades individuals would make in the absence of transaction costs is unlikely to serve the constitutionalist well. The fundamental issue is not whether we can ever have knowledge of the sorts of trades individuals would make in the absence of transaction costs; it concerns, rather, the limits of our knowledge of such trades. What abandoning elements of its realism as well as its subjectivism means to the possible success of the constitutionalist enterprise is what remains to be explored.

PART III

Torts, crimes and settlements

6. Crimes, kickers and transaction structures

These remarks are occasioned by Alvin Klevorick's very thoughtful essay "On the Economic Theory of Crime."[1] The economic approach to law, Klevorick notes, has had a far wider and deeper impact on areas of the private law – especially torts, contracts and property – than it has on the criminal law. The reason: Economic analysis simply fails (or has failed so far) to elucidate central features of the criminal law. In some ways, Klevorick's essay attempts to identify the weak link in the chain of economic reasoning about crime. Klevorick does not stop at identifying what he takes to be the problem; he offers a tentative solution to it. In the end, however, he finds even aspects of his solution wanting and gives an all too brief, but provocative, explanation of why *all* economic theories of the criminal law are likely to prove unsatisfying.

Just where is the weakness in the economic theory of crime? We can begin by considering where the economic analysis of crime has proven most fruitful. In general, economists have done well at setting optimal penalties for criminal conduct and at determining how much of a community's resources ought to be spent on enforcing criminal prohibitions. In both endeavors, the economist takes as given that a certain aspect or category of conduct has been designated criminal. In the first instance he wants to determine just how much punishment is necessary to reduce to an efficient level conduct that has been independently identified as criminal. In doing so, the economist relies on basic models of individual rational choice, usually under conditions of uncertainty. The criminal is a rational utility maximizer deciding, among other things, whether or not to engage in criminal activity. The economist's concern: Given that the probability of apprehension is less than 1.0, just what penalty is necessary to induce the rational potential criminal to live a life beyond reproach – or at least one more or less in conformity with the dictates of the criminal law? It would be nice if we could impose sanctions on criminal mischief such that the actor's expected marginal cost of engaging in criminality was set equal to his expected marginal gain so that each criminal would have no good reason for preferring criminal activity to a noncriminal alternative. The problem is that most communities cannot afford the expenditures necessary to eliminate crime entirely. So a community must determine just how much of its resources to devote to the criminal justice system. To the economist, this concern translates into the question: What is the optimal use of resources in controlling crime? The answer depends on a number of variables. For example, suppose a community wanted to put a virtual end to jaywalking but did not want overly to tax its resource base to do so. Instead of employing resources to increase the rate of detection, it might simply impose a very heavy sanction on jaywalking. If we assume that potential jaywalkers are risk-neutral, then they have just as much reason to avoid a $1,000 fine they are unlikely to incur as they have to avoid a $10 fine they are a hundred times more likely to get.[2] The likelihood of being apprehended and sentenced is a partial function of the amount of money the community is prepared to spend on detecting and convicting jaywalkers. So a reduction in expenditures may call for an increase in the weight of the sanction. But then sanctions for those apprehended and sentenced are unlikely to fit the offense, and thereby to depart from the requirement that the penalty fit the crime. This departure from the ideal is for the economist a cost – the cost of injustice – which, however, is not to say that it ought not be reckoned with. Moreover, as the "price" of an offense increases, the social cost of a mistake in judgment increases. It is one thing to impose a $5 fine mistakenly; another to impose a life sentence. And as the level of expenditure drops, the likelihood of mistakes increases, thus further increasing the expected social costs of punishment. Economists concerned about the allocation of resources to the criminal justice system are concerned primarily with determining the costs and benefits of various allocations decisions in the light of the kinds of factors I have just mentioned. Again, however, part of the fruitfulness of these efforts is due to the fact that the allocation decision – the decision about how much crime is permissible – presupposes an independently defined category of criminal conduct.

According to Klevorick – and he is surely right – economic analysis has proven least fruitful in explaining the very existence of a criminal category. What economic reasons, if any, do we have for making certain conduct criminal? Put another way, there is an economic theory of undesirable actions – acts whose costs (however conceived) outweigh their benefits (however conceived). These are actions economists think ought to be curtailed, limited or, in some cases, if the costs of doing so are not too high, eliminated entirely. Any number of mechanisms for reducing the incidence of socially undesirable activity are worth exploring. We might counsel against mischief; or we might implore, cajole, persuade, plead with, even beg doers of dastardly deeds to forbear. We can ostracize and condemn. Or we can tax, impose tort liability or criminalize. Why do we ever criminalize? Why do we set out a category of conduct, designate it as criminal and thereby subject violators to a particular kind of sanction? Is there a particularly economic argument for our doing so?

Here is one way in which economists have thought about the need for a criminal prohibition against certain activities. Suppose *A* harms *B*. Now what? Should we prevent future *A*s from harming future *B*s, by giving *B* the right not to be harmed; or should we put future *B*s on notice that the losses will lie where they have fallen, by giving *A* the right to harm *B*? To the economist this is a perfectly serious question that is not easily answered. Suppose in harming *B*, *A* causes *B* $10 worth of damage, but by doing so he secures $1,000 gain. Were we to prohibit *A* from harming *B*, *B* would gain $10 and *A* would lose $1,000. This seems hardly the rational thing to do, for few of us would forgo a thousand-dollar gain to avoid a ten-dollar loss. This suggests we should not prevent *A* from harming *B*. But it seems equally wrong to give *A* license to harm *B* whenever it is to his, *A*'s, advantage to do so. At this point perhaps you are inclined to say the difference between the original example and the rationality of an individual's decision not to forgo a large gain to avoid a small loss is that in the former case we are dealing with two persons, not one, each of whose autonomy must be respected. In that case, the economist has a suggestion that should satisfy you. Why not give *B* the right not to be harmed by *A*, but permit *A* to buy from *B* the right to harm him? Then *A* will harm *B*, but will do so at a mutually agreed-upon price. In effect, what we have done is decide both that *B* has a right not to be harmed by *A* and that *A* has a right to harm *B* as long as he secures *B*'s consent. In terminology that has been widely accepted by economists since the publication of the famous Calabresi–Melamed paper,[3] we have assigned the right to *B* not to be harmed and protected it by a *property rule*.

We could have assigned *B* the right not to be harmed by *A* and secured it in a different way, that is, by a *liability rule*. In that case, *B* would have a right that *A* not harm him, but *A* would nevertheless be free to harm *B* anyway, provided he paid *B* compensation *ex post* for whatever damage his harmful conduct occasioned. Under the property rule scheme, *A* and *B* must reach an agreement *ex ante* before *A* can harm *B* (act contrary to *B*'s right). Under the liability rule scheme, *A* need secure no agreement with *B*. He may act as he deems fit provided he is prepared to render *B* compensation *ex post*.[4]

In the traditional economic analysis, the point of assigning and protecting rights according to various options is to encourage individuals to engage in activities at their efficient levels. For example, suppose *B* has a right protected by a property rule that *A* not harm him. In our example, it would be inefficient for *A* not to harm *B*, since by not harming *B* there is a net loss of $990 (a forgone opportunity cost of $,1000 minus a savings of $10). The efficient result of *A* harming *B* is secured through a market transaction required by the property rule at *B*'s disposal. Sometimes efficient outcomes cannot be secured if rights are protected by property rules. There are two straightforward cases to consider. In one, the costs of negotiations are high. If the costs of negotiations exceed the difference in the value of the right to *A* and *B*, then no transfer will occur. So if it costs *A* and *B* $991 to reach agreement *ex ante*, *A* would have to incur $1,001 in costs for something he values at $1,000. Where negotiations are costly, it is sometimes necessary to substitute liability rules for property rules, since the former do not require *ex ante* agreements. The standard example is automobile accident law. Think how difficult it would be to track down all the individuals you might put at risk by your driving, let alone to negotiate with them.

The second sort of inefficiency in property rules arises from strategic behavior. If *B* knows that the value to *A* of harming him is $1,000, then he is unlikely to settle for $10. If *A* knows that the value of *B*'s damages is $10, he is likely to press for an agreement that gives *B* not much more than that. We have in these negotiations a bargaining game: a mixed game – mixed because it involves a redistributive and a productive element. A possible $990 of surplus exists to distribute, provided agreement can be reached. Agreement to *distribute* the surplus (the redistributive element) is necessary and sufficient to *produce* it (the productive element). If *A* or *B* holds out for a share of the gains from trade that is unacceptable to the other, no transfer will occur and the outcome will be inefficient. Once again, to avoid the pitfalls of negotiations, liability rules may be substituted for property rules.

We can follow a slightly different but no less standard line of economic argument to reach the same point in the overall argument. Most behavior has external effects, called externalities. The cost of externalities can either lie where they have fallen – on victims – or be shifted to those whose conduct occasions them – injurers. Economists believe that shifting of losses provides a powerful mechanism for inducing efficient behavior. For example, one way of inducing efficiency by shifting losses is to impose liability on the party whose conduct causes the externality. This process is called internalizing externalities; its effect is to force the injurer to take the social costs of his conduct into account. Ronald Coase's important article "The Problem of Social Cost"[5] may be read as demonstrating that certain conditions support a market solution to the problem of externalities. In other words, externalities may be internalized by private negotiations as well as by the imposition of liability. Roughly, the Coasian approach corresponds to the Calabresi–Melamed property rule approach. In both cases inefficiencies are eliminated in standard market ways. When the market approach is unavailable because transaction costs are high or the threat of strategic behavior is substantial, the liability rule approach is appropriately substituted. The purpose of the liability rule is to mimic the market solution, that is, produce the efficient result the costless market would have.

Now what does all this have to do with crime? Why criminalize when a perfectly good property rule–liability rule structure for responding to right violations or to other wrongful conduct is available? In classical economic theory, the criminal law is seen as a way to induce individuals to comply with the relevant rules of transfer, that is, to adhere to the property rule–liability rule distinction, or to pursue market solutions to externality problems where they are available and feasible.

In order to explore one way in which economic analysis tries to tie the criminal law to the property rule–liability rule distinction, consider the situation where no market solution to an externality exists. Then the liability rule method seems in order. It differs from the property rule approach not only in terms of *ex ante* versus *ex post* perspectives but also because liability rules raise the problem of detection. If someone has to buy *B*'s right from him, he reveals his identify to us through negotiations. But if anyone, including A, can simply injure *B* at will, then he has an incentive to avoid detection, since whether or not he has to render *B* compensation depends on his being caught. The probability of detection is less than 1.0. Therefore, in order to induce efficiency, the penalty imposed upon the injurer must exceed the actual damages he causes. The actual damages he pays represent the tort or liability rule remedy. The additional penalty necessary to induce compliance (because detection is imperfect) is what we think of as the criminal sanction.

In this view, the criminal law is parasitic upon tort law: Crimes are defined in terms primarily of torts. Criminal sanctions are "kickers" imposed in addition to tort liability to foster compliance. But if this is the basis of the criminal law, notice that it would become otiose if detection rates approached 1.0. This seems an implausible basis for the criminal law – even to economists.

Let us try something more sophisticated. Either there is a market (property rule) solution to such a problem or there is not. If there is a market solution to an externality problem, then one reason for imposing a criminal sanction is to induce individuals to opt for the market solution when it is available to them. So we criminalize theft, for example, because theft involves a coercive transfer of resources when a noncoercive one – exchange – is available. This is basically Richard Posner's explanation of the criminal category. The criminal is someone who chooses a non-market solution to a problem when the market solution is available, and the penal sanction is intended to encourage him to opt for the market solution.

The Calabresi–Melamed analysis differs only slightly from Posner's. The difference is that in Posner's view liability rules and property rules are used to promote efficiency only. On the Calabresi–Melamed theory, the rules promote a mix of social goals, including efficiency and justice. With this difference in mind, the two views proceed in almost exactly the same way. For Calabresi and Melamed the criminal sanction is necessary because tort liability by itself would in effect allow perpetrators to change property rules into liability rules at will. So we penalize theft not just because there is a market alternative – exchange – but because, if we required only that the thief pay damages, we would in effect give thieves the option of not taking property rules seriously. If a society wishes individuals to pursue market solutions to problems, then it cannot allow individuals the option of ignoring the property rule–liability rules distinction. The criminal sanction is the kicker added to keep individuals from changing property rules into liability rules at will, not a kicker added to the tort remedy to compensate for imperfect detection rates.

As Klevorick points out, however, neither Posner's nor the Calabresi–Melamed analysis handles the cases. A rule against selling oneself into slavery, in effect, prevents individuals from turning inalienability rules into property rules. Similarly, a rule against blackmail, by preventing an individual who owns information from exchanging it, might be aimed at preventing that individual from turning an inalienability rule into a property rule. A society might impose tort liability for pollution and not permit private agreements between the parties to circumvent the liability decision. In effect, criminalizing buy-offs would prevent the relevant parties from turning liability rules into property rules. What these examples show is that both the Posner and Calabresi–Melamed suggestions are too narrow. Posner's is too narrow because he sees the criminal law as directing actors to market solutions when their costs are acceptably low, whereas some criminal statutes may be aimed at prohibiting market transactions. Calabresi and Melamed go astray by overemphasizing the role of the criminal law in inducing individuals not to turn liability rules into property rules.

The moral Klevorick draws from all this is that the proper economic analysis would emphasize the criminal law's role in enforcing a general transaction structure rather than particular elements of it. As Klevorick puts it:

> In each instance, the act that is characterized as a crime involves the actor(s) forcing society to deal with a transaction in a way in which society did not want to treat it. What makes the act a crime is that the individual assaults the transaction structure that has been established by society. One could say, alternatively, that the individual coerces society into considering and coping with an exchange or transaction in a way that differs from the mode society had chosen. Finally, one might characterize the criminal as arrogating to himself the power or the authority to determine at least a part of the societal transaction structure, that is, appropriating to himself a power or right that society had reserved to itself. The criminal sanction is then a sanction to enforce the transaction structure that society has chosen as well as to compensate for the harms to individuals within the society.[6]

These are very suggestive remarks indeed. Notice, however, that Klevorick takes the basic insight of Posner and Calabresi and Melamed to be correct, namely, that the criminal law is defined in terms of offenses independently characterized elsewhere in the law, that it serves to redirect conduct to comply with requirements set forth elsewhere in the law (the property rule–liability rule distinction) and that the criminal law is concerned largely with the transfer of resources among individuals in a society. Klevorick's contribution is to generalize from particular inducements within a given transaction structure to the transaction structure itself. Next, what Klevorick adds to the traditional accounts is a "moral" vocabulary of "assault," "coercion" and "arrogation of power" that he claims is essential to the characterization of criminal conduct, but which is in fact nowhere implied or even suggested by the discussion to that point. I once suggested to Klevorick that we might describe what the criminal does as acting "contrary to the transaction structure," thus removing the essentially moral features of the characterization of criminality. Klevorick appears to accept my point, but underestimates it, for there is all the difference in the world between characterizing criminal behavior as action contrary to a prevailing transaction structure and as an assault against it or as involving an arrogation of power.

Klevorick's claim is that the economic analysis of crime is essentially unsatisfying to the extent that it does not adequately explain the criminal category itself. His particular objections to the Posner and Calabresi–Melamed accounts are of two sorts. The first is that the previous work emphasizes the role of the criminal law in providing particular inducements – usually to market behavior or to respecting property rules – whereas the proper account would see the criminal law as a mechanism for securing an entire transaction structure. To the extent that this is Klevorick's view, it is an essentially economic one.

Klevorick's other objection, the one I believe he takes to be the more important, is that an account of the criminal category involves an essentially noneconomic normative vocabulary: that of assault, coercion, arrogation of power; that while it may be possible to give an economic analysis of these concepts, such an account is likely to be artificial, uninformative and ultimately unconvincing. Klevorick's argument rests on describing the criminal's behavior in these morally charged terms, and there is nothing in the argument that supports such a characterization. Can anyone seriously believe that a jaywalker, auto thief, rapist or embezzler is essentially involved in a struggle over fundamental political power and authority – taking upon himself a power that is legitimately the state's – or that it is necessary to our characterizing his conduct as a crime that we describe it as such? For one reason or another – usually personal gain – individuals sometimes act contrary to the rules of the game. It's as simple as that.

Klevorick tacitly recognizes that he builds too much into his characterization of criminal conduct, because he shifts his objection to the economic analysis from the morality of the actor's as-

sault against the transaction structure to questions of the legitimacy of the transaction structure itself:

> One could simply say that the criminal acts contrary to the
> transaction structure society had established. But the critical
> observation is that the explication of why some acts are crimes
> while others are not requires an inquiry into the legitimation
> of the transaction structure. It forces one to confront ques-
> tions like: why does the collectivity have the right to decide
> the terms on which particular transactions will take place un-
> der different circumstances? Why do some rights reside in the
> individual while others rest with the state?[7]

No doubt these are good questions, but they do not bear on the
explanation of the existence of a criminal category. Rather, they
are questions about the legitimacy of the rules society lays down
to govern transactions. They are essentially normative, not analytic. Presumably a society could decide to criminalize conduct
even if the rules it sets forth to govern transactions were not ultimately defensible. In such a case we should be inclined to say that
the criminal law was being unjustly or wrongly used, and that
punishment for violations of its prohibitions would not be justified. But we might nevertheless have no difficulty in explaining in
purely economic terms (of the transaction structure sort) why that
society found it necessary to have a criminal law. In short, Klevorick's argument, though thoughtful and provocative, does not
move the economic analysis much beyond its previous frontier.

As an economist, Klevorick is taken by the transaction structure
analysis. His efforts to explain the missing ingredient in the economic account take the transaction structure model as basically
correct and seek to augment it either by explaining the criminal
category in terms of the moral or political nature of the criminal's
conduct ("assault," "coercion" or "arrogation of power") or in
terms of the legitimacy of the transaction structure itself. Efforts
of the first sort involve a leap not warranted by the evidence. Those
of the second sort confuse the problem of explaining the criminal
category with the problem of justifying particular instances of it.

For all that, I agree with Klevorick that the economic analysis
of crime gives a less than convincing account of the criminal category. The real problem, however, is that it is simply a mistake
to think of the criminal law as an enforcer of resource transfers.
Moreover, the key moral notions of criminal responsibility – of
guilt and fault – are simply absent from the economic infrastruc-

ture. Let me close by saying something brief and sketchy on behalf of both points.

First, the economic theory goes wrong by seeing the criminal law primarily as a mechanism for securing a transaction structure. A good deal of the criminal law has nothing to do with transactions or the transfer of resources. What, for example, do murder, rape and treason have to do with the exchange or the transfer of resources? Consider two cases. In one case, B and A reach an agreement *ex ante* whereby A will kill B, in exchange for which A will pay a substantial sum to B's family. It is plausible in this case to describe the prohibition against such agreements as a refusal to permit individuals to turn inalienability rules into property rules. One's right not to be murdered cannot be bargained away; it is inalienable. In the other case, A simply murders B. Presumably, what A did constitutes a crime. Now, it cannot possibly be the explanation of the crime of murder that were murder not a crime we would be allowing individuals to turn property rules into liability rules, since the previous case demonstrates that the right not to be murdered is protected not by a property rule but by an inalienability rule instead. Nor can we describe it as an effort to prevent offenders from turning inalienability rules into liability rules at their discretion, since the point of inalienability rules is that they limit the freedom of those who possess rights from bargaining them away either *ex ante* or ex post, that is, whether by contract or by compensation *ex post*.[8]

Consider rape. Can anyone seriously argue that rape is criminal because otherwise individuals have the option of changing property rules into liability rules? What could possibly be the market (or property rule) equivalent of rape? Sex? Sex plus dominance? If it is either, then how do we make sense of the prohibition against prostitution, that is, a prohibition against placing certain exchanges in the marketplace? Is it plausible, therefore, to think of it as an effort to induce people not to turn inalienability rules into property rules? What is the right that is said to be protected by an inalienability rule: the right to one's sexual organs? Presumably that right entails control over one's organs and their use. It may be that one cannot relinquish ultimate control of one's sex organs – though even that may be false – but one can surely negotiate their use in all sorts of contexts. The criminal law is a set of prohibitions – mandatory legal requirements. And it is a very impoverished view of the range of human interaction that analyzes all such constraints on behavior in terms of directives based exclusively on exchange relations.

Second, the criminal law states legal requirements and prohibitions, not prices. The economist misses important features of the criminal law by conceiving of it as a pricing mechanism. The criminal law sets out prohibitions that are themselves perfectly intelligible, and meant to serve as guides to behavior quite apart from sanctions for noncompliance being attached to them. The sanction is of secondary importance and comes into effect only when the criminal law fails sufficiently to deter behavior. It is wrong to murder, to rape or to assault, and society is right to prohibit such conduct, whether or not the prohibition is backed by a threat of sanction. So it is fundamentally mistaken to try to understand the criminal category by trying to explain the uses to which one can put the criminal sanction.

Klevorick is in fact neither alone nor first among economists in trying to explain the criminal category by a mixture of economic and moral terms. Even Posner's analysis has an essential moral dimension. His view is that the main reason we punish is to induce criminals to substitute, where they are available, voluntary market transactions for coercive transfers. Since it is an empirical question whether voluntary transfers are more efficient than involuntary ones, the grounds for preferring market to nonmarket transfers is the moral one – the value of voluntary over coercive transfer.

Posner is closer to the way we ordinarily think about crime when he puts the argument in terms of criminal conduct's (usually) being coercive: one party imposing his or her will on another. Of course, not all crime involves a person's acting contrary to the will of another. In some cases there are no victims in this sense; in others, an activity may be criminal even if the "victim" consents. Where criminal law is concerned with coercion, it is concerned with an individual's coercion against others, not the kind of coercion against an institutional arrangement of the variety Klevorick has in mind.

Striking in both Posner's and Klevorick's analyses is the absence of a discussion of the conditions of responsibility as a requirement of criminal liability. If the criminal law is simply a mechanism for inducing compliance with a transaction structure, why the enormous emphasis on guilt as a condition for imposing the sanction? Indeed, why the criminal sanction as we know it? Why, in other words, do incarceration and the deprivation of liberty seem appropriate responses to criminal misconduct if the purpose of the criminal law is to encourage respect for a transaction structure? Perhaps a course in economics would be a more suitable punishment.

The criminal sanction is not imposed unless fairly rigid standards of personal responsibility or culpability are met. With few exceptions involving strict liability, these standards are more rigid than those required to impose tort liability. This emphasis on individual culpability cannot be explained in terms of the inducement function of the criminal law. If a body of law cannot serve its inducement or deterrent function unless individuals have available to them a wide range of possible excusing conditions, then tort law, as well as the law of crimes, should be replete with discussions of excusing conditions. As we know, tort law does not recognize a wide range of excuses, but the law of crimes does. Moreover, strict liability is rare in criminal law, and a general theory of strict criminal liability has never been seriously advanced. In contrast, in torts strict liability is on the increase, and even the rule of fault liability has several dimensions of strict liability embedded in it. For example, in negligence law, an individual may be at fault for the harm his conduct occasions even if his failure to comply with standards of due care is not his fault: even if he did the vest he could. Negligence (in torts), as the jurisprudent Terry pointed out seventy years ago, is "conduct, not a state of mind." Indeed, it is the essentially nonmoral character of negligence in torts that has led economists like Posner to develop a plausible economic analysis of torts based on Learned Hand's famous characterization of negligence in *U.S. v. Carrol Towing*. It is precisely the essentially moral aspect of the conditions of responsibility in the criminal law that makes an economic analysis of it so fundamentally implausible.

Put another way, in crimes the question is whether the state has the right to deprive a particular person of his liberty by incarcerating him. In torts, it is whether the state has sufficient grounds for shifting a loss from the party upon whom it has initially fallen to another individual, when the loss must fall on one or the other of them. In the first case, the state must be satisfied that the individual deserves to be punished. In the second, it must feel that there are good reasons as between two parties (one of whom is bound to be made worse off) to have one rather than the other shoulder the costs. No equivalent situation exists in the criminal law. There is no individual who must be punished – whose liberty must be constrained; there is no loss or cost that must be borne by somebody. So, in order for the state to take the extraordinary step of imposing this burden on someone, it must show that in some sense he deserves it. That argument requires an inquiry not only into what a person does but also into his responsibility and guilt for having done it. These are essential features of the criminal law, and it is not surprising that an economic analysis of crimes that focuses on the inducement aspect of the criminal law in terms of securing compliance with transfer mechanisms should miss it entirely. Such a theory has no place for the moral sentiments and virtues appropriate to matters of crime and punishment: guilt, shame, remorse, forgiveness and mercy, to name a few. A purely economic theory of crime can only impoverish, not enrich, our understanding of the nature of crime.

7. The morality of strict tort liability

1. INTRODUCTION

Accidents occur; personal property is damaged and sometimes lost altogether. Accident victims are likely to suffer anything from mere bruises and headaches to temporary or permanent disability to death. The personal and social costs of accidents are staggering. Yet the question of who should bear these costs has turned the heads of few philosophers and has occasioned surprisingly little philosophic discussion. Perhaps that is because the answer has seemed so obvious; accident costs, at least the nontrivial ones, ought to be borne by those at fault in causing them.[1] The requirement of fault at one time appeared to be so deeply rooted in the concept of personal responsibility that in the famous *Ives*[2] case, Judge Werner was moved to argue that liability without fault was not only immoral but also an unconstitutional violation of due process of law.[3] Although Judge Werner's arguments have long since lost whatever appeal they might have had within the legal community, the view persists among philosophers that strict liability is an unjust or immoral standard of responsibility in torts. This chapter argues not only that strict tort liability is not unjust; it claims that strict liability is at the core of all tort liability.

2. LIABILITY AND FAULT

In his great work *The Common Law,* Oliver Wendell Holmes wrote that a loss ought to lie where it falls, that is, on a victim, in the absence of a compelling reason for shifting it to another party.[4] One could, of course, maintain precisely the opposite initial liability rule: In the absence of a sound reason for leaving a loss with a victim, it ought to be transferred to an injurer.[5] Indeed, in products liability as well as other areas of tort law, this is the initial liability rule we have adopted.[6] As a general rule, however, losses in tort litigation lie where they fall, thus creating a burden on victim–plaintiffs to show why they ought not remain there. Holmes believed that the justification for this initial liability rule is that it is administratively less cumbersome and therefore less costly than the feasible alternatives.[7] Thus, the primary liability rule is rooted in considerations of administrative cost avoidance. But losses do not always remain where they have fallen; nor, apparently, should they. It is not surprising, therefore, that what has come to be called tort theory is composed largely of attempts to fashion general principles of compensation popularly termed liability rules, specifying the conditions under which losses ought to be shifted.[8]

The following arguments, alone and in combination, have been advanced to justify a system of liability rules. (1) Under a retributive rationale, accident costs are shifted from victims to injurers to penalize blameworthy or faulty injuries.[9] On this theory of liability, compensation is likened to punishment or penal sanctions and is said to be required by our notions of retributive justice. (2) Under a compensatory rationale, faulty injurers are liable for their victims' losses, not to ensure that those at fault are punished, but to see to it that fault-free victims are compensated for what are undeserved or otherwise unjustifiable losses. On this view, principles and ideals of compensatory justice rather than those of retributive justice are the touchstone of a system of liability rules.[10] (3) Under a risk-spreading argument, accident costs ought to be allocated either to spread them maximally over persons and time or to ensure that those individuals best able to bear them do so.[11] (4) Under a deterrence argument, accident costs should be allocated to provide incentives for the party best able to avoid the accident to do so, or, if we are unaware or unsure of who is the best or cheapest accident avoider, the costs should be borne by that party best able to decide if an accident ought to be avoided; that is, if it is worth its costs.[12]

The traditional view is that whereas the retributive and compensatory rationales appear to require both fault-based liability rules and a case-by-case determination of liability, the risk-spreading and deterrence justifications for a system of liability rules require neither. That is, to be liable, the party with the deepest pocket need not be the individual responsible for the accident, and the individual best suited to avoid the accident or best able to judge if it ought to be avoided need not be the party at fault in causing it to be liable for its costs. For example, factory owners, by introducing safety measures, might prove to be better and cheaper accident avoiders than their careless and negligent employees. It is entirely possible that the goals of deterrence, cost spreading, and wealth distribution *may* involve fault-based liability rules, for example, when the party at fault is also the best risk spreader or cost avoider. However, unless one equates being at fault with being the cheapest cost avoider, as Guido Calabresi appears to do, [13] the goal of accident cost avoidance does not require that liability for the costs of accidents be determined by the criterion of fault. The same can be said of the other instrumentalist goals of tort law.

I have argued at length elsewhere that we need not adopt a fault system or a case-by-case determination of liability to secure the goals of penalization and compensation in torts.[14] In short, neither justice nor utility requires that liability by based on fault. The argument that justice does not require fault-based liability rules has two thrusts. On the one hand, if there is sufficient fault on an injurer's part, principles of retributive justice may require that an appropriate penalty be imposed upon him. However, retributive justice does not require a faulty person to bear the costs of any accidents he causes.[15] On the other hand, compensatory justice requires the elimination of undeserved or otherwise unjustifiable losses caused by the fault of another. Thus, a victim is entitled to recompense as a matter of justice for those losses caused by his injurer's fault.[16] The considerations that ground an individual's right to recover, however, need not coincide with those that root an obligation to provide compensation. Although the presence of causally efficacious injurer fault may suffice to ground a victim's right to compensation, to be just the obligation to annul or eliminate a victim's loss need not be discharged by the injurer at fault.[17] In short, although principles of retributive justice may justify penalizing wrongdoers and principles of compensatory justice require elimination of wrongfully inflicted losses, neither standard of justice requires that the costs of individual accidents be borne by those at fault in causing them. These considerations demonstrate not only that fault-based liability rules are not required to secure whatever punitive or compensatory aims we might have but also, perhaps more important, that the role of fault in a system of tort liability may not best be explained by reference to these ideals of justice.[18]

If the fault principle is not required to satisfy either punitive or compensatory ideals, how might an accident law that would secure these goals be constructed? First, all conduct that is at fault without regard to the presence or absence of harmful causal consequences might be lumped together.[19] Once the category of conduct that is at fault is considered generally, appropriate penal-like sanctions could be implemented, measured by the degree of culpability or dangerousness in faulty conduct of different sorts rather than by the standard index of harm actually caused.[20] While culpability was being penalized through penal-like sanctions, compensation of faultless victims could be secured through a system of private insurance contracts or from general tax coffers by which individual victims protect themselves against losses they might suffer at the hands of the faulty. This form of protection might be limited only to faultless victims. In that way, although everyone who engages in an activity would be free to purchase an insurance policy against activity-related losses, the protective device would be triggered only when a victim could establish the unjustifiability of a loss. For reasons of administrative and economic efficiency, insurance could be extended either to the class of faultless victims who are injured through no one's fault or to the general class of persons engaged in the activity whether they are at fault or free from it. Although such an expansive approach would not be required by ideals of compensatory justice, insurance schemes of this sort would nevertheless be consistent with such ideals. Thus, although principles of compensatory justice need not confer an entitlement to compensation on individuals who have suffered losses through their own fault or through no one's fault, these considerations do not bar faulty parties from indemnifying themselves against the costs of their own misdeeds.

This is not to suggest that compensatory justice comports with every possible no-fault allocation of losses. Principles of compensatory justice are best viewed as equilibrium or steady-state principles of justice in that they protect a distribution of wealth against unjustifiable gains and losses by requiring the annulment of both. Thus, justice requires that those at fault forfeit the gains imputable to their misconduct; a no-fault allocation of losses in which there is wrongful gain or advantage would not be compatible with this ideal of compensatory justice. The maxim that one ought not profit from one's own wrongdoing and corresponding prohibitions against unjust enrichment are therefore elements in a completely satisfactory account of compensatory justice.

This brief summary of the relationship of fault to justice in tort liability leaves a number of questions unanswered. Foremost among them are the following: If fault-based liability rules are not required to secure the goals of justice in tort law, what justification exists for a fault system? If shifting losses on the basis of fault is not required either to compensate victims or to penalize injurers, what could possibly be unjust about a system of strict liability that imposes liability without regard to fault? The question is less paradoxical than it appears at first. From the conclusion that our principles of justice do not *require* the fault system, it follows neither that every no-fault alternative to the fault system comports with our notions of justice nor that the fault system is not morally inferior to certain no-fault alternatives. Even if the fault system is not required by considerations of justice, the question remains whether it is nevertheless morally superior to the rule of strict liability.

3. THE STRICT LIABILITY DIMENSION OF FAULT

Apparently, most of those unfamiliar with the case law and many of those familiar with it believe that tort liability is based on the criterion of fault. According to the fault principle, the costs of an accident ought to be borne by that party whose fault caused it.[21] Given this basic liability rule, one can then distinguish among four categories of limitations on the scope of fault as a basis of tort liability.

In cases of the first sort there is defendant fault, but the victim nevertheless is denied recovery because of some real or imputed shortcoming in the victim's conduct. Thus, a plaintiff may be denied recompense for his losses caused by a defendant's fault if he is contributorily negligent[22] or if the contributory negligence of another is imputed to him.[23] In cases of the second sort, the defendant is at fault, but the plaintiff fails to recover either because the plaintiff assumed the risk[24] or because the relationship between the defendant's fault and the victim's injury is insufficiently proximate to justify compensation.[25] In these cases there is no defect, real or imputed, in the plaintiff's conduct, yet he fails to recover either because the defendant's fault fails to reach far enough or because of some contractually assumed or otherwise voluntarily accepted level of risk on the plaintiff's behalf. Cases of denied recovery because of *victim status,* rather than victim misconduct, also could fall into this category. For example, a defendant's fault may not reach far enough to protect a trespasser though the trespasser's loss would not have occurred but for the defendant's fault.[26] Cases falling into a third category differ from those in the first two in that the defendant is immune from liability either to the instant plaintiff or to all possible plaintiffs. Examples of *defendant status* immunity include family[27] and charitable[28] immunities.

These categories of exceptions to the fault principle overlap and might be put in other terms. Generally, however, exceptions to fault–based liability within the fault context are grounded either in plaintiff or defendant status, contractual agreement, or plaintiff misconduct or in the insufficient reach of defendant fault. In each of these categories, a defendant is at fault and his fault is causally responsible for a victim's losses, yet the victim goes uncompensated and the defendant escapes liability. As an empirical matter, these limitations on the reach of the fault standard ought to shed some doubt on the widely held view that the fault system aims primarily to compensate the victims of fault or to punish the perpetrators of it.

Each of these limitations on the availability of compensation to victims presupposes a basic commitment to the criterion of fault as a standard of liability in torts. They represent limitations on the extent to which satisfaction of the fault requirement determines liability even *in a fault context.*

In contrast, there is an ever expanding body of tort law in which the incidence of a loss is said to be determined without regard to the criterion of fault. This fourth category of exceptions to the fault standard commonly is referred to as strict liability. It includes the law governing workmen's compensation,[29] abnormal or ultra-hazardous activities,[30] nuisance,[31] and products liability.[32] First-party, no-fault accident law is a special kind of strict liability in which each litigant is strictly liable for his own losses, not for those of another.

The categories of cases now decided on a strict liability basis are so diverse that the most interesting current literature on tort law has been devoted to trying to establish a family resemblance among them.[33] These efforts will, I hope, be enhanced by drawing certain distinctions that bear on the application of strict liability theory.

First, the procedural and substantive aspects of strict liability can be distinguished. On the one hand, strict liability is primarily a theory about evidence, burdens of proof and standards of recovery; on the other hand, it is a liability rule about where losses ought to fall. As a procedural matter, strict liability dictates that it is not relevant to a plaintiff's claim for recovery that he establish the fault of the defendant in causing his injury. Although the defendant may well be at fault, the plaintiff's right to secure compensation from him does not depend on showing to the satisfaction of a judge or jury that he is. Substantively, the strict liability rule is that even an injurer who is not at fault is responsible for a victim's loss. So, on the one hand, strict liability is a series of rules

about the kind of cases a plaintiff–victim must make out in order
to trigger the application of a liability rule; on the other hand, it is
the liability rule that is triggered thereby.

In those categories of cases governed by the strict liability rule,
cases in which there is in fact defendant fault and those in which
the defendant is free from fault are indistinguishable from the point
of view of standards of proof and threshold requirements of liability. Yet there is the obvious distinction that in some cases the
defendant is at fault and in others the defendant is not at fault. At
first blush, it seems somewhat illogical to treat some cases in which
there is defendant fault less like other cases in which there is defendant fault and more like cases in which the defendant is faultless.
Of course, if one has reason to believe that in areas of the law
governed by the strict liability rule the goals of tort law are advanced by ignoring the requirement of fault, then abandoning fault
is a perfectly plausible strategy. The point can be put more generally. The law develops by categories. If a category of cases can
be delineated that is best dealt with on a no-fault basis and if a case
falls within the boundaries of the category, it makes perfectly good
sense to apply the strict liability rule to it even if in the instant case
the criterion of fault is or could be satisfied. But to ask why, in
certain kinds or categories of cases but not others, the presence of
defendant fault is absolutely necessary to trigger the application of
a loss-shifting liability rule is simply to raise in another form the
question of what the goals of tort law are.

Although the procedural aspect of strict liability compels us to
ignore the criterion of fault even when it is present, the substantive
or liability aspect of it may require us to impose liability upon
individuals who cause harm through no fault of their own. The
substantive aspect of the strict liability rule therefore raises this
difficult question: Why does failure to find defendant fault constitute a complete bar to recovery in some areas of tort law, whereas
in other cases absence of defendant fault is no bar at all to recovery? Indeed, when strict liability is the rule, not only does the
absence of fault fail to bar liability, but failure to find even a causal
relationship between the defendant's conduct and the plaintiff's
injury may not be a defense against liability.[34]

Although the issues raised by the procedural and substantive
elements of the strict liability rule are very similar, they are not
identical. The procedural component raises the question of why
we would abandon fault as the criterion applicable in some cases
but not in others when fault is present in both. The substantive
element of the strict liability rule asks us to justify the imposition

of liability in the absence of fault. If strict liability always involved only an abandoning of fault when, as a matter of fact, fault was present, the strict liability rule doubtless would prove less troublesome to those who object to it from the moral point of view. But as a matter of fact, adherence to the strict liability rule means that at least some of the time liability will be imposed upon individuals who are absolutely free from fault. Thus, strict liability may require individuals to bear the costs of accidents that are not their fault.

We must now distinguish between the two senses in which liability may be imposed strictly. There are two fundamental components in all fault judgments. To be at fault, (1) an actor's conduct must fail to satisfy a standard of reasonableness and (2) an actor's conduct must be imputable to him as his own doing in some sense. The distinction between these elements in fault attributions is illustrated best by the positive defenses one can offer to them: justifications and excuses. Briefly, a justification is proffered to establish that the conduct in doubt indeed meets required standards. An excuse is offered not to contest the failure to measure up, but to deny responsibility for it. An appropriate justification defeats a fault attribution because a justification shows that the attribution is grounded in a mistaken allegation of failure to measure up to standard. An excuse defeats an ascription of fault by pulling the rug from under the claim of responsibility implicit in it.[35]

This distinction demonstrates that there are two senses in which liability in torts can be said to be strict, that is, imposed without regard to fault. Liability is strict if it is not defeasible by an excuse. That is, an actor may be held liable when, in Hart's words, he "could not help doing what he did"[36] (though lack of capacity constitutes but one sort of excusing condition). In strict liability of this sort a defendant may be liable for the costs of accidents caused by his conduct even though he could show to the satisfaction of the trier of fact that he lacked substantial capacity to comply with the required standards of care. This is liability for excusable conduct. On the other hand, liability without fault may be liability for conduct that is reasonable or that satisfies standards of due care. In other words, in strict liability of this sort, an actor may be accountable for injuries caused by his perfectly acceptable conduct. This is liability for justifiable risk taking.

This chapter is concerned primarily with strict liability in the latter sense and with the accusation that liability for the harmful causal upshots of reasonable conduct is unjust.[37] I want to argue that, at best, this criticism of strict liability is overstated and that, at worst, it is fundamentally misconceived.

4. FAULT LIABILITY AS STRICT VICTIM LIABILITY

The simple truth is that even in the fault system individuals may be required to bear the costs of accidents that are not their fault. This is an important consequence of those limitations on the scope of fault discussed in some detail above.[38] But the nonfault element in the fault system extends beyond these technical limitations on the scope of the criterion of fault. To see that this is true, we have to reconsider the initial liability rule of the fault system, that the costs of accidents ought to lie on victims. This liability rule enables a victim to shift his costs to his injurer when it can be established that the injurer was at fault in causing the harm. What that implies, of course, is that victims bear accident costs when they are unable to establish that the criterion of fault is satisfied, even when they themselves are entirely free from fault. This is not merely a matter of evidence, but of substantive law. If neither litigant is at fault, the fault system is designed so that the faultless victim bears the costs. That is a direct consequence of the initial liability rule. The upshot of the initial liability decision, rooted, if we are to follow Holmes, in considerations of administrative cost avoidance,[39] is a far-reaching no-fault component in the fault system. This no-fault element requires no more and no less than does its counterpart in the strict liability rule.

In a system of strict liability, the opposite initial liability rule operates. The injurer bears the costs of accidents unless he can show some defect in the victim's conduct sufficient to free him from liability. If he is able to do so, the costs of the accident are transferred to the victim. Failing that, however, the injurer must bear the costs even if he is entirely without fault. Thus, in both strict and fault liability, an individual may be required to bear the costs of accidents that are not his fault.

This point should not be overstated. It is very plain, but overlooked, that in both a fault and a strict liability system there are circumstances in which an attribution of liability cannot be defeated by the positive defense of freedom from fault. At the same time, the point should not be underestimated. What has been shown is that both the fault system and the strict liability rule are committed at their core to liability without fault.[40] Thus, the charge that what is peculiarly wrong with strict liability is that it does not permit an individual to free himself from the burdens of liability by the defense of faultlessness may be simply misplaced or at least overstated.

Although absence of fault is not a defense in any area of strict liability law, different categories of strict liability may be distinguished from one another on the basis of the sorts of *plaintiff-related* defenses a party held strictly liable may offer to defeat an ascription of liability. In some cases, the presence of victim negligence or contributory fault is a defense to strict liability.[41] In other areas of tort law, such as workmen's compensation, plaintiff negligence is not a defense, though willful misconduct by a plaintiff may be.[42] In products liability, misuse of product or unforeseen usage may be a defense,[43] though plaintiff fault may not be.[44] Yet in other kinds of cases, no plaintiff-related defense will succeed, at least once certain minimal conditions of liability are met.[45]

It would be fruitful, therefore, to distinguish four general systems of liability: (1) the fault system; (2) strict injurer liability with the defense of plaintiff (victim) fault; (3) strict injurer liability with no defense of plaintiff misconduct; and (4) strict victim (plaintiff) liability with no defense of injurer wrongfulness. Categories (3) and (4) above may be labeled *absolute injurer* and *absolute victim* liability, respectively.

The first thing to note about these categories is that (2) is merely (1) in reverse. This is a point already well made by Guido Calabresi.[46] Substantively, the two theories of liability differ only with respect to whom liability will be attributed to initially, and consequently where it will fall if the fault-based liability provision cannot be met. When the fault system decides in both cases against the victim, the system of strict liability with the defense of plaintiff fault decides against the injurer.

Secondly, under both an absolute victim liability system and a fault system, the victim would bear the loss if there were no fault on the part of either litigant. But in the same circumstance, the injurer would bear the loss under a strict injurer liability system; this would be so whether or not the system was one that allowed victim misconduct as a defense.

Thirdly, in both absolute injurer and absolute victim liability systems, not even misconduct by a victim or injurer, respectively, would suffice as a defense. In that respect, the absolute liability systems differ most significantly from their nonabsolute counterparts.

We now can begin to evaluate the claim that strict liability is an immoral theory of responsibility in torts. Several questions are involved here. First, is there a moral reason for preferring the fault system to strict liability with a defense of plaintiff fault? As both systems of liability transfer losses to the party at fault when there is fault, they differ only with respect to who bears the loss when there is no culpable litigant. The question ultimately becomes whether there is a moral reason for favoring one no-fault decision over another, that is, for systematically favoring the no-fault decision against victims over the same decision against injurers.

Following Holmes,[47] one might argue that the no-fault decision against injurers is the administratively costlier alternative of the two. Because administrative costs are wasteful and lead to an inefficient allocation of resources, and because waste and inefficient resource use is morally undesirable, the fault system is to be preferred to a system of strict liability. I am not prepared to deny that inefficiency in the economic sense is a moral shortcoming in a system of liability rules.[48] Yet it hardly follows from the fact that transferring losses from victims to injurers is costly that doing so is invariably not worth its costs. Surely the question is not whether a liability rule involves incurring administrative costs but whether the rule is worth its costs.

Alternatively, one could argue, as Holmes appears to,[49] that the injurers are the doers: the industrialists, the opportunity seekers and the providers. Consequently, on this view they deserve the advantage created by an initial liability rule favorable to them. The argument rests on the dubious initial premise that as a class injurers are doers, and that victims, as a class, are merely passive agents. More important, absent a moral accounting of the entire lives of categories of victims and injurers past, present and future, there is absolutely no reason to believe that injurers rather than victims have earned or merited a favorable initial liability rule.

Perhaps the most intriguing argument for preferring as a general rule that the no-fault decision favor the injurer rather than the victim relies on the premise that in strict liability, but not in the fault system, an act of compensation is involved; the defendant must make good the victim's loss if neither is at fault.[50] On the other hand, the no-fault element of the fault system requires only that the victim make good his own losses. Though there is a no-fault component in both theories of liability, only in strict liability does the no-fault decision translate into an act of compensation. Indeed, in the fault system the no-fault decision against the victim requires neither compensation nor an attribution of liability. When the victim is unable to establish the fault of the defendant, we do not characterize his having to bear his own losses as his *being held liable* for them, though we might describe him as *being liable* for them.

Compensation is required as a matter of justice when it is necessary to annul or to eliminate an unjustifiable loss; that is, to make good a loss caused by the fault of another.[51] But compensation also may be a vehicle for expressing public attitudes of disapproval or, in extreme cases, of condemnation toward the conduct of the offending party. More likely, compensation may serve as a private law remedy by which injurers take responsibility for, or declare as their own, actions that cause harm to others. Or perhaps compensation is a useful social instrument through which injurers express their regrets and apologies to the victims of their misdeeds. If that is so, strict liability may be an immoral standard of liability, because it requires a morally inappropriate act. By requiring an injurer to compensate his victim, strict liability may compel an injurer to offer apologies when he has done nothing for which he ought to apologize. What may be wrong with strict liability as a standard of tort responsibility is that the act of compensation it compels is a source of "undeserved responsive attitudes and unfair judgments of blame."[52]

There are really two closely allied arguments here. First, strict liability is immoral because it requires the injurer to express morally inappropriate feelings of regret, shame, guilt, fault or the like. Secondly, because attributions of liability imply judgments of blameworthiness, strict liability involves making formal, official pronouncements of culpability in a judicial context. It requires us, in short, to impute blame to blameless conduct.

Arguably, however, only infrequently does tort liability invoke feelings of contrition, regret, shame, guilt, remorse or the like on the part of the party required to render compensation. For the most part, compensation as a remedy in torts is impersonal and usually is transacted through insurance mechanisms. To illustrate the diverse nature of compensation as a tort remedy, consider the case of a polluting feedlot, a simple nuisance. In the absence of an injunction, the polluter may be free to operate his nuisance provided he compensates (often on an ongoing basis) those individuals whose property values are adversely affected by the nuisance. In cases of this sort, the compensation rendered by the offending party is more accurately characterized as an operating cost of the feedlot or as recompense required under a takings-like doctrine[53] than as the vehicle through which the wrongdoer is made to express his nuisance cases, compensation may be simply the price an offending litigant must pay to be free to victimize his neighbors. As long as the neighbor's entitlement to be free from pollution is not protected by an injunction against the polluter, paying compensation on an ongoing basis may be one of the ways in which the polluter may purchase from his neighbor the right to pollute.[54]

For the economist, compensation may be required in such cases to ensure that the impact of the pollution on resource use is reflected adequately in the price of the manufacturer's goods. Were the polluter not required to compensate his victims, they in turn would be forced to internalize the costs of pollution and the polluter would be free to pollute costlessly.[55] Because he would not be required to internalize pollution costs, the prices of his goods would give systematically misleading cues or information to the consumer with respect to the marginal rate of transformation of resources into goods. The price he would charge could be significantly lower than the marginal rate of transformation, thus leading to both an inefficient allocation of resources and to more pollution.

To fail to see compensation and liability rules in this broader context is to miss entirely the role of tort liability in pursuing Pareto-optimal[56] and/or just distributions of resources.

But to see compensation this way is to recognize that disputes settled by compensation are not always best framed by and in terms of the interests of the individual litigating parties only. The more often compensation is required by liability rules governing areas like environmental control, in which disputes often are *not* best formulated by or in terms of the interests of litigating parties, the less likely is compensation to retain the personalized meaning that has come to be associated with the term by virtue of its usage in the nonlegal context.

The second thrust of the moral argument against strict liability, that it imputes blame to individuals or to conduct unworthy of blame, rests on the premise that an attribution of liability is itself either a judgment of blame or a source of it. When liability is based on fault, an attribution of liability is often a shorthand for ascribing blame for the faulty conduct. But if our liability rules do not require fault, an ascription of blame need not be implicit in an attribution of liability. To hold someone strictly liable is not necessarily to blame him for what he has done. Instead, the liability decision may be the result of a delicate balancing of non–fault-related considerations, for example, the relative ability of litigants either to bear risks or to evaluate the worthiness of accident-causing conduct.[57] That moral stigma or blame attaches to the judgment of fault rather than to the attribution of liability may be illustrated by an example from case law.

In *Western & Atlantic Railroad v. Henderson,*[58] the Supreme Court struck down, as a violation of the due process clause of the Fourteenth Amendment,[59] section 2780 of the Georgia Civil Code, which created a nearly irrebuttable presumption of *fault*[60] against railroads in the event of "any damages done to persons, stock, or other property by the running of the locomotives, or cars, or other machinery of such company, or for damage done by any person in the employment and service of such company."[61] On the other hand, in *St. Louis & San Francisco Railway Company v. Mathews,*[62] the Court upheld a Missouri statute that made railroads strictly responsible "in damages to every person and corporation whose property may be injured or destroyed by fire communicated, directly or indirectly, by locomotive engines in use upon the railroad owned or operated by such railroad corporation."[63]

Liability based on an irrebuttable presumption of *fault,* at least at the turn of the century, was thought to violate the due process clause of the Fourteenth Amendment. Except for the decision in the anomalous *Ives* case,[64] strict tort liability never has been thought to constitute an unconstitutional violation of due process. Yet the only meaningful element that seems to underlie the different holdings in *Henderson* and *Mathews* is that in the former case the statute provided for liability to be imposed on the basis of fault that was irrebuttably presumed to exist. In *Mathews* no judgment of fault was required to establish liability. When the cases were decided, they stood for the proposition that it is not unconstitutional to impose liability without regard to fault, though it may be unconstitutional, in the same circumstances, to impose liability on the basis of fault irrebuttably presumed to exist. The distinction is most plausibly explained in terms of stigma: An attribution of liability with no pretense of fault as its basis imputes no stigma to the party held liable, but an unwarranted imputation of fault reflects unfavorably and unfairly on the character of the accused.

To summarize, two very different sorts of moral criticisms of strict liability have been considered, neither of which, I have argued, succeeds. First, critics contend that strict liability is an immoral standard of responsibility in torts because it imposes the costs of accidents on individuals who are not at fault in causing them. In other words, absence of injurer fault is not a defense to strict liability. However, because the type of strict liability considered here allows the defense of plaintiff misconduct, it imposes liability on faultless injurers only when neither they nor their victims are at fault. Moreover, the fault system is committed to imposing liability on faultless parties in the very same circumstances; when neither litigant is at fault, the faultless victim bears the costs. This traditional argument against strict liability, focusing as it does on the absence of fault as a necessary defeating condition of liability in any just theory of tort liability, ignores the plain fact that the fault system involves the same sort of strict liability decision.

As a second line of attack, critics attempt to define more narrowly the immorality of strict liability, arguing that there is at least a moral reason for preferring the no-fault decision in the fault system to the one in strict liability. To that end they advance considerations of administrative cost avoidance and injurer desert. But the desert claim is unfounded and the cost-avoidance claim is too weak. The most compelling argument advanced against strict liability at this level depends on the premise that only the strict liability no-fault decision involves an act of compensation. According to this argument, the requisite act of compensation is inappropriate, given the lack of defendant fault. But as we already have seen, compensation in torts only infrequently involves an expression of apology by the injurer to his victim. In brief, the argument rests on an inappropriate transposition of the ordinary concept of compensation to the legal context.

5. THE MORALITY OF ABSOLUTE LIABILITY

The question remains whether there is a moral reason for preferring the fault system to the *absolute* liability rule as a general matter. What, if anything, is unjust or immoral about absolute liability?

There are two distinct kinds of absolute liability rules: absolute victim liability and absolute injurer liability. Absolute *victim* liability maintains not only that the costs of accidents ought to fall on victims initially, but also that they ought to remain there. Thus, absolute victim liability is nothing more than the initial liability rule of the fault system taken as an ultimate liability decision.[65] Absolute injurer liability is simply strict liability without the defense of plaintiff fault or misconduct. Thus, it is the initial liability rule of strict liability, again taken as a final liability rule.

The clearest example of a *de facto* absolute liability system is provided by workmen's compensation schemes that allow no plaintiff-related defenses to employer liability. In such statutory systems an employer may be required to bear the costs of his employees' on-the-job injuries even when these accidents are the fault

of the employee.[66] Whatever reasons of deterrence there might be
for adopting an absolute liability rule when the party held liable is
the one best able to avoid the accident, it is at least arguable that
there is a certain element of injustice in the rule.

But can we clearly define the injustice that may be present in
the absolute liability rule? Schematically, the rule maintains that
X, who is free from fault, must bear the costs of an accident sustained by Y and caused by Y's fault. Sometimes X also is held
liable for the cost of accidents that Y's fault causes Z to suffer.
Absolute victim liability is simply a special instance of the latter
formula in which X and Z are the same person. The absolute liability rule may require that a fault-free party bear the costs of an
accident when a party whose fault caused the accident is available
for liability. Is there anything unjust about such an arrangement
of responsibilities? Joel Feinberg, in his article "Sua Culpa," claims
that there is a principle of weak retributive justice that holds that
if a loss must fall on either of two parties, one of whom is at fault
in causing it and the other of whom is faultless, the party at fault
ought to bear the loss, all other things being equal.[67] Feinberg's
principle of weak retributivism is grounded in the requirement
that innocence or lack of fault ought to be protected, not in the
view that those at fault ought to be penalized.

The weak retributive principle admittedly has a limited scope
and force. It does not purport to decide the incidence of a loss
when both parties are at fault, nor does it determine liability when
neither party is at fault. Moreover, the principle does not require
that the party at fault bear the loss if his fault is inconsequential or
if it does not contribute to the harm. Furthermore, the "all things
being equal" escape clause means that even if the fault requirement
is met by one party but not the other, conceivably in some situations it would not be unjust for the party free from fault to bear
the loss. Apparently one such situation is when the party free from
fault contractually agrees to bear the loss.

One argument against the absolute liability rule could rely on
Feinberg's principle. Thus, under this argument, the absolute liability rule may require that someone who is free from fault bear
the costs of injuries suffered by the party whose fault is responsible
for them, but justice requires that the party at fault bear the costs.
Therefore, absolute liability goes awry by violating this principle
of weak retributive justice.

Feinberg's principle requires only that when the sole relevant
moral difference between litigating parties is that one, but not the
other, is at fault in causing the harm, liability ought to be imposed

on the party at fault to protect the innocence of the faultless party.
In contrast, the absolute liability rule, in some circumstances, would
reach the opposite liability decision. What may be unjust about it,
then, is that in the absence of a moral difference it could require
the party free from fault to bear the costs of accidents caused by
another's fault. I do not mean to suggest that one cannot envision
instances in which the circumstances were such that it would not
be unjust to require the faultless to bear the losses caused by another's fault. I mean to say only that in the absence of such circumstances, the absolute liability rule may be unjust.

The same point could be put another way: What is wrong with
absolute liability is that it requires an individual free from fault to
serve as the insurer of the faulty. Moreover, it imposes this obligation of insurer not by contractual agreement but by liability rule.
Although it may not be unjust for an individual to assume the role
of an insurer by contract, it may be unjust to impose that role
upon him through a liability rule in the absence of a standard liability trigger mechanism, such as fault.[68]

The traditional view is that strict liability is an unjust theory of
responsibility in torts because it does not allow the defense of freedom from fault to defeat an attribution of liability. I have argued
that in both the fault and strict liability systems, an individual may
be required to bear the costs of accidents that are not his fault.
Moreover, if there is a moral shortcoming in strict liability, it is
not an injustice in strict liability generally; instead, it is an injustice
in the absolute liability rule only. It is the narrow injustice that one
who is without fault is required, in the absence of a contractual
agreement, to be the insurer of one who is at fault. Thus, absolute
liability may violate the principle of justice that holds that in the
absence of such an agreement, or conditions of similar effect, the
party at fault should bear the loss.

The plain but almost universally unappreciated fact is that in
tort law we are dealing with losses − with activities and their accident costs. The question with which we began is the question
with which we conclude: Who should bear these costs? My argument has been that the preoccupation with fault as an essential
element in a just theory of torts has obscured significant structural
similarities between the criteria of fault and strict injurer liability.
Foremost among these similarities is that we can conceive of the
fault system itself as a form of strict victim liability with the defense of injurer fault.[69]

Once we conceive of traditional fault and strict injurer liability
as structural analogues, the importance of another issue comes to

the fore, because these standards of liability differ primarily only with regard to who bears losses in the absence of fault. The fault principle, whether it is employed to justify transferring losses from victims to injurers (in the fault system) or from injurers to victims (in strict injurer liability), cannot provide a moral reason for preferring one standard of liability to the other. That issue can be resolved only by first attempting to fashion general principles for allocating losses in the absence of fault.

My arguments here have been that we cannot decide, without reference to particular kinds of categories of cases, which no–fault decision to make. Indeed, once we consider cases, we are likely to discover that in certain instances the strict liability rule is morally superior to the criterion of fault. For example, in workmen's compensation cases and products liability cases, considerations not of compensatory justice but of distributive justice could support imposing the burden of bearing accident costs on the employer or manufacturer rather than on the employee or consumer. But a thorough inspection of cases is left for another occasion. My point is simply that by focusing on the presence of fault in a just theory of liability, moral philosophers largely have ignored the question of who should bear a loss when no candidate for it is at fault. Consequently, philosophers have stopped contributing to the dialogue at that very point where their contribution is needed most.

8. Corrective justice and wrongful gain

1. INTRODUCTION

Richard Posner's essay "The Concept of Corrective Justice in Recent Theories of Tort Law"[1] falls into three distinct but related sections. In the first part of the paper, Posner attempts to characterize the principle(s) of corrective justice. In the second part, he criticizes the efforts of a number of other tort theorists, including George Fletcher, Richard Epstein and myself, who have attempted to ground the law of torts on a foundation of corrective justice. Having himself previously advanced an efficiency-based conception of the law of torts, Posner goes on to argue in the third part of the essay that the principle of corrective justice is itself required by the principle of efficiency. By laying an economic foundation for the principle of corrective justice, Posner argues not only for the compatibility of the most promising line of moral defense of tort law with the dominant economic one, but for the primacy of the latter as well.

Posner has graciously provided me with the opportunity to respond to his paper. In a series of essays, some of which have appeared in philosophy journals,[2] others of which have surfaced in law reviews[3] and one of which has appeared as a chapter in a very overpriced book,[4] I have explored the moral foundations of tort law. It would not be unfair – indeed, it may be too generous – to say that in these essays I have advanced a theory of torts based on the principle of corrective justice. In what follows I first summarize (in a very compressed fashion) my view of the role of corrective justice in tort theory, then briefly contrast it with those of Epstein and Fletcher, and finally consider Posner's objections to it.

1.1. Liability, recovery and a conception of corrective justice

Central to my account of torts is the distinction between the grounds of liability and recovery – in other words, between the two questions: (1) What are the grounds necessary and sufficient to justify a victim's claim to recompense? and (2) Under what conditions ought an injurer be obligated to provide compensation to his victims?[5] That the grounds of recovery and liability are at least analytically distinguishable is illustrated by the fact that a society could establish an insurance scheme to compensate all accident victims, while only those injurers who are at fault in causing an accident would be required to contribute to the insurance pool. Were we to separate liability and recovery in this way, being at fault in causing harm would be a necessary condition of liability, but not of the victim's case for recovery. Whether a system that separated liability from recovery in this particular way would be just or efficient remains to be worked out. For now the point is simply that the considerations that ground a claim to recompense need not coincide with those that ground the obligation to repair.

Once the distinction between the foundations of recovery and liability is drawn, the next question concerns the role of corrective justice in each. This in turn requires a conception of corrective justice. In my view, corrective or compensatory justice is concerned with the category of wrongful gains and losses. Rectification, in this view, is a matter of justice when it is necessary to protect a distribution of holdings (or entitlements) from distortions which arise from unjust enrichments and wrongful losses. The principle of corrective justice requires the annulments of both wrongful gains and losses.[6]

This conception of corrective justice puts a great burden on the concepts of wrongful gain and wrongful loss. Without offering a set of conditions necessary and sufficient for a loss or gain to count as wrongful, I tried in my previous work to characterize the basic idea by examples. Within the category of wrongful losses are those one suffers through the fault or wrongful conduct of another; within the class of unjust enrichments are those one secures through one's wrongdoing, as in many instances of fraud and theft. A compensable or undeserved loss need not, however, be the result of another's wrongdoing. Sometimes the justifiable (i.e., nonwrongful) taking of what another has a well-established right to justifies a claim to rectification.[7] An instance of a justifiable taking that creates a compensable loss is given by this example of Joel Feinberg's:

Suppose that you are on a backpacking trip in mountain country when an unexpected blizzard strikes the area with such ferocity that your life is imperiled. Fortunately, you stumble on an unoccupied cabin, locked and boarded up for the winter, clearly somebody else's private property. You smash in a window, enter and huddle in a corner for three days until the storm abates. During this period you help yourself to your unknown benefactor's food supply and burn his wooden furniture in the fireplace to keep warm. Surely you are justified in doing all these things, and yet you have infringed the clear rights of another person.[8]

Feinberg argues, and I concur, that in spite of the justifiability of what you have done, you owe the owner of the cabin compensation for his food and furniture.

Although these examples do not define in any strict sense the operative notion of wrongfulness, they help to characterize it sufficiently to make the notion a useful one.

Given this general conception of corrective justice and the instances above of wrongful gain and loss, as well as the central distinction between the grounds of recovery and liability, I can begin to spell out my account of the role of corrective justice in tort theory.

In torts a distinction is drawn between rules of fault (or conditional) and strict (or unconditional) liability. In fault liability, a victim is not entitled to recover his loss unless it is the result of another's fault, and an injurer is liable only for those harms that are his fault. In strict liability, neither the victim's claim to recompense nor the injurer's responsibility to make repair requires that the injurer's conduct be at fault.

1.1.1. Corrective justice and the fault principle. Consider first the role of corrective justice in grounding recovery and liability under the fault principle. Under the fault principle a victim is entitled to repair only if his loss results from another's fault. A loss that is the consequence of another's fault is, in the sense just characterized, a wrongful one. Since the principle of corrective justice requires annulling wrongful losses, it supports the victim's claim to recompense in fault liability.

The relationship between corrective justice and the principle that an individual ought to be liable for the untoward consequences of his fault is somewhat more complex. There are two kinds of cases in which the principle of corrective justice gives direct support to the principle of fault liability: (1) those cases in which an individual's fault results not only in another's loss but in his gain as well and (2) those cases in which an individual secures a wrongful gain through his fault, though his gain is not the result of another's loss. Unjust enrichment through fraud is an example of a wrongful gain secured at another's expense; non–harm-causing but nevertheless negligent motoring is often an example of conduct that creates wrongful gain in the absence of a corresponding wrongful loss.

Consider the case of negligent motoring more carefully. Negligent motoring may or may not result in an accident. Whether or not it does, individuals who drive negligently often secure a wrongful gain in doing so, namely, the "savings" from not taking adequate safety precautions – those required of the reasonable man of ordinary prudence. This form of wrongful gain is not, *ex hypothesi,* the result of anyone else's wrongful loss. On the other hand, if a negligent motorist causes another harm, he normally secures no *additional* wrongful gain in virtue of his doing so. In this respect faulty motoring differs from the usual case of fraud or theft. Because harmful negligent motoring does not generally result in any wrongful gain (apart from that which is the result of negligence itself), the obligation to repair the victim's wrongful loss cannot be entirely grounded on a foundation of corrective justice. There is, in other words, no wrongful gain correlative of the wrongful loss the faulty injurer imposes upon his victim, and no reason, therefore, as a matter of corrective justice alone for imposing the victim's loss upon his injurer. The wrongful gain negligent motorists secure is logically distinct from any loss they may cause others, and so the occasion of another's loss cannot be the moral basis for annulling these gains as a matter of justice.[9]

This is bound to appear controversial; some additional distinctions might make it appear less so. A full theory of justice in tort liability and recovery would distinguish among four issues: (1) the foundation of a claim that a person has suffered a compensable loss, or that he has secured an unjust gain; (2) the mode of rectification – that is, the manner in which unjust gains and losses are to be eliminated;[10] (3) the character of rectification – that is, whether a particular form of compensation (e.g., money) is always, sometimes or rarely appropriate; and (4) the extent of rectification – that is, just how much of a person's loss (or gain) ought to be eliminated.[11]

The central claim of my thesis is the rather straightforward one (I believe) that determining whether a gain or loss is wrongful determines the answer only to the first of these issues. If there is a wrongful loss, it ought to be annulled; the same goes for wrongful or unwarranted gains. Nevertheless, the principle of corrective justice which enables us to identify compensable losses and unjust enrichments does not commit us to adopting any particular mode of rectification. The principle that determines which gains and losses are to be eliminated does not by itself specify a means for doing

so. Presumably there is more than one way of rectifying undeserved gains and losses. So when I claim that if an injurer who
through his fault imposes a wrongful loss on another but who
does not thereby gain has an obligation to repair, his obligation
cannot derive directly from the principle of corrective justice, I
mean only to be emphasizing the obvious fact that he has secured
no gain which would be the concern of corrective justice to rectify. His victim's claim to recompense is on the other hand a matter of corrective justice. And if we feel that the injurer should rectify his victim's loss, it must be for reasons other than the fact that
doing so is required in order to annul his gain.

Once we have adopted a system of tort liability, we have committed ourselves to a particular mode of rectifying wrongful gains
and losses – a method that imposes victims' losses on their injurers
whether or not losses occasion wrongful gain. That particular mode
of rectification is in no sense required by the principle of corrective
justice. There may be reasons other than those which derive from
a theory of corrective justice for imposing an innocent victim's
loss on his injurer. Consider three such arguments. First, one might
argue from the principle of retributive justice for the imposition
of liability on faulty injurers. Such an argument would hold that
wrongdoing, whether or not it secures personal gain, is sinful and
ought to be punished or sanctioned. Imposing liability in torts is a
way of sanctioning mischief. Therefore, liability is imposed on the
faulty injurer not to rectify his gain – of which there may be none
– but to penalize his moral wrong.[12] Or one could argue from the
principle that claim rights impose correlative duties to the conclusion that the victim's right, which is grounded in corrective justice, imposes a correlative duty to repair on his injurer.[13] Or one
might take yet another tack and seek to ground the injurer's obligation to repair in considerations of deterrence or accident cost
avoidance. This argument might take the following form. To be
at fault is to act in an inefficient manner; it is to fail to take appropriate accident-avoidance measures when the cost of doing so is
less than the cost of the harm to the victim discounted by the
probability of its occurrence. An injurer who is at fault in harming
another is obligated to make restitution because his doing so provides him with an incentive to take such precautions as are reasonable and necessary in the future, and because doing so in general
has the long-term effect of reducing the sum of accident and accident-avoidance costs.[14] Were one to take an economic approach to
the liability of the faulty injurer and a corrective justice approach

to the right of his victim to secure recompense, the net result would be a merger of economic and moral theories of fault liability, albeit a more narrowly defined one than Posner contemplates.

1.1.2. Corrective justice and strict liability. Consider now the relationship between the principle of corrective justice and liability and recovery under the rule of unconditional or strict liability. The conception of unwarranted or wrongful gain and loss central to the principle of corrective justice includes losses and gains that result from justified "takings." Unlike the wrongful losses in fault liability, the unwarranted losses in these cases are not the result of wrongdoing in the ordinary sense. The taking itself may be reasonable or justified, as it is in Feinberg's example, and as it is in cases like *Vincent v. Lake Erie Transportation Company*.[15] Consequently, there is no wrong in the doing; were there any wrong at all, it would consist in taking what another has a legitimate right to (under specifiable circumstances) and not rendering adequate compensation for having done so.

Understood in this way, corrective justice may explain those strict liability cases that can adequately be modeled on the idea of a taking. Corrective justice might therefore explain *Vincent v. Lake Erie,* but probably not strict liability for either ultrahazardous activities or defective products. Just how much of strict liability the principle of corrective justice explains will depend on the proper analysis of what constitutes a taking – and that is no easy matter.

Again, one has to be careful to avoid misunderstanding the claim. It does not follow from what I have said that those areas of strict liability, like ultrahazardous or product liability, which do not involve takings in the ordinary sense cannot be justified or rationally explained. My point is simply that appealing to the principle of corrective justice – once it is properly understood – will not help explain them. There may be other considerations, both of morality and economics, that neatly rationalize existing strict liability law. My purpose is simply to determine which, if any, of the existing law of torts might be defensible within a certain conception of corrective justice. If it turns out, as I think it does, that only certain well-defined areas of tort law can be comprehended by a single principle, so much the better for my view, for it demonstrates theoretically what we knew pretheoretically – namely, that the law of torts is extremely complex and that it resists simple analysis.[16]

2. EPSTEIN AND FLETCHER ON CORRECTIVE JUSTICE

Considerations of corrective justice ground four claims related to liability and recovery in torts: (1) the claim to recompense of a victim of another's fault, (2) the liability of a faulty injurer who gains through his mischief, (3) the claim of a victim in strict liability for a takings-like loss and (4) the injurer's liability for a taking. In contrast, both Epstein and Fletcher appear to believe that all, or nearly all, of torts can be explained by subsumption under a theory of corrective justice. The interesting question concerns how it is that the three of us, each of whom believes that corrective justice is central to an adequate analysis of torts, reach such different conclusions.

There really is not much of a mystery, however. The key difference is that both Epstein and Fletcher share a strategy that is first to identify an element common to both strict and fault liability, then to argue that this common element is central to liability and recovery, and finally to confer normativity upon this feature of both fault and strict liability by subsuming it under a particular conception of corrective justice. Fletcher and Epstein disagree about which element is the operative shared component in strict and fault liability. For Epstein it is the fact that in both fault and strict liability the injurer causes the victim's loss;[17] for Fletcher it is the fact that the injurer harmed the victim through his nonreciprocal risk taking.[18]

Epstein's arguments are motivated in part by a desire to deemphasize the role of fault in determining both liability and recovery. The desire to eliminate the centrality of fault to torts must be understood against the background of a failed moral theory of fault liability and an increasingly accepted economic account of it. Let me explain. At one time the prevailing moral theory of torts seized upon the introduction of the fault requirement in the mid nineteenth century as a shift away from the amoral criterion of strict liability to a moral foundation for liability. Instead of imposing liability without regard to the culpability or blameworthiness of the injurer – as was the case in strict liability – fault liability injected a concern for the moral character of the injurer's conduct into the formula that was to determine the appropriateness of imposing another's loss upon him.

The concern of torts for the moral character of the injurer's conduct has always been rather minimal, however. It is the lesson of *Vaughan v. Menlove*[19] that an individual may be at fault in torts even if he is not morally at fault for his conduct, his fault being determined by his failure to comply with a standard of reasonable care whether or not he is capable of compliance. Because moral culpability is not a condition of fault in torts, previous efforts to provide a moral account of fault liability have stalled. Moreover, by the early 1970s the prevailing view had become that the only plausible, coherent account of fault in torts was an economic one: To be at fault is simply to fail to take the precautions necessary to avoid an inefficient (in cost–benefit terms) harm. In short, the standard of fault liability that moralists had hoped would anchor a moral theory of torts appeared not only to escape moral analysis but also to be firmly rooted in economic theory. Theorists intent on defending a moral account of torts were faced with a choice: Either they could provide an alternative moral account of the fault principle, or they could reexamine, even eliminate, the role of fault in a moral theory of torts. (I have pursued the former route; Epstein and Fletcher have taken the latter.)

In reducing the role of fault liability Epstein focuses his attention on the fact that wherever liability is appropriate, someone has caused another harm. The moral freight which, in the traditional view, had been carried by the fault requirement is borne, in Epstein's view, by the causal condition. Unlike a theory of torts that relies on fault, a theory that relies on the causal condition can theoretically (at least) ground all of tort law under a comprehensive moral principle, since the causal condition, unlike the fault condition, is a necessary element in both fault and strict liability.

Though Epstein has always emphasized the causal condition as central to a moral account of tort liability, his view about the principle that confers moral significance on the causal condition has undergone subtle but significant changes.

In his early essay "A Theory of Strict Liability,"[20] Epstein appears to have held the view that the best way to understand and (where possible) justify tort liability is by rooting it in a more comprehensive theory of personal responsibility. Tort liability is justly imposed provided the conditions of tort liability conform to the requirements of an agent's being responsible for his conduct. Epstein's view is that a satisfactory account of personal responsibility must be developed in terms of an analysis of causation and volition.

Running alongside the responsibility thesis in Epstein's early work is a little-developed argument which relies on corrective justice as the basis of tort liability. Prior to the incidence of harm, individuals are in a state of "equilibrium" or "balance." Liability in torts provides the mechanism for redressing imbalances caused by harmful conduct: Liability and recovery in torts reestablish the previously existing equilibria. The causal condition remains central to a just theory of liability, since the principle of corrective justice requires annulling gains and losses caused by harmful conduct.

Both the responsibility thesis and the simple corrective justice accounts of tort liability are seriously flawed. I have argued that although considerations of personal responsibility are relevant to a full theory of torts, Epstein is mistaken in thinking that the analysis of responsibility (which would be a normative theory) could be adequately developed in terms of an analysis of causation (which would involve a natural or scientific theory).[21] One can be responsible not only for what one does, but for what one fails to do as well. If a person wrongly fails to act, he may be culpable for his failure to prevent harm. Although it would be confused to say that his failure to act caused the harm, there might be sufficient reasons for ascribing the resulting harm to him as his responsibility.

The problem with the theory of corrective justice that relies on the fact that *A* caused *B* harm as sufficient both for (*prima facie*) liability and recovery (respectively) is simply that not every way in which *A* harms *B* is wrongful. Not every loss *B* suffers at *A*'s hands is a wrongful one; not every gain *A* secures at *B*'s expense is an unjust one.

Epstein's most recent view emerges from these lines of criticism. In answering the charge that *A* may have a duty to prevent harm to *B* so that both his failure to do so may be wrongful and the resulting harm to *B* his responsibility, Epstein denies that *B* has any *right* to rescue against *A*. And in answering the objection to the corrective justice theory that not every harm creates a wrongful loss, Epstein's response is that only those harms that involve invasions of property *rights* are compensable. In short, the emerging Epstein view is that corrective justice requires annulling only gains and losses owing to the invasion of an individual's rights.[22]

This account of corrective justice maintains a commitment to the causal requirement as central to a just theory of liability not because causing harm is sufficient to trigger the principle's application, but because the concept of a "right invasion" is to be spelled out in causal terms. Causation, then, is necessary to liability but no longer sufficient to justify even the *prima facie* case. For it is also necessary that the injurer's conduct invade one or more of the victim's rights.

I take up Epstein's latest view elsewhere,[23] so I shall confine these remarks to a few observations. One way of understanding this view is as follows: Epstein has simply adopted my general conception of corrective justice – that wrongful gains and losses are to be annulled. He has then chosen to analyze the difficult and troublesome notion of wrongfulness in terms of the more basic idea of a property right violation. Wrongful losses are those that result from the invasion of a property right. So what a judge in a tort case is deciding upon is whether *B* has a property right against *A* which *A* has failed adequately to respect. If the claim "*A* invaded *B*'s right" is true, then it follows on this view that *B* has a further right against *A* to recompense for whatever loss *A*'s invasion occasioned.

My view, which I shall not defend here, is that the latest Epstein account is both too strong and too weak. It is too strong because it makes the fact that the victim's loss resulted from a right invasion a necessary condition of liability, whereas in fact not every compensable loss requires that the harm for which one seeks recovery results from the invasion of a right. It is too weak because it maintains that if a person's property rights are violated it follows that he is entitled to recompense, whereas it does not follow either as a matter of logic or moral argument that every right violation triggers a right to repair.

For Fletcher, the guiding principle in determining liability and recovery is the principle of nonreciprocity of risk. A person is entitled to recover whenever he is the victim of harm caused by another's nonreciprocal risk taking; an individual is liable in torts whenever he has no excuse for having caused another harm through his nonreciprocal risk taking. An individual imposes a nonreciprocal risk on others whenever it is different in degree or kind from those risks others impose on him. Examples of nonreciprocal risk taking include engaging in ultrahazardous activities and keeping wild animals on one's property (while one's neighbors confine their affections to traditional domestic pets). The principle of nonreciprocity of risk therefore explains strict liability for harms that result from such activities. Strict liability is appropriate in those cases in which one risk taker imposes risks different from those others in general impose upon him.

There are other activities, however, in which individuals generally impose a certain level or risk on one another. Motoring is one. Liability is not imposed whenever an individual motorist harms another. In Fletcher's view that is because activities like motoring involve a level of reciprocal risk taking. For such activities, liability is not strict. In order for liability to be imposed, a motorist must negligently harm another. In other words, liability is appropriate only for risks that exceed the general level of shared risk. These nonreciprocal risks are all that is meant, in Fletcher's view, by negligence.

In fault as well as in strict liability, the key to recovery is nonreciprocity of risk. The difference between fault and strict liability is to be understood in terms of the level of risk that constitutes the "background" against which the criterion of nonreciprocity is to be applied. The fault criterion is appropriate to activities of mutual involvement, like motoring, in which there exists a shared level of background or reciprocal risk taking. A faulty or negligent risk is one that exceeds the level of common or background risk. In activities that do not by nature involve participants' imposing similar risks on one another, activities like blasting, strict liability is the appropriate criterion.[24]

Fletcher is considerably less clear about what it is that confers moral significance on nonreciprocity of risk. He cites Aristotle on corrective justice as the source of nonreciprocity of risk's claim to moral significance, but the actual argument he advances on its behalf relies on Rawls. The difference is important. Whereas Aristotle is concerned with corrective justice, Rawls is concerned with principles of distributive justice.

Citing Rawls, Fletcher argues for nonreciprocity of risk by constructing a principle of distributive justice that he takes to be an analogue of Rawls's first principle of justice. Fletcher contends that each individual is entitled to the maximum degree of security compatible with a like level of security for all. (The "analogy" is to Rawls's principle that each individual is entitled to the most extensive liberty compatible with a like liberty for all.) Fletcher goes on to define security as freedom from harm without compensation. So defined, everyone has a right not to be harmed without being compensated. If we take Fletcher at his word, it is the fact that one has suffered harm that entitles one to recompense, not the fact that one's harm results from another's nonreciprocal risk taking. The principle that is supposed to impart moral significance to the criterion of nonreciprocity of risk actually has the effect of eliminating it. With nonreciprocity as a condition of liability out of the way, Fletcher's view collapses into Epstein's – in fact, into a less defensible version of Epstein's, since Epstein is committed to the weaker proposition that causing harm is sufficient to establish the *prima facie* case for liability only.

To maintain the centrality of nonreciprocity of risk in Fletcher's theory, one must reformulate the principle that is to confer moral significance on it. This can be accomplished in a number of ways, each of which is problematic. First, one might redefine the notion of security more narrowly as freedom from exposure to nonreciprocal risk taking. An individual's right to security is then the freedom from having nonreciprocal risks imposed on him. If the right one has is to freedom from nonreciprocal risks, then the right to recover that is based upon it does not require that one actually suffer a harm. Exposure to nonreciprocal risk, whether or not it results in harm, triggers the right to recompense. The effect is to eliminate as central to liability what is currently necessary in both strict and fault liability: the requirement that one who seeks relief must establish a loss, not just the threat or risk of loss.

It will not do to redefine security even more narrowly as freedom from harm due to nonreciprocal risk, for that would trivialize the enterprise by restating the criterion of recovery as the principle that is supposed to justify it: People are entitled to recover for harms caused by nonreciprocal risk taking because there is a principle that people have such a right.

I want to develop a more sympathetic reading of Fletcher that involves ignoring his efforts to ground the principle of nonreciprocity of risk in a Rawlsian conception of distributive justice. I prefer to read Fletcher as follows: First, assume that he has adopted a conception of corrective justice like mine or Aristotle's. Then understand the criterion of nonreciprocity of risk as his way of characterizing wrongful gains and losses. In other words, ascribe to Fletcher the position that justice requires annulling wrongful gains and losses; then interpret his account of nonreciprocity of risk as a characterization of what it is that makes a gain or loss wrongful. Our views would then be much closer than they otherwise appear to be. The advantage of his would be that by identifying wrongful loss with losses that result from nonreciprocal risk taking, he can provide a criterion of wrongfulness that is applicable to all of tort law – both strict and fault liability. My conception of wrongfulness is considerably more narrow and explains only a small area of strict liability law. The problem with his view might then be that the notion of nonreciprocity of risk is too broad a characterization of wrongfulness to function within the principle of corrective justice.

To sum up: Epstein, Fletcher and I reach different conclusions regarding the extent to which the principle of corrective justice could figure in an adequate theory of liability and recovery in torts for the following reasons. Epstein advances both a simple and a more complex theory of corrective justice. According to the simple theory, corrective justice requires annulling losses caused by harmful conduct. This conception of corrective justice is broad enough to make the fact that *A* caused *B* harm sufficient to trigger its application. Since causing harm is (presumably) a necessary element in both strict and fault liability, Epstein's conception of corrective justice turns out to be sufficient to ground all of liability and recovery in torts.

According to the more complex theory of corrective justice, the fact that *A* harmed *B* and that in doing so *A* invaded a right of *B*'s are both separately necessary and jointly sufficient to justify rectification. The best way to read this amendment to the simple view is as resulting from Epstein's sensitivity to the objection that not every harm one suffers at the hands of another creates a compensable loss. To meet that objection to the simple view, Epstein restricts compensable losses to those occasioned by the invasion of a property right. Because Epstein must also believe that as a matter of fact all recoverable losses in torts involve property right invasions, he can maintain the view that the principle of corrective justice grounds most, if not all, of tort law.

Fletcher does not explicitly put forward a conception of corrective justice, but it would be fair to ascribe to him a much narrower conception of it than the one Epstein first put forth, for example, one like mine or Aristotle's which requires that a loss or gain be wrongful in order to trigger its application. Fletcher and I differ because we have different conceptions of what makes a gain or loss a wrongful one. Because Fletcher believes that nonreciprocity of risk is central to both strict and fault liability, and because nonreciprocity of risk is one way of fleshing out the notion of wrongfulness in the principle of corrective justice, Fletcher, like Epstein (but for different reasons), is led to the conclusion that corrective justice explains most of torts.

When the emerging Epstein view and the principle of reciprocity are understood in the way in which I have been suggesting, it would be fair to ascribe to both Epstein and Fletcher the same conception of the principle of corrective justice I have advanced. The differences between us could be pinpointed as involving the ways in which each of us analyzes the notion of wrongfulness. Whereas Fletcher and I may be said to adopt the same principle of corrective justice, the principle of nonreciprocity of risk constitutes a much broader conception of what makes a gain or loss compensable or wrongful than does the account I have been developing. Epstein's theory of wrongful losses as involving invasions of property rights is both broader and narrower than my

own. It is narrower in the sense that my view allows compensation for losses even where the invasion of a property right is not
established; it is broader in the sense that he believes that as a matter of fact every compensable loss in torts involves the invasion of
a property right.

Let me close this section by saying something about the difference between my view and Aristotle's. In my view, the principle
of corrective justice explains a good deal more of tort law than it
would for Aristotle. While Aristotle's conception of corrective
justice is very similar to mine, he appears to have held that a
wrongful gain or loss requires that a wrong has been done. In that
case, the principle of corrective justice could not explain any of
strict liability. In contrast, my view is that a loss or gain may
sometimes be wrongful, as in a justified taking, even if the conduct that creates it is not wrongful. Moreover, Aristotle appears
to have further limited the notion of a wrong to deliberate or intentional wrongdoing. In that case the principle of corrective justice would be unable to account for much of fault liability, in which
liability is imposed for what one unintentionally but negligently
does.

3. POSNER'S OBJECTIONS

I come finally to Posner's objections. Though Posner appears to
find much to recommend the position he ascribes to me, he finds
fault with three related components of my argument. Two of his
objections concern the limitations I place on the argument for liability from the principle of corrective justice; the third concerns
the question of whether requiring potential victims to purchase
first-party insurance coverage actually enables them to secure full
compensation in the event of injury.

One of the central points of my thesis is that, whereas the victim
of another's fault has a claim as a matter of corrective justice to
recompense, the obligation to make him whole may or may not
be as a matter of corrective justice the injurer's responsibility. Objecting to this claim, Posner asks rhetorically, "If the injurer is not
the source of the compensation, someone else, who is innocent,
must be, and why is not that innocent party a victim of the
wrongdoer's injurious conduct?"[25] Again, after ascribing to me
the view that "the victim of an accident in which the injurer was
at fault is entitled to compensation . . . the injurer is not required
as a matter of justice to be the source of compensation because he
does not gain by his wrongful act, as he would if we were speak-

ing of a theft rather than an accident," Posner argues that because
faulty injurers avoid the costs of taking adequate safety precautions, they in fact gain by their injurious conduct.[26] Because they
gain by their wrongdoing, liability is appropriately imposed upon
them.

In sum, Posner's objections are: (1) If a faulty injurer is not the
source of compensation, some "innocent" third party must be,
and this constitutes an injustice; and (2) each faulty injurer gains
from his wrongdoing in a sense sufficient to warrant imposing the
victim's loss upon him as a matter of corrective justice.

Taken together, these points constitute a serious challenge to
central features of my argument. Consider the second objection
first. Surely Posner is right in thinking that by and large faulty
injurers gain by their failing to satisfy the standard of reasonable
care. In fact, their gain, the savings from failing to exercise the
care required of others, is a wrongful one, since it is the consequence of their fault. Nevertheless, as I have already pointed out
in this chapter, this gain in savings is secured by negligent individuals whether or not their negligence results in another's loss. The
gain in savings is not triggered by the harm a particular individual's negligence causes another. In contrast to a theft, it is not a gain
that results from another's loss. Posner acknowledges the distinction but goes on to say that he fails to understand the importance
of distinguishing between wrongful gains that result from another's loss and those that do not in determining whether a person's
conduct is wrongful.[27]

Posner misses the point, however. The distinction is not relevant to determining if an individual's gain from his actions is
wrongful; I did not suggest that it was. The distinction may play
an important role, however, in determining whether the victim's
loss should be imposed upon his particular injurer. In making *that*
determination it is relevant to inquire whether the injurer's gain is
correlative of the victim's loss, for if the injurer's gain exists independently of the victim's loss, then it is not the victim's loss that
provides the moral basis for annulling the injurer's gain.

Furthermore, there are ways other than imposing the victim's
loss on him of annulling the gain a faulty injurer secures by avoiding the costs of adequate precautions; for example, by imposing a
fine for negligence. Indeed, because the gains owing to taking inadequate precautions accrue to all negligent individuals, it is in fact
more appropriate to annul the gain in savings by fines imposed on
each. In this way we can treat this category of wrongful gains
similarly by not imposing any additional burden on those partic-

ular faulty injurers who, though they do not gain further by their mischief, are unfortunate enough to cause another harm. In short, Posner is right to insist upon the fact that wrongful gain is sufficient to impose as a matter of corrective justice a victim's loss on his negligent injurer.

Posner's other objection is that if the faulty injurer is not required to compensate his victim, an innocent individual – either the victim or some third party – will be forced to do so, and that imposing the loss on an innocent individual constitutes an injustice. (Indeed, Posner goes so far as to refer to these innocent individuals as "victims" of the faulty party's conduct.) This objection goes astray from the start. It simply does not follow in a system in which faulty injurers were not made liable to victims of their mischief that innocent individuals would be coerced into doing so in their stead. Surely it is at least logically possible that everyone would agree *ex ante* to distribute accident costs without regard to fault – for example, in accordance with a deep-pocket or risk-spreading principle. In such a system, individuals other than those at fault in causing particular accidents would help to pay for the costs of accidents, though no injustice of the sort Posner imagines would exist. Alternatively, the costs of accidents as they accumulate over time could be allocated among faulty individuals – whether or not the fault of each results in harm – without any individual's being liable to any particular victim of his fault. Instead, each negligent motorist, for example, would pay according to the degree of his fault rather than according to the extent of the damage his fault causes. (After all, minor faults often occasion major damage, and serious wrongdoing may result in little, if any, damage at all.) In both counterexamples to Posner's objection, the negligent motorist is not obligated to his victim, yet the result is not that some innocent third party is unjustly held liable instead.

Both of these counterexamples imagine modes of rectifying wrongful losses other than the tort system. Perhaps Posner's objection is more telling if we limit ourselves to the tort system. Then his objection appears to be the following: In torts, the victim of another's wrongdoing has a right to recompense. This right constitutes a valid claim against someone. If the obligation to repair is not imposed upon the faulty injurer, the victim's loss will fall on some innocent party or other. According to Posner, my view is that if the faulty injurer does not gain from his conduct, he has no obligation as a matter of corrective justice to render compensation. Absent such an obligation, the victim's loss must indeed fall on someone else (i.e., an innocent person). Therefore (given the tort system as the appropriate mode of rectification), my position generates injustice.

Though more promising, this line of argument fails as well. It begins by assuming a particular mode of rectification, namely, that the desired way of annulling undeserved gains and losses is by conferring on victims a right to redress and by imposing on their injurers the corresponding obligation to repair. There is nothing in my view that is incompatible with establishing a tort system to annul wrongful losses. Given the tort system, it would be my view that the obligation to repair the victim's loss falls upon his faulty injurer. It is also my view, however, that it cannot logically be any part of the reason for imposing the duty to repair on the faulty victim in such cases that in doing so we rectify or annul his wrongful gain. He simply enjoys no gain that needs to be rectified. The duty to repair his victim's loss, in other words, may be rightly his responsibility in a tort system, though it is not a duty of corrective justice.

These objections to my view rest on an ambiguity concerning whether the tort system as a particular mode of rectification is to be assumed, or whether instead it needs some sort of justification. I take the latter approach; and because I do, I emphasize the fact that in the absence of wrongful gain the tort system will not be required by corrective justice. Some other principles must therefore ground our choice of this particular mode of rectification. Posner's last objection to my argument takes the tort system as given, and then chides me for not being able to explain the faulty injurer's liability as rooted in corrective justice, and accuses me of imposing the obligation to repair on an innocent third party. But if we take the tort system as given, my view does in fact impose the obligation to repair upon the faulty injurer; and though it imposes the obligation to repair upon the faulty injurer, it does not explain that obligation as required by the principle of corrective justice itself. Instead, whatever principle it is that leads us to adopt the tort system as the desired means of rectification (and I am not sure we should be driven in that direction) will be the principle that explains why we impose the victim's loss on his injurer. But to deny that the relevant principle is one of corrective justice is not tantamount to asserting that I cannot provide an explanation of the injurer's liability.

Given the tort system, one might object that I am making far too much of these subtle distinctions among the various ways of grounding the injurer's liability. After all, or so the argument might go, I am not denying that (under these circumstances) the faulty injurer has an obligation to make his victim whole. Provided the injurer is obligated to repair, why should it matter whether the duty derives from corrective justice, from deterrence or from a principle like Posner's? It does matter, however, for two very different reasons.

First, the concern of my work has been in part to explore the limits of the corrective justice theory of torts. The limits on the role of corrective justice in imposing liability are therefore important. Second, it is important, I think, to distinguish between the question of whether a particular individual has a duty and the question of whether justice requires that the encumbered individual, rather than someone else, discharge the duty. If the faulty injurer's duty to repair is a matter of corrective justice, that entails, in my view, that he has secured a wrongful gain. If someone else discharges the duty on his behalf, that is, compensates his victim, an injustice remains, since the injurer's gain is left unrectified. In contrast, if the faulty injurer's duty does not derive from the principle of corrective justice, that means that his victim's loss does not translate into his wrongful gain. If someone other than the faulty injurer fully compensates the victim, no corrective injustice is done, since there exists no wrongful gain that is left unrectified.

The distinction I insist on among the various sources of one's obligation to repay is relevant in determining whether principles of justice permit or prohibit various means for compensating victims. Certain debts of repayment, like the criminal's debt to society, cannot, consistent with principles of justice, be discharged by others – for example, through an insurance scheme for criminal liability. The debt of repayment one has in virtue of the wrongful gain one secures at another's expense is another debt that must as a matter of justice be discharged by the encumbered party. Failure to discharge the debt leaves a wrongful gain unrectified. On the other hand, if I am right, the debt of repayment a faulty injurer who does not gain by his mischief owes his victim is one that can, consistent with the principle of corrective justice, be discharged by another. This feature of the debt of repayment in torts is, I have argued, central to any defense of no-fault insurance schemes.[28]

9. Justice in settlements

1. INTRODUCTION

In any society relatively few disputes are brought to judges for resolution. Most are handled informally or forgotten. Fewer still are cases that go to trial. Most are settled. Compromises are reached even in cases where issues are hotly contested and where millions or billions of dollars in damages are claimed. Recently, for example, one of the most controversial lawsuits of our time, the Agent Orange case, was settled.[1] In that case, veterans of the Vietnam War, their spouses and their children alleged that a defoliant – Agent Orange – used in Southeast Asia contained dioxin and was responsible for deaths, debilities, miscarriages and birth defects suffered by members of the plaintiff class. Class members argued that the manufacturers of the defoliant, seven major chemical companies, knew that it was tainted and should be made to compensate them for their injuries, claiming billions of dollars in damages. The case received national exposure and became a rallying point for veterans, a means they hoped to use to publicize their plight and to spur Congress to come to their aid. On the eve of trial, the case was settled. The defendants, who denied liability throughout the pretrial period, agreed to pay the veterans $180 million. In turn, the plaintiff class agreed to drop the suit. Thus ended a controversy which not only presented novel legal issues and tested the ability of the federal courts to handle complex lawsuits, but concerned the well-being of a large number of veterans, their spouses and their handicapped children as well.[2]

Most lawyers, judges and law professors think it is good that so few cases are tried.[3] Many want to reduce the amount of litigation even further.[4] To this end, they have invented and incorporated into the legal system a variety of devices that encourage parties to settle. For example, the *Manual for Complex Litigation*[5] and the *Federal Rules of Civil Procedure*[6] encourage judges to hold pretrial conferences at which they are to invite the parties to come to terms. And a proposed amendment to Federal Rule of Civil Procedure 68 would require "a party who rejects a settlement offer and then receives a judgment less favorable than that offer [to] pay the [postoffer] attorney's fees of the other party."[7] The reasons most commonly given for discouraging trials are that settlements conserve resources and enable parties to resolve their differences amicably. Settlements are said to reduce attorneys' fees and court costs, free space on crowded dockets, speed relief to injured plaintiffs and avoid the need for judges to decide difficult legal questions.[8] These beliefs are so widely accepted that even legal encyclopedias – the most conservative of authorities – recite them.[9]

The consensus within the legal community notwithstanding, settlements are by no means unproblematic. Whenever cases settle, plaintiffs get less than they want and either more or less than they would receive at trial. Defendants give more than they want and, again, either more or less than they could be required to pay. Plaintiffs therefore either get more or less than they deserve, and almost never just what they deserve. Defendants pay more or less than they ought to, and almost never just what they owe. If justice requires giving each party his or her due, that is, his or her desert, then settlements almost never satisfy this principle of justice. One concern, then, is the extent to which parties can legitimately or justifiably negotiate around the requirements of justice, and the extent to which legal institutions that encourage their doing so – that is, institutions that encourage and facilitate settlements – are desirable and defensible.

Owen Fiss raises several other objections to the institutions that foster settlements and to settlements themselves. In general, he argues that settlements are inferior to judgments and, therefore, ought not to supplant them.[10] For Fiss, settlement is a "highly problematic technique for streamlining dockets," the "civil analogue of plea bargaining" and a "capitulation to the conditions of mass society [that] should be neither encouraged nor praised."[11] In this chapter, I shall introduce the terms of the debate over the morality of compromises and settlements and contribute to the literature in this important field. I shall begin by setting out some of my reasons for thinking that settlements may sometimes be morally objectionable. This discussion will familiarize readers with some of the procedures and principles settlements involve. I shall then show that a particular practice now standard in the federal courts – that of dividing settlement funds among the members of a plaintiff class – cannot be defended on the ground usually given for it, which is that justice, the principle that people ought to be compensated for wrongfully inflicted losses, entitles class members to payments.

Before moving to the arguments, however, I wish to emphasize the conditional nature of the claims that follow. My view is that trials offer advantages that are often overlooked and that cannot be procured by means of settlements, not that all disputes should be tried or that all means of resolving disputes informally should be abolished. I realize that the advantages adjudication provides come at a price, and that often the price may not be worth paying. But, as I endeavor to show in the pages that follow, settlements also exact a price, one that may sometimes be sufficiently high to call into question the advisability of institutions that encourage settlements.

2. WHY SHOULD WE WORRY ABOUT SETTLEMENTS?

Although procedures vary from jurisdiction to jurisdiction and even from courtroom to courtroom, a lawsuit is settled roughly in the following way.[12] Some time after a suit is initiated, the judge assigned to it will call the attorneys into chambers for the purpose of exploring the prospects for settlement.[13] The conference will be informal. Only the judge's sense of propriety and the attorneys' desire to play their cards close to the vest will act as constraints. The attorneys will describe the case to the judge, highlighting its strengths and weaknesses. The judge will then ask counsel for the plaintiff whether the case can be settled and, if so, at what price.[14] At this point, negotiations will begin. Usually, plaintiff's counsel will suggest a figure well above the amount the defendant is willing to pay. Opposing counsel will then make a counteroffer, and it will be up to the judge to narrow the distance between the parties.[15] Of course the judge can bridge the gap either by encouraging the defendant to come up or the plaintiff to come down, or both. The choice of strategy will depend on the judge's views of the merits of the case, the ability of the defendant to make a larger payment, the extent of the plaintiff's need and perhaps other factors. Moreover, the judge will always be conscious of the need to clear the docket. Primarily by playing on counsels' hopes and fears – for example, by suggesting that close calls may be decided for or against a particular party, by praising the quality of counsels' efforts, and by emphasizing the common interest the judge and counsel have in settling the case and moving on to other matters – the judge will broker the settlement. When the parties agree on a price, everyone will reenter the courtroom and, assuming counsel have their clients' consent, the case will be dismissed. The plaintiff's attorney will then prepare a release which states that the plaintiff agrees to renounce the suit in return for a payment from the defendant. When the release is executed and the payment made, the case will be at an end.

A settlement, then, is a contractual exchange.[16] Parties settle because they expect settlements to make them better off than they would be if they continued to litigate. A plaintiff may prefer settling at a particular price now to the risk of losing at trial or to the prospect of waiting years to recover. A defendant may want to avoid the risk of liability or to be free of the burdens of litigation. And both parties want to keep legal fees and court costs to a minimum. Since there is room for mutual gain, and since there may be strong pressure from the judge to settle, the parties negotiate an exchange in which the plaintiff gives up the right to sue and the defendant makes a payment to, or performs a service for, the plaintiff. Because aspects of the exchange extend into the future, the exchange is regulated by a contract – a release or a consent decree. A defendant may be required to make a series of payments, to reform its employment policies or to refrain from monopolistic practices. A plaintiff may want to renew a suit, for example, because alleged injuries have worsened or because newly acquired evidence strengthens the case against a defendant. Each party will therefore want a means of binding its counterpart to the settlement. Moreover, each will want to commit itself to an agreement as a means of persuading its opponent to do the same. Finally, if after compromising the lawsuit the parties disagree about their rights and duties under the settlement, a judge will look at the contract and interpret it according to standard contractual principles when resolving that and any related subsequent dispute.[17]

2.1. Justice versus efficiency

It is worth noting that settlement agreements bind parties irrespective of the legal validity of a plaintiff's claim, that is, regardless of the outcome that would have been reached or ought to have been reached at trial. Although the parties' and the judge's perceptions of the merits of a case affect the price at which it settles, the validity of an underlying claim is never adjudicated.[18] No facts are found, no conclusions of law are drawn, no judgment is entered, and no opinion is written. The agreement binds as long as the

claim it settles was disputed in good faith, "even if [the] claim . . .
is actually invalid and its invalidity is not even doubtful in legal
contemplation."[19] The law reaches this result because, in general,
contracts bind whenever one person confers a benefit on another
who knowingly receives it. And since defendants gain whenever
suits against them are withdrawn – if only because they are allowed to live in peace – settlements bind in virtually all cases.[20]

It should come as no surprise that settlements preclude adjudication. First, settlement would be a poor means of economizing
resources and preserving relationships if plaintiffs were required
to demonstrate even the *prima facie* validity of their claims at trial.
If a minihearing on the merits were held, for example, evidence
would have to be gathered, documents read, depositions taken,
witnesses prepared, arguments and strategies mapped, a hearing
held and an opinion entered. This would raise the cost of settling
a case substantially, and could further impair the parties' relationship. Moreover, the hearing would likely be a sham. Given the
parties' mutual interest in settling a case, an adversarial presentation of views could not reasonably be expected.

Secondly, there is a sense in which everyone knows that "to
settle for something means to accept less than some ideal."[21] Plaintiffs and defendants often emerge from settlement conferences with
mixed emotions. On the one hand, they may be relieved to set
aside a lawsuit and to avoid the worst possible outcomes. On the
other hand, they may be upset at being denied justice. A defendant
may think that a plaintiff's claim is groundless, that a trial would
have proved its invalidity and that the legal system enables plaintiffs to extort settlement payments by threatening defendants with
litigation costs. A plaintiff may think that victory at trial is likely,
that settlement is a bargain for the defendant and that the legal
system disadvantages plaintiffs by using costs and delays to ham-
per their pursuit of justice. In short, both sides may believe that
for all practical purposes the private and social costs of adjudicating the validity of an allegation prevent them from pursuing the
justice of the matter, and that justice is sacrificed for efficiency.[22]

Another way to put the matter is to note that in a world with
zero litigation costs, we should want the validity of all complaints
to be adjudicated. This is so because what we should really like to
see is the payment of no compensation to those whose charges are
false. Equally, we should like to see all and only defendants who
commit wrongs brought to justice. In a world where lawsuits could
be maintained without expense, we should come as close as possible to achieving these goals by trying every complaint. How-

ever, since we live in a world where costs cannot be ignored, and where litigation severely strains relationships, we tolerate a state of affairs in which most plaintiffs get more or less than they deserve, and most defendants pay more or less than they ought. In other words, we sacrifice justice for the sake of efficiency and peace.[23]

By saying that we should come as close as possible to achieving justice in a costless world by trying every complaint, we mean to suggest only that there is a high correlation between vindication at trial and the actual validity of a claim, and that the strength of that correlation would reach its highest point if trials were conducted in light of all potentially relevant information about a claim. Even then, however, we do not think that adjudication would be an infallible means of identifying valid claims. Our ability to gather and process information may be limited even in a costless world. Still, in the real world we are a long way from reaching the limits of our ability to gather and process information. Because settlements are encouraged, far less money is spent investigating issues than would be spent if more cases went to trial. Since we could better achieve justice in our world by investing more heavily in information, the policy of encouraging parties to settle, that is, of conserving resources at the expense of doing justice, stands in need of a defense.[24]

2.2. Unfair bargaining

Institutions may be defensible on balance even though they trade off justice against efficiency. It could be argued that the policy of permitting and encouraging settlements is justified because settlements make people better off (even though they sacrifice justice for efficiency) and, moreover, because people consent to them. In other words, the sacrifice of justice for efficiency may be justified on both consensual and Paretian grounds.

Not every bargain that is voluntarily entered into is beyond reproach, however. The literature on the law of contract tells us that people are forbidden to carry out some exchanges on certain terms and to enter into others entirely. It is well known, for example, that courts will invalidate contracts by which people would sell themselves into slavery or bind themselves to perform immoral acts, and that courts will release minors and incompetents from the agreements they sign. It is less well known that courts will refuse to enforce agreements by which people would waive the right to marry, to divorce, to sue for relief under the bankruptcy laws, to alienate labor freely or to require a landlord to provide an apartment that meets minimum standards of habitability.[25] Moreover, even contracts that regulate permissible transactions may be unenforceable if their terms or the circumstances in which they are negotiated are objectionable. Courts routinely ignore "boilerplate" provisions in contracts and void contracts that result from fraud, deceit or duress.

Many reasons can be given for finding fault with contracts or even for invalidating them. Of particular interest for our purposes is the possibility that the parties to an agreement may not be in a position to bargain with one another on fair terms. A landlord, for example, will often know much more than a prospective tenant about the condition of a rental unit, and the prospective tenant may not easily be able to redress the imbalance. Consumers usually have far less experience than automobile dealers and department store managers with credit agreements, and may suffer an unfair bargaining disadvantage as a result. Contracts that are negotiated against a background of unequal bargaining power are said to be "adhesive," and judges often feel bound to alter their terms or, in extreme cases, to nullify them entirely.[26]

There is reason to think that parties to settlement agreements sometimes possess unequal bargaining power. In some respects, this may not be a bad thing. An inequality that reflects the objective merits of the parties' claims may be unobjectionable. In other respects, however, disparities call into question the moral acceptability of a settlement. Although the bargain struck in any given case will reflect in part the parties' predictions of the likely outcome of a trial, it will also reflect the parties' relative abilities to finance a lawsuit, to tolerate delays, to withstand adverse publicity, to spread losses among others and to tolerate risk, and many other extralegal factors.[27] For example, a personal injury case may pit an unemployed plaintiff who faces mounting medical and personal expenses against an insurance company.[28] Or a class action alleging antitrust violations may threaten a corporation with treble damages – a potentially staggering loss even in cases where the harms suffered by individual class members are small.[29] When one party has a significant resource or threat advantage over the other, it is reasonable to question the acceptability of the terms on which they agree to settle their dispute.[30]

2.3. Agreements contrary to public policy

It would be a mistake, however, to focus attention solely on the circumstances in which bargaining takes place. In some cases the fact that a bargain is struck at all should cause concern. This is so, for example, when parties use settlements to do things they are otherwise legally forbidden to do by means of contracts. When this occurs, a settlement provides for a result that is contrary to public policy, even if it is in keeping with the parties' wishes.

To take an example with far-reaching implications for corporate behavior, consider the case of *Globus v. Law Research Service, Inc.*[31] In *Globus* a jury convicted the name defendant, Law Research, and its underwriter, Blair and Company, of securities fraud. The convictions reflected the jury's belief that the companies knew that an offering circular misrepresented the value of securities issued by Law Research. Both companies were therefore required to compensate the purchasers of the securities for losses they incurred as a result of the fraud. After paying the judgment against it, Blair and Company sued Law Research, claiming that the underwriting agreement obligated Law Research to make good any loss Blair and Company suffered as a result of the fraud. The trial judge disagreed, holding that the indemnification provision of the underwriting agreement violated public policy and was unenforceable. He argued that if Law Research reimbursed Blair and Company, the latter "would have less of an incentive to conduct a thorough investigation and to be truthful in the prospectus distributed under its name."[32] The Court of Appeals concurred, noting that "it is well established that one cannot insure himself against his own reckless, willful or criminal misconduct."[33]

Indemnification agreements are a mainstay of corporate life. Not only underwriters but also officers and directors of corporations, investment bankers, brokers and accountants try to insulate themselves from liability from material misstatements made in connection with the purchase or sale of securities.[34] Possibly all of these arrangements are contrary to public policy,[35] but they are unenforceable only when fraud is proved. That is, if a case alleging securities fraud is settled, a defendant can collect an indemnity.[36] After all, the defendant will not have been convicted of fraud. This almost certainly means that many people who commit frauds go unpunished, that many plaintiffs receive settlement payments even though their allegations would fail at trial and that the incentives in the securities market are not what they might be.

An even more surprising possibility is that indemnities can be paid even in cases where fraud is proved. In *Globus,* for example, it would not have been abnormal for Law Research and Blair and Company to settle their dispute instead of exhausting the appeals process.[37] In this event, Law Research would have paid an indemnity smaller than that requested by Blair and Company but larger than that permitted by public policy. In other words, the defendants would have achieved by settlement a result they were prevented from achieving by contract.[38] Thus, whenever a securities fraud case involving multiple defendants is settled, the public policy behind the securities laws may be impaired.[39]

In fairness, it must be said that judges can refuse to permit settlements that violate public policy, and they can invalidate existing settlements for the same reason. Nonetheless, many objectionable agreements may go unnoticed. First, judges cannot expect parties to call attention to questionable aspects of settlements. Once parties form an agreement, their interest is to get a judge to approve it, not to invite an inspection of its terms. After a settlement is approved, the parties to it will raise the issue of its acceptability only if one of them thinks it is worthwhile to begin the trial of the dispute anew. Even in this event, however, it may be difficult for a judge to decide whether a settlement is contrary to public policy, because the issues presented by the underlying dispute will not have been aired. Second, institutional pressures discourage judges from acting *sua sponte* to invalidate settlements. As the amount of civil litigation grows, judges must process cases more quickly. Consequently, they have less time to familiarize themselves with the facts and issues cases present and must rely more heavily on counsels' opinions and recommendations. As a result, judges are more likely to miss objectionable elements of settlements. Third, parties can sometimes appeal a judge's decision to refuse to dismiss a case, which means that a judge who interferes with settlements sometimes risks being reversed by a superior court.[40] Thus, although judges can take steps to ensure that settlements accord with public policy, there is no cause for optimism that they will succeed.[41]

2.4. Third-party effects

Settlements may also be of concern for reasons other than that parties may use them to do things they are forbidden to do by contracts. For example, if a complaint alleges that the process of selecting books for classroom and library use at a public school discriminates against minority students, a settlement will affect all students at the school, not merely those involved in the lawsuit. This is so because the settlement agreement will determine how limited funds are allocated among competing goals and needs. The same problem would exist in a case in which it was alleged that a welfare agency may not lawfully cancel a recipient's payments without first providing the recipient an opportunity to be heard. Money spent holding hearings for some people cannot be used to provide benefits for others. In many cases, then, settlements affect third parties, and there is reason to worry that third parties' interests may be neglected.[42]

Thus, settlements may be open to the same objections that have been leveled at contracts. Indeed, the range of possible objections is larger than we have suggested here. For example, we have said nothing about the problem of generating consent to settlements in cases that involve classes of litigants, a matter Fiss discusses at length.[43] Nor have we raised the issue of paternalism: Is it ever appropriate to prevent a person from settling a claim, against his wishes but for his own good? Although I lack space to discuss these issues in this essay, it would be silly to pretend that they do not exist. It would be equally foolish to give an unqualified endorsement to policies that discourage trials, for example, policies like that called for by the proposed amendment to Rule 68, until all of these issues are raised and settled.

2.5. Underproduction of public goods

To this point, I have argued that the practice of permitting settlements may involve a sacrifice of justice for efficiency, and that the sacrifice may not be adequately defended on the ground that settlements serve parties' interests or that parties consent to them. A rational bargain is not necessarily a voluntary one, and even when the voluntariness of a contract is not at issue, settlement agreements may permit individuals to do what they otherwise would be legally prohibited from doing, or they may have objectionable third-party effects.

I now want to ask whether the policy of encouraging settlements promotes efficiency as fully as its advocates suggest. Even if it is admitted that justice can sometimes be traded off against efficiency, it hardly follows that policies that promote neither justice nor efficiency should be adopted. And there is at least one reason to think that institutions that encourage settlements may be inefficient. The reason is that trials often produce opinions and precedents – public goods – that benefit not only the parties to a lawsuit but third parties as well. Public goods are positive externalities. Opinions and precedents are public goods because they are sources of information about the things that can and cannot lawfully be done in a society. Lawyers and others whose lives are affected by law use them when planning their affairs and when advising others. When cases settle, judges have no opportunity "to explicate and give force to the values embodied in authoritative texts such as the Constitution and statutes."[44] For this reason, settlements do not increase the amount of information or the number and variety of legal precedents available to the public, and policies that encourage settlements decrease the rate at which these public goods are produced. Had the co-defendants in *Globus* settled the claim for indemnification, for example, the opinions that case produced would never have been written.

That settlements reduce the number and variety of legal opinions has two implications. First, it means that the public subsidizes litigants. Even cases that settle consume public resources. Although litigants are required to pay court costs, taxpayers defray the fixed costs of keeping the judiciary running.[45] The net result is that forums for dispute resolution are made available to settling parties at prices that fail to reflect their full social cost.[46]

There may be nothing wrong with subsidizing people who settle civil cases, but the practice requires a defense. An argument that has been made for using tax monies to support the judiciary is that since lawsuits produce positive externalities – information in the form of opinions and precedents – the public should encourage litigation by making forums for the resolution of civil disputes available at subsidized rates.[47] One could also argue that, in fairness, taxpayers should bear part of the expense of producing public goods simply because taxpayers consume them.[48] Obviously, neither argument justifies the practice of subsidizing litigants who settle their claims. When cases settle, the public gets little or nothing in return for its investment in the court system, because in general settlements produce neither opinions nor precedents.[49] And since the vast majority of cases settle, subsidies may be better thought of as wealth transfers than as investments in public goods. It is therefore reasonable to ask why public funds are used to provide forums for the settlement of private disputes.[50] In other words, it may be reasonable to require people who settle their cases to reimburse the public for the full social cost of supporting the courts while permitting people who take their cases to trial to pay only a fraction of that cost.

The second implication of the fact that settlements produce neither opinions nor precedents is that institutions that encourage settlements may cause too few public goods to be produced.[51] For example, the proposed amendment to Rule 68 would require a plaintiff who refused a settlement offer and who then received a judgment smaller than the offer to compensate a defendant for attorney's fees incurred after the offer was made. Under the new rule a plaintiff who refused a settlement offer of $500,000 and was then awarded only $400,000 in damages would have to pay the defendant's post-offer attorney's fees. Obviously, if the amendment is adopted, plaintiffs will become more receptive to settlement offers and settlement prices will decline. Less obviously, if the new rule reduces the frequency of trials, our society's capital stock of information will be affected, because precedents will be produced at a slower rate. The need for precedents, however, will remain unchanged at best. Uncertainty will continue to exist, precedents will continue to become obsolete and disputes will continue to arise. A new increase in litigation may therefore occur. This is so because, as circumstances change and precedents obsolesce, litigants will become less sure of the outcomes of lawsuits and will file more complaints as a result. As Posner notes, "Litigation would seldom occur were there no uncertainty concerning the outcome. . . . Only if each disputant expects to do much better in the litigation than the other disputant expects him to do are the parties likely to fail to agree on [a] settlement . . . ; and uncertainty is a necessary condition of such a divergence of estimates."[52] In other words, a possible explanation of the increase in litigation that so many writers find so deplorable is that the policy of encouraging settlements results in the underproduction of opinions and precedents. If this explanation is valid, institutions that foster even higher rates of settlement will only make matters worse.

The problem with devices like the proposed amendment to Rule 68 is that they discourage litigation by increasing its cost, not by attacking its cause – controversy. Those who would raise the price of using the courts do not see that precedents help people figure out their legal rights and obligations, plan for the future and interact smoothly with others. In other words, precedents reduce transaction costs by reducing the amount of time people have to spend planning their affairs and by reducing the amount of uncertainty that sets in when unforeseen events occur. For example, precedents that clarify the meaning of words and phrases enable lawyers, contractors, testators, lessees, legislators, underwriters – everyone who uses legal language – to carry out their aims effectively and cheaply. When language is standardized, forms can replace tailor-made documents, people can spend more time performing their obligations and less time hammering them out, and disputes are both less likely to arise and more easily managed.

It is easy to forget the value of precedents as public goods. The gains they provide are spread across millions of interactions. We

are so accustomed to dealing with others without a lot of fuss that
we fail to notice the ways in which the common law smoothes out
the wrinkles in our affairs. By contrast, litigation costs are easily
remembered. They provide a rude and unwelcome shock to
everyone who brings a case to court. This is the reason so many
people think that lawsuits ought to be discouraged, and in a sense
I agree. It would be nice if people spent more time being productive and getting along and less time arguing. It is just that I think
it is more appropriate to seek this end by enabling people to avoid
disputes than by denying them access to the means of justice when
disputes arise. I am therefore skeptical of devices that would reduce the litigation rate, especially when they increase the amount
of uncertainty that attends human affairs.

One could reply to my claim that the number and variety of
precedents may fall to a suboptimal level in two ways. First, one
could argue that the relationship between uncertainty and litigation is self-equilibrating. As uncertainty grows, more lawsuits go
to trial, more precedents are produced and more information is
made available. After the tide of litigation rises, then, uncertainty
will diminish and the flow of new lawsuits will ebb. On this view,
uncertainty and litigation feed back upon each other; and as a result a suboptimal level of precedent production cannot persist for
long.[53] Second, one could argue that too much information is as
bad as too little. Beyond a certain point, information may be of
little, no or even negative value. For example, a precedent that
obscures a "bright line" rule may create uncertainty where none
previously existed, and the information value of a precedent that
simply reaffirms a well-entrenched legal doctrine may be too low
to justify the cost of its production. Thus, too much information
may be a problem, and it is wrong to assume that the production
of precedents is always a good thing.[54]

Although both of these theses have merit, neither of them fully
allays the fear that institutions that encourage settlements may cause
too few public goods to be produced. The view that uncertainty
and litigation maintain an optimal supply of information assumes
that relevant features of the legal system remain unchanged over
time. It assumes, for example, that judges who are appointed by
Republican presidents and judges who are appointed by Democratic presidents exert roughly the same amount of pressure on
parties to settle. Otherwise, changes in administration would alter
the rate at which precedents are produced. However, as the proposed amendment to Federal Rule of Civil Procedure 68 makes
abundantly clear, legal institutions may change in relevant ways

over time. The amendment to Rule 68 was offered because of concern over rising rates of litigation.[55] If the amendment is adopted, and if it discourages trials as its authors hope it will, the balance between uncertainty and litigation will be altered. Specifically, fewer precedents will be produced at a given level of uncertainty than before the amendment was proposed. On the other hand, if the amendment is rejected, or if it fails to reduce the rate of litigation,[56] the same people who proposed it can be expected to invent other means of discouraging trials. Thus, even if uncertainty and litigation feed back upon each other, the possibility remains that too few precedents will be produced.

In response to the thesis that too much information is as bad as too little, I note only that I have not claimed that too few precedents are in fact produced. I advance the weaker thesis that institutions that encourage settlements *may* cause too few public goods to be produced. Whether legal institutions currently produce a supraoptimal, optimal or suboptimal flow of information is an empirical matter we are not in a position to resolve. It is, however, a matter of importance that ought to be studied before unconditional approval is given to devices that increase the settlement rate. If, as seems plausible, the recent surge in litigation that has so alarmed scholars and judges is a result of the historical underproduction of legal precedents, we should be ill advised to place additional burdens on parties who are inclined to take their cases to trial. Alternatively, if more lawsuits are being brought because too much information is available, it may be reasonable to alter existing rules as a means of encouraging settlements. In either event, the factual issue cannot be resolved from the armchair, and until it is resolved by investigation, there is no reason to dismiss the possibility that precedents are in fact, or are likely to be, underproduced.

Moreover, even if precedents are currently overproduced, it would not necessarily follow that trials ought to be discouraged. Although trials often produce precedents, they need not and do not always do so. Cases are sometimes decided without opinion, and opinions are not always published. If trials are advantageous for reasons other than that they are sources of public goods – for example, because they achieve justice more fully than settlements do – we may want to encourage trials even though we also may want to reduce the flow of information to the public. In this event, the appropriate course of action would be to regulate the number and variety of precedents, not to encourage settlements.

3. MAKING JUST USE OF
CLASS ACTION SETTLEMENT FUNDS

In the preceding section I argued that institutions that encourage settlements may sacrifice justice to efficiency. I also argued that this trade-off may be inadequately defended on certain grounds. In this section I shall suggest that even if the trade-off can be defended, that is, even if it is reasonable to encourage settlements, considerations of justice continue to play a role in the settlement process. Once a case is settled and a gain in efficiency is achieved, questions of justice may arise in a new form.

Some lawsuits, for example, simple contract and tort cases, pit a single plaintiff against a single defendant. Others have a far more complex party structure. As we mentioned above, in the Agent Orange case a plaintiff class containing hundreds of thousands of members opposed seven corporate defendants. When a simple two-party case is settled, money flows from one person (the defendant) to another (the plaintiff). When a case involving a plaintiff class settles, something entirely different occurs: Money is paid to a group of people the vast majority of whom never appeared in court and were probably unidentified at the time of the settlement. Whenever a class action settles, then, a question of justice not presented by a simple two-party case may arise. The question is: What, in justice, should be done with the money paid to settle the case?

Judges have answered this question by saying that since justice requires that people who are injured wrongfully be compensated, settlement funds should be used to reimburse class members for their losses.[57] On the basis of this reasoning, judges have required that monies paid in settlement of class actions be divided among class members in proportion to the size and strength of their underlying claims.

We think that justice does not require this use of class action settlement funds, even if it does require that people be compensated for losses that are wrongfully inflicted upon them. Since our arguments presuppose a bit of familiarity with the law, we shall take a moment to describe class actions before setting out our reasons for thinking that the principle of compensation does not warrant the practice of dividing settlement funds among class members.

3.1. Class action procedures

The class action is a procedural device for adjudicating in a single lawsuit similar claims that are held by many different individuals.[58] For example, the residents of Bhopal, India, who were injured or killed during the 1984 disaster there have similar claims against the Union Carbide Company. Although the nature and extent of their injuries may vary enormously, each resident would have to prove that the chemical leak caused an injury and that Union Carbide should be held liable. If each resident initiated a separate lawsuit, then, the same issues of fact and law would have to be decided thousands of times, at considerable expense to both the plaintiffs and the defendants. To economize on litigation costs, Federal Rule of Civil Procedure 23 permits a single representative plaintiff to sue on behalf of all other persons who are similarly situated. Any injured Bhopal resident could hire an attorney and file a suit on behalf of all potential claimants. If the suit was successful, the costs of bringing it would be assessed against the fund recovered by the class. In other words, litigation costs would be distributed pro rata among all class members.

The preceding discussion is misleading in one respect. Although all class actions involve persons whose claims are similar, class actions may differ in a variety of respects. For example, class members are permitted to opt out of some classes but not others.[59] For our purposes, the size of members' claims is an important dimension along which class actions vary. In some cases, for example, the Bhopal case, class members would sue on their own even if the class action device were unavailable. In others, members' claims are so small that it makes sense to press them only as a group.[60] In *Phillips Petroleum Company v. Shutts,* for example, members' claims averaged only $100 per plaintiff. As Justice Rehnquist noted in the majority opinion in that case, when claims are this small "most of the plaintiffs would have no realistic day in court if a class action were not available."[61]

As the law now stands, monies defendants pay to settle class action lawsuits must be divided among class members. Ordinarily, the amount each member receives is determined by the putative size and strength of that member's claim. For example, if members A and B allege injuries worth $10,000 and $50,000, respectively, and both claims stand an equal chance of success on the merits, B would receive five times the amount A receives from a settlement fund. Likewise, if A and B assert equal claims, but A's stands only a 10 percent chance of success while B's stands a 50 percent chance of success, again B would receive five times as much as A.

The reader may now want to know how legally similar claims could stand unequal chances of success on the merits. This possibility arises because claims need not be identical to be grouped in a class – they need only raise common issues of fact and law. For example, in a class antitrust action, some claims may be older than others and may have to surmount a statute-of-limitations barrier that newer claims do not confront,[62] and some purchasers may have better records than others.[63] In a class tort action like Agent Orange, some class members' injuries may be direct and others' indirect. In that case, veterans claimed to have been harmed by being exposed to dioxin, while their spouses and children alleged that the primary exposure of veterans had adversely affected them, too. The claims of spouses and children were therefore more difficult to prove than those of the veterans themselves.[64] Thus, even though class members' claims must be similar, they may differ in size and strength.

3.2. Does the principle of compensation require that class members receive settlement payments?

What grounds are usually given for dividing settlement funds among class members in amounts that reflect the putative size and strength of their claims? Oddly, no one has offered a comprehensive defense of the practice. Even judges have advanced few arguments for it.[65] However, when judges do give reasons, they usually argue that justice requires the payment of compensation to class members. Compensation is said to be warranted either because settlements partially validate members' claims[66] or because members are stripped of the right to sue when a class action is settled.[67] In the next two subsections I shall show that neither of these arguments supports the practice of dividing settlement funds among class members in paradigm class actions. Paradigm class actions possess the following trait: Class members' claims are too small to litigate individually but are sufficiently numerous to be worth litigating as a group. We call these cases paradigm class actions because no one would bring them if the class action device were unavailable. This would entail a failure of both compensation and deterrence.[68] By contrast, cases in which members' claims are large would be brought even in the absence of Rule 23. They would be styled as individual actions, and of course they would be more expensive for plaintiffs and defendants to deal with. Thus, in what follows I shall argue against a practice that is part of the core of Rule 23.

3.2.1. Do settlements validate class members' substantive claims? The argument that settlements confer partial validity on class members' claims has never been fleshed out fully. We are therefore called upon to reinvent the rationale used by judges who take this view. A plausible argument for their position runs as follows: Defendants settle to limit their liability; that defendants face any liability at all indicates that class members' claims have some merit; indeed, if their claims wholly lacked merit, a judge would have a duty to dismiss the lawsuit; therefore, the fact of settlement indicates that plaintiffs' claims have some merit; therefore, each class member is entitled to a settlement payment by virtue of the partial validity of his or her claim.

This argument fails for three reasons. First, defendants often settle cases for reasons that have nothing to do with the validity of the charges against them. Defendants settle to limit attorneys' fees, court costs, unfavorable publicity, uncertainty in financial markets, lost managerial time, discovery costs (including invasions of privacy) and other expenses. In the Agent Orange case, for example, one observer estimated the defendants' litigation expenses at approximately $1 million per week during the period immediately prior to the settlement,[69] and another observer set their costs at $75 million overall.[70] It is also worth noting that the Agent Orange defendants managed to settle for far less than the damages claimed and consistently denied being at fault. In view of Judge Weinstein's subsequent dismissal of the suits brought by veterans who opted out of the Agent Orange class, the chemical companies' plea of innocence has considerable plausibility.[71]

Second, even if settlements confer informal recognition on class members' claims, they do not legally validate those claims.[72] As indicated above, settlements bind even in cases where plaintiffs' claims are legally invalid.[73] Moreover, settlements preclude adjudication, the ordinary means of establishing the validity of allegations. This is stated explicitly in the cases, where it is held that when approving a class settlement neither a trial court nor an appellate court has "the right or the duty to reach any ultimate conclusions on the issues of fact and law which underlie the merits of [a] dispute."[74]

The relevance of the fact that settlements preclude adjudication stems from the assumption we made above that winning at trial and having a valid claim to compensation are highly correlated. If this assumption is valid, the fact that a person wins at trial gives us good reason to think that that person is actually entitled to compensation. All we are claiming in this section is that settlements are less probative of the validity of claims than are trials. In other words, we think that the evidence for the validity of settled claims is in general less compelling than the evidence for the validity of claims that prevail at trial, not that settled claims are necessarily invalid claims. When a case settles, neither the facts surrounding an alleged injury nor the theories in light of which its wrongfulness is to be assessed are developed. For this reason, our confidence that plaintiffs who receive settlement payments deserve to be compensated should in general be weaker than our confidence that justice is served when plaintiffs who prevail at trial are awarded damages.

Third, and finally, even if it is admitted that settlements partially validate class members' claims, when cases settle judges are poorly placed to estimate the relative size and strength of those claims. This is so because judges often learn little about a case before trial. The discovery process that plaintiffs and defendants use to build their cases is ordinarily self-executing, and in complex cases disputes that arise during the course of discovery may be resolved by a special master rather than a judge. Also, different judges may preside over a case as it moves toward trial. Moreover, as I have mentioned, the adversarial presentation of views that sharpens a judge's understanding of a case is strikingly absent from the process that produces plans for dividing settlement funds among class members.[75] Given the small size of their claims, absent class members cannot be expected to show up and defend their interests. And neither class representatives nor class counsel have an incentive to oppose plans that are unfair to absent members.[76] Thus, even if settlements partially validate class members' allegations, judges' ignorance of the merits and the absence of the adversarial process all but guarantee that they will gauge the relative size and strength of members' claims inaccurately and that no one will know how far wide of the mark their guesses really are.

At this point, it might be argued that if class members were not compensated for their losses when cases settle, they would take their claims to trial, at considerably greater expense to the parties. Even if this is admitted, all that follows is that class members should receive payments sufficient to discourage them from continuing to press a lawsuit. At best, this amount is only contingently related to the size and strength of members' claims. It is also a function of the benefits members hope to gain by opting out of classes and by objecting to proposed settlements. In other words, on the assumption that class members are rational, they will settle if they are paid just a bit more than they can expect to receive if they do not settle. But in paradigm cases, refusal to settle has a negative expected value. To begin with, class members' claims are small, so that even a class member who would achieve a complete recovery by refusing to settle has a weak incentive to put up a struggle. Moreover, it is expensive to oppose a proposed settlement or plan of distribution. Members who would lodge successful objections must sift through discovered documents, read depositions, construct arguments, file briefs and appear in court. Those who would opt out carry an even heavier burden. They must exclude themselves from a class, and if they are to receive anything at all, they must file a separate lawsuit. Since the expected returns from objecting and opting out are negative, we doubt that the failure to make settlement payments to individual members on the basis of the relative size and strength of their claims would move class members to refuse to settle.

Further evidence for this view can be found in the literature on attorneys' fees. By and large, paradigm class actions are conceived and initiated by the plaintiffs' bar, not by class members themselves. This should come as no surprise. After all, class members' claims are too small for them to litigate individually. Lawyers therefore bear the primary responsibility for ferreting out instances in which small losses are wrongfully imposed on large numbers of people. That lawyers are also the main force behind the settlement of class actions may come as more of a surprise, but it is no less true. Counsel may get nothing if they lose a case at trial, and the amount they get if they win may not be sufficiently larger than the fee they receive if they settle to offset the risk of coming away empty-handed.[77] Since we do not propose to do away with attorneys' fees or to change the way they are awarded, we doubt that the failure to make settlement payments to individual class members would increase the rate at which class actions go to trial.

In response, one might say, "Look, even if settlements don't validate members' claims, and even if payments to members don't facilitate settlements, surely class members, like plaintiffs in ordinary cases, must have contractual rights to payments by virtue of settlement agreements." Strictly speaking, this claim is false. Although members have rights to payments when plans for dispensing benefits are written into agreements, often the plans are formulated after the contracts are signed and the controversy concluded. And it is no answer to this to say that the solution is to require attorneys to incorporate such plans into all settlement agreements. To propose this solution is to argue that we should insist on contractual provisions because otherwise class members will lack rights to settlement payments. This, of course, merely assumes what must be proved, namely, that settlement funds ought to be divided among class members.

Another way to approach this matter is to ask why counsel have any control whatsoever over this aspect of settlements. Although counsel are permitted (and even encouraged) to formulate utilization plans, to the best of our knowledge the only argument given for this practice is that it relieves the court of "the almost impossible task of determining the distribution of the settlement fund among the myriad claimants and can be desirable if . . . representatives have information sufficient to allow them to formulate a reasonable division."[78] Obviously, this is a weak argument. For one thing, it concedes that judges are unable to supervise settlements effectively and that the risk that arbitrary utilization plans will be chosen is great. For another, it fails to tell us why either judges or lawyers are busying themselves with this task. In response to the question "Why should settlement funds be divided among class members?" the answer "Because lawyers do a better job of apportioning payments than judges" is no answer at all.

Finally, the reader may want to respond to our argument that settlements preclude the validation of claims by pointing out that plaintiffs can legitimate their allegations simply by insisting that appropriate stipulations be written into settlement agreements. In other words, one might say that, even if class counsel should be forbidden to formulate utilization plans, they should certainly be permitted to convince defendants to concede the validity of class members' charges, and when they succeed in doing so class members ought to be compensated.

The obvious deficiency of this argument is that settlement agreements rarely stipulate the validity of plaintiff claims. On the contrary, defendants usually disclaim fault and liability. Moreover, courts typically treat settlements as "effort[s] to obtain peace rather than as admission[s] of the validity of another party's claim."[79] Thus, even if settlement agreements can validate the claims of settling classes, most often they do not, and the problem of justifying the division of funds among class members remains.

A less obvious weakness is that validation by adjudication and validation by agreement differ in a relevant respect. A claim is validated at trial when a judge applies laws to a set of facts. A claim is validated by agreement when parties bargain for this result. This difference is important because arguments for compensating people whose claims are valid undoubtedly turn on the means by which the validity of those claims is established. For example, assume that compensation may reasonably be paid to plaintiffs who win in courts that operate within the confines of significant procedural, evidentiary and precedential safeguards. Does it follow that compensation ought also to be paid to plaintiffs who win in courts where judges decide cases by tossing dice? No. Nor does it follow from the fact that we compensate plaintiffs who succeed at trial that we must also compensate those who prevail at the bargaining table. The institutional framework within which settlements are negotiated differs markedly from that which regulates class action adjudications. Arbitrary, extralegal factors like litigation costs, need and degree of risk averseness of the parties figure far more prominently in settlement negotiations than they do at trial. Thus, although class members who win at trial may deserve compensation, those whose claims are validated by agreement may not.

For the same reason, it would also be wrong to argue, as Judge Flaum did in the Folding Carton antitrust case, that because the class action device is supposed to enable people to recover on claims that are too small to litigate individually, class members ought to recover on claims that are settled.[80] The problem with this argument is that its premise is ambiguous. Is the class action device a means of enabling people to recover on all claims, or only on valid claims? If the latter, then the device will serve its intended purpose if compensation is paid to class members whose grievances are supported by convincing evidence and rationalized in terms of adequate theories of wrongfulness. Since in most cases both facts and theories are poorly developed at settlement, and since the rules of evidence are largely ignored during the pretrial discovery process, very often there is little reason to think that a settled claim is valid. Unless one is willing to contend that the purpose of the class action device is to enable people to collect on all claims, including those which are largely unproven, one cannot argue that class members are entitled to settlement payments simply by virtue of their participation in a class action.

At this point, one might argue that it is impossible to know before trial whether allegations are valid, and that it is inappropriate to penalize people who possess potentially valid claims for settling rather than pressing on with a lawsuit. This argument is very disturbing. Its force stems from the assumption that at least some members of settling classes have legally valid claims, for only if one assumes that a class would have won at trial does it make sense to say that members are penalized when they are denied settlement payments. But of course this assumption is inconsistent both with the law of settlements and with a basic principle of our legal system – the principle that plaintiffs' claims are not presumed to be valid unless proven to be.

At this point one might fall back on the weaker line that class members who can present a *prima facie* case for their claims should be permitted to share in a settlement. This argument is akin to the statement often heard from the bench that only class members who possess colorable claims against a defendant may participate in a distribution.[81] Obviously, this gambit leaves open the possibility that some class members – those who cannot make a *prima facie* showing – may reasonably be denied settlement payments. For this reason, the argument does not justify the current practice of dividing settlement funds among class members in all cases. Moreover, this move would require judges to decide questions of fact and law, tasks that, as we have seen, they are ill-placed and legally forbidden to undertake at this stage of a proceeding. And if it is suggested that a minihearing on the merits should be held prior to settlement, then one must ask how great the savings from settlements would be, whether an adversarial presentation of views could reasonably be expected and what threshold of legality would entitle plaintiffs to compensation. If, as seems likely, the savings would be small and the hearing a sham, then this suggestion ought to be rejected. Further, it is possible that any standard short of full legality would fail to justify compensation. Many plaintiffs who ultimately lose at trial successfully demonstrate the *prima facie* plausibility of their claims, for example by defeating motions for summary judgment. These plaintiffs are denied compensation nonetheless. Therefore, were a court to use a summary judgment standard at a minihearing on the merits, it would not follow that plaintiffs who prevailed would deserve to be compensated.

Thus, the argument that class members are entitled to settlement payments because settlements confer partial recognition on their grievances fails. This is not surprising. After all, the argument fails even to explain why plaintiffs who settle ordinary, non-class actions are entitled to payments. As we saw above, their entitlements stem from the contracts that end their cases. Plaintiffs can contract around their disputes and bargain for settlement payments because it is an established policy that trials are to be discouraged, not because settled claims are valid claims. It is only because judges unthinkingly went about distributing benefits to members of settling classes that they now find themselves engaging in specious arguments about the partial validity of members' claims. I think the time has come to admit that neither class members' unproved allegations nor the policy of encouraging settlements entitles them to share in class action settlement funds.

3.2.2. Should class members be compensated for the loss of the right to sue? As I have mentioned, judges sometimes argue that since each member of a class forfeits the right to sue when a case is settled, each should be compensated for the loss of that right. The intuitive appeal of this argument is apparent. It raises several related questions. First, do class members forfeit the right to sue when class actions settle? Second, if class members' rights are extinguished, do they have claims in justice to compensation? Third, if class members are entitled to compensation, how much compensation should they receive? We shall consider each of these questions in turn.

(i) Do settlements deprive class members of legal rights?

The argument that class members are entitled to settlement payments in compensation for the loss of the right to sue obviously presupposes that members in fact forfeit that right on the settlement of a class action. It is certainly true that class action settlements are binding on class members in the sense that they preclude members from continuing to sue, and from launching separate lawsuits, on settled claims. Is it therefore also true that settlements deprive class members of the right to sue? Not necessarily; it depends on how we think about the nature and scope of the relevant right. The content of the right to sue may just be that one can sue or settle. Consider what happens when an ordinary lawsuit is settled. A plaintiff files a complaint, agrees to withdraw it in return for a payment and is barred from bringing another action on the settled claim from that point on. One way to construe this series of events is to say that a plaintiff who settles forfeits the right to sue on a claim. Another, equally plausible, reading is that the plaintiff was entitled to sue or to settle, but not both. In other words, instead of saying that a plaintiff forfeits the right to sue by settling, one could say that a plaintiff exercises the right to sue by settling. By analogy, class members can be said to have fully exercised their rights to sue when a class action is settled. Their rights entitle them either to sue as a class or to settle as a class, but not both. If this description of the content of class members' rights is accurate, it is false that settlements deprive class members of the right to sue. Settlements merely deprive class members of the opportunity to sue, an opportunity they have no legal right to exploit given that their case was settled.

At this point the reader may wonder whether we have undermined the case against dividing settlement funds among class members by suggesting that the right to sue is exercised when a plaintiff settles. After all, on the construction of the right to sue we have offered, does not that right entitle class members to settlement payments in the event that the option of going to trial is foreclosed? To ask this question is to miss the point of the discussion entirely. Judges have argued that justice requires that class members be compensated because they forfeit the right to sue when a case is settled. Our reply to this argument is that class members may not forfeit a right (even if they pass up an opportunity) and that, therefore, they may not have a claim in justice to compensation. Of course, the practice of dividing settlement funds among class members endows them with rights to share in those funds. We do not mean to deny this fact. We mean to deny only the arguments given in support of the practice of dividing settlement funds among class members. One such argument is that settlement plans that confer legal rights on individual members to share in a settlement are justified as compensation for the loss of the right to sue. This is the claim with which we take issue. If the right to sue as a class is understood as the right either to sue as a class or to settle as a class, then in settling no individuals' rights have been forfeited. Instead, the right to sue, correctly understood, is fully exercised. Current compensatory schemes might nevertheless be justified, but not on the ground that they are required in order to compensate for a forfeited right. In our understanding of the right to sue, settlement and trial are both options within its ambit. Choosing to settle is to avail oneself of one option and necessarily to forgo others. But it is not to forfeit the right. It is to exercise it.

But suppose we are wrong to argue that the content of the right to sue is that class members can sue or settle. Would it then be true that class members forfeit a legal right when a case is settled? Again, not necessarily; the fact that settlements bar class members from suing on a claim can be construed as the effect of a voluntary transfer of either the right to sue itself or the authority to exercise that right, rather than as a forfeiture. As we noted above, in paradigm cases potential class members are given an opportunity to exclude themselves from a class before the class is certified. It is both plausible and consonant with the case law on class actions to say that class members voluntarily transfer the right to sue to a class, or that they voluntarily empower a class to exercise the right to sue on their behalf, by failing to opt out. Both authority to exercise legal rights and legal rights themselves are often alienable, and, as innumerable cases on contracts suggest, the conditions under which transfers of authority and legal rights occur vary widely. All we are suggesting is that a voluntary transfer of the right to sue, or of the power to exercise that right, may occur when class members fail to exclude themselves prior to class certification. If this view is correct, then class members' inability to sue on a settled claim is the natural consequence of their having voluntarily transferred their rights, or the power to exercise their rights, to a class, not an indication that members forfeit the right to sue on the settlement of a class action.[82]

(ii) Does the loss of the right to sue entitle class members to compensation?

Suppose that both the suggestion that class members' rights are exercised when a class action is settled and the suggestion that class members voluntarily transfer their rights to a class by failing to opt out are mistaken. In this event, it would be correct to say that class members forfeit the right to sue and that the occasion of their loss is the settlement of a class action. Even so, it would still be reasonable to ask whether the loss of the right to sue is the kind of loss that gives rise to a claim in justice to compensation. Corrective justice, the principle that people ought to be compensated for losses that are wrongfully inflicted upon them, does not require that compensation be paid every time anyone suffers an injury. For example, a pedestrian who picks up a loose five-dollar bill thereby deprives other passers-by of the opportunity of doing so, but the loss the others suffer is not one for which in justice they ought to be compensated. No compensation is required, because the loss is not wrongfully inflicted.

To establish that a loss is compensable as a matter of corrective justice, then, one must show that it is a wrongful loss. A loss may be wrongful if it is occasioned by a harm illegitimately imposed or wrongfully inflicted. Several reasons for counting the loss of the right to sue as compensable come to mind. The first is simply that it is wrong to extinguish an individual's legal right or, alternatively, that doing so is justifiable only if compensation is paid.

Are class members injured wrongfully when they are stripped of the rights to sue? By itself, the fact that they forfeit a legal right does not show this to be the case. There are lots of instances in which people are properly deprived of legal rights and are neither entitled to nor paid compensation for the loss. For example, plaintiffs who wage conventional lawsuits can select their attorneys, veto settlements unilaterally and decide on forums in which to sue. Class members have none of these rights. But they are not compensated for these losses, and there is no reason why they should be. The rights mentioned are procedural rights. They enable people to invoke the law on their behalf. In ordinary lawsuits these rights serve important purposes. But in class actions they are entirely out of place. Their exercise by individual class members would render class actions unmanageable and inhibit the pursuit of justice. It is therefore appropriate to deprive class members of these legal rights, and the fact that they suffer a loss does not entitle them to compensation.

Substantive legal rights may appropriately be extinguished, too. As more and more states raise the legal drinking age, people who were once free to purchase alcoholic beverages lose the right to do so. The passage of the Antipeonage Act in 1867 deprived masters of the legal right to compel indentured servants to perform labor contracts. Manufacturers who were once free to constrain trade are now denied the right to do so by the antitrust laws. Civil rights laws deprive employers of the right to discriminate in hiring and promotions. Convicted criminals are denied an extraordinary variety of legal rights. The list could be extended indefinitely.

Thus, the claim to repair requires more than just a showing that class members are deprived of a legal right; in addition, it requires a showing that it is wrong to deprive class members of the right to sue. But is it? An argument that it is wrong might run as follows. The right to sue is a property right protected by the Fifth Amendment to the Constitution. The Fifth Amendment provides that no one shall be "deprived of life, liberty, or property, without due process of law." But to deprive class members of settlement payments is to deprive them of a property right without due process. Therefore, class members who are stripped of the right to sue are injured wrongfully and have a claim in justice to compensation.

This argument is based on a confusion about due process. It is one thing to say that class members cannot be deprived of the right to sue without due process of law. It is quite another thing to say that, when their rights are extinguished, due process entitles class members to compensation. Although the former is true, the latter is clearly false. When class actions are lost at trial, all members are afforded due process of law, but none is compensated for the loss of the right to sue as an individual litigant. This outcome accords with due process because due process requires only that class members' interests be adequately represented. It does not require that class members be compensated if they lose the right to sue, notwithstanding the fact that their interests are adequately represented.

Likewise, due process does not establish that class members who lose the right to sue when a case settles are injured wrongfully. On the contrary, due process impels one toward the conclusion that there is nothing wrongful about this loss. As *Newberg on Class Actions* states, "The Supreme Court has held that a class action . . . satisfies due process . . . as long as the class has been adequately represented."[83] This requirement is often met when class actions settle. When classes are certified, it must be shown that a representative's claim is typical of the claims of a class, that class counsel are experienced, that an adversarial relationship obtains between the parties and that class members' interests are otherwise adequately protected. When class actions are settled, it must be shown that negotiations have been free of collusion, that sufficient discovery was conducted to enable counsel and the court to act intelligently, that objectors are few in number and that their complaints lack merit, and so forth. What this means is that when a class action is settled, class members receive all the process to which they are entitled. In other words, it is wrong to say that class members are denied due process of law when, on the settlement of a case, they are barred from launching another lawsuit. And since class members receive due process, the Fifth Amendment cannot be invoked to show that class members were injured wrongfully. Supporters of the practice of dividing settlement funds among class members must look elsewhere for evidence that class members have a claim in justice for compensation.

It could also be argued that class members' loss of the right to sue is wrongful because they are deprived of the right without their consent. Ordinary lawsuits cannot be settled over a plaintiff's objection, but class actions are often settled in the face of opposition from class members. It might be claimed, then, that class members are forced to forfeit the right to sue regardless of their wishes and that their loss should therefore be regarded as wrongful.

This objection raises two issues: Are class members deprived of the right to sue without their consent, and if they are, are they therefore injured wrongfully? Both questions must be answered in the negative. When considering the first question, one must keep in mind that the law takes many different things as evidence of consent. For example, partial performance of an obligation is often said to evince a contractor's consent to an exchange, even in the absence of an express agreement. In class actions, absent members are deemed to consent to representation and to all that it entails unless they opt out of a class. The law employs what one judge called the Book-of-the-Month Club technique of inferring consent from silence.[84] Thus, as far as the law is concerned, class members who fail to exclude themselves from a class agree to be bound by existing class action procedures, one of which empowers a judge to permit a settlement over class members' objections.

In response to the claim that class members consent to representation, it could be argued that actual, full-fledged consent and legally implied consent are two different things. The idea here is that although judges may imply consent right and left, a person can truly be said to consent only under certain conditions, for example, when he is fully informed of all relevant contingencies and options, is free to withhold consent, is of mature years and so forth. This line of argument is, then, that although judges say that class members consent to representation for legal purposes, for purposes of justice it is inappropriate to hold that merely by failing to respond to a notice a person can consent to representation.

Although it may make sense for some purposes to distinguish full-fledged consent from consent implied at law, I think judges are right to hold that class members who remain silent consent to representation. Class members cannot be expected to monitor paradigm class actions closely or to develop sophisticated views of the legal issues their cases present. Often their claims are too small to motivate them even to respond to notices of settlement. Moreover, if the positive consent of all class members were required before a case could settle, class actions would be unmanageable and uneconomical. In some cases, the cost of tracking down members and mailing them notices would use up a sizable portion of a settlement fund. And if a unanimity rule were in effect, class members would have an incentive to withhold their consent in an effort to garner a larger share of a settlement for themselves. Since members of paradigm classes are usually uninformed, and since class actions would be unworkable if members were required to indicate their consent affirmatively, judges are right to imply members' consent from their silence.

Even if the use of the Book-of-the-Month Club technique is inappropriate, however, one would still have to show that the failure to gain class members' actual consent before settling a case imposes a wrongful loss on them before one could claim that members are entitled to compensation. Not all nonconsensual forfeitures of rights qualify as wrongfully inflicted losses. Convicted criminals, for example, are not injured wrongfully when they are imprisoned, although they are deprived of many rights without their consent.

It is difficult to see that class members are injured wrongfully even if they are stripped of the right to sue without their consent. As the following replies to notices of the settlement reached in the "Antibiotics" case[85] indicate, members of paradigm classes usually take little or no interest in their lawsuits, hold unsophisticated views of legal issues and are unable to monitor class counsel effectively.

> Dear Mr. Clark: I have your notice that I owe you $300 for selling drugs. I have never sold any drugs, especially those you have listed; but I have sold a little whiskey once in a while.

> Dear Sir: I received this paper from you. I guess I really don't understand it, but if I have been given one of those drugs, nobody told me why. If it means what I think it does, I have not been with a man in nine years.

> Dear Sir: I received your pamphlet on drugs, which I think will be of great value to me in the future. I am unable to attend your class, however.

> Dear Mr. Attorney General: I am sorry to say this, but you have the wrong John Doe, because in 1954, I wasn't but three years old and didn't even have a name. Mother named me when I got my driver's license. Up to then, they just called me Baby Doe.[86]

Even if justice requires that people who are well informed be deprived of their legal rights only with their consent, this requirement may not apply when people are largely ignorant of relevant information. It seems especially unlikely to apply to members of paradigm class actions, because their interests will be protected even if they are deprived of the right to sue without their consent; indeed, even if a lawsuit is conducted entirely without their consent. It is, then, far from clear that a wrong is committed when a paradigm class action settles and class members are made to forfeit the right to sue without their consent.

Another reason for thinking that the loss absorbed by each class member who forfeits the right to pursue a claim further in litigation ought to be compensable is that the forfeiture frustrates legitimately held expectations. The market value of these expectations is their expected value. Thus, each class member is entitled as a matter of justice to a payment that reflects the relative expected value of his or her claim in court. There are several problems with this line of argument.

One problem is that from the fact that a claim has a particular expected value at trial it does not follow that the person who holds that claim has any expectations at all. The claim holder may know neither that the claim exists nor that under existing laws the claim stands a chance of being vindicated in court. As the responses quoted suggest, class members are usually completely in the dark as to the nature and legal merits of their claims. If this is so, then class members' expectations cannot be frustrated when they are deprived of the right to sue, because they have no expectations to begin with. In this respect, class members differ from contractors, and the arguments that are normally advanced for compensating contractors whose expectations are dashed cannot be invoked in defense of the practice of giving class members settlement payments. For example, one could not claim that class members ought to be compensated because they, like contractors, rely on their expectations to their detriment. Nor could one argue that class members ought to be compensated because they, like contractors, will act in inefficient ways if their expectations are ignored. These approaches fail because contractors, unlike class members, actually have expectations about things that may happen in the future.

Notwithstanding the fact that, in paradigm cases, most class members usually know next to nothing about their claims and the lawsuits that are brought on their behalf, in every lawsuit some class members may be well informed and may have definite expectations about the outcome of a trial. Does the disappointment these individuals experience when a suit is settled entitle them to compensation?

Before answering this question directly, it is worth noting that if a frustrated class member has a claim to compensation, justice would require only that compensation be paid to class members who are in fact disappointed. It would not require that settlement funds be divided among all class members or that members be paid amounts that reflect the putative size and strength of their claims. In other words, the disappointment some class members experience cannot justify the practice of paying all class members amounts that reflect the putative size and strength of their claims.

Moreover, disappointment occasioned by frustrated expectations is rarely a sufficient condition for recovery at law or in morals. Buyers who lose at auctions are not entitled to payments from buyers who win. Frustrated gamblers have no legal claim to compensation even though their fondest hopes may be staked on a losing spin of a roulette wheel. Even people who reasonably and rationally rely on their expectations often have no legal claim to compensation when they are disappointed. An individual who visits a post office and finds it closed cannot recover in the courts. Nor are plaintiffs who rely on a hope of winning at trial entitled to compensation when they lose. More important for our purposes, class members who find that a settlement gives them less than they expected to receive cannot sue to recover for the pain of disappointment. When a settlement and a plan for distributing benefits are approved, class members are deemed to have received everything they are legally entitled to, their personal views on the adequacy of their payments being of no moment.

In short, class members may in fact have no expectations the frustration of which could conceivably call for remedial relief. Moreover, even if they had conditional expectations, that is, expectations which they need not actually have at any time but which they would have if they attended to the relevant circumstances, it still would not follow that failure to compensate for those frustrated expectations constitutes an injustice. Not every expectation, not even every legitimate expectation, gives rise to a claim to repair in the event of its frustration. The case for compensation, then, must rely upon the relevant expectations being secured by, or being associated with, a legal right. But then it is the loss of the right, not the fact of disappointment alone, that is fundamental to the claim to compensation, and we have already shown that lines of argument resting on this fact fail to support the prevailing practice.

Is there any other reason to think that class members are injured wrongfully when, on settlement, they are stripped of the right to sue? As far as we can tell, no other reason exists. This may seem surprising, but it should not. After all, no one claims that the reason plaintiffs who settle ordinary cases are entitled to payments is that they suffer wrongful injuries when they are deprived of the right to sue. Plaintiffs who settle conventional lawsuits are permitted to bargain for and to receive payments because it is public policy to encourage settlements, and because the truth is that conventional lawsuits will settle only if plaintiffs are paid to end them. In other words, the policy of encouraging settlement payments to be made in conventional cases is rationalized on the ground of economy, not on the ground that justice entitles settling plaintiffs to compensation for the loss of the right to sue. In view of this, it is odd to think that any justification other than economy could be found for the practice of compensating class members when their claims are settled. And as we have seen, since paradigm class actions will settle even if members are paid nothing, even economy gives us no reason to divide settlement funds among all class members.

On the contrary, it we want to conserve resources, we ought to abandon the practice of paying members of paradigm classes amounts that reflect the putative size and strength of their claims. The requirement that settlement funds be distributed in this manner causes judges and lawyers, and sometimes even class members, to waste a lot of time, money and energy figuring out who is entitled to how much and implementing the plans they devise. Judges must hold fairness hearings, write opinions in support of the plans they adopt, and oversee the claim-filing and distribution processes. Lawyers must estimate the value of claims that may allege different injuries and that may confront different obstacles to proof; they must formulate plans for distributing scarce settlement dollars; they must appear in court and argue for those plans; and they must compose and distribute notices, locate absent class members and serve as administrators until all the proceeds are paid out or all claims are satisfied. If unclaimed funds remain in a settlement fund – and they usually do when class members' claims are small – litigation over the ownership of those funds may erupt, and class counsel will again be drawn into court. On occasion, even class members get into the act, though admittedly, and expectedly in view of the size of their claims, this is a rare event. In the Agent Orange case, for example, thousands of veterans attended fairness hearings and spent many hours telling Judge Weinstein how they wanted the settlement fund to be used.[87] In my view, the resources consumed during the process of designing and implementing distribution plans could often be more usefully invested in other projects.

That these resources are wasted becomes even clearer if one keeps in mind that the payments distributed are often vanishingly small. In the Hilton Hotel telephone surcharge case, future guests at Hilton and other hotels received a discount of fifty cents a day on their room rates as a result of the settlement.[88] In *Ohio Public Interest Campaign v. Fisher Foods*,[89] residents of several northeast Ohio counties received one-dollar food coupons redeemable at the rate of two every six months for five years. The settlement of *Grossman v. Playboy Clubs International, Inc.*,[90] a state court case, entitled each lifetime member of the Playboy Club in California to receive an eight-dollar chit redeemable over a two-year period.[91] The settlement approved in the Barbri antitrust case gave class members, the bulk of whom were practicing attorneys, $9 in cash, a transferrable discount coupon worth $25 for an exam preparation course, and $50 in book discounts.[92] It strikes me as odd that so much work should be done, so much expense incurred and so many arguments twisted to provide people with so little.

(iii) If class members are entitled to compensation, how much compensation are they entitled to?

To this point, I have argued against the view that class members forfeit the right to sue on the settlement of a class action, and also against the view that class members are entitled to compensation in the event that such a forfeiture occurs. In this section we shall assume that the views I have argued against are in fact correct. That is, I shall assume that class members are deprived of the right to sue when a class action settles and that this loss, because it is wrongful, gives rise to a claim in justice to compensation. We now want to ask how much compensation class members ought to receive, given that they suffer a wrongfully inflicted loss when a class action settles. In particular, we want to know whether the amount of compensation class members are entitled to varies with the putative size and strength of their claims, as the current gloss on Rule 23(e) suggests.

It should be apparent that, by itself, the principle that people must be compensated for wrongfully inflicted losses establishes only that class members must be paid something for the loss of the right to sue, not that they are entitled to payments that vary with the size and strength of their underlying claims.[93] The amount of compensation a class member is entitled to depends on the extent of the injury that person suffered when stripped of the right to sue. However much that turns out to be, there is no reason to think that it will always, or ever, be a function of the size and strength of that member's claim. This is so because the right lost is not a right to the expected value of a claim at trial.[94] The right lost is a right to sue on a substantive claim, and from the fact that one is legally entitled to sue it does not follow that one is legally entitled to a payment based on one's estimate of how one would fare at trial. One may be able to bargain for such a payment when one settles a case, but what one can get and what one is legally entitled to are two different things. Thus, even if it is admitted that class members ought to be compensated for the losses they incur when a case is settled, it does not follow that the payments

they receive ought to vary with the size and strength of their substantive claims.

In response to this it might be suggested that the expected value
of a claim at trial is an objective measure of harm occasioned by
extinguishing the right to sue. That is, one could argue that even
if class members are not legally entitled to payments that vary
with the size and strength of their claims, these variables accurately measure the harm they suffer when they are stripped of the
right to sue the defendants, and justice may be said to require that
people be compensated for the losses they endure.

It may be helpful to think about this argument in the following
way. In a world without transaction costs and in which plaintiffs
could freely alienate their claims, claims would fetch roughly their
expected value at trial. Given this, the objective loss a person suffers when deprived of the right to sue should also be measured in
terms of the expected value of a claim at trial. In other words,
since the size and strength of a claim would determine its price in
an open market, the same variables should determine the size of
the payments class members receive when their claims are settled.

Suppose we admit that, in the absence of transaction costs, the
size and strength of claims would affect their retail value. Does it
follow that we ought to use these variables as legal measures of
the loss a class member suffers when stripped of the right to sue?
No. The price at which a good trades is only one of many possible
objective measures of the injury a person suffers by being deprived
of that good. Correlatively, a rule that ties the level of compensation to the market value of a good is only one of many possible
compensation rules. For example, in tort law the cost of producing a good is often used as a measure of the loss incurred when a
good is accidentally damaged or destroyed, and the same measure
is often incorporated into appropriate damage rules. In the class
action context one could formulate an alternative measure of loss
by asking how much one would have to pay to deter class members from opting out of a class. In other words, instead of looking
to the prices claims would fetch in open markets, one could ask
what class members' real opportunity costs are. The opportunity
cost of remaining in a class is the value of the next best alternative
available to a class member. That alternative is to opt out of a
class. But since class members' claims are small, we know that it
is uneconomical for them to press their claims individually. This
means that any nonnegative payment would persuade them to remain in a lawsuit. In turn, this means that if the opportunity cost
of remaining in a class is taken as a measure of loss, members who

lose the right to sue are entitled to little or nothing by way of compensation, and the amounts they ought to receive do not vary with the size and strength of their claims.

Since at least two measures of loss and an equal number of compensation rules exist, an argument must be given for taking the expected value of a claim at trial, rather than the opportunity cost of remaining in a class action, as the legal measure of loss. Can a suitable argument be made? The rationale usually advanced for expectation-based damage rules is that they promote efficient behavior of some sort. An expectation-based contract remedy, for example, is said to encourage people to breach agreements only when it is socially wealth maximizing to do so.[95] By analogy, it may be possible to argue that paying class members the expected value of their claims at trial would encourage them to act efficiently in some respect. The two most likely applications of the argument are that payment plans that take into account the size and strength of members' claims would stimulate efficient initiation and settlement of class actions. Unfortunately, neither application seems promising. As indicated above, the incentives that influence the rates at which class actions come and go operate whether benefits are conferred on all class members or not. Lawyers' fees and the interests of named plaintiffs are the strongest inducements to both activities, and their lure is unaffected by the decision to allow each individual class member to share in a settlement fund.

Moreover, whether one can invoke efficiency at this stage of the argument turns on one's reason for thinking that people should be compensated for wrongfully inflicted losses in the first place. If one thinks that people should be compensated because a system of compensation encourages efficient investments in accident avoidance, then one may appropriately fall back on efficiency as a reason for paying members of a settling class the expected value of their claims at trial. But if one thinks that people who are harmed should be compensated because it would be unjust not to compensate them, one cannot now shift to the argument that to encourage efficient rates of class action initiation and settlement we ought to pay members of a settling class the expected value of their claims at trial. One can argue only that it would be unjust to pay class members anything less than the expected value of their claims, because the size and strength of a claim uniquely measure the loss a person suffers when deprived of the right to sue on that claim.

In arguing for the division of settlement funds among class members, judges have appealed to considerations of justice, not efficiency. Arguments from efficiency, therefore, cannot now be invoked in their defense. Of course, there is no reason to prevent the judges from changing horses in midstream, and if they were to do so, the argument for efficient initiation and settlement of class actions would be in order. Still, the new horse is unlikely to carry the argument very far. Given that the rates at which paradigm class actions are brought and settled are determined by things other than the size of class members' settlement payments, the argument from efficiency has little chance of success. Moreover, as I have indicated, in view of the amounts class members stand to receive when paradigm class actions are settled and because of the cost of distributing settlement payments, it is likely that efficiency is poorly served by the practice of dividing settlement funds among class members.

3.2.3. What ought to be done with monies paid in settlement of class actions? What I have shown in section 3 of this essay is that justice, the principle that parties should be compensated for losses that are wrongfully imposed upon them, does not require that class members receive payments when their cases are settled. Neither the existence of their underlying claims nor the fact that settlements deprive them of the right to sue drives one to the opposite conclusion. Another way to put the matter is to say that justice does not preclude the possibility that settlement funds may be used in ways that do not benefit class members at all. There may be other reasons for paying class members when cases settle,[96] but if only justice is at issue, we are free to consider all of the uses to which money can be put, and that is a large number of uses indeed.

Although we are far from the point of dismissing all other options, we think it is plausible that monies paid in settlement of class actions should escheat to the federal government. The argument for escheat is simple. If we are right that class members are not entitled to compensation, then although a class as an entity has a claim in contract (by virtue of a settlement agreement) to receive a payment from a settling defendant, neither individual class members nor class members as a group have any claim to class action settlement funds. If this is correct, then it seems reasonable to treat class action settlement funds as unclaimed funds that have been left on deposit with a federal court. Under existing federal law,[97] unclaimed funds escheat to the United States Government five years after the date of their deposit with a court.

The escheat option has a variety of attractive features, chief among which is that it economizes on the cost of devising and implementing plans for distributing benefits among class members. But I put forward escheat merely as a proposal. Justice, efficiency or some other principle entirely may weigh against the use of the escheat statute. In this essay I mean to show only that the practice of dividing settlement funds among class members in amounts that reflect the putative size and strength of their claims, as intuitively plausible as it seems, cannot be defended on the ground that class members are entitled to compensation. I have suggested an alternative way of disposing of monies paid in settlement of class actions that seems to me defensible, but I do not wish it thought that even that proposal has my unqualified endorsement.[98]

4. CONCLUSION

I have raised doubts about policies that encourage people to settle lawsuits and about the practice of dividing settlement funds among class members. In neither case have my arguments been conclusive. The arguments against settlement merely question the widely held view that settlements are always preferable to trials; they do not show that that view is wrong. The arguments against dividing settlement funds among class members demonstrate only that the practice cannot be defended on the grounds that are usually given for it, not that the practice is indefensible. But even though I have shown only that the waters are deeper than the proponents of settlements suspect, I am satisfied with the result. Litigation is, after all, the primary and often the sole means by which people can use political authority to work for justice. It is therefore appropriate that the advocates of settlement bear the burden of justification. The job of others is to see that the burden is carried, not shirked.

PART IV

Markets, morals and politics

10. Market contractarianism

1. INTRODUCTION

This essay is part of a larger project exploring the extent to which the market paradigm might usefully be employed to explain and in some instances justify nonmarket institutions.[1] The focus of the market paradigm in this essay is the relationship between the idea of a perfectly competitive market and the rationality of political association. The market theory of political association I intend to discuss I call market contractarianism.

2. MARKET CONTRACTARIANISM

There are two forms of market contractarianism. In one form, political cooperation is rational to resolve problems arising from prisoners' dilemmas, externalities, public goods, asymmetries of information, extreme inequalities in bargaining power, and other sources of market failure. In this view, political action is necessary to bridge the gap between the suboptimal equilibrium of interaction that has the payoff structure of the prisoners' dilemma and the optimal equilibrium of perfect competition. In the alternative market contractarian view, political association is necessary not only to compensate for market failure but to realize the conditions necessary for market success as well. For convenience, I shall refer to the version of market contractarianism that grounds the rationality of political association in the failure of perfect competition as the *thin* form of the theory. The version of market contractarianism that sees the need for political association in realizing the conditions of market success as well as in overcoming market failure I shall call the *thick* form of the theory.

2.1. The first and second theorems of welfare economics

The best way to illustrate the basic claims of both the thin and thick forms of market contractarianism is first to spell out the idea of perfect competition, including the conditions necessary for its realization, and then to explore ways in which various problems of interaction lead to market failure. I shall begin by specifying the conditions of perfect competition, and then I shall define three basic concepts: Pareto optimality, Pareto superiority and the core.

(D_1)   An economy is perfectly competitive if and only if:
- (C_1)   There exists a stable, private allocation of resources. (All resources are privately held and decisions about their use are reserved to those who hold them.)
- (C_2)   Force and fraud in exchange are prohibited.
- (C_3)   There are a sufficient number of buyers and sellers so that no one person's behavior can affect prices.
- (C_4)   All consumption is private. Each person's consumption enters only his utility function. This condition is alternatively expressed as "nontuism," i.e., each person is uninterested in the interests of others; or as the requirement that individuals have "selfish utility functions"; or as the requirement that no externalities exist.
- (C_5)   Transactions are costless.
- (C_6)   All utility functions are monotonic.

(D_2)   A state of affairs (S_n) is Pareto optimal provided there exists no state of affairs (S_i) Pareto superior to it.

(D_3)   A state of affairs (S_i) is Pareto superior to another state (S_n) if and only if no one prefers S_n to S_i and at least one person prefers S_i to S_n.[2]

Every distribution of resources in the core is Pareto optimal, but not every Pareto-optimal allocation is in the core. Suppose we think of exchange as a two-person game. Mutual exchange is one of the possible solutions to the game. It is also a Pareto-optimal one. Suppose, however, that the rules of the game do not prohibit theft. Then both individuals could do better by stealing than by exchanging. The exchange solution is Pareto optimal, then, but not within the core. Generally, an allocation is not within the core even if it is Pareto optimal whenever one party or a coalition (including the coalition of the whole) can do better independently, on his (or its) own.

(D₄)   An allocation of resources (S_i) is in the core if and only if it is Pareto optimal and no person or coalition (including the coalition of the whole) can do better independently.

Thus, in a game that does not prohibit theft, the exchange solution is Pareto optimal but not within the core. My interest in the core is limited to its application within markets, especially within perfectly competitive ones. Under perfect competition, theft is prohibited; all exchanges must be voluntary. If exchange is voluntary – as it is in perfect competition – the exchange solution to the game is not only optimal, but within the core.

Restricting the discussion of the core to the market introduces the notion of initial endowments. If all exchanges must be voluntary, an individual's initial endowments define how well he can do independently. He will block (veto) any exchange that does not leave him better off than he would be by acting independently. In an exchange economy where force and fraud are prohibited, the core depends on an initial set of endowments, whereas the set of Pareto-optimal allocations does not.

The relationship between optimality and the core can be illustrated by an Edgeworth box. The set of Pareto-optimal points in a two-person, two-good economy can be represented as points on the contract curve. (See Figure 10.1.)

Points *a, b, c* and *d* are the tangents of *A*'s and *B*'s indifference curves. The line connecting these four points is the contract curve. Points on the contract curve are Pareto optimal; that is, they are points to which *A* and *B* would voluntarily trade, and from which they would not voluntarily depart. The set of attainable Pareto-optimal points can be specified without first specifying an initial distribution of the commodities between *A* and *B*. Suppose, however, that the initial allocation of goods is represented by w_1. Therefore, *A* would be better off acting independently, that is, by not cooperating. Given *A*'s and *B*'s indifference curves and the initial distribution w_1, only points between *a* and *b* fall within the core.

With resources initially distributed at w_2, only points on the contract curve between *b* and *c* would fall within the core. Shifts to other Pareto-optimal allocations, for example, those between *a* and *b*, would be blocked by *B*; shifts to those between *c* and *d* would be blocked by *A*. Given any initial allocation of resources, only those Pareto-optimal points that make both *A* and *B* better off are within the core. Under conditions of perfect competition, an economy will secure a Pareto-optimal distribution of resources

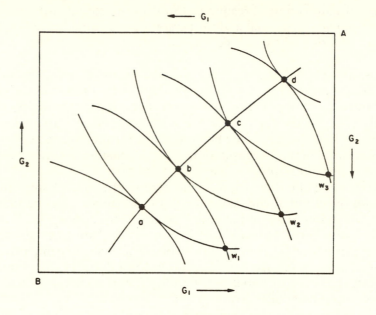

Figure 10.1. Edgeworth box

that is Pareto superior to the initial allocation. Everyone is better off than each was when trade commenced, and trade ceases when no further mutual gains can be had – when, in other words, the surplus has been exhausted. The first theorem of welfare economics is that the outcome of trade under conditions of perfect competition is in the core.[3]

Suppose *A* and *B* begin trade from a grossly unequal position. Because the optimal allocation they secure through trade is determined by the initial allocation of resources between them, inequalities that appear in the initial allocation are simply entrenched in the core solution. In general, free trade is mutually beneficial, but only within the domain of possibilities determined by the initial allocation. Left unfettered, perfectly competitive mechanisms are compatible with a great deal of inequality. Can the "distribution" problem be overcome in a way that is compatible with the competitive mechanism? The second theorem of welfare economics claims that it can.

The general problem can be illustrated graphically by representing the contract curve of the Edgeworth box as a utility possibility or Pareto frontier. (See Figure 10.2.)

The points *a, b, c, d, e, f, g, h* and *i* represent Pareto-optimal

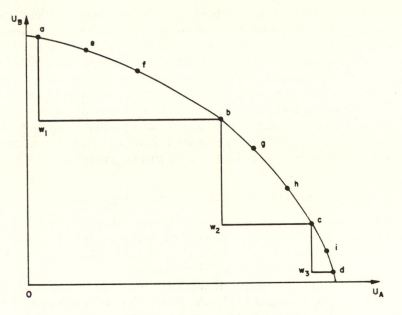

Figure 10.2. Pareto frontier

allocations of the total resource base. If trade originates at w_1, then
A and B will trade voluntarily until they reach a point on the frontier between a and b. If trade begins at w_2, A and B will eventually
reach a point on the frontier between b and c. Suppose we have
independent reasons for believing that points between c and d are
more desirable than those between a and b or those between b and
c. How can we get to a point on the frontier between c and d?

Points between c and d are Pareto optimal but, were exchange
to begin at either w_1 or w_2, not within the core. That is, points
between c and d are securable from w_1 or w_2 only by violating the
condition of individual rationality. We can, however, reach a point
between c and d either by lump–sum wealth transfer *ex post* or by
rearranging holdings between A and B *ex ante*. The net effect, in
either case, is that an area on the frontier is attainable that would
constitute a core solution to trade originating at w_3. From w_3, points
within c and d satisfy both the individual and collective rationality
conditions. The second theorem of welfare economics holds that,
for any allocation of resources on the frontier, there exists a set of
lump–sum wealth transfers that can move the economy to it.

The conjunction of the first and second theorems of welfare
economics implies that a competitive mechanism modified by a

zero-sum costless wealth transfer system can yield efficient and just allocations of resources. In claiming this, welfare economists can be understood to be asserting: (1) that in competitive markets rational self-interested behavior secures a social optimum; (2) that this social optimum can be adjusted to match any desired pattern of distribution by a zero-sum game involving costless lump-sum wealth transfers; and (3) that the optimum secured under conditions of perfect competition is the result of fully voluntary exchange. Together, the first and second theorems provide the standard normative defense of laissez-faire market economies.[4]

2.2. The two theorems and the nonintegration thesis

The first theorem of welfare economics specifies the efficiency of competitive mechanisms; the second specifies the distributive property. What do the two theorems together claim is the relationship between efficiency and distribution?

It is clear that the concepts of efficiency and wealth (or resource) distribution are distinguishable. An allocation of resources may be efficient without being distributively just, or it may be distributively just without being efficient. On the other hand, because an efficient allocation of resources is, after all, a distribution of resources, every allocation of resources will necessarily have both efficiency and distributive dimensions. It will either be efficient or not; and it will either satisfy certain distributive ideals or it will not. In an obvious and unproblematic way, then, considerations of efficiency and distribution are at once conceptually distinct and necessarily connected.

There is, however, a more interesting sense, suggested by the two theorems, in which efficiency and wealth distribution are distinguishable from one another. Suppose we decided to implement policies or institutional mechanisms sufficient to move the economy toward efficiency. Then, if the first theorem is correct, all we need to do is to put in place a perfectly competitive market mechanism. When the gains from trade are exhausted, the Pareto-optimal allocation that emerges will possess a distributive property. But no need exists to integrate a particular distributive ideal into our planning to obtain an efficient distribution of resources. To secure efficiency, we need not have taken any account of the distributive dimension of the Pareto-optimal allocation that emerges. We need only make competition, albeit perfect competition, possible. By the same token, were we to seek to satisfy a particular principle of wealth distribution – say, a principle of equity – we might follow the guidance given by the second theorem, paying no heed whatsoever to what steps must be taken for our distribution to be efficient. The resulting distribution will be either efficient or not; but promoting distributive principles, by whatever light, does not require that we integrate into the mix those policies or instrumentalities that promote efficiency. This is the simple but chief inference to be drawn from the first and second theorems about the relationship between efficiency and wealth distribution: namely, that in order to pursue either it is not necessary that we integrate considerations of the other sort. When pursuing efficiency, we may be blind to distributive inequalities; and when rectifying perceived inequities, we may be blind to considerations of efficiency. We can first secure the frontier and then move along it *ex post* until we come upon an allocation that is both efficient and just.

In spite of its obvious plausibility, the Nonintegration Thesis is at best uninformative and very likely misleading or false. It is uninformative for the following reasons. The Nonintegration Thesis is entailed by the two theorems of welfare economics that are themselves derivable only under conditions of perfect competition. But the welfare economic theory of rational political association – what I call thin market contractarianism – states that political association is in each person's rational self-interest to overcome market failure. Under conditions of market failure the two theorems do not obtain. Instead, in order to overcome market failure it is necessary to integrate considerations of efficiency and wealth distribution. Or so I shall argue.

Because the Nonintegration Thesis implies that under conditions of perfect competition concern for relative distributive shares need not be integrated into the pursuit of efficiency, it may be misleading. The Nonintegration Thesis obtains under conditions of perfect competition. If the argument I alluded to above is sound, however, it does not obtain under conditions of market failure. In the thick market contractarian view, however, perfect competition is itself a bargained solution to what I shall call premarket market failure. So market success is itself made possible by solving a market failure problem in which the thesis cannot be sustained. There is a sense, then, in which the failure of the Nonintegration Thesis is logically prior to its success.[5]

2.3. Competition and rational political association

The point of focusing on the perfectly competitive market and its theorems is that thin market contractarianism holds that political association is rational only if the conditions of perfect competition are not satisfied. Thick market contractarianism holds that political association is rational, not just to overcome market failure, but also to realize the conditions necessary for market success.

The remainder of this essay falls into two parts. The first part explores the plausibility and difficulties of both forms of market contractarianism. The general line of argument in both cases will be as follows: Markets fail (as do premarket "markets"). When they do, it is not possible to secure an efficient allocation of resources noncooperatively. The alternative is a cooperative approach to market failure. Cooperation entails both efficiency and distributive components, and they are necessarily linked in a way that undermines the Nonintegration Thesis. Agreeing to a cooperative or joint strategy requires agreement on the division of the gains obtainable by overcoming market failure – and sometimes a good deal more as well. There are, therefore, two problems in cooperative action: The first is securing agreement through rational bargaining; the second is securing compliance with bargains that are reached. Problems of both sorts will be discussed, as will their importance and the relationship between them. The second part of the essay explores the properties of a unanimity rule for collective choice. If commitment to the market paradigm entails a market contractarian approach to the rationality of a political domain, does it also entail commitment to a unanimity rule as a political decision rule within that domain?

3. MARKET AND PREMARKET FAILURE: THE CASE FOR RATIONAL POLITICAL ASSOCIATION

3.1. Market failure

In this section, we begin by assuming that a market economy is in place. In a market, rational individual utility maximizers take prices as given and seek to advance their own interests noncooperatively. If the market economy in place were a perfectly competitive one, it would give rise to a Pareto-optimal allocation of resources. If certain of the conditions of competition are not satisfied, however, consumers and producers in an economy might reach and remain stabilized at inefficient outcomes. When rational, self-interest behavior leads to a suboptimal equilibrium, that is, a nonoptimal equilibrium, market failure occurs.

The standard example of suboptimal equilibrium in the game-theoretic, not the market, setting is the single-play prisoners' di-

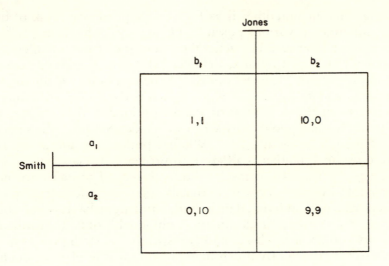

Figure 10.3. Single-play prisoners' dilemma

lemma game characterized by a payoff matrix like the one in Figure 10.3. The joint play a_1, b_1 is the dominant outcome. That is, both players do best, no matter what the other player does, by playing a_1, b_1. Smith can play either a_1 or a_2. With this in mind, Jones must decide whether to play b_1 or b_2. Suppose Smith plays a_1. If Jones plays b_1, he secures 1; had he played b_2, he would have secured 0. Now suppose Smith plays a_2. If Jones plays b_1, he secures 10; had he played b_2, he would have secured 9. No matter which play Smith makes, Jones does best by playing b_1. Similarly, Smith does best by playing a_1. If Jones plays b_1, then, by playing a_1, Smith secures 1 instead of 0; and if Jones plays b_2, by playing a_1 instead of a_2, Smith secures 10 rather than 9. Jones and Smith play a_1, b_1 because in doing so each does the best he can no matter what the other does. Both Jones and Smith would have done better, however, by playing a_2, b_2. Because it is possible to imagine a state of the world, that is, a_2, b_2, which makes both Jones and Smith better off, the state at which they find themselves, that is, a_1, b_1, is not Pareto optimal. The outcome of rational, utility-maximizing behavior in the single-play prisoners' dilemma is a stable, suboptimal equilibrium. Sometimes individual utility-maximizing behavior is self-defeating.

Every outcome of the prisoners' dilemma but a_1, b_1 is Pareto optimal. Only the move from a_1, b_1 to a_2, b_2, however, constitutes a Pareto improvement. The relevance of the Pareto relationships among the four outcomes is as follows. Suppose we think of the four outcomes as various possible starting points for future negotiations or exchanges. The general point of the prisoners' dilemma is that we shall end up at whichever cell of the game we take as the starting point for negotiations. In the cases of a_1, b_2 and a_2, b_1 and a_2, b_1 and a_2, b_2, that is because each is Pareto optimal, and it follows from the definition of Pareto optimality that no further mutually advantageous trades can be made. Suppose, however, that we begin trade at a_1, b_1. Whereas both a_1, b_2 and a_2, b_1 are Pareto optimal, neither is a Pareto improvement relative to a_1, b_1. Only a_2, b_2 promises gains for both players. The gains are not obtainable by trade, however: that is, they are not securable by noncoordinated, individual utility-maximizing behavior. For both players there exists a dominant individual utility-maximizing strategy – and it is to play a_1 and b_1 respectively. Both players may agree to play the jointly maximizing or optimizing play, a_2 and b_2, respectively, but the dominant strategy is for each to defect from the agreement he has made.[6]

This discussion illustrates two important features of the suboptimal equilibrium of the prisoners' dilemma. The first is that inefficiency results from defection or noncompliance. Where communication is possible, there is no reason for the parties not to agree to the jointly maximizing strategy; the problem is that in the single play, defection from one's agreement is the dominant, utility-maximizing strategy. Second, a_2, b_2 represents a net gain for both players from a_1, b_1. It is a mutually advantageous optimum. Moreover, these gains are not obtainable noncooperatively, in the context of the prisoners' dilemma. They can be secured instead only by compliance with a cooperative strategy. We can think of the difference between a_1, b_1 and a_2, b_2 as a "capturable cooperative surplus."

We might draw a further distinction between cooperation and the cooperative surplus. The cooperative surplus is the difference between the suboptimal equilibrium and the efficient equilibrium. In a purely voluntary exchange or market setting, the surplus cannot be captured noncooperatively. That is one way of reading the message of the prisoners' dilemma. Cooperation is one way of securing the surplus. If our options for securing the surplus are limited to forms of voluntary interaction, it is the only way. Once we allow coercive measures, or create other sorts of institutional mechanisms – for example, demand-revealing devices – it may be possible to capture the cooperative surplus in ways other than through voluntary cooperation. In short, the cooperative surplus is definable as the gains to be had by overcoming suboptimal equilibria; and cooperation is one way to secure them. In the present context, in which only voluntary measures motivated by rational self-interest are options, it is the only way of doing so.

To sum up: The prisoners' dilemma provides the most vivid illustration of the way in which rational, self-interested noncooperative behavior may lead to stable inefficiencies. In the prisoners' dilemma, inefficiency results from noncompliance or defection. It does not result from an inability among the parties to reach an agreement to cooperate. Agreement, albeit insincere agreement, is rational; compliance is not.

3.2. Market failure and the prisoners' dilemma: the problem of defection

Because the prisoners' dilemma arises in contexts in which individuals act noncooperatively as rational utility maximizers, it is not surprising that economists have analyzed standard cases of market failure in terms of the prisoners' dilemma. Markets, after all, are the paradigm of noncooperative utility-maximizing interaction. Under conditions of perfect competition, market behavior is efficient. If the conditions of perfect competition are not satisfied, rational utility maximization may lead to stable suboptimal equilibria, just as in the prisoners' dilemma. It is now fashionable to see all such market inefficiencies as resulting from prisoners' dilemma interactions. I want to illustrate this line of argument by considering two sources of market failure: public goods and externalities.

Let us first consider the problem of pure public goods. A pure public good has two salient properties: One person's consumption of the good does not reduce another person's ability to enjoy it; and once the good is produced there exists no principled or efficient way of excluding anyone from consuming it. National defense is a public good; an apple is a private good. My "consuming" national defense does not prevent others from doing so; whereas, unless one holds a bizarre view about the reincarnation capacities of apples, perhaps fashionable only in California, my eating the apple usually precludes others from doing so. These features of public goods create free-rider problems. To see this, consider the matrix of the collective goods problem given by Russell Hardin.[7] A collective good is presumed to be produced by a collection of individuals: ten individuals in Hardin's example. Suppose also that each unit of contribution yields two units of the

Collective

	Contribute	Decline
Contribute	1,1	−.8, .2
Decline	1.8, .8	0, 0

Individual

Figure 10.4. Public goods as prisoners' dilemma

public good. The payoff for each individual is equal to his benefits net his costs. Each individual must decide whether or not to contribute to the provision of the good. Hardin provides the matrix shown in Figure 10.4 to characterize the decision problem facing a potential contributor.

If ten people contribute, twenty units of the commodity are produced at a cost of ten units. There is a net benefit of ten units from the provision of the good: a gain of one unit per person. If everyone contributes, that is, both Individual and Collective, then the payoff is 1, 1. If Individual fails to contribute and the nine others do, eighteen units are produced, but because the good is nonexcludable, all ten persons can share in its benefit equally. The benefit per person is 1.8, but the cost of provision for everyone other than Individual is 1. The net gain for Individual is 1.8; for everyone else it is 0.8. If Collective contributes, Individual does best by declining.

Consider Individual's potential strategies should Collective fail to contribute. If Collective does not contribute, then by failing to contribute, Individual gains and loses nothing. But if Individual contributes when no one else does, two units of the good are produced to be distributed among ten persons, yielding a benefit of 0.2 to each. Everyone else free-rides on Individual's contribution, and his payoff is a net loss of 0.8. If Collective fails to contribute, then so should Individual; but if Collective contributes, Individual should decline to do so. In either case, Individual does best by declining to contribute to the provision of the public good.

The calculus of Individual's choice is the rational calculus for each individual member of Collective. For each person contemplating whether or not to contribute to the provision of the good, the rational strategy is to decline the contribution and to seek to be a free-rider. Under these conditions, the collective good will not be provided. The logic of rational choice in the public goods problem is the same as that in the prisoners' dilemma. Cooperation provides a gain for everyone, but the rational strategy is to defect or, in the case of public goods, to decline to contribute to their provision. In a private competitive market setting, where individual act strategies are made noncooperatively, public goods tend to be provided at suboptimal levels. The failure to optimize constitutes the classic case of market failure. The difference, then, between the stable but suboptimal equilibrium of market failure and the *ex post* optimal equilibrium of perfect competition constitutes a capturable cooperative surplus.

Public goods are positive externalities. Externalities are by-products of one person's consumption or production which affect the welfare of others. Externalities may be negative, as in pollution, or positive, as in a lighthouse. To secure an efficient level of an externality-causing activity, the social costs (or benefits) of the activity must be reflected in the private cost (benefit) calculation of the externality-causing activity. This is just another way of saying that optimality requires that marginal cost equal marginal benefit. To see this, consider the rancher–farmer example all too familiar to followers of the law and economics literature.[8] As the rancher's cattle graze on the farmer's land, each additional cow causes marginal damage to the farmer's land. If the social costs of ranching on farming are not reflected in the rancher's decisions about how many cows to raise, he will raise an inefficient number of cows (too many) and the farmer will grow too little corn.

But how are we to determine that too many cattle are being raised and too little corn farmed? What, in other words, is the basis for the claim that the externality leads to inefficiency? The objection can be met by supposing that both the ranching and farming activities are under the direction of one person, who owns both adjacent plots of land and who asks himself, "How many cows and how much corn ought I to raise?" For this reason, there is no avoiding the costs of ranching on farming or farming on ranching; he bears the benefits and costs of both. We might say, therefore, that the externalities are internalized by this example. In the case where externalities are internalized, it is obvious that the rancher will raise fewer cows than he would were he not responsible for the social costs of ranching on farming. Indeed, because he will cease raising cattle at the point at which an additional cow results in greater forgone benefits (to him) obtainable by shifting resources to farming, his decision is efficient.

There is no real difficulty in seeing that both the provision of public goods and the existence of externalities lead to suboptimal equilibria or market failure. It is also easy to see how, following Russell Hardin, the public goods problem can be analyzed in terms of the prisoners' dilemma. It is more difficult to characterize the problem of externalities in terms of their involving a surplus securable by mutually advantageous cooperative strategies. It can be done, however, and here is how.

The key is to see the externality problem as one in which both the individuals whose conduct generates negative externalities and those who are harmed by them stand to benefit by their elimination; but in the absence of adequate incentives, they are unable to do so. The best illustration of the possibility of mutually advantageous gain through the elimination of externalities is provided by the Coasean approach to externalities. Suppose that had the rancher and the farmer actually become one person – rancher–farmer – he would have raised fifty cows. The fifty-first cow, and each subsequent one, would have cost him more in forgone corn-crop profits than he would have gained by raising additional cows. This means that when there are two distinct persons, a rancher and a farmer, and the rancher raises an inefficient number of cows, say, fifty-one, the farmer loses more than the rancher gains. By negotiating to reduce the number of cows to fifty, both parties gain. To make the example concrete, suppose the fifty-first cow brings the rancher a net gain of $500 but causes the farmer $600 in crop damage. If an accord is struck between the two that provides the rancher with somewhat more than $500 and costs the farmer somewhat less than $600, both are made better off through cooperation, the net effect of which is to reduce the number of cows to an efficient number – in this case fifty. Not only are externalities inefficient; as for public goods, there are mutually advantageous gains to be had by eliminating them. Externalities exist and persist precisely when these gains are not secured; that is, when there is a failure to realize the cooperative surplus.

Externalities can create a capturable cooperative surplus. In the Coasean approach, these gains can be captured voluntarily among small numbers of individuals through bargaining. The bargain is, in effect, an exchange: a reduction in output for a negotiated price. But exchange itself has the payoff structure of the prisoners' dilemma; and in the single play, the dominant strategy is to defect. (See Figure 10.5, where Smith does best by withholding the orange from trade no matter what Jones does, and Jones does best, no matter what Smith does, by withholding the apple. It is a fair question why exchange ever proves successful. There are at least

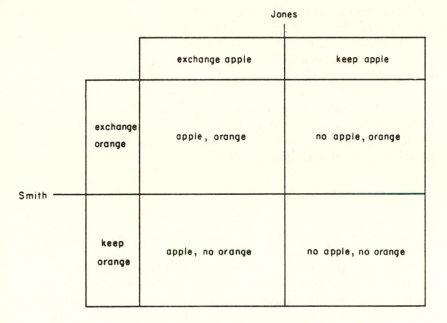

Figure 10.5. Exchange as prisoners' dilemma

two good answers: Exchange is iterated, and we have a law of contract to enforce agreement by changing the payoff for defection.)

Externalities, then, are fully analyzable in prisoners' dilemma terms. Their existence is inefficient, thus creating a potential cooperative surplus that can be distributed so as to make each person better off. Nevertheless, the agreement to distribute those gains, once secured, is subject to the problem of defection.

It is possible to recast other sources of market failure, including monopoly bargaining power, in the same way. Roughly, the idea is that consumers form coalitions to bargain with a monopolist, thereby inducing him to sell his product or service at what would be the competitive market, that is, the efficient, price. There are potential gains for both sides by overcoming the source of market failure. The gains to the consumers result from the reduction in prices to the competitive level; the gain to the monopolist comes from the "bribe" consumers pay him to reduce his prices. Monopoly bargaining power is, therefore, also analyzable in prisoners' dilemma terms. Overcoming the inefficiency created by monopolies provides potential gains for everyone. The agreement drawn between monopolists and consumers is in the interest of each, but once again defection is the dominant strategy in the single play.

In order to understand forms of market failure as prisoners' dilemmas, it is necessary to show (1) that there are mutually advantageous gains to be had by structuring the problem in order for it to have a cooperative solution and (2) that any agreement to cooperate, because of the nature of the problem involved, is subject to the problem of defection. In the previous discussion, I drew attention to the prisoners' dilemma component in market failure, thereby emphasizing the defection problem.

3.3. Market failure and the prisoners' dilemma: the problem of agreement

Focusing too closely on the prisoners' dilemma as the basic structure of market failure may mask several ways in which public goods or externality problems are more complex than the prisoners' dilemma. In the prisoners' dilemma, inefficiency results from noncompliance. There is, moreover, a specified distribution of the gains from cooperation. Agreement on the distribution of those gains is never at issue, never itself the source of failure. In contrast, in the standard market-failure case, there is no efficiency unless the parties can agree on the division of the gains from cooperation or on a mechanism of division. There is no specified division of those stakes, and failures of bargaining are as likely to result in market failure as are problems of defection or noncompliance. Moreover, if we focus entirely on the prisoners' dilemma defection dimension of market failure, then we are likely to see the rationality of political association in terms only of securing, or coercively enforcing, rational agreements to cooperate. We shall, then, underestimate the difficulty of securing such agreements and the role political institutions and mechanisms might play in encouraging agreement – say, by demand revelation mechanisms[9] – as well as the role they play in enforcing agreements once completed.

I want to emphasize in this section that problem of rational cooperation and market failure inadequately addressed by the standard prisoners' dilemma analysis of market failure, that is, the problem of rational bargaining, of agreeing on the division of the gains.

I want to make good on two modest claims. First, agreeing on the gains from cooperation is a necessary condition of securing the cooperative surplus. Secondly, the problem of securing agreement is not trivial. In the section on premarket market failures, I shall attempt to extend the argument to show that securing agreement in some contexts may be nearly impossible and, moreover, that even when agreements are reached, they may be unstable. For now, I shall be content to demonstrate the more modest claims suitable to this context: in particular, that agreement on the gains from providing public goods and eliminating externalities is necessary to achieve efficiency, but difficult to obtain.

First, let me begin by making clear the sense in which market failure integrates considerations of efficiency and distribution in precisely the way these considerations are presumed separable under the conditions of perfect competition. In the case of market failure, there are gains to be had which, *ex hypothesi,* are not capturable by purely voluntary exchange. Securing these gains requires an agreement to act jointly, to cooperate. Efficiency can be secured, then, only if the parties agree to cooperate on a joint strategy. But the rationality of each person's willingness to cooperate depends on his accepting a particular division of the gains. Efficiency, in this context, cannot be secured other than by securing agreement on the division of the cooperative surplus. No agreements on the division of the gains, no gains. No gain, no efficiency. To see this, just recall the rancher–farmer example. Reducing the number of cows to their effective level, that is, fifty, depends entirely on the rancher and farmer's agreeing on a division of the $100 surplus (the difference between the $500 gain and the $600 loss associated with the fifty-first cow). Should bargaining fail, inefficiency will remain. Bargaining, moreover (in this context at least), is over the division of the gains and nothing else.

We might put this point as follows. In the circumstances of market failure, individual utility-maximizing behavior can go only so far in securing the Pareto frontier. When the market falls short of reaching the frontier, cooperation is necessary. Market failure creates the opportunity for everyone to play a mixed bargaining game. The game is mixed because it has both redistributive and productive dimensions. Moreover, success in securing the productive goals depends on reaching an accord over the distribution of the productive or cooperative surplus. In the case of overcoming market failure by cooperation, the Nonintegration Thesis simply does not apply. Consequently, the model of perfect competition has limited force in explaining the nature and scope of rational political association.

The problem we want to focus on is the difficulty of securing agreement. We begin by assuming that a political order or state will enforce whatever agreement individuals reach to overcome

externalities. In deciding how to go about overcoming the inefficiency of externalities, everyone recognizes that externalities can
be overcome by bargaining, liability rules, taxes or subsidies.
Consider taxes first: the Pigouvian solution. Tax the offending
party at a rate equal to the marginal damage caused by the externality. This will cause the offending party to internalize his costs
and, therefore, to bring the level of his output down to the efficient level. Then, if the revenue from the tax is transferred to those
harmed by the externality, gains that were left uncaptured by virtue of the externalities are captured and distributed completely to
one side. Efficiency is obtained through taxation, not cooperation.

Efficiency could also be secured by subsidy. In that case, in order to reduce the level of its output, the offending party would be
paid a subsidy equal to the marginal gain it secured by imposing
the externality. Once again, the efficient or, loosely speaking, the
cooperative solution is achieved noncooperatively. And in the event
a tax is imposed on those who were harmed by the externality
in order to raise the revenue to subsidize externality-reducing subsidies, the gains would be distributed largely to the advantage
of those who cause the harms rather than to those who suffer
them.

Both the tax and subsidy schemes overcome the inefficiency of
externalities, but they distribute the gains from doing so in vastly
different ways. Alternatively, our rational bargainers might contemplate a Coasean approach to externalities. In that case, efficiency would be secured through voluntary exchange, but in each
case whether efficiency was in fact secured would depend on the
success of individual bargaining. That, in turn, would depend on
the costs of negotiations, the incentives to reveal information, and
the like. Each approach can theoretically overcome the inefficiency of market failure, but which approach would be rational to
adopt depends primarily on nonefficiency properties, particularly
on the ways in which various schemes distribute the cooperative
surplus.

There is another way to illustrate the problem. If individuals
choose to solve externality problems in a Coasean way, then, provided transaction costs are acceptably low, whether externalities
will be overcome depends in each case on the success of bargaining
over the cooperative surplus. On the other hand, if individuals opt
for a nonmarket or Pigouvian approach, there is no problem of
securing agreement on the division of gains in each case, because
the parties do not enter negotiations. On the other hand, there is
the problem of securing pertinent information. If the externality-

causing activity is to be taxed and the revenues are to be transferred to the harmed individuals, members of the latter group have an incentive to overstate the value of the harm they experience. If the level of the negative externality is reduced by subsidizing the offending party, he has an incentive to misrepresent the extent of its benefit.

We are imagining the following: rational bargainers seeking cooperatively to overcome a market failure caused by externalities. They have the following feasible options: taxes, subsidies, bargains, liability rules. Consider the first three. Suppose all are efficient and thus are capable of capturing the surplus. The solutions differ in how they distribute the gains. Subsidies distribute the gains favorably to those who cause harm; taxes distribute the gains favorably to those who suffer harm. Under Coasean bargaining, the cooperative gains are negotiated among individuals or small groups. These alternatives also differ with regard to other morally relevant characteristics. Both the tax and subsidy approaches capture and distribute the surplus noncooperatively, whereas the Coasean approach distributes the gains according to a principle of voluntary, negotiated settlement. So the problem is complex. Overcoming market failure requires seeking agreement over alternative mechanisms. Without introducing any artificially imposed conditions of uncertainty into the bargaining process, it is hard to imagine that individuals could come to an agreement over alternatives with such different distributional and other properties.

The problem of agreeing on the division of the gains is strictly analogous to the problem of revealing information. It is a problem that is particularly troublesome with respect to public goods. Public goods are positive externalities; their provision by anyone benefits everyone – at least potentially. Consequently, the problem of preference revelation arises. Individuals who stand to gain by the provision of a public good have an incentive to understate the benefit of the good to them whenever the good is to be paid for by some form of benefit tax.

The general issue raised by considering the bargaining problem is that market failure may result in inefficiency; there are potential states of the economy capable of making everyone better off. But obtaining those states may require bargaining, as in the Coase theorem; or they may require taxation, subsidies, liability rules; or in the case of public goods, they may require a choice among a variety of demand–revelation mechanisms. The rationality of bargaining to any of these mechanisms or institutions depends on a theory of the rational division of the surplus. In the absence of agreement on the division of the cooperative gains, inefficiency remains.

In the thin market contractarian conception of rational political association, the state is necessary to overcome market failure. In the case of the prisoners' dilemma, that just amounts to enforcing compliance. In the case of more complex market failures, political association may entail institutions for encouraging honest revelation of preferences and other inducements to successful negotiations. Failure to reach agreement on the division of the gains from trade is as likely a source of market failure as is failure to comply with agreements once reached. Focusing on the Prisoners' Dilemma aspect of market failure encourages a theory of rational political association that emphasizes the role of the state in enforcing agreements by changing the payoff structures facing each other. It does little to highlight the problem of agreement formation and, therefore, does little to motivate the rationality of those political institutions designed to reveal information and encourage negotiations; the rationality, in other words, of schemes of collective decision.

Whether or not one shares my doubts about rational bargaining, it is important to see that the entire process of choosing these political associations of a specific sort that emerge both in securing agreement and in enforcing compliance is itself analyzable as a mixed bargaining game. By a mixed game, I mean one that has both productive and redistributive elements. Rational political association is a mixed game in that it holds out the possibility of overcoming market inefficiencies – and is, in that sense, productive – provided an agreement upon the division of the surplus can be secured.

I want to close this section by emphasizing how different this view of rational political association (as both productive and redistributive) is from the standard view. Political theorists like Lester Thurow who model politics game-theoretically have claimed that political association is redistributive only. They argue that decisions pertaining to allocational efficiency are made elsewhere in a well-ordered society, and that politics is therefore a pure redistribution game. If what I have said so far makes sense, this view is fundamentally mistaken.

3.4. Premarket market failure

Thin market contractarianism finds in market failure the rationality of political association. Political institutions are rational, in that view, not only because they enforce compliance with rational bargains, but because they encourage rational bargaining as well. Rational bargaining is necessary to overcome market failure. Overcoming market failure by rational bargaining requires agreement on the division of the cooperative surplus. If agreement is not reached on the distribution of the cooperative surplus, negotiations or bargaining fails, and market failure remains.

Thick market contractarianism sees the need for rational political association not just in overcoming a variety of market failures, but in seeking to realize the conditions of perfect competition as well. Perfect competition requires the existence of a property rights scheme. The property rights scheme is itself a bargained solution to what I call a premarket market failure problem. The remainder of this section presents the argument for this claim and explores its implications.

A property rights scheme specifies the domain of an individual's rightful possessions and enforces certain claims individuals have with respect to objects in that domain. Borrowing from the law-and-economics literature, then, we might think of the property rights scheme as consisting of property rules, liability rules and inalienability rules, as well as a criminal law that serves to enforce the transaction structure specified by the property–liability–inalienability rule distinctions.[10] We might think of the property rights scheme, therefore, as involving a law of property which sets out the domain of rightful possessions – and a law of contract (property rules) which gives individuals the right to trade resources as they see fit. A property rights scheme also involves a law of tort (liability rules), which provides individuals with compensation for invasions of those rights and which, on the standard economic view, specifies the conditions under which others can invade the domain of someone's rightful possessions; and it includes a law of crimes to enforce the resource transfer mechanism just discussed.

Where markets exist, they are subject to market failure. Markets cannot exist, however, in the absence of a system of private property rights. The emergence of a system of property rights occurs, then, in what we might think of as a premarket setting. In the premarket setting, there are at least two reasons rational, self-interested parties might have for trying to create a property rights scheme: The first is to make possible the gains from trade realizable in a market economy; the other is to reduce the costs of protecting premarket holdings.

Suppose that individuals have holdings – possessions – but have no rights to these possessions that are themselves secure and enforceable. This is a premarket state of nature. In this premarket setting, individuals spend a share of their real resources in defending their holdings from attack and some of the rest of their resources in attacking others. Their decisions about how to live their lives – in effect, what strategies of defense and attack to adopt – can be represented game-theoretically. Each individual has a bundle of property or holdings (H), which he can protect at a certain cost (p) or which he can seek to increase by attacking at a certain cost (a). To simplify the subsequent argument, let us make four additional assumptions: (1) The value of all persons' holdings is equal, so that in a successful attack, one's holdings increase from H to $2H$; (2) the probability of successful attack is .5; (3) everyone is risk-neutral, and is thus concerned only with the expected payoffs of alternative strategies; and (4) the probabilities of successful attack and defense are independent. The payoff matrix for this "state-of-nature" game is represented in Figure 10.6.

Given the payoff structure described, the expected value to individuals of playing the state-of-nature game of "attack and defend" is equal to the sum of the values of each outcome discounted by the probability of its occurrence. Because the probability of successful attack (or defense) is .5, the probability of each outcome, which involves both an attack and a defense element, is equal to the product of the probabilities of each, or .25. The expected payoff of the game can be calculated as follows:

(1) Let $C = p + a$
(2) $EV = .25\,(2H - C) + .25\,(H - C) + .25\,(H - C) + .25\,(C) =$
(3) $EV = (.50H - .25C) + (.25H - .25C) + (.25H - .25C) + (.25C) =$
(4) $H - C$, where $C = p + a$ and $EV = H - (p + a)$

Suppose that there are increasing economies of scale in the joint production of protection; that is, the cost per unit of producing n units of protection is less than that of producing $n - 1$ units.[11] The marginal cost of providing protection, that is, of establishing a property rights scheme, will decrease as protection is provided for more individuals. Let us label the unit cost of protection charged to each person O.

If $(p + a) > O$ for any i, as it must be if we assume linearly increasing economies of scale, each person stands to save the difference in costs by agreeing to a property rights scheme.

There is an inefficiency in the premarket state of nature remediable by providing a property rights scheme that recognizes certain possessions as rightful and enforces claims in regard to them.

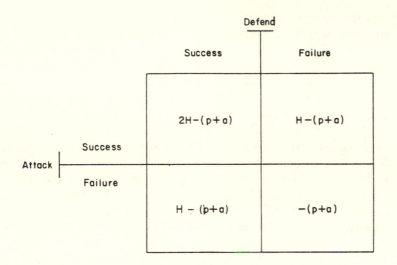

Figure 10.6. Attack and defend

Because the property rights scheme is capable of improving the lot of everyone by saving unnecessary protection costs, we might think of the premarket state as inefficient in the standard welfare-economic sense.[12]

There are gains to be had by overcoming the suboptimality of a premarket system of nonrightful holdings. The way to do so is to create a property rights scheme. As long as the costs of providing protection cooperatively are lower than the costs of doing so individually, the property rights scheme is in each person's rational self-interest. Thus, we should expect individuals to seek an agreement to provide the necessary good. On the other hand, as long as exclusion is impossible (which it probably is not) or costly and inefficient (which it probably is), each person has an incentive to be a free-rider – to enjoy the savings in protection costs made possible by a property rights scheme without incurring any of the costs of provision. Thus, we should expect problems of rational defection, as in the prisoners' dilemma, to surface. Once again, this time in the context of overcoming premarket market failure, we are faced with the two basic problems in finding a cooperative solution to a market failure situation. These are the problems of reaching agreement and of enforcing compliance.

3.4.1. Premarket market failure and the problem of compliance. In the section on market failure and thin market contractarianism, I devoted some attention to the problem of compliance. The point I emphasized was that defection, not compliance, is the rational strategy in the collective goods context. I argued from that to the need for a coercive mechanism, that is, a state, capable of enforcing agreements to cooperate. I did not ask whether the state could itself emerge as the outcome of a rational bargain. But that is precisely the question we must face now.

The property rights scheme not only makes markets, including perfectly competitive ones, possible. It also constitutes a legal order – a set of enforceable claims and the institutions to vindicate them. In asking, them, whether a property rights scheme can emerge by rational bargaining, I am asking whether the agreement to have a legal order is self-enforcing, or whether, instead, enforcing the agreement to have an enforcement mechanism itself presupposes such a mechanism.

The only agreements that demand compliance are self-enforcing; and an agreement is self-enforcing if compliance is the dominant strategy for each person or a Nash equilibrium. More typically, there are incentives to defect from whatever agreement one has made. This is especially true in public goods cases; and this is the way the prisoners' dilemma problem of defection surfaces in the public goods context, particularly in the context of trying to create a property rights scheme. Rational bargaining may be necessary, but it is not sufficient to overcome premarket failure.

The problem is that no adequate enforcement mechanism in the premarket market setting exists; the very point of the agreement is to put into place such an enforcement mechanism. In short, the problem is this: Because the agreement to create a legal order, whatever its benefits and however they are to be distributed, is not self-enforcing, it must be coercively enforceable by an already existing coercive mechanism. But the object of the agreement is to create that mechanism precisely because in the premarket state-of-nature setting no such instrumentality exists. Consequently, while it is possible to demonstrate the rationality of political association as necessary to overcome premarket market failure, it may be impossible for individuals acting as rational utility maximizers to bring about what each recognizes to be in his rational self-interest, that is, a legal order.

3.4.2. Premarket market failure and the problem of rational agreement. This point is familiar, and it is common to attribute it to Hobbes. I want to take up a part of the problem that has received a good deal less attention: securing agreement on the gains rational political cooperation makes possible. For if we assume that compliance could be enforced, there remains the question of exactly what the terms of the agreement would be. Indeed, there is a sense in which the problem of reaching an agreement and specifying its terms is more fundamental than the problem of enforcing it. Suppose we could specify the terms of an agreement to produce and divide the gains made possible by overcoming premarket market failure. Then we might argue as follows. If there is a state (or enforcement mechanism) – even if its emergence could not be reconstructed as the result of a series of rational, utility-maximizing choices – it could resolve the premarket market failure problem in a particular way, namely, according to the terms of the agreement reached by rational bargainers in the premarket market context. So, even if rational choice theory cannot provide an account of the actual emergence of political institutions, it might nevertheless provide an account of the contingent rationality of political association (that is, a theory about why the move from anarchy to polity is rational) and an account of the specific conditions or principles of rational political association (that is, a specification of the outcome of the rational bargain that takes place in order to overcome premarket market failure).

The problem of securing agreement, however, is a good deal more difficult than one might suppose, and in the remainder of this section I want to discuss some of the formidable obstacles to securing meaningful rational agreement in the premarket bargaining context. In exploring the bargaining problem, I want first to call the reader's attention to a point I made in the preceding section in connection with ordinary market failure, namely, that in overcoming market failure through cooperation it is necessary to integrate considerations of wealth distribution and efficiency. The point takes on additional significance in the context of bargaining to overcome the suboptimality of premarket interaction. The argument in the section on market failure warranted the conclusion that the Nonintegration Thesis does not apply in cases of market failure. Here a stronger influence is warranted. The issue is market success, not market failure. Market success is possible only if premarket market failure can be overcome by an agreement to a property rights scheme. Putting such a scheme into effect is a collective-action problem that requires bargaining over the division of the gains made possible by an exchange economy. Bargaining to realize the conditions minimally necessary for competitive equilibrium requires the joint pursuit of efficiency and wealth distribution. Therefore, even the conditions of perfect competition logically presuppose the necessity of integrating efficiency and wealth distribution. In short, while there is no denying that we can distinguish between efficiency and wealth distribution, that feature of competitive markets is simply irrelevant to the kinds of problems that on the market model make political association necessary. On the market model, failures to achieve efficiency may motivate political cooperation; solving the problem of inefficiency, however, requires attending to both efficiency and distributive aspects of the problem.[13]

Let us set this point aside and return to the problem of securing an agreement on the division of the gains obtainable by a property rights scheme. These gains are of two sorts: (1) the savings made possible by jointly providing protection and (2) the gains made possible by perfect competition – indeed, even the gains associated with the most rudimentary forms of exchange.

To explore how difficult reaching agreement might be, I want first to focus in some detail on the problem of capturing and dividing the savings that will emerge by taking advantage of increasing economies of scale in the joint provision of protection, thus setting aside for the moment the much more complex problem of settling on a property rights scheme to secure the gains from exchange. Any person thinking about what share of the savings it would be rational to accept should take notice of the following problem. Suppose there are no defection problems, and suppose that the property rights scheme is in place. Further, suppose that, once in place, it enforces whatever division of the savings in protection costs everyone has bargained for.[14]

Let us inspect more carefully some of the salient properties of any property rights scheme. First, because it is a public good, the property rights scheme includes everyone. Still, its membership consists of two classes: providers and consumers. All providers of the public good are consumers as well; but not all consumers are producers. First, let O be the unit cost of producing and providing protection. The tax imposed on any consumer in order to raise revenue sufficient to provide protection can be set below, equal to or above O. The providers can price-discriminate. Let B equal the total cost of providing protection. Provided the revenue raised by the tax equals B, what each person can be taxed depends on the value to him of the costs of attack and protection. No person has an incentive (individually) to leave the coalition, provided his tax share is less than the sum of protection and attack costs. For each person, provided $(H-O)>(H-C)$, the coalition remains rational. Because the tax enables price discrimination, it has a built-in redistributive capability. Moreover, though cooperation in the form of a joint effort to provide a public good (in this case, an enforceable system of property rights) is in each person's rational self-interest, it does not follow that everyone is equally advantaged – in either absolute or relative terms – by cooperation. The collective rationality of the coalition, in other words, can be maintained even if its fruits are differentially distributed. This redistributive aspect of the property rights association derives from its capacity to tax individual subscribers differentially; the only constraint on the extent of differentiation is that for each person the value (H minus the tax on him) must be greater than the cost (H minus C for him).

This argument assumes a balanced budget: that is, the total costs of provision are equal to the total revenue collected. This assumption is too strong. If we assume that the providers of the property rights system constitute a monopoly within a particular geographic sphere, then they can tax to an extent greater than that minimally necessary to provide the good. The tax on each subscriber, then, will approximate the cost to him of his second-best option, namely providing the good by himself ($p + a$) or in concert with others. Because we assume economies of scale, such a tax will lead to revenue in excess of that needed to provide the public good. The budget surplus means that, in addition to a public goods element in the state budget, there will exist a "redistributive" element as well. Moreover, redistribution will go from consumers (who are not themselves providers) to providers. Providers are, therefore, also members of what we might think of as a sharing coalition. The additional proceeds from the tax are distributed among the members of this coalition in order to reduce the costs to each of the public good. In the extreme case, the public tax revenues will offset the full costs of providing the good to members of the sharing coalition.

Each subscriber to the property rights scheme has an incentive to remain in the coalition, provided the tax he incurs is less than the cost of providing the good himself or in concert with others. The same is true for the entire subgroup of subscribers who are not themselves members of the sharing coalition. The only constraint on the absolute level of public tax is set by the costs individual subscribers would have to incur to provide the public good on their own or in concert with others outside the sharing coalition.

The maximum dollar value of the redistributive component of the public tax is the sum of the differences between the unit cost of providing the public good and the cost of each subscriber's second-best alternative. Where exit is costless, the total is the sum of the differences between the marginal costs of providing the good within the coalition and the marginal costs of providing it either alone or in concert with others.

There are obvious incentives to seek membership in the sharing coalition. It is rational for individuals to spend real resources in order to pursue a piece of the redistributive budget. (This is the essence of rent seeking.) Membership in the sharing coalition reduces the costs of the public good, and as a consequence it increases the marginal costs of providing the good for those outside the coalition. One question is whether members of the sharing coalition have an incentive to minimize the size of the coalition, that is, to keep others out. The answer is surprising.

Provided additional members do not reduce the share of the redistributive surplus going to existing members, existing members will be indifferent to increases in the size of coalition. If the total redistributive budget remains constant, the benefits of the coalition decrease to existing members. Moreover, by increasing the absolute number of individuals in the sharing coalition, there is a reduction in the number of those subscribers who must bear the additional tax burdens. The costs of increased membership, then, must fall on the ever decreasing number of those who remain outside the coalition; and their tax burden must increase to provide the public good and to maintain the shares existing members of the coalition already receive. As it happens, taxes on those outside the coalition can increase to the extent to which the cost of providing the good in their own increases. Because the group outside the sharing coalition decreases in size, and because there are economies of scale in the production of the public good, individual and group costs increase. Thus, taxes can increase accordingly. Provided the increase in taxes is sufficient to offset new memberships in the sharing coalition, membership increases, taxes increase and the overall institution remains rational. Only when the costs of exit and self-provision are less than the adjusted tax rate, thereby making exit rational, will the sharing coalition cease growing or will the entire institution become unstable.

Any individual considering whether or not to accept a particular division of the gains must be aware that whatever he agrees to is likely to be undermined by price discrimination, monopoly taxation, the existence of a redistributive element in the budget and the subsequent rent-seeking behavior it encourages. The rent-seeking dimension of the problem is especially interesting. First, rent seeking may simply nullify the substance of an agreement, by destabilizing it or by substituting distributions quite different from those originally agreed to. Moreover, because rent seeking involves the expenditure of real resources on nonproductive uses, it is inefficient.

Theoretically, the purpose of agreement is to overcome market failure and to promote efficiency in a way that secures agreement on the division of its fruits. But if the provision of the public good is by a monopoly – as it must be if the good is "the legal order" – then we have something to learn by switching our mode of analysis from "public or rational choice" to "public finance." What we have to learn is discouraging. If there is a redistributive component in the budget – and indeed, there are likely to be at least two different ones – rent seeking becomes a rational strategy. But rent seeking may render the terms of the agreement otiose, and to the extent potentially productive resources are employed to seek a larger share of the distribution budget, it is inefficient.[15]

In light of these sorts of considerations, it is hard to believe that individuals will reach a meaningful agreement, even on the savings made possible by taking advantage of economies of scale in the provision of protection. Because of what the future holds, once a property rights scheme is in place the premarket bargain is likely to be superseded almost immediately by strategic manipulation and rent-seeking behavior. Let me be blunt. The point of the bargain is to distribute and make possible gains associated with an efficient provision of protection. The net effect, however, of the dynamic mechanism and incentives put in place is to promote inefficiency and to undermine the terms of the original agreement. So even if bargaining is successful, in the sense that agreement is reached, it may turn out that the terms of the bargain are meaningless and the purpose of the bargain left unfulfilled. If a potential agreement is likely to prove unstable, then it may be irrational for the parties to bargain in the first place.

The problem of securing a meaningful agreement does not get any easier if we focus on allocating once and for all a set of property rights, thereby defining the core and the gains competition makes possible. Perfect competition results in a core solution to exchange – a Pareto-optimal allocation of resources that is Pareto superior to the origin. Making possible the conditions of perfect competition is in each person's rational self-interest. If the other conditions of perfect competition are satisfied, then the establishment of a property rights scheme will guarantee that market behavior leads to the frontier. The location on the frontier that obtains from perfect competition is entirely a function of the *ex ante* allocation of property rights. It may be rational to seek to establish a system of property to fill the gap between the suboptimality of the premarket market and the optimality of a perfectly competitive market. But the agreement to do so depends crucially on agreeing upon an *ex ante* distribution of property rights. Every mutually advantageous property rights system possesses the Pareto-optimality and Pareto-superiority properties. But which scheme any person would rationally assent to is a function not only of the fact that he can secure gains from trade he otherwise would have been unable to (or which would have been extremely costly to secure) but also of his expected share of the gains from trade under alternative property rights schemes. This may be just another way of making a point I have made elsewhere in another context: except at the margins, every Pareto improvement involves potential surplus as well as the potential for efficiency; and so, embedded in all institutional arrangements that provide the opportunity for mutual gain is a bargaining game over relative shares.[16] The fact that gains are potential does not mean they will be realized, or even that rational people will take the first steps toward their actualization by reaching an accord on their division. Let us explore the problem more deeply. We shall need to make two distinctions: one between alternative formal theories of the rational bargaining process and the other between two conceptions of the bargaining problem.

We have two options in thinking about the bargaining process over property rights. First, we might imagine this bargaining game as settling once and for all the allocation of property rights – except as those rights might be redistributed through post-bargaining contracts. We might alternatively imagine it to be an initial bargaining game settling on a distribution of property rights that will be in effect over a specified period of time, but subject to continual renegotiation. According to the second option, bargaining over property rights is subject to continual renegotiation; in the first, bargaining is a one-shot deal.

Next, it is possible to characterize this and other bargains formally. There are currently any number of axiomatic treatments of rational bargaining. The best known is the extended Nash–Zeuthen theory. Its most serious challenger is the Kalai–Smorodinski–Gauthier account. Nash bargaining is bargaining from threat advantage; the unique rational solution to any bargaining problem is that distribution of the gains that produces the greatest product of the utilities of the parties to the bargain. According to Gauthier, the unique solution to any bargaining game is given by the principle of minimax relative concession.[17] There is no need to explore the details of the various theories, for two reasons. First, even though axiomatic theories of bargaining each claim to provide a unique result for the bargaining problem, there is, in fact, no one theory of rational bargaining. In each case, only one principle of bargaining satisfies the axioms; but even slight changes in the axiomatic characterization of the problem yield a different "unique" solution to the problem. This result is important because it means we cannot legitimately impose a formal structure on the bargaining problem and thereby generate a unique solution to it.[18]

Second, the problems of rational bargaining that I want to focus on, for example strategic behavior and rent seeking, plague any dynamic bargaining process. Even if there were a unique solution to the bargaining problem, the problems I draw attention to would surface and render agreements inefficient or unstable. Because it does not matter which formal model we use, I shall treat the bargaining process as proceeding along the lines suggested by the more widely known Nash–Zeuthen account.

Consider, in Nashian terms, the one-shot-deal conception of the bargaining problem. In extended Nashian bargaining, a noncooperative game is embedded within the cooperative or bargaining game. The noncooperative game establishes the parties' relative threat advantages. Bargaining commences from this point of noncooperation, and in the event negotiations fail, this is the point to which the parties return. The allocation of the cooperative surplus is in this model a function of the relative strength of the parties' threat advantages. People in weaker threat positions run the risk of entering an agreement that although it makes them better off relative to the status quo, does not make them as well off as others who enjoy a greater threat advantage. A person in a weaker position, however, is not without options. He can hold out. Gaining his assent to the bargain might be worth something to those of stronger threat advantages, who might themselves have more to gain by securing agreement. The longer the delay, the more real resources are wasted and the greater the risk of a decrease in the gains securable by cooperation. In short, in the hopes of inducing those possessing greater threat advantages to give up some of their advantage, the least advantaged might hold out. By the same token, those with stronger threat values can seek to exploit their relative strength. Recognizing that the least well-off are particularly vulnerable, the stronger may hold out, hoping to squeeze even more of the surplus. Both sides have incentives to hold out.

But hold-out behavior can lead to inefficiency. No agreement may be reached. This is especially true in large groups. Indeed, in large groups the problem of misrepresentation or strategic behavior is more formidable. Even if agreement is eventually reached, the expenditure of resources to improve one's relative position through hold-out behavior or rent seeking may mean that the outcome of the agreement is not efficient.[19]

Moreover, as Ned McClennen has pointed out to me, agreement that results from the physics of threat advantage bargaining is not underwritten by genuine consensus. So, even if Nashian bargaining succeeds in producing an agreement to create a property rights scheme, those who are relatively disadvantaged by the agreement will seek to destabilize it by engaging in post-contractual rent-seeking behavior. As the discussion of the properties of property rights schemes illustrates, there are ample opportunities for rent seeking. In Nashian bargaining, hold-out behavior may make agreement impossible, or if successful, inefficient. On the other hand, since Nashian bargaining is not based on genuine consensus, even if it is successful the agreement may not endure. Moreover, whatever agreement is reached, those who feel they are exploited will seek to destabilize the agreement, and there is ample opportunity for them to do so. This problem is not significantly met by other theories of bargaining – even those like Gauthier's, in which rational bargaining secures outcomes that have the appearance of being fair or impartial. The reason is that rent-seeking behavior is motivated by self-interest and will occur regardless of the perceived fairness of the terms parties bargain to.[20]

The Buchanan model of continual renegotiation is problematic as well. The motivation for it seems clear and well founded. Individuals may be unsatisfied with the deal they originally make, and if there are no opportunities for renegotiation, they will try to destabilize or undermine the terms of the original bargain. By requiring continued renegotiation, the parties attempt to keep the existing agreement reasonably stable while in force. There are several problems here. First, renegotiation by itself does not guarantee that those who receive the short end of the stick the first time will do better the next. Indeed, if continued rounds of bargaining involve Nash bargaining, that is, from a threat advantage, the outcome of each round of bargaining continues to entrench relative disparities in threat advantage. Renegotiation does not guarantee an improvement in the status of those dissatisfied the first time around. But if individuals are aware of the need to improve their relative threat advantage for the upcoming bargain – and if their threat advantage is determined by their initial threat advantage plus the gains achieved by the existing agreement – then both those with weaker and those with stronger advantages have incentives to behave strategically at each agreement, including the first. In that event, the continual renegotiation alternative simply collapses into the one-shot deal. If, however, renegotiation continually begins from a new initial bargaining position and thus ignores the relative advantages secured under previous bargains, it may have negative incentive effects, and, in any case, it is grossly inefficient. Why not negotiate just once, from what we might think of as a fair starting point, thereby reducing envy and providing the possibility of stability based on genuine consensus?[21] Finally, if continual renegotiation proves successful, it turns out to be entirely redistributive, providing no gains in efficiency. The point of continual renegotiation, after all, is not to overcome inefficiency but to redistribute the stakes. In that case, rational political association is largely a zero-sum game. Surely, such an arrangement is inefficient.

Rational cooperation, in sum, is necessary to overcome market failure in the market contractarian theory of political association. Market failures are of two sorts: standard market failure and pre-market market failure. Examples of the first sort include attempts to provide privately basic medical research and national defense. The property rights scheme itself is an example of the latter. In seeking to overcome market failures of both types, cooperation is rational. Rational cooperation has three features relevant to the relationship between politics and economics. First, rational cooperation has strongly integrated efficiency and distributive elements. Thus, the Nonintegration Thesis is unhelpful, misleading and perhaps false. Moreover, where rational cooperation takes the form of political association, politics is both productive and redistributive. Thus, the view of politics as purely redistributive, and the welfare economist's view of social change as consisting only in efforts to identify a proper welfare distribution once the Pareto frontier has been secured, is fundamentally mistaken.[22]

Second, in order for rational cooperation to succeed, an agreement, usually on the division of the cooperative surplus, must be achieved; and third, compliance with the agreement must be widespread. In this part of the essay, while I have discussed the more well-known problems of compliance, I have sought primarily to focus on problems in obtaining meaningful and enduring agreements. The problems of securing agreement in any bargaining circumstance involving large numbers of persons are formidable. In the case of putting a property rights scheme or legal order in place, they may be insurmountable. The problem of compliance, moreover, may be insurmountable in the premarket setting, where no enforcement mechanism exists and where the very point of bargaining is to reach an accord on putting such a mechanism in place. If that bargain is not self-enforcing, it may be impossible to give a rational choice or market account of the emergence of rational political institutions.

The upshot is that bargaining in the premarket setting may be irrational or, if not irrational, at least radically uncertain. If bargainers are inadequately disposed to comply with their agreements, that is, if agreements are unstable, bargaining itself is irrational. For it is simply a waste of time. If compliance is rational, which it can be only if agreements are likely to be stable, then bargaining can be rational. But it is not at all obvious that given the stakes, namely distribution of the gains erected by markets, bargaining will prove fruitful. The process itself cannot rule out strategic and hold-out behavior or misrepresentation of information. The incentives for rent seeking at this stage may be great enough to make the enterprise itself futile, and the possibility of rationally reconstructing a market economy embedded in a liberal legal structure implausible; implausible in the sense of reconstructing a minimal legal structure as the outcome of a rational bargain taking place in a hypothetical premarket market setting.

One way of reading this discussion, then, is that if we take the rational choice perspective seriously we see the state and a market economy as a solution to the problem of market failure: premarket market failure. This just means that a market embedded in a legal order is rational for each agent and collectively rational as well. But which market embedded in which legal order? That is, the real task for the market *contractarian* is *not* to show that a market economy embedded in a legal order is rational as compared with the absence of both. He has, rather, to make plausible the emergence of markets as the outcome of a rational bargain; and this, or so I have argued, is a much more difficult task than contractarians have taken it to be.

11. Unanimity

1. INTRODUCTION

Thin market contractarianism is the view that political association is a rational means to overcome market failures. Thick market contractarianism is the view that political association is a rational means to overcome both market failure and premarket market failure, thus making possible the conditions of market success. In both conceptions of rational political association, politics has both productive and redistributive dimensions. Rational political association might then be viewed as a mixed bargaining game, the outcome of which specifies the conditions of political association.

To say that the terms of rational political association are specified as the outcome of rational bargaining is not to say that all political decisions are to be resolved by bargaining. That depends on whether, in either constitutional or post-constitutional bargains, bargainers would agree that the best way to overcome a particular market failure is by bargaining. It is perfectly plausible that rational bargainers seeking to overcome market failures owing to externalities might prefer a tax, subsidy or liability approach to a bargaining or Coasean approach; or that bargainers in a public goods context might agree to implement a demand-revelation mechanism[1] rather than try to settle on the level of provision by simple majority vote.

The bargainers are seeking a mechanism that will secure an efficient allocation of resources and divide the gains in a way that will obtain the agreement of all. The mechanisms open to rational bargainers in their efforts to overcome market failure include: bargains, social choice or collective decision rules, demand-revelation or incentive-compatible mechanisms, taxes or subsidies, and the property rule–liability rule transaction structure.

One of the options open to rational bargainers is to agree to solve certain inefficiencies by adopting a collective choice rule, such as voting. In this essay I want to explore the argument for one kind of collective choice rule, namely, unanimity. Unanimity is democratic in a particularly strong sense. Moreover, unlike majority rule, unanimity is connected to efficiency in supposedly obvious ways. Its efficiency property alone makes unanimity attractive to rational bargainers seeking to overcome market failure. Its democratic features might be attractive to those aiming for stable or enduring agreements. Finally, unanimity is conceptually connected to the idea of the market, in particular to the concept of liberty of exchange. It is, therefore, the social choice rule naturally suggested by a commitment to the market paradigm.

Not without plausibility, advocates of unanimity have argued that the unanimity rule is both efficient and strongly democratic. Indeed, when leveled against the unanimity rule, the argument that collective choice rules are coercive because they impose policies on those who disagree with the majority decision is simply a nonstarter. Under the unanimity rule, no policy can be adopted if anyone votes against it. Furthermore, the unanimity rule appears to replicate in the political sphere not only the efficient or optimal outcome of competitive markets but the Pareto-improving character of free exchange as well. There are, I believe, at least four arguments for the unanimity rule suggested by these brief remarks, and in what follows I want to tease them out as best I can, even if in a somewhat preliminary way.

2. UNANIMITY, PUBLIC GOODS AND WICKSELL–LINDAHL TAXES

The paradox of public goods is that *ex ante* they benefit everyone; and so providing them is in each person's rational self-interest. Nevertheless, if each individual acts to promote his rational self-interest, it is virtually certain that less than the optimal level of any public good will be provided. The fact that public goods are potentially to each person's advantage, however, provides the basis for one argument for the use of the unanimity rule to decide on the provision of public goods. This argument has its roots in the work of Knut Wicksell,[2] and it has been further developed by Erik Lindahl.[3] The basic idea behind what has been called the Wicksell–Lindahl tax is very simple. Because the provision of public goods is capable of making each person better off, there should be a way of providing and distributing their benefits and costs that can secure each person's agreement. There should exist, in other words, a public good–tax package tailored to each person which will secure his consent. In the aggregate, there is a relationship between the optimal provision of public goods and unanimity.

In the Wicksell–Lindahl scheme each person is asked to vote on a tax package applicable only to him. The tax package links a particular level of public good with a benefit tax. The purpose of the package is to match each person's marginal benefit from a public good with his marginal contribution to the costs of providing it. The point of matching benefits and costs follows from general equilibrium analysis of private goods: In optimal equilibrium, marginal private cost equals marginal private gain. The Wicksell–Lindahl scheme seeks to replicate in the realm of public goods what is essential to an efficient allocation of private goods: linkage of marginal benefit and marginal cost.

Each person has a demand schedule for public goods. As his tax share decreases, his demand for public goods increases. Theoretically, there exists an allocation of tax shares and units of the public good that meets with each person's approval. An illustration of this property of public good–tax packages is provided in Figure 11.1, originally given by Dennis Mueller.[4] The horizontal axis represents the levels of output of the public good, G. The vertical axis represents A's share of the tax, T, necessary to provide the good at various levels. B's tax burden is equal to $(1 - A$'s share), for any level of provision. Both A's and B's demand for the public good is inversely related to their tax share: the lower the tax, the higher the demand.

The graph is complex in the following way. The indifference curves for A and B (labeled A_1 and B_1) specify respectively A's and B's utilities in an economy without public goods, that is, a private goods economy. Each point on the other indifference curves (A_2 through A_5 and B_2 through B_5) represents a preference for a mixture of public and private goods at various tax levels, given various budgetary constraints. C' is the contract curve. The difference between this graph and the standard Edgeworth box representation of a two-person, two-commodity exchange economy is that in the standard case A would prefer to be on an indifference curve farther from the origin, whereas B would prefer to be on an indifference curve closer to A's origin. By contrast, in this graph, A prefers to be closer to his origin and B farther from it. That is because as A moves closer to the origin his tax share drops; and as B moves farther out from the origin his tax share declines.

We can say that the graph is bounded by the lens formed by the intersection of A's and B's indifference curves, A_1, B_1. Any level

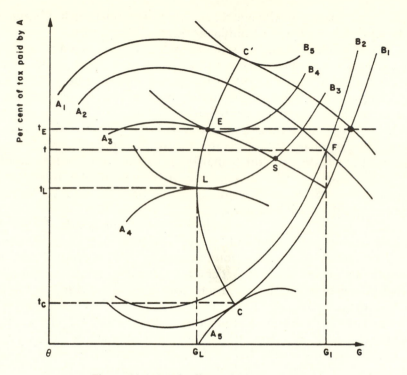

Figure 11.1. Wicksell–Lindahl tax scheme

of provision of a public good is desirable for both A and B only if it promises to make both better off than they would be in the absence of public goods. The status quo point, then, is represented by the boundary A_1, B_1. A public good–tax package is Pareto improving for A and B only if it is represented by a point that falls within the boundaries formed by the intersection of A_1 and B_1; otherwise it is not.

Following Mueller, begin by assuming the relevant government agency offers both parties a package that consists of a level of public good and a corresponding level of taxation necessary to provide the good. Either the offer falls within the lens formed by the intersection of A_1 and B_1, as it would if the government packages were represented by F, or it does not. If the package falls outside the lens, either A or B or both will reject it. If the package falls within the lens, then both A and B will vote for the package, since at that level of taxation and public good both are better off than they would be in the absence of the public good.[5] F represents a Pareto improvement, but it is not itself a point on the contract curve. Another tax package is therefore offered. Only tax packages offered that fall within the lens created by the intersection of A_2 and B_2 are acceptable to both parties. Therefore, F represents the new veto point in the same way as the intersection of A_1 and B_1 represented the original veto point. Only public good–tax packages Pareto superior to it can secure the consent of both parties. One such package is represented by S. If S is offered, it is accepted and replaces F as the veto point. The process continues until a point on the contract curve is reached which is preferable to the previous veto point and cannot itself be improved upon. Such points fall on the contract curve and lie between E and L.

The Wicksell–Lindahl tax scheme appears to solve the public goods problem. It does so by replicating in the "public sector" the central features of exchange in the private sector: the linkage of marginal cost and marginal gain. Moreover, the process of securing an efficient or optimal level of public goods and public expenditures just described is based on giving each person a veto over all possible tax packages. The collective choice rule, then, that is employed to guarantee that the political process yields an optimal level of public goods is the unanimity rule. The argument from the Wicksell–Lindahl tax scheme is one argument for the unanimity rule based on its efficiency. It is not, however, the only argument for unanimity that relies on the relationship between it and Pareto efficiency.

2.1. Unanimity as efficiency

James Buchanan is perhaps the most influential defender of the unanimity rule for collective choice.[6] He views himself, above all else, as a defender of unanimity on Wicksellian grounds. Even his severest critics, for example, Brian Barry, grant Buchanan this historical link to Wicksell.[7] I believe, however, that in an important sense Buchanan's conception of the relationship between unanimity and efficiency is not Wicksellian. The difference between the two views is important.

Buchanan's view is that unanimity is the test of efficiency. As I have argued elsewhere, this claim is ambiguous, because the term "test" may be given either an epistemic or a semantic rendering.[8] In the epistemic sense, unanimity is (perhaps the best) evidence of efficiency, but whether or not a state of the world is efficient depends on its satisfying some other criterion. In the semantic sense, to say that a state of the world is efficient is just to say that it has secured unanimous agreement. In this sense, unanimity is not simply evidence of efficiency; it is criterial of it. My view is that Buchanan is committed to the criterial, semantic or ontological conception of the relationship between efficiency and unanimity, and not to the epistemic one. For Buchanan, unanimity constitutes efficiency: that is, unanimity is both necessary and sufficient for efficiency. Buchanan has accepted my characterization of his conception of unanimity and of its relationship to efficiency. Let us call Buchanan's view the subjectivist criterion of efficiency.

Given a loose reading, the subjectivist account of efficiency has some initial plausibility. Suppose one person vetoes a proposal. Then we can say that he does so because implementing the proposal would make him worse off. If no one vetoes a proposal – if a proposal secures unanimous agreement – then it makes no one worse off. Because it makes no one worse off, it is efficient. Anything less than unanimity is inefficient. Not only is the argument plausible, it has happy consequences as well. If the point of political association is to mimic the perfectly competitive market by securing optimal allocations of resources, then one way to insure success in the political enterprise is to require unanimity. Unanimity entails efficiency; and efficiency is the goal. So one way of overcoming market failure is to get individuals to agree unanimously on policy recommendations.

What people agree to, however, may vary from what is in their rational self-interest. Presumably someone may be motivated by moral considerations to agree to a diminution in his well-being for the good of others. Unanimous agreement itself, even voluntary agreement, does not entail Pareto efficiency in the usual sense. In the standard, welfarist conception of efficiency, a state of the world that makes someone worse off cannot be efficient. So there is no necessary connection between what people agree to, even unanimously, and what is Pareto efficient or welfare enhancing.

The subjectivist theory of efficiency is not the one purportedly employed to demonstrate that the Lindahl–Wicksell tax scheme for public goods is efficient. Nor is the relationship between efficiency and unanimity in the Lindahl–Wicksell scheme the same as the one in Buchanan's argument for unanimity. In the tax scheme, the notion of efficiency is the standard one, employing the common conceptions of rational self-interest, Pareto superiority and the core. The idea is that there exists a tax package for public goods tailored to each person capable of making each person *better off,* that is, capable of increasing his welfare, and therefore capable of securing each person's consent. The package is efficient because it is welfare-enhancing; and because it is welfare-enhancing, each person will agree to it. Unanimity follows from efficiency, not the other way around. In contrast, in the Buchanan conception of efficiency, unanimous agreement constitutes efficiency, even if what people in fact agree to, say, in the allocation of public goods, does not satisfy the Samuelson condition.[9] A state of the world that is efficient in the subjective sense need not be in the "objective" welfare sense. On the other hand, a state of the economy that is efficient in the Samuelson sense, and therefore is in each person's rational self-interest, may not be unanimously agreed to and therefore may not be efficient in the subjectivist sense.

These two arguments for the unanimity rule are based on two very different conceptions of efficiency and of the relationship between it and unanimity. Though Buchanan thinks of himself as above all else a Wicksellian, the differences between them may be more impressive than are the similarities. In Buchanan's argument for the unanimity rule, we infer efficiency from unanimity; in the Wicksell–Lindahl scheme, we establish efficiency and then infer unanimity from it. In both cases, different conceptions of efficiency are at work. In both cases the inference may be unwarranted.

Once one appreciates the subjectivism of Buchanan's view, several serious problems emerge. The most pressing is the following. Return to the rational bargain. Suppose rational bargainers opt for a unanimity rule to overcome market failures. The problem is that there is no reason to believe that policy measures adopted unanimously are efficient in the same sense of the term in which market failures are inefficient. There is, in other words, no guarantee that a policy efficient in the subjectivist–Buchanan sense overcomes the market failure, which is inefficient in an entirely different sense. But it was the very point of the unanimity rule that it held out the promise of solving the problem of market inefficiency.

The Wicksell–Lindahl scheme employs the useful sense of efficiency. The problem with it is that there is no reason to think that the scheme will eventually lead to an efficient level of public goods. The reason is really quite simple. In order to secure an efficient level of public goods, the government needs consumers to reveal their true preferences for them. If the good is provided, everyone has the opportunity to benefit from it. So each person's rational strategy is to understate the benefit to him of the public good and hope thereby to benefit from its provision without incurring the full marginal costs of provision. Thus, each person has an incentive to withhold information. Therefore, the Wicksell–Lindahl scheme fails for the very same reasons private markets fail to provide optimal levels of public goods: inadequate honest information. In both the Lindahl–Wicksell and Buchanan arguments for the unanimity rule, the connection between efficiency and unanimity is a good deal less persuasive than advocates of the unanimity rule would have us believe.

There are two final points to be made about the unanimity rule and efficiency, both based on the fact that unanimity leads to strategic behavior. One consequence of a unanimity rule is that an individual may hold out in hopes of forging a better deal. Strategic behavior plagues unanimity and promotes inefficiency. Holding out wastes real resources. So there is at least one clear and uncontroversial sense in which unanimity may lead to inefficiency. The irony here is that critics of majority rule claim it is inefficient, and it is;[10] but turning to unanimity need not obviate the problem of inefficiency.

The fact that the unanimity rule is subject to strategic behavior implies a much deeper objection to it. Either the unanimity rule fails to secure efficiency or it is otiose; it is either unnecessary or ineffective. The argument is this. Where unanimity leads to efficiency, as in the idealized Wicksell–Lindahl scheme, it does so because individuals willingly reveal their preferences for public goods at various tax levels. Where it fails, it does so because individuals withhold pertinent information. But notice that the unanimity rule in the Wicksell–Lindahl context succeeds under precisely those conditions necessary for the optimal private provision of the public good. On the other hand, the unanimity rule approach fails precisely where, and for the same reasons, the private market fails in the provision of public goods.[11] Unanimity schemes have the same incentives that create private market failures. On the other hand, a unanimity rule works when individuals do not act strategically – when instead they reveal their true preferences for public goods. But under those conditions, a unanimity rule of collective choice may be otiose, since the market itself can secure an efficient allocation of public goods. In short, it appears that no unanimity rule can rest on what seems its most promising foundation: its alleged connection to efficiency, or its capacity to overcome market failure.

2.2. The argument from liberty of exchange

The unanimity rule replicates the exchange aspect of the competitive market in two ways. First, in a competitive market, exchange is voluntary. No one is required to exchange unless he chooses to do so. Let us refer to this property of markets as "liberty of exchange." The unanimity rule of collective choice is liberty of exchange writ large. Just as in the market no one is compelled to exchange, the unanimity rule of collective choice guarantees that no person is required to commit his resources to public measures he disapproves of.

There are at least two arguments for liberty of exchange here and, therefore, at least two arguments for the unanimity rule of collective choice that embodies it. The first argument appeals to its "prospective" value; the second to its "retrospective" value. In markets, rational exchanges are made only if they are from an *ex ante* perspective mutually advantageous, that is, Pareto superior. Only unanimity guarantees that no person is made worse off by collective policy. Unanimity replicates the Pareto-superiority aspect of market exchange. Liberty of exchange guarantees Pareto superiority. Unanimity does so as well – and for the same reasons – or so one might argue.

There is a difference, however, between liberty of exchange and Pareto superiority that surfaces both in market exchange and in the unanimity rule of collective choice. The former is connected to the idea of autonomy; the latter to welfare, well-being or utility. It may be irrational to agree to be made worse off, but it is not logically incoherent to do so. Because markets embody liberty of exchange, they may pave the way for Pareto improvements; Pareto superiority, however, is not a logical consequence of the liberty-of-exchange component of markets. Pareto superiority follows from the conjunction of liberty of exchange and the assumption of rational self-interestedness, not from the former alone. The same applies to the unanimity rule. Unanimous agreement entails neither Pareto optimality nor Pareto superiority. This is the point I made above, and it has been made by others as well.

One might respond to this objection as follows: In the same sense as that in which market behavior reveals one's preferences for commodities, voting reveals one's preferences for outcomes. Consequently, if exchange is efficient because it is preference maximizing, so should be unanimity. Unanimous agreement in the voting context is Pareto improving.

The problem here is that, under conditions of perfect competition, market behavior is a reliable index of preference; voting behavior is not. The reason is that, under conditions of perfect competition, there is little, if any, room for strategic behavior. In the voting context – especially under a unanimity rule – opportunities for strategic behavior are manifest. There is just too much room between a person's vote and his honest preference for outcomes in the voting context to infer either Pareto superiority or Pareto optimality from any voting rule – even unanimity (and even assuming rational self-interestedness).[12]

In free markets, no individual is required to give up that to which he already has a legitimate claim. The unanimity rule provides each person with a veto over any policy that imposes net costs on him or anyone else. This feature of the unanimity rule is usually discussed favorably in the context of bargaining over the terms of the constitutional contract specifying the conditions of the move from anarchy to polity.

Individuals come to the constitutional contract (or, in my terms, to the bargain to solve the problem of premarket market failure) with a set of holdings. In terms of the extended Nashian bargaining model, these preconstitutional holdings determine the threat advantage of each individual. The point of negotiations is to settle on the division of the gains made possible by cooperation. It takes place, in a Nash model, within the context of threat values secured noncooperatively. In any case, at the constitutional level no one is required to remit any of his or her preconstitutional holdings. To say, however, that preconstitutional entitlements are not up for grabs is not to say that those assets are frozen. Individuals may exchange what they have acquired preconstitutionally. The key here is that any redistribution must be agreed to by those affected by it. In effect, each person has a veto over the transfer of his preconstitutional entitlements. No one can obtain them other than by consent.

The liberty-of-exchange model suggests a way of securing preconstitutional holdings against public measures that would encroach upon them, namely, by providing constitutionally that policy measures must be agreed upon unanimously to be adopted. While there is no way of separating (at the constitutional level) once and for all time objects in the domain of collective policy from those outside the domain, there exists in the unanimity rule a guardian of preconstitutional holdings. Policy that encroaches on someone's preconstitutional holdings (or that fails, at least in that person's eyes, to confer sufficient offsetting benefits) is subject to veto. The unanimity rule is insurance that, once set, the domain of collective policy is properly maintained. This is the second way in which liberty of exchange, both in the market and in the unanimity rule of collective choice, is thought to be morally desirable. Liberty of exchange has the alleged prospective virtue of ensuring that exchange and the adoption of public policy based on exchange, that is, unanimity, will be Pareto improving. It also has the retrospective virtue of securing a distribution of holdings against forced transfers. But is the latter really a virtue of the unanimity rule and of liberty of exchange generally?

One objection to this line of argument is that unanimity may freeze, or at least entrench, what is in fact a very unjust distribution of preconstitutional holdings.[13] In the thick version of market contractarianism, the allocation of initial property rights is the subject of a preconstitutional contract necessary in order to solve the collective action problem of premarket market failure. The initial assignment of rights is itself the outcome of rational bargaining. It will not follow, however, even on the thick theory, that the allocation of property rights, and of the gains from trade made possible by them, is morally unassailable. That is because the allocation is the outcome of rational bargaining, and the rational distribution of resources that results from a bargain need not be a moral one.[14] So not even the thick theory of market contractarianism can ensure that the application of the unanimity rule at the stage of collective action will lead to a just pattern of holdings. On the other hand, it does not follow that unanimity will entrench injustice. Since everything depends on the justice or injustice of preconstitutional holdings, we might remain agnostic about whether the conservative features of unanimity are a good or a bad thing. What we can say with confidence may simply not be helpful, and that is: If forced redistribution through public measures is desirable, then we are unlikely to achieve it under unanimity; whereas if existing patterns of distribution are desirable, then unanimity is one device for protecting the patterns of distribution from distortion through the implementation of publicly financed projects. This, of course, is a much weaker claim on behalf of unanimity than its defenders – who imbue the status quo with objective value[15] – have been prepared to advance.

The first argument for the liberty-of-exchange feature of unanimity seeks to connect free exchange to Pareto superiority; the second seeks to connect it to the protection of a system of holdings. Both arguments are inconclusive: the first because free exchange is not necessarily Pareto improving, the second because existing patterns of holdings are not necessarily worth protecting.

2.3. Unanimity, externalities and moral skepticism

I want to close by considering an argument for the unanimity rule that is suggested both by liberty of exchange and by moral skepticism. The argument is as follows: Suppose that collective choices are made by a rule requiring less than unanimous agreement, for example, a simple majority. If politics is a pure redistribution game, then majority voting would consist entirely in transferring wealth from the minority to the majority. It would also very likely turn out that social choices would cycle as everyone offered up splits of the social pie in efforts to become a member of the wealth-sharing majority.[16] In the redistributive game, it is very clear that anything less than unanimity would impose costs on members of the minority: costs that members of the minority had not in any obvious sense agreed to have imposed upon them. (Of course, in a pure redistribution game, a unanimity rule might have the undesirable property of freezing the status quo.) We can capture this aspect of voting rules that require less than unanimous agreement by saying that they impose "voting externalities." The claim that simple majority rule, for example, imposes externalities is really just the claim that a policy adopted by some is coercively enforceable against all, including those who do not favor it. At some level this is just the claim that the minority is required to act for the collective good and against what they perceive to be their own interest. Without some further justification, this may be simply unjustified coercion. Externalities in this sense occur under any voting rule that requires less than unanimity. Externalities are coercive. Coercion is *prima facie* wrong, and wrong full stop unless an overriding justification for it can be found.

One kind of justification for imposing coercive externalities might be that the majority is simply right about what ought to be done on a given collective matter. If it is, or if majorities tend to be right, then imposing coercive externalities on minorities is justified.[17] Defenders of the unanimity rule might agree. Indeed, they might agree that moral knowledge about what is right is all that could ever justify imposing voting externalities. Unfortunately, or so they often agree, this sort of argument does not work, because moral knowledge is not attainable. Indeed, most defenders of unanimity, like Buchanan, are moral skeptics. Without moral knowledge, the best one can do is secure consensus. Consensus or unanimity is as close as we can come to objective moral truth – it may even be all that we mean by truth. Moreover, consensus precludes the imposition of nonconsensual external costs.

There is a good deal in this argument that is problematic. I want to consider three problems with it. First, it is questionable whether being on the losing side in a vote is equivalent to having an externality imposed upon one. This is plausible only if we assume that individuals always vote their *interests* rather than their *judgment* about what the correct public decision ought to be. Only if votes are expressions of preferences can it be even minimally plausible that a policy adopted contrary to a person's vote imposes external costs upon him.[18] Second, this argument from unanimity assumes that the only ground for justifiably imposing externalities is either the consent of the party who suffers the externality or the moral rightness of the policy in question. Since advocates of the argument we are considering deny the possibility of moral knowledge, the only option is consent. But consent as a condition for justifiably imposing external costs is equivalent to unanimity. Indeed, there is a sense in which consent does not justify imposing externalities, but logically precludes them. If I consent to having the costs put on me, then in making that decision I take into account the effects of those costs on me; I internalize the costs.

Third, although wholesale moral skepticism might lend itself to a unanimity rule, unanimity cannot rest comfortably on general moral skepticism. For if skepticism about moral truth is in fact warranted, the advocate of the unanimity rule who claims that it is wrong to impose external costs on others without justification is advancing a self-defeating argument. If we cannot know what is morally true, then we cannot know that it is wrong without justification to impose voting or other externalities.

But it need not be wrong to impose voting externalities, for several reasons. It is a mistake to believe that voting externalities can be justified if and only if adopting the policies that impose them can be shown to be morally right. First of all, voting externalities may be defensible provided that the collective decision-making procedures are themselves "fair." Fair procedures are compatible with mistaken results. Hence a fair procedure may justify the adoption of the policy and the subsequent imposition of voting externalities. Secondly, an unfair decision-making procedure may invalidate even a correct decision. However we conceive of this argument for the unanimity rule – as rooted in moral skepticism or in a theory about the conditions under which voting externalities can be legitimately imposed – it falls far short of the defense of unanimity we seek.[19]

12. Democracy and social choice

The problem of justifying democracy arises when a society sees the need for cooperative, collective action. Collective action may be needed to solve coordination problems, public goods problems, prisoners' dilemmas and other structural problems of human interaction or perhaps to realize common ideals of justice in concrete political institutions.

Once the need for collective action is established, one must ask how the goals of a cooperative endeavor are to be secured. Cooperation requires that individuals, at least over a specified range of activity, pursue a joint strategy. To ensure *voluntary* compliance in a joint venture, cooperation must be to each person's advantage. However, each person may have an incentive to induce others to cooperate and to defect from the joint strategy in the hope of enjoying the fruits of cooperation without incurring the opportunity costs of compliance. This is the essence of the prisoners' dilemma, and considerations of this sort suggest that if collective action is to succeed, policies or strategies formed collectively must be coercively enforceable.

Coercion, however, requires justification. Because solving the problem of rational noncompliance requires that collective decisions be coercively enforceable, the rules by which collective decisions are reached require justification. Douglas Rae neatly puts the problem of justification that emerges when political solutions are coercively enforceable as follows: "Once a political community has decided which of its members are to participate directly in the making of collective policy, an important question remains: 'How many of them must agree before a policy is *imposed* on the community?' "[1] This is essentially the question to which the principle of democratic rule provides an answer: By what process are collective decisions to be made?

Answering Rae's question requires a normative framework. We could say that a procedure for making collective decisions is justified if and only if the procedure is one that the parties in the collective – that is, those who will from time to time be required to act contrary to their own preferences – would choose. Let us call this the *contractarian* or *rational choice* approach to the justification of collective decision rules.[2] Alternatively, we could say that a collective decision-making procedure is justified if and only if the procedure is one that promotes efficiently the goals of the collective enterprise. Let us call this the *instrumentalist* or *consequentialist* approach to the justification of collective decision. Finally, we could identify a set of ideals with which any collective decision-making procedure ought to comply. We might think of these as procedural ideals, and a process of collective decision making would be more or less justifiable depending on the extent to which it satisfies them. Let us call this the *proceduralist* approach to the justification of collective decision.

Characterized this way, proceduralism is inadequately distinguished from both instrumentalism and contractarianism. The instrumentalist could be taken as holding that the correct procedural ideals are those that identify a decision-making procedure that produces desired consequences; and the contractarian can be understood as claiming that the correct procedural ideals are those that identify a decision-making procedure that would be agreed to *ex ante* by members of the collective. Indeed, any theory of the justification of a decision-making procedure could be construed in proceduralist terms.

What, then, distinguishes proceduralism from other modes of justification? Proceduralism holds that what justifies a decision-making procedure is strictly a *necessary* property of the procedure – one entailed by the definition of the procedure alone. In other words, the justification of a procedure depends on the nature of the mapping from the original preference orderings of the collective to the outcome. This characterization distinguishes the proceduralist from the instrumentalist and the contractarian. For both instrumentalists and contractarians, the justification of a procedure is logically independent of its definition. In one case, justification depends on the consequences that will arise from following the rule, while in the other it depends on how these consequences would be evaluated *ex ante* – two contingent properties of decision-making procedures.

The modern theory of social choice contains a number of attempts to develop a defense of particular voting or collective decision procedures by appeal to axioms aimed at characterizing one or another aspect of procedural fairness. Social choice theorists are, in general, committed to the view that the appropriate project for democratic theory is to develop and justify the constraints that can serve to represent our fundamental notions of fair or legitimate procedures. Social choice theory attempts this essentially proceduralist project through axiomatic constructions.

Perhaps the best attempt to examine proceduralist justifications of democratic institutions drawn from the theory of social choice was propounded by William Riker in his book *Liberalism against Populism*.[3] What makes Riker's book so important is that, among social choice theorists, he is the first to attempt self-consciously to explore the implications of social choice theory for fundamental problems in political theory, in particular the justification of democracy.

Riker argues that the project of social choice theory is hopeless. Roughly the argument is this: Every voting system that satisfies the requirements of minimal procedural fairness necessary for democratic choice produces arbitrary or meaningless social choices or outcomes, outcomes that are essentially unrelated to the preferences of the members of society. Because the outcomes are arbitrary in this sense, they can be given no justification other than the purely procedural one that points to the institutional processes that produced them. But those institutions are themselves inadequate to preclude arbitrary outcomes, and because they are, procedural modes of justification, at least so far as they can be rendered axiomatically, are themselves inadequate. Riker argues, then, not only that attempts to justify decision rules on procedural or axiomatic grounds fail, but also that proceduralism is itself an inadequate basis for evaluating collective decision-making institutions.

Having abandoned proceduralism, we are led, therefore, to employ either contractarian or instrumentalist justifications for democratic institutions. By moving to either a contractarian or instrumentalist approach, the choice of a particular family of democratic institutions can be justified, and another rejected. According to Riker, the uniquely defensible institutions are those associated with constitutionally limited representative democracy, what he calls liberal democracy; those he rejects are majoritarian or direct democracy unfettered by constitutional guarantees of regular elections and individual rights, what he thinks of as populist democracy.

Crucial to Riker's argument are the claim that all voting procedures produce arbitrary outcomes and the implicit claim that constitutional limitations restrict the range of arbitrariness of outcomes in a way that populist institutions do not. Neither of these claims can be sustained, however. On the first point, a number of recent results in social choice theory suggest that fair procedures are likely to produce constrained outcomes – while there may be some ambiguity, its range is small. If this is so, the rejection of populism in favor of liberal democracy on the ground that populist institutions produce arbitrary outcomes may be premature. On the second point, there are as yet no established theoretical grounds for the belief that choices made by liberal institutions are any less arbitrary than those produced by populist ones. In short, it is unclear that constitutional limitations on voting eliminate arbitrariness in social choices, and it is also unclear that the range of arbitrariness expected under populist democratic institutions warrants their rejection. Constitutional limitations aimed exclusively at reducing the scope of arbitrariness of outcomes may be unnecessary or unsuccessful or both. At the very least, we have no satisfactory theory establishing that they are necessary or adequate. Lacking such comparative institutional knowledge, we think that Riker's endorsement of liberal institutions is premature. Without a theory of the performance of liberal institutions, we do find unconvincing the claim that rational individuals would impose constitutional limitations on democratic procedures. Thus, the move from proceduralist to contractarian modes of justification may not warrant the endorsement of liberalism and the rejection of populism.

This is not to say that there are no good reasons for preferring liberal to populist institutions. Rather, such reasons would rest on considerations of practicality, such as the cost of monitoring officials and the size of a polity, not on the formal properties of choice mechanisms.

1. PROCEDURAL CONSTRAINTS

Social choice theory structures collective decision problems by imposing a set of constraints on collective decision procedures. The question in each case is whether there exists a procedure or mechanism that satisfies those constraints. Social choice theorists tend, therefore, to be proceduralists about the justification of democracy. In social choice theory, democracy itself is analyzed as a subset of institutions for aggregating individual preferences into social choices; that is, democracy is a kind or set of voting rules. In aggregation problems, social choice theory treats individual preferences as basic and as given. Voting, in this view, expresses "tastes" or preferences; it does not consist in the formation of a collective judgment. In Riker's view, what distinguishes demo-cratic voting procedures from alternatives is their commitment to the ideals of equality, liberty and participation. Commitment to these ideals gives rise to more particular constraints on collective decision rules. Satisfaction of the derivative constraints justifies a collective decision procedure because the constraints are deducible from or otherwise justificationally connected to the more funda-mental commitments to equality, liberty and participation.

What do participation, liberty and equality mean for the social choice theorist, and how do these ideals give rise to concrete pro-cedural constraints on voting? "The crucial attribute of democ-racy," Riker writes, "is popular participation in government."[4] Participation, in turn, is analyzed in terms of voting. "Although the institutions of participation have been many and varied, they have always revolved around the simple act of voting."[5] Democ-racy requires participation. Participation entails voting. But "vot-ing is not equivalent to democracy, only voting that facilitates popular choice is democratic. . . . Or, voting is a necessary, but not a sufficient, condition of democracy. To render them equiva-lent, voting must be surrounded with numerous institutions like political parties and free speech, which organize voting into gen-uine choice."[6]

Of the connection between liberty and collective decision, Riker writes, "The historic purpose of . . . fundamental democratic lib-erties has been *not* to provide freedom as an end in itself, but to render effective both political participation and the process of choice in voting."[7] In the same connection, citing Rousseau, he writes that "liberty resides in participation in government, not in rights distinct from government."[8]

Equality, Riker writes, "originated in some rough sense as an instrument of voting. Voting would not mean much if each per-son's vote were not counted in the same way. . . . Its logical base lies in the instrumental value of making voting work."[9] Accord-ing to Riker, democratic rules are the only collective decision rules that satisfy these three abstract criteria, satisfaction of which is both necessary and sufficient to justify them.

> In a society characterized by democratic justice, people are free (by reason of democratic liberty) and have the chance (by reason of democratic equality) to seek self-respect and self-control (through some kind of democratic participation). The democratic method that is supposed to achieve this idea . . . is the process of participation, specifically through voting, in

the management of society, where voting is understood to include all the ancillary institutions (like parties and pressure groups) and social principles (like freedom and equality) that are necessary to render it significant.[10]

Riker argues that the essence of the commitment to democratic choice is captured by its commitment to the abstract ideals of participation, liberty and equality. The problem is to work from these abstract commitments to specific constraints on possible social choice rules necessary and sufficient to justify them. These more particular constraints appear to be of two distinct sorts: normative and semantic.

On the one hand, justified social choice (or voting) procedures must be fair, provide for full and equal participation, and allow for autonomy in the Rousseauean–Kantian sense, according to which an autonomous agent complies with dictates or constraints of his own choosing. On the other hand, autonomy in this sense presupposes full participation because full participation is necessary to guarantee that the voting rule produces outcomes that express the collective or general will. This line of analysis brings us to the cognitive or meaningfulness criterion. In order to be *meaningful*, the social choice must be unambiguously interpretable in terms of individual wills, preferences or voter profiles.

Only democratic choice procedures are capable, even in principle, of satisfying both conditions. The problem social choice theory raises for democratic theory is that any democratic voting procedure that is fair in the appropriate sense will be normatively defensible but not meaningful, that is, its outcomes will be arbitrary. Only voting that is meaningful and fair can be justified. Unfortunately, no voting procedure can be both.

2. THE PROBLEM OF AMBIGUOUS INTERPRETATION AND PARADOXICAL OUTCOMES

We can distinguish between two defects in voting rules, either of which would be sufficient to render voting meaningless. If a voting rule can generate a paradoxical ordering of preferences, it is said to be *unstable*. Generally, we refer to theorems that establish paradoxical orderings or cycles as instability, disequilibria or chaos results. The voting paradox,[11] Arrow's theorem[12] and McKelvey–Schofield results[13] are instability results. However, an outcome which, in social choice theory, is itself a complete ordering of preferences need not be paradoxical to be deeply troubling. An

Table 12.1. *Imaginary ordinal and cardinal utilities for five choices and five persons*

Rank order (highest to lowest)	Voter 1	Voter 2	Voter 3	Voter 4	Voter 5
1	a (1.00)	d (1.00)	e (1.00)	b (1.00)	b (1.00)
2	d (.90)	a (.61)	c (.80)	d (.90)	e (.96)
3	b (.60)	b (.60)	a (.70)	a (.75)	c (.70)
4	c (.55)	e (.59)	b (.55)	e (.74)	a (.60)
5	e (.50)	c (.50)	d (.50)	c (.50)	d (.50)

Note: Cardinal utilities are in parentheses.
Source: Reprinted from Riker, *Liberalism against Populism*, p. 37.

outcome is also troubling if it is not *unique*. An outcome, O_R, is not unique if, given a profile of preferences, D, another outcome, O_S, might have obtained had fair aggregation rule S rather than fair rule R been employed. In such a case, O_R is said to be *ambiguous*. Ambiguity concerns us only if there are no independent grounds for preferring R to S when aggregating preferences in D. We refer to defects of the first sort as instabilities and to those of the second sort as ambiguities. The bulk of Riker's argument attempts to demonstrate the *meaninglessness* of voting by establishing generalized instability or ambiguity results.

In addition to the distinction between instabilities and ambiguities, we can distinguish among different kinds of implications we might draw from either. Riker employs the instability and ambiguity results to demonstrate the meaninglessness of voting. One could just as well take these results as bearing on the normative defensibility of voting rules, because both ambiguity and instability create opportunities for differential influence over outcomes that is incompatible with the democratic ideal of equality. Thus, if different outcomes result from different rules, then access to the agenda increases – at least potentially – one's influence over outcomes. We shall return to these problems in due course. For now, we want to focus on Riker's claim that instability and ambiguity demonstrate the meaninglessness of voting. We first address the ambiguity argument.

According to the ambiguity argument, the result of applying rule R, namely O_R, is ambiguous if a different outcome, O_S, might have obtained had we applied rule S. Because O_R is ambiguous, we do not know what meaning to assign to it – what to make of it as a collective choice. For example, given a profile of preferences among voters, four methods of amalgamation or summation – the Borda count,[14] cardinal utility comparison,[15] multiplicative cardinal utility comparison[16] and ordinal pairwise comparison[17] – can result in different social choices. Each voting procedure satisfies a general, minimal conception of fairness, and there is no theoretical basis either to assert that only one of these rules is capable of accurately revealing public sentiment or to deny that any one of them can. Riker argues for this claim by examining the example in Table 12.1.[18]

It turns out that, among the five choices in Table 12.1, *a* is the Condorcet or pairwise winner, *b* is the plurality winner, *d* is the ordinal utility winner and *e* is the multiplicative cardinal or Nash winner. All four methods are plausible choice rules.

The same profiles of preferences can yield several quite distinct "winners," depending on the aggregation procedure employed. So even if outcome *a* in Riker's example wins in pairwise comparisons against each other alternative, there is no reason to interpret *a* as the choice embedded in the preferences of the voters. Had another choice procedure been employed, another outcome would have been the winner. The question is: What interpretation can we plausibly give to this argument? By his own account, Riker has "been very much impressed with this deep ambiguity" in the "process of aggregating preferences."[19]

There are at least two ways to interpret the argument. One interpretation is consistent with the concerns voiced by Riker, the other is not. In one sense, that a social choice is a function both of the profiles of preferences and the aggregation rule does not imply that the choice has ambiguous meaning or significance. The meaning of a social choice can be reconstructed in terms of the interplay of the data base and the decision rule. That other winners may have emerged under different decision rules is simply not relevant either to interpreting the outcome or to assessing its merits. Consider the problem of aggregation in another context. In American football, teams are awarded six points for a touchdown, three for a field goal, one for an extra point and two for a safety. The outcomes of football games depend on these assignments of points for events. A different assignment of points for events or a different way of aggregating them might well lead to different outcomes: Some wins would become losses and vice versa. (Different scoring rules would, of course, lead to changes in *strategy,* but changes in aggregation procedures, if known, would also affect voting strategies.) Even though we could score football games differently – according to different rules – it does not follow that the

outcomes of football games are ambiguous or that the score does
not reveal what occurred in the game. Just showing that different
outcomes result from applying different procedures, all of which
are minimally fair or plausible on other grounds, is not enough to
establish a troubling result for democracy.

There is, however, a different sense in which the fact that, given
the same profiles of preferences, different outcomes result from
different social choice rules can be problematic. The problem is
not that the outcomes lack meaning or significance. Instead, the
problem is that it is impossible unambiguously to interpret an outcome as *uniquely representing the popular will.* We can make sense of
this interpretation of the argument only if we assume that in every
set of voters' preference profiles there "exists" a unique popular
"will" defined and revealed by voting, and that voting is not
meaningful or significant unless it uniquely identifies this will. In
this view of collective decision, voting is important because it
specifies or defines the popular will, and the ambiguity problem is
troubling because, although voting is supposed to reveal a unique
general or popular will, the will that is revealed by a social choice
is as much a function of the method of choice as of the initial
profile from which the choice emerges. Thus, one can never know
that the outcome of an election reflects the popular or collective
will, because, in general, one always has good reason to believe
that a different outcome would have been produced by applying a
different, equally plausible aggregation procedure. But if a voting
procedure, in particular a democratic one, is defensible only if its
results meaningfully reflect a unique public disposition or will,
then it is natural to be skeptical about the legitimacy of any voting
procedure.

The revised ambiguity argument is as follows: Voting is meaningless if its outcome is ambiguous; the outcome of voting is ambiguous if it does not uniquely reveal the popular or general will;
because different rules produce different outcomes, voting cannot
unambiguously define the popular will. We note that this argument relies upon the claim that democratic theory is committed to
(1) the existence of a unique popular will in all electoral matters
and (2) the constraint that that will is defined by voting. Are these
conditions plausible constraints on democratic theory?

For Riker they appear to be. Recall his claim that voting is *democratic* only if it expresses popular will or sentiment. Democracy
grounds the requirement of full participation, the constraint of
fairness and the protection of speech, association and the like.
Democratic institutions, the constraints they impose and the free-

doms they create are alleged to organize choice meaningfully, that is, to ensure that a social or public choice reflects public sentiment. If Riker is right about this characterization of democratic political institutions and particularly about the role constraints on voting procedures play in the theory of democracy, then the ambiguity problem is serious. For, as he sees it, *democratic* voting must express a unique public sentiment or preference. But the fact that different voting rules express different sentiments, given the exact same data base, means that no voting rule can uniquely determine the public will.

Riker appears to treat these two constraints – that in any election there exists a unique popular will and that that will is defined or specified by voting – as part of the meaning of democracy. Otherwise, the argument from ambiguity would fail to establish the meaninglessness of democratic voting. Since only democratic voting rules are adequately fair, their meaninglessness suffices to shed doubt on all collective decision procedures.

At this juncture in the argument, Riker's distinction between two conceptions of democracy becomes relevant. In the end, Riker does not claim that all forms of democratic voting are indefensible. What he previously treated as commitments of all democratic theories he now claims are commitments of only one sort of democratic theory: democratic or constitutional *populism*. Populist democracy is then distinguished from constitutional liberalism or *liberal* democracy. According to populism, each election reveals a popular or general will. The point of elections is to define and uncover the general will so that, by complying with laws, individuals act in accordance with their own will. The liberal sees elections in an entirely different way. For the liberal democrat, for example James Madison, the point of elections is the possibility of removing officeholders.[20] The claim Riker ultimately advances is that the results of social choice theory undermine populism but not liberalism. Liberal democracy alone withstands the challenge of social choice theory.

3. POPULIST DEFENSES

Several avenues of defense are open to a populist who seeks to meet the challenge of social choice theory as it is construed by Riker.

First, a populist can deny that a general will must exist in all electoral matters. Following Rousseau, a populist might accept the existence of a general will over a certain domain of electoral issues (such as those concerned with the provision of public goods) while denying that there is a general will in all matters that may be brought up for a vote. Next, over the domain of issues in which it is alleged that a general will exists, a populist can deny being committed to the claim that the general will is unique. Rather, just as welfare economists need not subscribe to the idea of unique efficient outcomes, the general will may only specify a set of acceptable outcomes. Populists may, therefore, be committed to a general will, but they need not assert its uniqueness or its existence in all electoral matters. Against this defense, Riker's criticisms of populism are telling only if he can show that the range of ambiguity is so large that the general will is essentially vacuous.

As Riker implies, a number of recent results in the theory of collective choice have been construed as ruling against this defense.[21] Under quite general conditions, the range of instability of any voting rule is large enough to encompass all the feasible alternatives. A voting procedure is liable to pick any alternative, and so the general will must be entirely unconfining.

Whether the general instability results preclude a populist from pursuing this line of defense depends on the proper interpretation of those results, and that is a matter of some dispute. Our view is that the implications of the instability results are somewhat overdrawn. While voting procedures are able to produce any feasible alternative as an outcome, they may be very unlikely to do so.[22]

Secondly, a populist might argue that in those electoral matters in which there exists a general will, it is not specified by voting. This line of defense relies on specifying the relationship between voting and the general will in a *nonsemantic* or *noncriterial* way. One alternative is to view the relationship between voting and the general will as *epistemic*. (Again, this appears to have been Rousseau's view.) Moreover, such a view requires treating voting over issues involving a general will as consisting in *judgments* – which can be either true or false – rather than in expressions of preferences – which are neither. Like an advocate of the first line of defense, the epistemic populist need not hold that there is a uniquely good or most reliable voting procedure for all electoral matters, nor need he hold that there exists a general will in all matters. Rousseau, for one, appears to have held that the range of issues in which there is a general will is limited; that the relationship between voting and the general will over those matters is epistemic; and that no particular voting rule is optimal in all cases.

The epistemic populist begins, then, by distinguishing between those electoral issues in which there exists a general will and those in which there is no reason to believe that there is a general will or disposition. For all those electoral issues in which no general will exists, the ambiguity argument of social choice theory poses no special problems for a populist. Where no general will exists, electoral outcomes can be meaningful even if they are not unique.

We therefore restrict the remainder of this discussion to those cases in which the populist is committed to the existence of a general will. Over these issues there is a correct judgment about what a collective ought to do. By voting, individuals express judgments about what ought to be done. One's judgment about what ought to be done by way of providing public goods need not coincide with one's own preference; in any case, one's vote is not intended to express one's preference. Voting brings together judgments. Different voting rules amalgamate those judgments in different ways. Voting rules are then to be justified in terms of their capacity to provide evidence of the general will. And, as in other contexts, different rules will be more or less well suited to this task.

The epistemic populist denies that there is a necessary connection between the results of voting and the general will. He holds that the general will is not entailed by the result of a vote, and so he escapes the implications of social choice theory. However, he accepts, along with the criterial populist, that the results of a vote can give *evidence* of what the general will is. This presents the epistemic populist with a problem not faced by the criterial populist. The problem is explaining why the results of voting provide evidence of the general will. This explanation is simple for the criterial populist. Voting provides evidence of the general will because voting defines the general will. No such explanation of the evidential connection between voting and the general will is open to the epistemic populist. What sort of account of the evidential relationship between voting and the general will can a populist offer?

One explanation, but by no means the only one, open to the epistemic populist is to argue that voting provides evidence of the general will if there exists a *reliability* connection between voting and the general will. The desirability of a voting rule will then depend on its reliability – the extent to which the collective judgments it generates converge with what is in fact the correct judgment. The key features of a voting rule would then relate to its capacity to discriminate among various levels of voter competence in making judgments and in its capacity to encourage voter competence in forming the correct judgment.

One might be tempted to object to the reliabilist analysis of the evidentiary property of voting as follows: In any epistemic account, the general will transcends voting. There is a correct answer in regard to the issue at stake whether or not a vote is taken. The voting procedure is a device to help citizens discover what is the correct thing to do. If there exists an independently specifiable general will, however, then either we can uncover what it is on a particular issue or we cannot. If we cannot determine what the general will is, then voting, understood epistemically, is uninteresting. If, however, we can discover the general will, then we can do so by voting only, in some other way, or both by voting and in some other way. If, on the one hand, we can identify what is in the general interest over a domain of issues without regard to voting, then it cannot be part of the justification of voting that it is necessary to reveal the general will. On the other hand, if the general will can be revealed only by voting, then we appear to lack an independent criterion for assessing the reliability of various voting mechanisms. The problem, for an epistemic interpretation of voting, is that we need either an independent means for identifying the general will – in which case voting, for this purpose, is otiose – or independent criteria with which to assess the reliability of various voting procedures which do not themselves rely upon the existence of an alternative mechanism for identifying the general will.

These remarks contain two different objections to this particular form of epistemic populism. Both rely on the following claim. The reliability of voting rules depends on our having independent access to the nature of the general will. Either we have such access or we do not. If we do, then voting is otiose, if we do not, then we cannot determine its reliability. Both objections can be met. First, it need be no part of an epistemic theory of voting that voting should be the only way of gaining insight into the nature of the general will. What recommends voting is neither its epistemic uniqueness nor its privileged status. It may lack both features. Instead, voting may give evidence of the general will in a particular way – by public forum, discussion and participation. And in matters concerning the coercive authority of the state, these features of voting are not insignificant. Second, while it is true that if we have no independent access to the nature of the general will, then we may be unable to determine whether or not a voting rule is in fact reliable, the epistemic populist is trying to specify the conditions under which a voting rule could be justified, not the conditions under which we would know that it was. The voting reliabilist would deny that in order for a voting rule to be justified we must also know that it a reliable guide to the nature of the general will. It simply must be reliable, independent of our knowledge of its reliability.

Nonuniqueness and epistemic populism are not the only ways in which a populist might attempt to meet the challenge of social choice theory. A populist might seek to avoid the implications of the instability and ambiguity results by arguing that there exists a uniquely defensible voting rule. In this way, even if the outcome of an election is thought to define the general will and not merely to relate to it evidentiarily, problems of ambiguity will not arise, because only one rule is admissible. Perhaps the best-known such attempt to meet the challenge of social choice theory along choice theoretic lines is Kenneth May's characterization of majority rule with two alternatives.[23] If the implications of May's theorem are accepted, admissible choice on larger sets of alternatives would be made by voting rules that are extensions of binary majority rule.

Leaving aside for the moment what would constitute an extension of simple majority rule, we must ask if May's defense of his axioms is in fact sufficient to preclude all alternatives to simple majority rule. In our view, May's formal statement of his axioms is stronger than the defense that may be offered for them. One example is sufficient to illustrate this and to undercut this line of argument.

In the presence of May's other axioms we can restrict our argument to the case of special majority rules. Within the class of special majorities, only simple majority satisfies May's strong monotonicity condition;[24] yet special majorities, including unanimity, are weakly monotonic. If we drop the strong monotonicity condition in favor of weak monotonicity as a condition on voting rules requires an argument that only it expresses some more fundamental demand of collective decision. The plausible candidate for this deeper demand would be that only a strongly monotonic function could specify a general will. But as we have seen, a populist wants a choice rule to do two things: (1) rule out perversity and (2) specify a general will. Weak monotonicity suffices to rule out perversity. Special majorities are weakly monotonic, and, moreover, they are more likely than simple majorities to constitute what we would normally think of as expressions of popular or general sentiment. The strong monotonicity requirement is inadequately motivated; weakening it, however, precludes uniqueness.[25]

Something like the uniqueness argument is required by a pop-

ulist who is committed to a criterial conception of the relationship
between voting and the general will. Unfortunately, it appears
that no such argument can be sustained.

If May were right, simple majority voting would be the preferred social choice procedure in binary choice situations. As Riker
notes, however, there are almost always more than two natural
alternatives. Simple majority over more than two alternatives is
unstable. Consequently, to avoid instability, the alternatives must
be reduced to two. But every method of performing this reduction is subject to strategic manipulation, and this fact reintroduces
ambiguity into the process. In this sense, then, the uniqueness of
simple majority voting is either mythical or useless.

The responses I have thus far offered assume that social choice
theory presents a serious problem for populism. The problem is
this: Voting is meaningless. If the outcome of a vote is meaningless, how can it be thought of as defining anything, let alone the
general will? Populism, even in its modest forms, is committed to
a general will, at least over some electoral issues. Populism is committed to nonsense or, worse, is itself nonsense.

Taking the results of social choice theory at face value, as deeply
problematic for populism, I suggested how populists might yet
defend their position by advancing what we call epistemic populism. I also suggested that a criterial populist might deny the
uniqueness of the general will. In short, populism might be defended by accepting that the relationship between voting and the
general will is definitional, by denying uniqueness or by denying
that the relationship between voting and the general will is definitional.

We have not fully considered two other, related alternatives.
The first is that perhaps the results of social choice theory are as
problematic for liberalism as they are for populism. The second is
that the implications of the social choice literature are subject to
dispute and, in particular, that neither liberal nor populist political
institutions behave as poorly as the instability theories would have
us believe. I shall turn now to considering each of these alternatives.

4. LIBERAL DEMOCRACY

I shall begin by summarizing Riker's argument for liberalism. Only
democratic institutions can satisfy minimal standards of fairness.
But democratic institutions produce arbitrary social choices. A
radical skepticism about voting is therefore warranted. Three things

appear to follow from this skepticism about voting. First, no purely proceduralist defense of democracy can be sustained, for whatever the virtues of participation or procedural fairness might be, one cannot defend the morality of what is either paradoxical or otherwise unintelligible. It hardly counts in favor of a procedure that participation is fair, full and equal if the outcomes of every application of the procedure turn out to be unintelligible. Second, the argument for autonomy and democracy is undercut, since democratic voting procedures do not necessarily yield expressions of the general will; so complying with measures that result from democratic voting procedures is not tantamount to acting in compliance with rules of one's own making. Thus, radical skepticism about the meaningfulness of voting requires that democracy be defended on nonprocedural grounds having nothing to do with the relationship between democratic collective choice and the aims of collective policy. "All elections do or have to do is to permit people to get rid of rulers. The people who do this do not themselves need to have a coherent will. . . . The liberal interpretation of voting thus allows elections to be useful and significant even in the presence of cycles, manipulation and other kinds of 'errors' in voting. . . . The kind of democracy that thus survives is not, however, popular rule, but rather an intermittent, sometimes random, even perverse, popular veto. . . . Liberal democracy is simply the veto by which it is sometimes possible to restrain official tyranny."[26]

Thus, third, the virtue of liberal democracy is that it promotes liberty by veto. "Suppose freedom is simply the absence of governmental restraint on individual action. Then the chance to engage in vetoing by rejecting officials and the chance that the rejection actually occur are the very essence of this freedom."[27]

Voting outcomes are either deeply ambiguous, unstable or both. That turns out not to matter, however; voting does not have to be meaningful. It simply has to be *effective* in a well-defined way. The voting process need only make it possible for an electorate to remove officials from office. In doing so, democratic voting is the guardian of liberty. Liberty is the absence of governmental constraints or coercion. Liberty is maximized when coercion is minimized. Voting helps to reduce coercion by increasing the costs to legislators of imposing coercive legislation, that is, by making real the possibility of their removal from office. Voting as the guardian of negative liberty, not as the expression of popular will, is the essence of liberal democracy.

In fact, we can flesh out a bit more the possible connections between liberty and democracy and identify exactly which relationships between the two the liberal democrat, at least for Riker, is committed to. Riker has in mind three ways in which the ideals of democracy and liberty might connect in a liberal theory of democracy. The first concerns the relationship between voting and those concrete liberties of, say, association and expression that render voting possible and judgments over alternatives informed. The next concerns autonomy, or Kantian liberty. Here, liberty consists entirely in complying with prescriptions of one's own making. The third sort of liberty is negative liberty, the absence of governmental constraints. In the full theory of the state that ultimately emerges from the social choice theory of democracy, democracy as popular will, as autonomous agency, does not survive. What does survive is a theory of the liberal state in which negative liberty is maximized or ensured through popular elections and where the liberties necessary for the franchise to be meaningfully exercised are constitutionally guaranteed.

The liberal democrat, it appears, is committed to a skeletal version of classical liberal constitutionalism. A constitution exists that specifies not only the terms of collective decision making but guarantees a set of fundamental political liberties. These concrete, political liberties, for example of association and speech, derive from the need to make political decisions informed and reasoned. Whatever rule of collective decision making emerges in the constitutional process is necessary to reduce the possibility of political tyranny and to maximize, thereby, negative political liberty. The choice of voting rules is then to be made exclusively in the light of this goal. For these reasons, liberal democracy, so conceived, survives the challenge of social choice theory. But does it?

Let us begin by noting that this defense of liberal democracy is based not on a proceduralist criterion of assessment but on both instrumental and contractarian ones. There is no claim made that liberal democratic collective decision procedures are justified because they satisfy a certain set of ideals or constraints. Quite the contrary. Liberal democracy appears to emerge precisely because no voting procedure – at least in Riker's view – satisfies any plausible set of such constraints. Instead, liberal democratic institutions have the desired effect of allowing individuals to remove officeholders, and this maximizes (negative) liberty. That is their instrumental value. Moreover, each potential voter, thinking through the choice of collective decision rules *ex ante,* would prefer liberal voting institutions precisely because they have this property.

But do the ambiguity and instability results of social choice theory distinguish between populist and liberal democracy sufficiently to render the rejection of populism and the defense of liberalism plausible? Consider the ambiguity arguments first. To the extent that the outcomes of social choice are ambiguous, they render liberal democracy just as incoherent as populist democracy. If it is impossible to interpret the outcomes of elections in a reasoned way, officials removed from office under election system P might not have been removed under process Q, and so on. How then can we interpret the removal of officials as an expression of dissatisfaction with their performance? How can we expect officials to take account of such ambiguous signals in deciding how to behave?

The problem with Riker's argument goes even deeper than this. If he is right about the implications of the social choice theory, namely, that all voting is meaningless, then what follows is that *no* set of collective choice institutions – *liberal or populist* – can be defended on proceduralist grounds. Recall that, as Riker interprets proceduralist modes of justification, to be justified a voting rule must be both fair and meaningful. If he is right about social choice theory, no voting rules are meaningful. *No* institutions, liberal or populist, are therefore justifiable on proceduralist grounds. Justification must rest on instrumentalist or contractarian approaches. But if this is so, it is not enough to give an instrumentalist or contractarian defense of liberal democracy; he must also show that liberal institutions are to be preferred to populist ones on these accounts. In other words, if it shows anything, social choice theory demonstrates that neither liberalism nor populism may be defended on proceduralist grounds. It leaves open the possibility that both can be defended on some other grounds. But Riker considers nonprocedural defenses only of liberalism, not of populism. He appears to believe that populism entails a particular form of justification, namely proceduralism, whereas liberalism also entails a unique form of justification, namely instrumentalism. Surely this is wrong. When Riker says that the meaninglessness of voting is compatible with liberalism, he should be saying that even if voting is not meaningful, it is still possible to justify its application on other grounds – that is, its good consequences. But then, a populist might make precisely the same argument. Voting, though meaningless in the sense of social choice theory, still strengthens allegiance, increases competence, develops a sense of community and the like. All of these are virtues of electoral systems that populists have generally endorsed. Elections have good populist consequences.

In fact, once the line of justification switches from procedural-ism to instrumentalism, it is not at all obvious that the liberal dem-ocrat, as he is construed by Riker, does as well as Rousseau's pop-ulist. For it surely cannot be a good consequence of voting that it randomly, that is, nonrationally, removes officeholders. So does sudden illness. But nonreasoned removal from office is precisely what follows if Riker is correct in interpreting the instability re-sults of social choice theory as demonstrating the meaninglessness of voting. If outcomes are arbitrarily connected to the preferences of the electorate, we cannot infer from his removal from office that an officeholder's conduct was in fact disapproved of by the voters. This is hardly the ideal of officeholders being put at risk by elections that we associate with liberalism. In short, if we take social choice theory's results as conclusive, as Riker does, then what we must give up is proceduralism, not necessarily populism. Moreover, in moving from proceduralism to instrumentalism, it may be that populism is more plausible than the sort of liberalism Riker advances.

Next, in our view, Riker overstates the implications of the in-stability results of social choice. The problem of ambiguity arises at two levels. As Riker first raises it, the problem is simply that the outcome is always relative to the collective choice rule; had a different rule been employed, a different outcome might have been reached. Understood in this way, ambiguity is troublesome nei-ther for the liberal nor for the populist. As long as there is a well-defined set of rules in place, the outcome of an election is inter-pretable within the given electoral framework. That an alternative framework could be thought of that would produce a different outcome is simply irrelevant.

The ambiguity problem resurfaces, however, in a systemic way. Consider that more than two alternatives are almost always avail-able. The application of any nonunanimity rule to the set of alter-natives may therefore lead to unstable outcomes. As all methods for reducing the set of alternatives to two are subject to manipu-lation, there is no guarantee that the electoral outcome will be related to the distribution of preferences. This is the sort of sys-temic ambiguity that is in theory at least problematic for both liberal and populist theories.

Putting the two ambiguity problems together suggests the fol-lowing. As long as the electoral framework is well defined, its outcomes are interpretable and only uninterestingly ambiguous. The problem is in deciding upon an electoral framework. The aim of any such framework is to generate outcomes that are systematically and coherently related to the distribution of preferences. If more than two feasible alternatives are available, the nature of this connection will depend on the institutional details of the electoral system. Rather than infer from the ambiguity argument that electoral outcomes are arbitrary, we ought instead to infer that institutions matter. They matter because their particular content and contour determine the extent to which electoral outcomes reflect popular preferences. From this perspective, the real intellectual need is for a workable theory of institutional behavior.

It is true, as Riker says, that if there are a large enough number of available alternatives, any voting rule that requires less than unanimity will produce large cycles for most configurations of popular preferences. But while such cycles usually exist, and all outcomes are unstable in the sense of being liable to defeat by some alternative, this does not imply that such cycles will be realized, or that the actual performance of the collective choice institutions will be chaotic in the ordinary sense of that term. While cycles may be ubiquitous and all outcomes unstable, some alternatives may be much more vulnerable than others, and the less vulnerable alternatives may turn out to be quite nicely connected to the distribution of preferences.

In fact, two recent lines of argument have been made in support of this claim. The first, due to Gerald Kramer[28] and to John Ferejohn, Richard McKelvey and Edward Packel,[29] shows essentially that, even in the presence of a global cycle, majority-rule "paths" or "trajectories" are well behaved in the sense of exhibiting stable, limiting properties. Intuitively, the arguments may be stated as follows: While alternatives that are disliked by nearly everyone may be reached in the majority-rule cycle, relatively few paths lead to these alternatives from any given alternative. Most paths lead toward alternatives that are attractive to large numbers of people, so that such paths tend to stay among relatively attractive alternatives. For this reason, majority-rule paths converge on relatively small sets of alternatives, which are "centrally" located in the sense that they are moderately attractive to large numbers of people.

The second argument is due to Nicholas Miller[30] and is developed further by Kenneth Shepsle and Barry Weingast[31] and Richard McKelvey,[32] and it shows that even when there is a global cycle, if the members of the electorate take full account of their strategic opportunities under the institutional rules governing consideration of alternatives, only a small subset of alternatives may arise as outcomes of the process. Thus, while each alternative may be defeated, only a small subset of them may arise as equilibria. Moreover, this set is "close" to the set found in the paper by Ferejohn, McKelvey and Packel. While neither of these lines of argument has been formulated in as general a setup as have the instability results, it seems likely that similar properties will be found in general models.

From the present point of view, the important thing about these results is that they apply to a wide variety of implementations of voting rules, liberal as well as populist. Thus, on the basis of this work, there seems to be no reason to separate the likely performance of liberal and populist institutions. If the one is unstable, so is the other, and the extent of instability seems likely to be similar. The instability results may be inadequate to preclude either liberal or populist institutions or, for that matter, proceduralist attempts to justify either.

5. CONCLUSION

Social choice theory is replete with theorems demonstrating the instability and systemic ambiguity of voting. Riker argues from these results to the incoherence of populist democracy and to the defensibility of liberal democracy. But the instability and ambiguity results do not distinguish between liberal and populist institutions. Whether these results are compatible with the defensibility of both or establish the incoherence of both remains the central question. Although I am troubled by the implications of instability theorems, I think it premature to see these results as establishing the arbitrariness of collective decision making. Rather, these results demonstrate the importance of gaining a fuller understanding of the likely performance of democratic institutions.

13. Morality and the theory of rational choice

1. INTRODUCTION

What is the relationship between morality and rationality? The answer to this question depends, of course, on how we characterize rationality and morality. We can begin with the definition of rationality found in contemporary microeconomics: Rationality is utility maximization. The rational actor seeks to maximize his net (expected) utility. Defining rationality in this way enables us to give a simple and minimal definition of morality: Morality is constrained utility maximization. The moral actor sometimes acts so as to constrain his utility-maximizing behavior. Given these definitions, rationality and morality are incompatible. The purely rational individual, at least sometimes, must act immorally; the purely moral individual, at least sometimes, must act irrationally. Recent work in the theory of rational choice, however, purports to demonstrate not only that rationality and morality are compatible but, moreover, that moral principles are *derivable* from rationality, once that concept is correctly analyzed.

It is common to distinguish between the *substantive* and *motivational* aspects of a moral theory. The substantive component specifies the content of the principles of morality; the motivational component explains why a rational person would comply with the principles specified by the substantive theory. If morality is to be derived from rationality, the theory of rationality must generate both the substantive and motivational components of moral theory. In what follows, we hope to show that rationality cannot generate the *substantive* component of a moral theory. But despite this skeptical goal, we are determined to take seriously the rational choice framework in which this debate takes place. Understanding this framework is essential in order both to comprehend the arguments that follow and to appreciate the relevance of rational choice theory to moral and political philosophy in general.

2. THE RATIONAL CHOICE FRAMEWORK

One way of framing the question of whether morality is derivable
from rationality is in contractarian terms: Under what conditions,
if any, would rational agents agree to constrain their utility-
maximizing behavior? We might begin answering this question by
answering another question first: Can circumstances be specified
in which imposing constraints on one's self-interested, utility-
maximizing behavior would be *irrational?* In this light, consider
the economist's concept of perfect competition. Under conditions
of perfect competition, the individually rational, self-interested
behavior of all agents induces a Pareto-efficient outcome. Pareto-
efficient states have no states Pareto superior to them. In optimal
equilibria, therefore, each actor does as well as he can – that is, his
utility is maximized subject to the utility maximization of others.
If, by acting purely self-interestedly, each agent does as well as he
or she can, then it would be irrational for any agent to impose
restrictions on the pursuit of his self-interest. If, given the utility
of others, I do the best I can by pursuing my self-interest, then I
will necessarily do less well by constraining my self-interested behavior. Under conditions of perfect competition, then, the rational actor has no incentive to adopt constraints, moral or otherwise, on his utility-maximizing behavior. Compliance with moral
principles would be irrational.

When markets fail, however (which, in the real world, they will
do without exception), and conditions of perfect competition do
not obtain, the self-interested, utility-maximizing behavior of each
individual leads to a Pareto-*inefficient* outcome – that is, one in
which at least some individuals could be made better off without
worsening the condition of others. The possibility then arises that
by constraining her utility-maximizing behavior, an individual may
be made better off than if she continues, unconstrained, to pursue
her self-interest. By introducing constraints on the utility-
maximizing behavior of individuals, it may be possible to secure
Pareto-*efficient* outcomes in which an individual fares better than
she would were she to act as an unconstrained utility maximizer.
There would then be a rational motivation for compliance with
normative, possibly even moral, principles which require constraint. Although the perfectly competitive market might be likened to what David Gauthier calls a "morally free zone" of "moral
anarchy," in which moral constraints are irrational, the imper-
fectly competitive market represents a "normatively constrained
zone," in which moral constraints might well be rational.[1]

Morality is a potential solution to the problem of market failure. Because morality is introduced to govern social interactions only under conditions of market failure, it is rendered fundamentally instrumental. The rationality of morality depends on its being a particular kind of solution to the problem of market failure, that is, one that secures a Pareto-efficient outcome by making each individual better off. To be a viable solution to the problem of market failure, morality must be both individually and collectively rational. Moreover, the case for morality generated by the market model is entirely contingent. But the contingency on which it rests is one virtually certain to obtain; markets are never perfectly competitive.

The market model of morality we are developing is not alone in employing the contingent fact of market failure as its theoretical point of departure. In affirming the need for political coercion, Hobbesian political contractarianism also relies on characterizing the state of nature as, in effect, a failed market. Within the market contractarian framework, morality and politics are alternative solutions to the same problem, that is, the suboptimality of the state of nature. Both morality and politics attempt to bridge the gap between the inefficient equilibrium of the state of nature and the potential Pareto-efficient equilibria unavailable if individuals act noncooperatively. Both moral and political contractarians recognize that efficient, mutually beneficial gains are available only when individuals constrain their utility-maximizing behavior. But while political contractarianism endorses a political or coercive remedy, moral contractarianism offers a moral one. Where political contractarians claim that state coercion is necessary to prevent individuals from unrestrained pursuit of their self-interest, moral contractarianism claims that individuals rationally and voluntarily will choose to constrain their behavior, thus rendering a political solution otiose.

I have, up to now, cast the rational choice approach to moral and political theory in terms of market failure. But the textbook illustration of conduct that is both individually rational and collectively irrational is the prisoners' dilemma (PD). It is common, moreover, to treat market failure as a PD; and Russell Hardin is widely credited with having demonstrated that certain sources of market failure (for example, the provision of certain collective goods) are themselves extensionally equivalent to n-person PDs.[2] Given the standard conventions, we might discuss the relationship between morality and rationality in terms of the PD.

Recasting the problem of market failure as the problem of escaping the PD emphasizes the relationship between the suboptimality of the state of nature and cooperation. Rational individuals in a PD *must* choose the noncooperative individual strategy available to them. Were individuals in the PD able to cooperate, they would, in principle, be able to secure the Pareto-efficient outcome. Cooperation in the PD amounts to agreement among all individuals in the dilemma on a *cooperative joint strategy*, which if complied with by all, will secure a Pareto-efficient outcome. We can characterize the object of agreement in this context as a set of collectively self-imposed constraints on individual utility-maximization, perhaps even as a set of moral principles. The problem of deriving morality from rationality, then, can be recast as the problem of determining the cooperative joint strategy on which all parties in the state of nature would agree and with which all would comply, a strategy the existence of which the political contractarian denies. The rational choice theory of morality must provide an account of the rationality of agreement and another account of the rationality of compliance. The theory of that agreement will provide the substantive component of morality; the theory of compliance with that agreement will generate the motivational component of morality.

How are we to model in rational choice terms the process and substance of agreement? We can think of the contract or agreement process as a *rational bargain*. Each actor would agree upon a set of principles only if compliance with them is efficient, that is, only if the principles of moral constraint captured the whole of the available surplus. (This is the collective rationality condition of bargaining theory.) Each actor, as a utility maximizer, however, seeks to maximize his or her share of the gain. (This is the individual rationality condition.) Because the choice problem has both efficiency and division aspects, it is natural to model it as a "mixed bargaining game." Cooperation is necessary to *produce* the surplus, which is in turn contingent upon agreement on the *division* of those gains. No agreement upon relative shares, no surplus. Moral principles are the outcome of a *rational* bargain so conceived.

The theory of compliance with the agreement on the joint cooperative strategy must explain why rational agents would *comply with* the joint strategy they bargain to. In agreeing on a joint strategy, agents have agreed to abide by normative, perhaps moral, principles. The problem, then, of explaining why rational agents would comply with a joint strategy becomes the problem of determining the motivational component in moral theory – that is, that part of moral theory which explains why it is rational to act in accordance with moral principles.

Compliance and agreement are inexorably linked in the rational choice framework. If rationality precludes compliance, there is no sense in pursuing agreement on a cooperative joint strategy. And there is no point to demonstrating the rationality of such compliance if rationality precludes securing agreement on a cooperative joint strategy. More important, it will not be enough for the rational choice model to demonstrate the rationality of agreement and compliance with *any* constraining principles. If they are to be *moral* principles, these principles must be fair and impartial. In this essay, I shall assume that there is some correct theory of the bargaining process whereby rational agents agree on *some unique principle or other,* and concentrate instead on the problem of demonstrating that rational agents will agree on *fair,* and thus *moral,* principles.

In a bargaining situation, failure to secure agreement returns parties to their prebargaining positions. The way in which the parties evaluate their prebargaining positions will naturally influence their bargaining behavior in ways that are likely to affect outcomes. If inequity or unfairness exists in the initial position, it is likely to be influential in the bargaining process, or even if it is not, it will be transmitted by the bargaining process to the outcomes, thereby raising doubts about the fairness of the resulting principles. The principles chosen in bargaining from unfair initial positions will almost certainly be unfair. On the other hand, the unfairness of the outcome of bargaining does not preclude its rationality. Rational bargains need not be fair ones. So why in the world would someone think that morality could possibly be the outcome of a rational bargain?

One solution to the problem of the *status quo ante* and its role in bargaining is to emphasize that morality is the outcome of a particular rational bargain, characterized in a particular way. The advocate of the bargaining theory approach need not make the foolish claim that every rational bargain is fair. Only certain rational bargains, struck under certain conditions, need be fair. But which bargains, under what conditions? One argument might be that rational bargains struck from fair initial conditions produce constraints that are fair and impartial in the sense necessary for them to constitute a morality. Why not, in other words, just preclude bargaining from unfair starting points? The point of the enterprise, after all, is to hit upon moral principles, and bargaining from unfair initial positions is unlikely to serve that purpose well.

This simple solution is, alas, too simple. In confining the bargaining problem to "fair" starting points, one cannot end up deriving morality from rationality alone; the best one can do is derive morality from rationality encased within an independently derived moral framework. Our objection is not that it is inappropriate in general to confine the choice problem or to define the environment or circumstances in which actors are viewed as bargaining. After all, every theorist gives a particular characterization of the choice problem, including a specification of the environment of choice and a characterization of the decision makers. Our objection is the narrow one that precluding unfair initial bargaining positions *a priori* simply undermines the enterprise of deriving morality from rationality *simpliciter*. Instead, it derives morality from rationality *cum* fairness. Other constraints on the bargaining problem might be perfectly acceptable. This one is not, unless one can show, rather than assume, that bargaining from unfair initial positions is irrational.

We shall return to the problem of characterizing the choice problem later. For now it is enough to note that the easy solution won't work. Let us consider a complicated one. The rational choice theory of morality faces two difficult problems. It must provide a theory of compliance and a theory of the fairness of the bargain. This much we know. Wouldn't it be especially impressive if both could be solved by the same argument? Certainly. Consider the following strategy. To solve the compliance problem one has to show minimally that it is rational to comply with one's agreements. Presumably these agreements or bargains are themselves rational. Not every rational agreement is a moral (or fair) one. Suppose, however, one could argue that it is rational to comply with agreements only if they are fair. Then the following argument would be available.

(1) Bargaining is rational only if compliance is rational.
(2) Compliance is rational only if the bargain outcome is fair.
(3) Therefore, bargaining is rational only if it is fair.
(4) Therefore, rational bargains must be fair bargains.
(5) Therefore, bargaining from whatever unfair advantages one may have *ex ante* is not rational. (The reason: Bargaining from unfair positions yields unfair outcomes with which it is not rational to comply. But if it is not rational to comply, then it is not rational to bargain.)

The upshot of the argument is that a particular solution to the compliance problem is sufficient to solve the unfair bargaining problem as well. Once both problems are resolved, the derivation of morality from rationality requires only a particular theory of rational bargaining. Moreover, if this argument is sound, the view that bargaining theoretic models of justice necessarily generate the principle "to each according to his threat advantage" turns out to be unfounded. This, then, is the argument one needs to make in order to derive morality from a bargaining theoretic conception of rationality. But is it an argument one can plausibly make? Apparently it is, for it is the central argument in David Gauthier's *Morals by Agreement*. Moreover, the fact that Gauthier comes closer to pulling off this "argument of a lifetime" than anyone could legitimately expect makes this book the most important contribution to moral and political theory since Rawls's *Theory of Justice*.[3] The fact that in the end the argument does not quite work makes the rest of this chapter worth reading.

3. FAIRNESS AND CONSTRAINED MAXIMIZATION

We noted earlier that any game-theoretic approach to morality requires a solution to the defection or compliance problem. As a general solution to the compliance problem, Gauthier advances the *theory of constrained maximization*. I do not take issue with the theory of constrainted maximization as such, but several of the arguments that follow require at least a rudimentary understanding of it and of several distinctions upon which it relies.

The question is whether it is rational to comply with bargains into which one has rationally entered. In the course of one's lifetime, one is likely to face this question many times over. In particular, one is likely to be faced repeatedly with PD-structured bargains, that is, bargains embedded within PDs. So one must ask oneself what sort of *disposition* toward compliance it would be rational to adopt. If one could rationally acquire a disposition which counseled compliance rather than defection in PD-structured bargains, then one could benefit repeatedly from collective action with others similarly disposed. The question is not simply whether it is rational sometimes, for strategic reasons, to comply with the bargains one strikes, but whether it is rational so to dispose oneself. Of course, the answer may be that it is not rational to adopt a disposition and thus to constrain oneself, that one will do better over time by behaving strategically on a case-by-case basis. Gauthier disagrees. He argues that under certain conditions it is in fact rational to dispose oneself to compliance. Basically his view is that it is rational to dispose oneself to compliance if a threshold number of similarly disposed persons exists and if individuals are neither "opaque" nor "transparent" but are instead "translucent" with respect to their dispositions for compliance.[4] In other words, if there is a reasonably good chance that you are negotiating with a similarly disposed person and the chances are pretty good that you will be identified for what you truly are (a complier or a defector), then it is rational to dispose yourself to compliance. To say it is rational to dispose yourself to compliance is to say that you will maximize your utility over time by doing so. Once you are rationally disposed, it will be rational for you to do what you are disposed to do – that is, to comply – even if you may be taken advantage of from time to time by defectors, or even if you might do better on occasion by defecting and thereby taking advantage of others. The idea is that the benefits from the collective action such a disposition makes possible outweigh these costs.

In what follows, I grant that constrained maximization is a correct solution to the compliance problem. The crucial issue, as we shall demonstrate, is whether *narrow* compliance, that is, (roughly) the disposition to comply only with *fair* bargains, is uniquely rational. So much for clarification on the matter of rational compliance and the motivational component of morality. Now, to the matter of fairness.

4. FAIRNESS AND BARGAINING

Moral principles are constraints. Not every constraint is, however, a moral one. Moral principles are constraints that are "fair and impartial." The outcome of a bargain is moral only if it is fair; and it is fair, according to Gauthier, only if it accords each party a share of the gains proportionate to his contribution, which itself must be a function of holdings fairly acquired in the initial position.

Considerations of fairness enter Gauthier's account at three distinct places. The first is within the theory of rational bargaining in which rational persons, it is argued, agree to a set of *fair* constraining principles as the result of following a uniquely rational bargaining principle. The second is within the theory of constrained maximization in which, it is argued, rational individuals dispose themselves to comply only with *fair* constraining principles. Bargaining, however, takes place within the context of prior relative bargaining (or starting) points. Consequently, Gauthier's defense of the rationality of morality requires, third, a theory of fair initial bargaining positions. For Gauthier, rational persons would only enter into bargaining from fair initial bargaining positions. It follows that there are two ways in which constraining principles might be unfair or biased and, therefore, not moral. First, the *bargaining procedure* itself might be unfair. If it is, the principles specifying the distribution of the cooperative surplus might allow some to gain in greater proportion to their contribution than others. Second, the *initial bargaining position* might be unfair, in which case even a fair bargaining procedure (i.e., one in which each individual gains in proportion to his contribution) will embed and transmit this unfairness to the constraining principles to which persons bargain.

Unfairness in the initial bargaining position may be transmitted to the outcome of bargaining in one of three ways. First, if as a result of an unfair initial position, some parties are able to contribute more to a cooperative venture than others, those advantaged individuals will be accorded greater shares of the cooperative surplus. Then, even if the bargaining process itself is fair in that it accords each a share of the surplus proportionate to his or her contribution, the resulting distribution is unfair because it transmits and amplifies the distortions created by unfairly acquired entitlements. Second, even if advantaged parties in the initial position do not contribute more to the bargain, and only contribute that portion of their entitlements which would have been acquired in a fair initial position, the outcome may yet be unfair for either of two reasons. Those unfairly advantaged in the initial bargaining position retain their unfairly acquired entitlements after the bargain. This is just to say that even a fair bargaining procedure need not rectify unjust prior distributions. Fair bargaining does not embed a principle of corrective or rectificatory justice. And it is also possible that those individuals whose entitlements were *fairly* acquired might have had more to bargain with in the initial position had no one else acquired entitlements unfairly. Third, advantaged parties in the initial position might use their advantage to "coerce," "railroad" or "extort" a bargain from the disadvantaged which fails even to accord the disadvantaged a share of the cooperative surplus proportionate to their contributions. Here, the unfair initial bargaining position induces an unfair bargaining procedure. In the first two kinds of cases the distortions existing in unfair starting points are transmitted to outcomes, thus polluting them, either because a fair bargaining procedure is unable to rectify or correct a prior unfair advantage, or because fair bargaining may actually exacerbate prior distortions. In the third case, prior unfairnesses are employed to distort, by "extortion" or "coercion," the bargaining process itself.

In order to derive morality from rational bargaining, the resulting principles must be fair and impartial. To demonstrate their fairness, Gauthier must argue that rational people will bargain only from fair initial bargaining positions, engage only in bargains whose procedures are fair and dispose themselves to comply with only constraining principles that result from a fair bargain originating in a fair initial bargaining position.

One last preliminary. Remember, Gauthier's argument is state-of-nature in character. That is what makes morality an alternative to political coercion. Both are potential solutions to the same problem: the suboptimality of the state of nature. Still, Gauthier is free to constrain somewhat the state of nature he has in mind. We shall have occasion to discuss aspects of his characterization of the state of nature in due course. For now, it is enough to note three aspects of his conception of state-of-nature theory. First, state-of-nature theory commits Gauthier to the *absence* of existing third-party enforcement. Bargaining takes place without the benefit of external means of enforcement adequate to induce compliance. If bargaining is to succeed, it must be because the outcome commands rational compliance on its own merits. Secondly, Gauthier is nowhere committed to the view that all rational bargains, under any conditions, are fair. He is committed only to the claim that rational bargaining in the state of nature yields fair and impartial outcomes. Finally, he explicitly rejects a Buchanan-like characterization of the state of nature in which individuals' initial bargaining positions are defined by a state of anarchistic equilibrium.[5]

These preliminaries strongly suggest the kind of strategy Gauthier pursues. Gauthier wants to argue that the only kind of bargains that can command rational compliance are fair ones; that bargaining from a position of anarchistic equilibrium will yield unstable results because the terms of the bargain will reflect the unfairness of the *status quo ante;* and that once third-party enforcement exists, the outcomes of rational bargaining need not be self-enforcing and, therefore, need not be fair. In effect, the bulk of Gauthier's arguments, therefore, seek to solve the compliance and the *status quo ante* problems simultaneously. The first, which is an argument from defection, claims that unfair bargains will be unstable, and since instability adversely affects the rationality of bargaining, only fair bargaining is rational. This argument contains the essence of what he finds wanting in Buchanan and Nash bargaining.

4.1. Fairness and stability

Gauthier begins his discussion of the initial bargaining position by considering a society of rational slaves and masters. In this society, the masters engage in costly coercion in order to force the slaves to do their bidding, while the slaves suffer the effects of coercion. Gauthier observes that this society is suboptimal: Alternative forms of interaction can enhance the well-being of some without making others worse off. In fact, there is a mutually advantageous bargain into which the slaves and masters might well enter. It would be rational, for example, for all to agree to continue their society as is, preserving the advantages and disadvantages of the caste system, while eliminating its coercive component. In such an agreement, masters are committed to eliminating coercion, and slaves are bound to serve their masters voluntarily. The bargain is Pareto improving, since masters could then enjoy life free of the costs of coercing, and the slaves would be free of the costs of being coerced. Gauthier notes, however, that once coercion has been banned by agreement and slaves and masters alike have improved their situation, the slaves will no longer find it rational to comply with their part of the bargain. They will simply walk away from the bargain, since in the absence of coercion they have no incentive to do the bidding of their masters. The bargain, though Pareto improving, is fundamentally unstable. By demanding pay for services, the slaves merely move the bargain along the Pareto frontier, giving them a greater share of the cooperative gains; whereas, were the masters to reintroduce slavery, both sides would return to the prebargain state, which would fall within the frontier and, therefore, would be inefficient. The slaves' walking away and demanding of pay are rational; the masters' threat to reintroduce slavery is not credible, since carrying it out would be inefficient. The slaves and masters end up with a situation in which the former slaves sell their labor to former slave owners. This is the stable outcome.

The conclusions Gauthier wants to draw from this example are: (1) that a bargain originating in an unfair initial position is unstable; and (2) that it is unstable because it is unfair; (3) that it is unfair because it involves "unproductive transfers"; and (4) that the stable outcome coincides with what would have been the outcome had the bargain originated in fair initial positions.

It is evident that the slaves would eventually find it irrational to continue to comply voluntarily with their agreement. The reason, as Gauthier puts it, is that they are being asked to make unproductive transfers. An unproductive transfer brings no new goods into being and involves no exchange of existing goods. It simply redistributes an existing good from one person to another. Thus, it involves "a utility cost for which no benefit is received, a utility gain for which no service is provided."[6]

The slaves have no incentive in the absence of coercion to continue making unproductive transfers. The masters are unable to reintroduce the former coercive arrangement in which slaves were slaves and masters were masters, since doing so would render everyone, including the masters, worse off then they would be under the implicit terms of the post-bargain, post-defection arrangement. The masters are stuck with a freer, more egalitarian society; the one, moreover, that all would have agreed to had the initial bargaining position been fair.

Perhaps Gauthier has isolated an example in which a bargain from an unfair initial position will result first in an unstable outcome and eventually in a stable one identical to that which would have resulted had bargaining originated in a fair initial position. It may also be true that the instability in the initial outcome is due to the irrationality, in the absence of coercion, of making unproductive transfers. Gauthier's argument for the rationality of morality requires, however, that the specific case be generalizable: that, in other words, all unfair but rational bargains in a state of nature will prove unstable. Unfair bargains must be unstable; that is, they must induce rational defection.

One reason for thinking that unfair bargains will occasion rational defection is that unfair bargains involve unproductive transfers, and making an unproductive transfer voluntarily is irrational. We can put the general argument more rigorously:

(1)   Unfair bargains always require unproductive transfers.
(2)   Therefore, absent coercion, compliance with unfair bargains will always require *voluntary* unproductive transfers.
(3)   An act is rational only if it is *directly* utility-maximizing.
(4)   An unproductive transfer is directly utility-maximizing only if it is *coerced.*
(5)   Therefore, absent coercion, compliance with unfair bargains must be irrational.
(6)   Therefore, unfair bargains between rational individuals are necessarily unstable.
(7)   Only stable bargains are rational.
(8)   Therefore, only fair bargains are rational.

Were it sound, this would be a great argument. It is surely an interesting one in any case. The problem is that it is unsound. Consider first the claim, (1), that unfair bargains always involve unproductive transfers. We earlier considered two ways in which an outcome of a bargain might be unfair. It might be the result of an unfair bargaining procedure, or it might be the outcome of a bargain from an unfair initial bargaining position. Recall that a fair bargaining procedure is one which distributes the cooperative surplus in proportion to the contributions of individuals. If we consider only those outcomes of bargains which are unfair because they are the result of unfair bargaining procedures, we might suppose that the first premise in Gauthier's argument is correct. After all, if the outcome of a bargain is unfair because it is the result of an unfair bargaining procedure, then some individuals are not gaining in proportion to their contribution and are instead transferring a portion of their fair share to others.

However, if we consider those outcomes of bargains which are unfair in virtue of the unfair initial positions in which they originate, we see that these unfair outcomes need not involve unproductive transfers. Outcomes which are unfair because of the unfairness of the initial bargaining position can be unfair for several reasons, only one of which requires unproductive transfers. This is the case where, as a result of an unfair bargaining advantage, one individual or group of individuals is able to use his (its) advantage to negotiate in an unfair bargaining process; in other words, bargains in which unfair initial positions induce an unfair bargaining procedure.

But unfair outcomes can result from unfair starting points for reasons other than the unfairness of the starting point's inducing extortion. These include outcomes that are results of a fair bargaining procedure but nevertheless either distribute the cooperative surplus according to contributions themselves made possible only because of unfairly acquired entitlements, or fail to rectify the unfairness of the initial position so that, though others have not gained in the bargain as a result of their unfair advantage in the initial position, they still retain their relative advantage in the postbargain state of affairs. Neither one of these unfair outcomes requires individuals to make unproductive transfers. If it is not rational for individuals to comply with these outcomes, it cannot be because it is irrational for individuals to make voluntary unproductive transfers, since no such transfers need to be made. It is not true, then, that unfair bargains always require unproductive transfers; (1) is false. Thus, it does not follow that, absent coercion, compliance with unfair bargains will always require *volun-*

tary unproductive transfers. In fact, they need not require *any* unproductive transfers, much less voluntary ones. Therefore, (2) is false.

Is it true, as is claimed in (4), that an unproductive transfer is directly utility maximizing only if it is coerced? Perhaps not. Whether an unproductive transfer can be directly utility maximizing in the absence of coercion depends on other available options, that is, on the opportunity costs of failing to make the unproductive transfer. We can, in fact, imagine cases in which unproductive transfers may be directly utility maximizing not because they are coerced but because the only alternative is a return to the initial bargaining position, an alternative that is mutually disadvantageous and thus irrational. Return to the initial bargaining position need not be the result of coercion; rather, it may be the result of contingent features of the nature of the joint strategy on which all parties agree. Nevertheless, it is a result rational parties must seek to avoid, even at the cost of making an unproductive transfer.

Gauthier believes that unfair bargains are inherently unstable because they involve unproductive transfers. Making an unproductive transfer is irrational because it is not directly utility maximizing. I have shown so far that bargains can be unfair without involving unproductive transfers. Just now, I suggested that unproductive transfers, given the opportunity costs of noncompliance, can be directly utility maximizing and, therefore, can be rational in the absence of coercion. But even if I am mistaken in claiming that unproductive transfers sometimes can be directly utility maximizing, it does not follow that unproductive transfers are irrational on that ground alone.

An act can be rational even if it is not directly utility maximizing, and for the very same reasons that Gauthier thinks that the disposition to comply with certain cooperative strategies, and thus compliance itself, can be rational. Simply recall Gauthier's solution to the compliance problem: the principle of constrained maximization. In the single-play or ordinary PD, defection is the dominant strategy. Consequently, rational individuals will not comply with the agreements they make because the agreements themselves have the logical structure of the PD. Agreement on a set of constraints will not produce the desired outcome, because defection will set in when agreement reaches closure. In order for cooperation to succeed, compliance with rational agreements must itself be rational. But defection, not compliance, is rational; or is it?

To solve the dilemma, Gauthier introduces a distinction between directly and indirectly utility-maximizing conduct. Compliance with PD-structured agreements, he argues, can be rational even when it is not *directly* maximizing. Why? Because compliance is particular cases is the result of choosing to have a certain *disposition* on the basis of directly utility-maximizing considerations. The rationality of compliance is a function of the rationality of the choice to dispose oneself to comply. Compliance with PD-structured bargains is rational, then, in virtue of the directly utility-maximizing choice of disposing oneself to compliance in PD-structured bargains. The disposition to comply is utility maximizing even if on occasion compliance is not *directly* utility maximizing. In Gauthier's view, the rationality of a course of conduct, the choice of a disposition – or anything, for that matter – simply cannot be determined entirely by inquiring whether or not it is directly utility maximizing.

Similar reasoning can be used to defend the rationality of other nondirectly utility-maximizing acts like unproductive transfers. Even if compliance with certain mutually advantageous joint strategies that require voluntary unproductive transfers is not directly maximizing, it may be rational to make such transfers in virtue of the rationality of the choice to *dispose* oneself to make such transfers. Gauthier's very own argument for the rationality of compliance shows that we cannot infer that certain actions or choices are irrational from the fact that they are not directly utility maximizing. If unproductive transfers are irrational, their irrationality does not follow from their not being directly utility maximizing, at least not if Gauthier's argument for the rationality of constrained maximization is compelling. So (3) is false.

The argument from the instability of unfair bargains is unsound. Were Gauthier seriously to defend the claim that only directly utility-maximizing behavior can be rational, he would be forced to abandon the argument for rational compliance. Were Gauthier to give up the argument for rational compliance, his entire enterprise would quickly unravel, and for the obvious reason stated earlier. If it is not rational to comply, it cannot be rational to bargain. It would appear that Gauthier would do better to hold onto the possibility that some nondirect utility-maximizing behavior can be rational, and to give up instead the argument from the instability of unfair bargains.

But there is another, potentially more attractive, line of argument for Gauthier which may allow him to have both constrained maximization and the argument from the instability of unfair bargains. This argument depends on a distinction he draws between two kinds of constrained maximization. In the end, Gauthier wants to argue not that constrained maximization in any form is rational but, rather, that it is rational to dispose oneself to comply with bargains only if they are *fair*. This is a particular form of constrained maximization, what Gauthier calls *narrow compliance*. Because narrow compliance is a form of constrained maximization, its rationality does not depend on its being directly maximizing. So Gauthier's commitment to the rationality of narrow compliance means that he is committed to the principle that nondirectly maximizing behavior can be rational. But in order to save the argument from the instability of unfair bargains, Gauthier has to give up reliance upon the claim that because unproductive transfers are not directly utility maximizing they are irrational. He can do this by claiming instead that nondirectly utility-maximizing behavior can be rational only when it is required by narrow compliance. Thus, unproductive transfers, which are involved in unfair bargains only, *cannot* be rational. They are not directly utility maximizing and are never required by narrow compliance. Moreover, given the unique rationality of narrow compliance, unfair bargains necessarily will be unstable, because it will be rational for all parties in unfair bargains to defect. They will not have the disposition to comply necessary to secure the success of PD-structured bargains.

If, however, narrow compliance is uniquely rational, then Gauthier's argument for the instability of unfair bargains is rendered entirely unnecessary. Because narrow compliance compels compliance only with fair bargains, unfair bargains, whatever their causes, are necessarily unstable. The entire discussion of the irrationality of unproductive transfers is beside the point. In short, if Gauthier is going to end up arguing for the unique rationality of narrow compliance, as in fact he is, it serves no purpose to show that unfair bargains unravel. The unique rationality of narrow compliance demonstrates a more fundamental flaw in them. Namely, it would not be rational to negotiate an unfair bargain, because it is not rational to bargain in the absence of compliance; and narrow compliance precludes abiding by the terms of anything other than fair bargains.

It is clear to me, and I hope to others, that the most important arguments in Gauthier's book are those presented on behalf of the unique rationality of narrow compliance. We therefore turn our attention to them.

5. BROAD AND NARROW COMPLIANCE

There is an important distinction between a person "who is disposed to cooperate in ways that, followed by all, merely yield her some benefit in relation to universal non-cooperation" and a person "who is disposed to cooperate in ways that, followed by all, yield nearly optimal and fair outcomes."[7] The former are *broad compliers,* the latter *narrow compliers.* As it stands, the definitions of broad and narrow compliance are seriously and importantly ambiguous.

Cooperation consists in both agreement and compliance. From what Gauthier says we cannot be certain if narrow compliers have the compound disposition *to agree to and comply with* fair bargains only, or if their disposition is *to comply with* whatever fair bargains they strike, though they have no particular disposition with respect to the striking of bargains, fair or otherwise. On both accounts, narrow compliers are disposed to comply with any fair bargains they make. The difference is that on the first account, the disposition they have is compound: It includes not only a disposition to comply with fair bargains, but a disposition to accept only fair bargains and to reject all others. Thus, for them the question of whether to comply with an unfair bargain into which one has entered never arises. Narrowly compliant persons of this sort just do not make unfair bargains. The disposition to be narrowly compliant in the second sense, however, ensures only that if a fair bargain is struck, a narrowly compliant person will abide by its terms. Narrow compliers, however, would be free to refrain from striking fair bargains *and* free to make unfair ones. They are not precluded from making unfair bargains, nor are they disposed to defect from unfair bargains. Their disposition is to comply with all fair bargains; but a disposition to comply with fair bargains is not at the same time a disposition to defect from unfair ones.

For the narrowly compliant person of the second sort, the decision whether or not to strike a particular bargain will be made on straightforward utility-maximizing grounds. Among the factors relevant to assessing the rationality of entering negotiations with others is the likelihood of their compliance with its terms. A narrowly compliant person in the second sense will strike either fair or unfair bargains only if she believes the compliance of others is likely. If compliance is likely and the bargain struck a fair one, the narrowly compliant person will cooperate. If the compliance of others is likely and the bargain struck an *unfair* one, the narrowly compliant person is not compelled to comply. This does *not* mean she is compelled to defect. She is compelled in no way at all. She is free either to comply or defect. If the bargain is embedded in a PD, she *will* defect. But her decision to defect follows from the PD structure of the bargain and the dominant rationality of defection in the absence of a disposition to do otherwise. If the bargain is not a PD, however, she can comply or defect depending on the counsel of straightforward maximization. If we restrict discussion to a state of nature in which all bargains are embedded in the PD, then she will always defect from unfair bargains she makes – but not because she is disposed to defect and not because she is disposed not to make unfair bargains.

Now reconsider the narrowly compliant person of the first sort. Because he is compelled to enter into and comply with only fair bargains, no decision he makes requires that he take into account straightforward maximizing considerations. Those factors enter only when he chooses so to dispose himself. From then on, he is compelled to turn his back on bargains that are unfair, even if the compliance of others is likely and the terms offered benefit him in disproportion to the gains accorded others.

In this essay I shall adopt the second formulation of narrow compliance and define broad compliance accordingly. *Narrow compliers* have the disposition to comply with fair bargains, though as a matter of their disposition they need not accept them in the first place. Because their disposition is confined only to fair bargains, they are dispositionally free with respect to their compliance decisions regarding unfair bargains. *Broad compliers* have the disposition to comply with any mutually advantageous bargains they enter, although they may choose not to enter certain bargains, fair or not.

We have adopted these formulations for three reasons. First and foremost, the theoretical motivation for constrained maximization is the PD. The adoption of a disposition to comply with bargains is motivated for rational agents as a strategy for avoiding the suboptimality of the PD. Rational agents can avoid the PD by the adoption of a disposition for compliance *simpliciter*. A more complex disposition which disposes agents both to comply and to accept bargains is unmotivated for rational agents, at least with respect to the defection problem. Secondly, the relevant disposition for compliance must be psychologically plausible. The disposition to comply only with certain bargains is psychologically more plausible, we believe, than the disposition to enter into and to comply with certain bargains only. Finally, Gauthier's own discussions of narrow and broad compliance in *Morals by Agreement* strongly suggest this interpretation. As concerns the arguments of *Morals by Agreement* and our criticism of them, however, the two definitions can be shown to be *extensionally equivalent;* so someone unpersuaded by our characterization of narrow compliance can substitute the more complex characterization in most arguments, *salva veritate.*

In order to solve the compliance and *status quo ante* problems simultaneously, the rational choice model of morality requires that narrow compliance be uniquely rational. In what follows, we distinguish among four arguments for the irrationality of broad compliance and the rationality of narrow compliance. These are arguments from predation, displaced costs, translucence and equal rationality. We consider each in turn.

5.1. Narrow compliance and predation

Gauthier writes:

> Someone disposed to comply with agreements that left untouched the fruits of predation would simply invite others to engage in predatory and coercive activities as a prelude to bargaining. She would permit the successful predators to reap where they had ceased to sow, to continue to profit from the effects of natural predation after entering into agreements freeing them from the need to invest further in predatory effort.[8]

It is irrational to dispose oneself to comply with less than fair bargains, because it would encourage others "to engage in predatory and coercive activities as a prelude to bargaining."[9] According to the argument from predation, it is rational to exclude from bargaining those individuals who have unfair initial entitlements, because doing so would discourage them from stealing as a prelude to bargaining. Narrow compliance, as we have defined it, ensures the exclusion of individuals with unfair entitlements from bargains with narrow compliers.

It is clearly desirable and rational to attempt to discourage individuals from attacking in the state of nature. Suppose there were so many narrow compliers in the state of nature who excluded those with unfair initial entitlements from the benefits of cooperation that the benefits from predation did not exceed the costs of exclusion from cooperation. Then, as Gauthier claims, it would be irrational to engage in predatory behavior, and individuals would be discouraged from doing so. But we cannot simply assume that there are, or always would be, a sufficient number of narrowly compliant individuals in the state of nature to make prebargain predation irrational. Even once a threshold population of narrow compliers has been reached and prebargain predation has become irrational, it does not follow that it is rational for any particular individual to be narrowly compliant.

Consider two possible scenarios. In one, the population of narrowly compliant individuals falls below the threshold necessary to induce others to refrain from predation. In the other, the population exceeds that necessary to deter predation. Should the threshold population of narrow compliers in the state of nature not obtain, there is no reason to think that the members of the narrow–compliance population will be spared from predation. Narrow compliance would be costly, since it would require someone to forgo certain mutually advantageous but unfair bargains; at the same time, the potential benefit of narrow compliance, that is, deterring predation, would not obtain. Thus, narrow compliance would not be rational, let alone uniquely so.

Now consider the case in which the threshold of narrowly compliant persons in the overall population is met or exceeded. When this condition is satisfied, it is rational to refrain from engaging in predatory behavior. But is it rational to be narrowly compliant? No. Whether or not an individual is narrowly compliant, others will not prey on him. If they do, they will be excluded from advantageous bargains with the narrow compliers. But being a narrow complier is not a necessary condition for cooperative interaction with narrow compliers. The only precondition is that one not engage in predation. Nonnarrow compliers who do not engage in predatory behavior will not be excluded from cooperative bargains with narrow compliers. It is rational not to be excluded. Broadly compliant persons also will be included as long as they are not predatory. Thus, broad compliance can be a rational disposition both when the number of narrowly compliant persons in a population falls below and when it exceeds that necessary to foreclose predation. The only circumstance in which it is uniquely rational to be narrowly compliant occurs when one's decision is decisive in reaching the threshold population in which predation becomes disutile and thus irrational. The probability that any one person's choice of a disposition toward compliance could be decisive is extremely low. And even where one person's choice could affect the expected utility of predation, the probability of any one particular choice being decisive in even lower. So the rationality of narrow compliance is simply not established by the argument from predation.

5.2. Displaced costs and rational compliance

The argument from displaced costs is really just Gauthier's earlier argument that because unfair bargains involve unproductive transfers, narrow compliance is uniquely rational. Gauthier writes:

> If interaction is to be fully cooperative, it must proceed from an initial position in which costs are internalized, and so in which no person has the right to impose uncompensated costs on another. For if not, the resulting social arrangements must embody one-sided interactions benefitting some persons at cost to others. Even if each were to receive some portion of the cooperative surplus, yet each could not expect to benefit in the same relation to contribution as his fellows. *Interactions based on displaced costs would be redistributive, and redistribution cannot be part of a rational system of cooperation.*[10]

The claim is that unfair bargains always result in displaced costs, and that because displaced costs are redistributive, they are irrational. Redistributive outcomes are irrational, according to Gauthier's earlier claim, because they require unproductive transfers. But recall that (in the instability argument) his argument for the irrationality of unproductive transfers, and thus redistribution, depended on the claim that unproductive transfers are not directly utility maximizing. However, as we earlier pointed out, Gauthier cannot claim that *any* act that is not directly utility maximizing is necessarily irrational, for his central thesis of constrained maximization, if correct, proves the exception: It is rational to dispose oneself *ex ante* to comply with certain bargains; thus, compliance with these bargains, even when not directly utility maximizing, is rational. In order to prove that unproductive transfers are irrational, Gauthier has to argue that only *one* brand of constrained maximization is rational, namely, narrow compliance. He could then hold that all nondirectly utility-maximizing behavior is irrational unless it is required by narrow compliance. Since unproductive transfers will never be required by narrow compliance, it follows that unproductive transfers cannot be rational. But this strategy cannot work. On pain of circularity, Gauthier cannot, in the displaced-costs argument, argue for the unique rationality of narrow compliance on the ground that the alternative of broad compliance involves unproductive transfers and is thus irrational, when his only argument for the necessary irrationality of unproductive transfers (made earlier in connection with the instability argument) relied upon the claim that narrow compliance is uniquely rational. We had best move on.

5.3. Translucence and compliance

The rationality of constrained maximization depends, in part, on the ability of constrained maximizers to recognize straightforward maximizers and other constrained maximizers. The easier it is to recognize what sort of maximizer an individual is, the more probable it will be that (i) constrained maximizers successfully bargain to mutual advantage with other constrained maximizers, (ii) constrained maximizers will not be exploited by straightforward maximizers and (iii) straightforward maximizers will be excluded from cooperative interaction. As the probability of (i)–(iii) increases, the expected utility of being a constrained maximizer increases and the expected utility of being a straightforward maximizer decreases.

A "transparent" individual is one whose disposition is unmistakable. Transparent individuals are always recognized correctly for the kind of maximizers they are. An "opaque" individual is one whose disposition is very difficult to detect. Opaque individuals are often mistakenly identified as constrained maximizers when they are in fact straightforward maximizers, and vice versa. Gauthier claims that in fact individuals are "translucent." They admit of various degrees of translucency, so that some individuals, who have finely honed skills of recognition, can do very well at recognizing constrained and straightforward maximizers, and most people stand a pretty good chance of recognizing individuals to be the types of maximizers they are.

We can reformulate Gauthier's claim about the relationship between the rationality of constrained maximization and the recognizability of constrained maximization as follows: The higher the degree of translucency, the less the potential benefit of cooperation must be in order for constrained maximization to be rational; or the lower the degree of translucency, the greater the potential benefit of cooperation must be in order for constrained maximization to be rational.

Gauthier claims that "as practices and activities fall short of fairness, the expected value of cooperation for those with less than fair shares decreases, and so the degree of translucency required to make cooperation rational for them increases."[11] The point is that it can be rational to be a constrained maximizer who accepts unfair bargains only as individuals approach transparency. The expected utility of constrained maximization is a function of the likelihood of interacting with constrained maximizers, the potential gain from such interaction and the potential loss from interacting with a straightforward maximizer. In turn, the likelihood of interacting with a constrained maximizer and not interacting with a straightforward maximizer is, in part, a function of translucency. So if it is going to be rational to dispose oneself to comply with unfair bargains, in which the potential gain need not be considerable, the likelihood of success must be very high. Thus, the rationality of disposing oneself to compliance with unfair, though mutually advantageous, bargains will be in part a function of translucency. Individuals will have to be very translucent in order for the expected utility of compliance with unfair bargains to be greater than the expected costs. Thus, a disposition to compliance with unfair bargains is *unlikely* to be rational.

Gauthier's account of the relationship between the rationality of the disposition to comply with unfair bargains and translucency is essentially correct. But the translucency argument fails to take *degrees* of unfairness into account. Surely not all unfair bargains are equally unfair. And where the stakes are large enough, even unfairly small portions of a surplus may be large enough to make the expected utility of broad compliance high enough to outweigh its expected loss. My principal objection to the translucency argument is that Gauthier cannot assume that all unfair bargains are ones in which the potential gain, the unfair share of the surplus, will be critically low. It may be sufficiently high if either (i) the bargain is not extremely unfair or (ii) the cooperative surplus is very large (even an unfair share of a million dollars may be significantly large). There will surely be some unfair bargains with which no rational person ought to comply. But from this it cannot follow that there are no unfair bargains with which rational persons ought to comply. The latter claim must be true, however, for narrow compliance to be uniquely rational.

5.4. Narrow compliance and equal rationality

In some sense, Gauthier's entire enterprise rests on his demonstrating the unique rationality of narrow compliance, that is, the disposition to comply only with fair bargains. It is one thing, though no small or insignificant thing, to establish the rationality of self-restraint; it is another thing to establish that compliance is rational only if the terms of an agreement are fair. Considerations of predation, displaced costs and the translucency of character do not appear to provide the argument Gauthier needs. The deepest and, in many ways, the most compelling argument for narrow compliance relies upon the concept of *equal rationality*. Basically the argument is this:

(1) Equally rational individuals will comply under the same conditions.
(2) Therefore, if some individuals comply under different conditions than others, these individuals cannot be equally rational.
(3) Therefore, if some people are narrowly compliant and others are broadly compliant, some individuals are not as rational as others.
(4) But all individuals are equally rational, *ex hypothesi*.
(5) Therefore, either everyone must be broadly compliant or everyone must be narrowly compliant.
(6) It is never rational for everyone to be broadly compliant.
(7) Therefore, it is uniquely rational for everyone to be narrowly compliant.

The argument rests on two extremely controversial claims. The first is that it cannot be rational for everyone to be broadly compliant, (6). The second is that, (1) equally rational individuals will comply under the same conditions; thus, broadly and narrowly compliant persons cannot be equally rational.

5.4.1. The irrationality of broad compliance. Gauthier's argument for the claim that it is not rational for everyone to be broadly compliant is:

(1′) "If you will comply for any benefit whatsoever, i.e. if you are broadly compliant, then in interacting with you I should dispose myself to comply with a bargain we strike only if it offers me, not a fair share, but the lion's share of the surplus."[12]
(2′) Therefore, "if some persons are broadly compliant, then others, interacting with them, will find it advantageous not to be broadly compliant, or even so much as narrowly compliant. It is rational for them (those demanding the lion's share) to be less-than-narrowly compliant."[13]
(3′) Therefore, "it is not and cannot be rational for everyone to be . . . broadly compliant."[14]

Consider premise (1') of the argument. According to Gauthier, constrained maximizers, whether narrowly or broadly compliant, cooperate only with people they have reason to believe are constrained maximizers. They want to make it costly to be a straightforward maximizer (by excluding such people from the benefits of cooperation) and beneficial to be a constrained maximizer. This will increase the desirability of being a constrained maximizer, and thus increase the number of constrained maximizers in the population. And this, in turn, increases the probability of constrained maximization's being rational. Now, suppose that you have the disposition to comply with any mutually advantageous bargains into which you enter and that I know this. That is, I know you are broadly compliant. Does it follow that I should dispose myself to comply only with agreements that afford me the lion's share of the cooperative surplus; that is, does it follow that I should be less than narrowly compliant? Surely not.

First, from the fact that you are broadly compliant it does not follow that you will enter into *any* mutually advantageous agreement. All that follows is that you will comply with any mutually advantageous agreement into which you enter. And were you to know that I am not even narrowly compliant (which you would be as likely to know as I am likely to know that you are broadly compliant), you would know that the only successful cooperative agreements between us would be ones that accorded me the lion's share of the surplus. You would enter into a bargain with me only if your squirrel's share of the surplus were sufficiently great to make such a bargain rational for you. Depending on your other opportunities, you may be inclined not to strike a deal with me at all. In general, broad compliers might well enter into few bargains with less than narrow compliers: those affording the broad compliers enough to make the bargain rational. And since less than narrow compliers are known not to comply with bargains affording them less than the lion's share of the surplus, broad compliers still find it rational to enter into bargains with them only when the surplus is so large that it is still worth their while to pursue their small share.

Whether it is worth pursuing depends of course on the opportunity costs. The range of unfair bargains worth entering into for those destined to receive an unfair, extremely small reward is nowhere near as large, we might reasonably suppose, as the range of unfair and fair bargains into which broad compliers might enter, for example, with one another. Were we both broadly compliant, the range of bargains with which each of us could count on the other to comply would be maximal, so we would probably strike more bargains and gain more as a result. Broad compliers faced with other broad compliers will know that they can successfully cooperate on a much larger set of joint ventures, and so will almost always find some strategy on which to agree. But broad compliers know that less than narrow compliers will have the disposition to comply only when they get the lion's share. Thus, it is less likely to be rational for broad compliers to interact with less than narrow compliers than it will be for them to interact with other broad compliers. If I am considering demanding the lion's share, then I must realize that one consequence of my doing so is that while you might be a broad complier, you might well decide not to bargain with me at all. So it may be *irrational* for me to be less than narrowly compliant even if I know you are broadly compliant. Certainly we can draw no inference about what it would be rational for me to demand of you in the absence of my knowledge of your other alternatives.

Second, even if it would be desirable for me to be a less than narrow complier when interacting with a broad complier, it does not follow it is rational for me to become a less than narrow complier. The dispositions of narrow and broad compliance are not conditional upon certain bargains *with certain sorts of people.* Individuals are either broad or narrow (or less than narrow) compliers, period. They cannot be broad compliers when interacting with some people but narrow compliers when interacting with others. Although I might rationally prefer to be a less than narrow complier while I am interacting with you, the rationality of my actually being a less than narrow complier will depend on the distribution of dispositions throughout the population with whom I interact. If everyone but you and I were narrowly compliant, then it would not be rational for me to be a less than narrow complier, even if you were broadly compliant.

The central premise in the argument, that is, (1'), is false. It does not follow from the fact that someone is broadly compliant that others ought to be less than narrowly compliant. In fact, the reverse might be true. Thus, (2') does not follow: If some people are broadly compliant, then it is not necessarily true that others interacting with them will find it advantageous not to be broadly compliant, or even so much as narrowly compliant. Proposition (3') is also false: It can be rational for everyone to be a broad complier. For being a broad complier may afford everyone the best opportunity to reach agreement and to benefit from cooperation.

5.5. Equal rationality and equal compliance

I have so far demonstrated that (6) in the equal-rationality argument is false: It can be rational for everyone to be a broad complier. Thus, the truth of (7) does not follow from the conjunction of (5) and (6), and the argument for the unique rationality of narrow compliance is now incomplete. But the crux of the argument, premise (1), so far remains intact: Equally rational individuals will comply under the same conditions; thus, everyone must be either broadly or narrowly compliant. Some people cannot be narrowly compliant and others broadly compliant. The "impossibility" is presumably a conceptual one, following from the definition of "equal rationality."

The equal rationality of the parties in the initial position, however, is largely irrelevant in determining the rationality of broad and narrow compliance. One's reasons for being a broad or narrow complier depend on one's bargaining advantage in the state of nature and the preexisting size of the populations of broad and narrow compliers. Given acceptable populations of broad and narrow compliers, if one is advantaged then one can afford to hold out for unfairly profitable bargains, but if one is disadvantaged then one may not be able to hold out for fair bargains. Opportunity costs will often force the disadvantaged to acquiesce in unfair bargains. Although parties in the initial position may be equally rational, they are not necessarily equally advantaged. Thus, they may comply with bargains under very different conditions.

For advantaged individuals, it will *never* be rational to be narrowly compliant, for the adoption of that disposition would preclude them from ever profiting from their advantage. The only question they must face is whether it is rational to engage in unfair bargains. Because anyone who gains unfairly in a bargain will be excluded from bargaining with a narrow complier, even advantaged individuals must weigh the benefits of using their advantage against the costs of being excluded from whatever population of narrow compliers exists or will exist in the future.

Ultimately, then, the only question an advantaged individual must confront is whether he ought to engage in unfair bargaining, not whether he ought *to be* a narrow complier. Under no circumstances will it be rational for an advantaged individual to be a narrow complier, for by becoming narrowly compliant he would forfeit the possibility of profiting from his advantage when the benefits of so doing outweigh the costs (i.e., of exclusion from bargaining with the population of narrow compliers). Individuals who are not advantaged will, of course, desire that there be a large enough population of narrow compliers so that advantaged individuals have incentive to engage only in fair bargaining. But as I earlier demonstrated, even from this it does not follow that any one particular disadvantaged individual ought to become narrowly compliant. In fact, unless his decision to become narrowly compliant can break through the threshold beyond which the costs of unfair bargaining for advantaged individuals outweigh the benefits, it is *irrational* for any single disadvantaged individual to be narrowly compliant. Broad compliance allows him to benefit from all bargains with narrow compliers *and* from those unfair bargains with advantaged individuals in which he gains the lesser, unfair, share.

What, then, can we say about the possibility of a population of equally rational individuals being divided between broad and narrow compliers? Simply this: In the absence of a preexisting large population of narrow compliers, it is not, and will never be, rational for *anyone,* advantaged or not, to become a narrow complier. For advantaged individuals, narrow compliance is never rational. For disadvantaged individuals, it is rational only when their choice to become narrowly compliant is decisive. Their choice's being decisive requires at least *some* preexisting population of narrow compliers. But if this is so, then there will never be *any* population of narrow compliers, for it will never be rational for any one individual to become narrowly compliant in the first place. Alternatively, if we *stipulate* the existence of a large population of narrow compliers, without explaining how it was ever rational for any of those narrow compliers to become narrow compliers, then it would still be irrational for any of the remainder of the total population to become narrowly compliant. They might just as well be broad compliers who restrict their bargains to fair ones. In this case, we see that a population of rational individuals could include both broad and narrow compliers, although the evolution of such a population would remain a mystery. In any event, equal rationality, it appears, does not entail equal compliance, and the last argument for unique rationality of narrow compliance has failed.

6. THE ARGUMENTS FROM RATIONAL AND COSTLESS BARGAINING

We cannot discuss every argument Gauthier advances for the rationality of morality. I am convinced that the arguments from narrow compliance are the most powerful available to him, and that is why I have focused on them in such detail. I want to close the main text of this essay by considering somewhat more quickly two other arguments available to Gauthier.

6.1. Rationality and fair bargaining

Suppose I am right in saying that the argument from narrow compliance is unsound. It can be rational to dispose oneself to comply with the rational bargains one strikes, even if those bargains are not fair. That is, we cannot derive the fairness or bargained outcomes as a consequence of a theory of rational compliance. This does not mean that we cannot derive it from a theory of rational bargaining. Suppose the correct theory of rational bargaining had as its consequence that a rational bargain was a fair one. Then, if moral principles must be fair ones, they might still be determined by the outcome of a rational bargain.

Gauthier advances a theory of rational bargaining, the principle of minimax-relative concession. According to this principle, each individual shares in the surplus proportionate to his relative contribution. Since fairness requires proportionate distribution, rational bargaining turns out to be fair bargaining. The outcome of every rational bargain is fair. Therefore, even if it is rational to be broadly compliant, the bargains with which one complies are fair ones.

The problem with this argument is that it ignores the potential unfairness of the initial positions. As we have repeatedly noted, even if the rational bargaining process itself is fair, it may exacerbate, and will in any event transmit rather than *rectify,* preexisting inequalities. Unless rational bargaining is rectificatory as well as contributorily just, the outcome of a rational bargain can be unfair even if rational bargaining is procedurally fair.

The possibility remains that this sort of unfairness need not concern the rational choice model of morality. After all, the substantive principles of morality will be fair; they just will not be rectificatory. But why think that correct moral principles ought to address issues of corrective justice? I think that a theory of morality that ignores corrective justice is unacceptable. But even if it were acceptable, a rational choice theorist of morality would still have to prove that the correct ideal principle of rational bargaining was a fair one. Gauthier claims to have done this, but his proof depends crucially on the characterization of the initial choice problem as taking place within the context of *costless bargaining.*

6.1.1. Costless bargaining. One of the commonest objections leveled against Rawls is that his characterization of the decision problem is not normatively neutral. Because it is not, the two principles of justice do not derive from pure rationality fleshed out as Rawls thinks it should be, namely, as individual rational decision under uncertainty. Instead, the principles are derived from rationality embedded within a Kantian normative framework. One way of understanding the rational choice model of morality is as an effort to derive morality from "pure rationality." This explains Gauthier's efforts to impose minimal constraints on the decision problem. The one important constraint he imposes, but inadequately discusses, is that bargaining in the state of nature is costless in terms of utility and time. This constraint is motivated by his desire to isolate pure rationality.

If bargaining is in fact costless in time and utility, it is possible to argue that rational bargaining will invariably lead to fair outcomes. Rational bargaining will give rise to unfair outcomes if initial inequities allow one party to extort shares that exceed his relative contribution, or if the inequities are simply transmitted in toto to the outcomes. If bargaining is costless, however, then those disadvantaged in the state of nature have nothing to lose by refusing to join in a cooperative effort unless the terms of the bargain are fair. At the same time, they cannot expect to receive terms more favorable to them than fair terms, since other cooperators will object and hold out for fair terms at no cost to themselves. Thus, everyone can expect fair terms, regardless of the initial distribution of holdings. Provided they are equally rational, all will get fair terms. Cooperation assumes that the contribution of others is necessary; the costlessness assumption guarantees that all bargaining will be on terms that are fair to all contributing parties. The costlessness assumption, which is aimed at isolating pure rationality, turns out to have extraordinary normative consequences. It nullifies all advantages and induces all parties to comply under exactly the same terms. It does what the arguments for narrow compliance could not do, that is, solve both the compliance and *status quo ante* problems. It has to be too good to be true, and it is.

The assumption enables Gauthier to derive morality from rationality, but at the cost of robbing the argument of its essential state-of-nature character. The motivation for rational individuals to cooperate in the state of nature, after all, is the existence of *costs*. These are forgone opportunities in the form of a surplus unattainable given the defection problem. If the state of nature were itself costless in Gauthier's sense, no need for a theory of rational bargaining would arise. Truly costless interaction would be efficient, and no need for a mechanism to solve a market failure problem would emerge. In a costless world, no market failures are in equilibrium. The entire state of nature enterprise unravels quickly once one introduces the costlessness condition.

A sympathetic reading of Gauthier sees the costlessness assumption as part of his attempt to isolate a concept of pure rationality. But we are not sure that the concept of "pure rational bargaining," by which is meant "costless bargaining," is coherent. Rational individuals who incur no costs for failing to reach agreement have, *a fortiori,* nothing to gain in bargaining. For if they did, there would be, *necessarily,* costs (opportunity costs) of forgoing, or delaying, agreement. Bargaining is rational, therefore, *only if* it takes place within the context of costs, and costless contexts necessarily render bargaining irrational. The costlessness assumption, far from being an innocent attempt to constrain the decision problem in a normatively neutral way, turns out to be too strong. It may even be incoherent.

7. CONCLUSION

I have invested a great deal of energy in presenting a series of complex criticisms of a complex view about the rationality of morality. There is, I believe, a significant theme that emerges from our discussion, and it is this: The very problems of collective action that cause the need for constrained maximization emerge again at the level of the choice between the alternative forms of constrained maximization, broad and narrow compliance. The rationality of narrow compliance utlimately depends on the incentives available for inducing individuals to be narrow compliers. And although we can imagine its sometimes being rational to want a population that is largely, if not exclusively, narrowly compliant, the problems of collective action prevent individuals from forming such a population. Only this time constrained maximization cannot be enlisted to overcome the problems of collective action. Once again, what is collectively rational is individually irrational. The conundrum of collective action, even when solved at one level, recurs at another, in this case foiling an ambitious attempt to ground morality in rationality.

Despite my objections to it, Gauthier's rational choice, moral contractarianism remains important. From a moral theorist's point of view, the importance of Gauthier's work is that he attempts to answer the moral skeptic. He does so by grounding moral theory in a particular conception of rationality. For analytic political theorists, Gauthier's work is important for two reasons: First and foremost, it demonstrates the importance of a unified theory of the social sciences – in the sense in which political theory, economics and political science are, at some level, the same discipline, namely, rational choice theory. Second, it is an impressive, extremely imaginative and thoughtful attempt to resurrect anarchism – an effort that rests neither on the implausible motivational theory of ideal communitarianism nor on implausible interpretations of the iterated prisoners' dilemma.

Notes

PREFACE

1 James Buchanan and Gordon Tullock, *The Calculus of Consent* (1962).
2 Jules L. Coleman, "Accidents" (unpublished manuscript in preparation).
3 Frank Easterbrook, "The Role of Consent in Consent Decrees," *Legal Forum* (forthcoming).
4 Jules Coleman and Charles Silver, "A Jurisprudence of Settlements" (unpublished manuscript in preparation).
5 Jules L. Coleman, "The Market Paradigm" (unpublished manuscript in preparation).

1. NEGATIVE AND POSITIVE POSITIVISM

1 Dworkin's claim that positivism is committed to a pedigree standard of legality is too narrow. What he means to argue, I believe, is that positivism is committed to some form of "noncontentful" criterion of legality, of which a pedigree standard would be one. For ease of exposition, I shall use "pedigree test" broadly to mean any sort of noncontentful criterion of legality.
2 See below, secs. 2 and 5.
3 The phrase "truth as a moral principle and a condition of legality" does seem a bit awkward. However, any other phrase, such as "morality as a condition of legality" or "moral content as a condition of legality," would be ambiguous, since it would be unclear whether the separability thesis was a claim about the relationship between law and critical morality or between law and conventional morality. My understanding of the separability thesis is as a denial of a constitutive relationship between law and critical morality. Other interpretations of the separability thesis are discussed in the text immediately following this note.
4 This seems to be the form of positivism David Lyons advances to meet Dworkin's objections to positivism. Cf. David Lyons, "Review: Principles, Positivism, and Legal Theory," *Yale Law Journal* 87 (1977): 415.
5 But see Rolf Sartorius, "Social Policy and Judicial Legislation," *American*

Philosophical Quarterly 8 (1971): 151, and Jules Coleman, "Review: Taking Rights Seriously," *California Law Review* 66 (1978): 885.

6   The following characterization of positivism in virtue of motivations for the separability thesis was developed after many discussions with Professor Dworkin. I am grateful to him for his remarks, but it is likely that I have not put the characterizations as well as he would have.

7   That is because legal realism is skeptical about the existence of legal facts. Legal facts are "created" by official actions; they are not "out there" to be discovered by judges. Scientific or metaphysical realism maintains exactly the opposite view of facts.

8   See above, note 5.

9   Often overlooked is the fact that there are two distinct arguments for discretion: One relies on the controversial nature of penumbral cases involving general terms; the other relies on the finiteness of legal standards. The first argument is actually rooted in a theory of language; the second, which would survive a rejection of that theory, relies on gaps in the law. See Coleman, above, note 5.

10   Dworkin does not explicitly distinguish among these various arguments, nor does he label any of them. The labels and distinctions are mine.

11   Sartorius, "Social Policy and Judicial Legislation." Dworkin himself discusses, but wrongly rejects, this possibility. See "Model of Rules I," in Ronald Dworkin, *Taking Rights Seriously* (1977), p. 977. See also C. L. Ten's useful discussion "The Soundest Theory of Law," *Mind* 88 (1979): 522.

12   There are two ways we might understand the notion of a social rule. Under one interpretation, not every rule of recognition would be a social rule; under the other, each would be. As both Hart and Dworkin use the term, a social rule is a practice, and the nature of the practice determines the scope of the rule and the extent of the duties it imposes. The rule that men must doff their hats upon entering church is a social rule in this sense. Not every rule of recognition, however, is a social rule in this sense, for two reasons. First, at least in some jurisdictions, the content of the rule may be specified prior to the existence of an appropriate practice. For example, the formulation of the Constitution of the United States did not require the existence of the relevant judicial practice; it preceded the practice. No doubt ambiguities and other uncertainties in the rule are resolved through judicial practice; nevertheless, the general form and nature of the rule had been specified without regard to practice. Second, whereas Dworkin's contrast between social rule and normative rule theories of law turns on the manner in which legal rules give rise to duties, the rule of recognition is not itself a duty-imposing rule. We might construct a broader notion of a social rule. In this sense a rule will be a social rule if its existence or authority depends, in part, on the existence of a social practice. Here the requirement is not that the rule's proper formulation be specified by practice. Instead, the claim is that the authority of the rule depends on the existence of a practice. The rule itself may be specifiable, at least in general terms and at some points in time, without regard to the practice. However, in the absence of the practice, the rule is empty in that it is incapable of providing justifications for action. In short, its normativity depends on the practice, though its content need not be specified by it. Every rule of recognition for the positivist is a social rule in this sense.

13 David Lewis, *Convention: A Philosophical Study* (1969).

14 Gerald Postema has been trying to develop an alternative to the social rule theory that relies heavily on Lewis's theory of conventions. See "Coordination and Convention at the Foundations of Law," *Journal of Legal Studies* 11 (1982): 165.

15 I have refrained from discussing the argument against positivism that Dworkin advances in his brilliant essay "Hard Cases," because in that essay Dworkin reveals himself to be much more of a conventionalist than he would have us believe. The main purpose of that essay is to provide a theory of adjudication that makes plain the sense in which right answers and judicial obligations exist in controversial cases. If Dworkin makes his case for right answers, positivism – at least versions of it that deny judicial duty in the face of controversy – must be mistaken. Moreover, Dworkin attempts to show that the theory of adjudication which provides right answers necessarily makes morality part of the concept of law. Some comments regarding at least this latter claim are in order. Dworkin's general theory of adjudication may be explicated as follows. A case, A, comes before an appellate judge. The judge must decide whether to give a decision in favor of the defendant (decision D) or in favor of the plaintiff, P. In making his decision, the judge notes that there exists a large body of settled law, S, that is suitably purged of its "mistakes." (Dworkin has a theory of the way in which judges identify mistaken decisions.) Once S has been purged of mistakes, it can be systematized. The judge is required then to construct a theory of law that best explains and justifies S by subsuming S under a set of general principles that constitute the best explanation of S. These principles constitute the soundest theory of the existing law *(STL)*. Dworkin employs the standard philosophic notion of explanation, so that if STL explains S, then S follows logically or theoretically from STL. Once STL is constructed, the judge must ask whether either D or P follows from it. If either statement follows logically from STL, the case presents no problem for the positivist. In the event that neither D nor P follows logically from STL, the case is one that, for the positivists at least, calls for discretion, since both conclusions are equally inadequately warranted by the existing law. Dworkin's theory of adjudication here departs from positivism. For while neither D nor P is entailed by STL, either D or P, but not both, "coheres" of "fits" best with it. While neither a decision in favor of the plaintiff nor one in favor of the defendant is a logical consequence of the soundest theory of law, one, but not the other, is a coherence consequence of it. Whichever is the coherence consequence is the "right" answer, the one the judge is obligated to provide. More important, in determining the right answer the judge is required to invoke consideration of morality, since the soundest theory of law not only explains the settled law but justifies it as well. While I have other systematic objections to the argument for right answers, I doubt that the theory of adjudication Dworkin outlines accurately describes judicial practice everywhere, or that it is a necessary feature of legal practice. More important for our present purposes, the claim that determining right answers necessarily involves a moral theory of law which is incompatible with the conventionalist account of law is simply mistaken. On the contrary, Dworkin's argument is thoroughly conventionalist in nature. First, Dworkin must be committed to some standard version of a rule of recognition, since he is committed to a judge's being able to identify the existing body of settled law. Like the positivists he criticizes, Dworkin is, therefore, committed to an epistemic rule of recognition – at least for determining settled law. In Dworkin's view, the judge must construct a theory of law that explains the settled law once it is discovered. The theory of law consists in a set of principles which explain and justify S. The argument for the claim that the soundest theory of law is a moral theory rests either on the requirement that the principles justify the law or on the claim that the principles which constitute the theory are moral principles. In neither case can the argument be sustained. Dworkin's argument for the justification requirement relies on a deeper principle of political responsibility; the judge must be able to give reasons in support of his decisions by showing a consistency between this and previous, similar cases. The notion of justification, however, is ambiguous. There are both weaker and stronger notions of justification. On the other hand, there is the notion of justification that is part of critical morality according to which if a principle or decision is justified it is morally defensible. In this sense, bad law can never be morally justified. But Dworkin (rightly) believes that bad law can be law nonetheless, so he cannot mean that the best theory of law justifies the existing law in the sense that it shows the law to be morally defensible. It is clear, then, that the principle of political responsibility requires the weaker notion of justification. This notion is institutional in nature and is akin to the requirement of consistency or formal justice. This notion of justification does not establish the link between law and critical morality necessary to undermine positivism. The argument that the best theory of law is a moral theory because it consists in a set of moral principles fails primarily because the principles which constitute the best theory do not do so because they are true, but because they best systematize the existing law.

2. RETHINKING THE THEORY OF LEGAL RIGHTS

1   Ronald Coase, "The Problem of Social Cost," *Journal of Law and Economics* 3 (1960): 1.

2   See Richard Posner, *Economic Analysis of Law* (3d ed., 1986); Jules L.

Coleman, "Economics and the Law: A Critical Review of the Foundations of the Economic Approach to Law," *Ethics* 94 (1984): 649.

3 Guido Calabresi and Douglas Melamed, "Property Rules, Liability Rules, and Inalienability: One View of the Cathedral," *Harvard Law Review* 85 (1972): 1089, 1105–15.

4 Spur Indus., Inc. v. Del E. Webb Dev. Co., 108 Ariz. 178, 494 P.2d 700 (1972) (court enjoined cattle feeding but required real estate developer to pay relocation or termination costs).

5 For example, one could argue that, given that there were only two litigants and the costs of the transactions were low, it is surprising the court did not choose to take a property, rather than a liability, rule approach.

6 Joel Feinberg, *Social Philosophy* (1973), pp. 55–9.

7 Jules L. Coleman, "The Foundations of Constitutional Economics," Chapter 6 in this volume.

8 This is the view, for example, of Charles Fried: "The regime of contract law, which respects the dispositions individuals make of their rights, carries to its natural conclusion the liberal premise that individuals have rights" (*Contract as Promise* [1982], p. 2 [footnote omitted]).

9 See generally A. Church, *Introduction of Mathematical Logic* (1956).

10 The content of particular legal rights will always be contingent upon the foundational theory, whereas the syntax of rights is independent of any commitment at the foundational level. This means that even if rights necessarily entail claims, the specific claims entailed will always depend on the foundational theory. Moreover, even a commitment to a utilitarian or welfare theory at the foundational level would not strictly entail that rights marked interests. Sometimes the best way to promote utility is to secure by rights a domain of autonomous control. Even within a utilitarian framework, institutional rights may sometimes mark liberties. Whether rights mark liberties or interests in this theory will depend on contingent features of the world and the structure of interaction. This is the kind of utilitarian theory of rights currently being pursued by Russell Hardin and, to some extent, by Jon Elster, Richard Epstein and Jules Coleman.

11 To say that legal rights are "markers" is to treat them as place holders. When interests or liberties are marked as rights, it is only as if an asterisk is placed by them. The right which secures them is as yet (analytically) content-free. The content is to be given in terms of claims.

12 For a lucid discussion of what it means to have a legitimate claim see Feinberg, *Social Philosophy*, pp. 64–7.

13 Jones has an interest in a job but no right to it. That is, he cannot prevent others from seeking the same job. But his interest in securing the job can be protected if he is given a claim against others that they not prevent him from pursuing it.

14 Alvin Klevorick, "The Economics Analysis of Crime," in *Criminal Justice: Nomos XXVII*, ed. J. Roland Pennock and John W. Chapman (1985), pp. 289, 301–4.

15 This characterization of the claims conferred by transaction rules follows closely their standard meaning since Calabresi–Melamed, with the important qualification that in our view transaction rules specify the content of particular rights.

16 Contemporary communitarians are quick to contrast the community conception of a legal order with a rights-based order. But in fact the contrast is too quick, as this analysis of transaction rules reveals. One possible norm of transfer might be that no one can exchange or trade without everyone's consent. Thus, the content of particular legal rights can be given in communitarian terms. We might then understand communitarianism not as an alternative to rights theory but as specifying a particular foundational view with implications for how the content of particular rights is to be given.

One trouble with the new communitarianism is that one never knows at what level of analysis communitarian ideals are supposed to enter. The problem is not insignificant. Consider that late in his life Frank Knight held the view that markets were desirable not because they are efficient (they may not be) but because free and equal persons recognizing the importance to the community of social consensus would desire above all else to restrict the occasions on which broad consensus was necessary for any form of social interaction. Consensus is hard to come by and fragile once reached. Nevertheless, it is the ultimate foundation of social communities. That is why it is important to minimize the extent to which our institutional life relies upon it. If Knight is right, then communitarianism at the level of institutional design could lead to many noncommunitarian institutions, for example, markets. For a general discussion of Knight's view, see J. L. Coleman, "Competition and Cooperation," *Ethics,* 1987: 76.

17 First, not every lawful claim is in fact enforceable by law, so that an entitlement cannot be analyzed entirely in terms of the forms of remedial relief available in the event of noncompliant behavior. Secondly, entitlements specify the conduct others must exhibit if they seek to conform to the relevant norms, not just the sanctions or liabilities they are likely to incur in the event their conduct fails to conform. Finally, it is unlikely, but possible, that the legitimate claims created by the transaction structure may be enforceable by an enlightened conscience or even by a constrained self-interest. More likely, it will be necessary to create formal institutions of enforcement. In doing so, distinguishing analytically between claims and the institutions that enforce them permits us to employ the claims as premises in arguments for the creation of appropriate institutions. By separating the enforcement mechanisms, like injunctions, from the claims being enforced, like those generated by property rules, we allow the maximal theoretical flexibility required to construct the system of institutions that most efficiently promotes the ends specified at the foundational level. For example, by treating as analytic the relationship between property rules and injunction or that between liability rules and tort-like compensation schemes (both of which are contingent and in need of substantive argument), the Realist interpretation of property and liability rules inadequately reflects the actual degree of flexibility available in creating institutions to enforce claims. At the same time, the Realist argument obscures the important point that the institutions created to enforce various claims always depend on the foundational theory and do not follow logically from the content of rights. We want to emphasize that the relationships between rights and their specific content on the one hand, and between their content and the institutions designed to protect them on the other, are all fundamentally contingent and normative. They are not logical or otherwise analytically derived.

18 In our view, then, property and liability rules differ in the liberties they afford entitled parties (as well as in other respects). If the content of an entitlement is specified by a liability rule only, then the entitled party is not free to seek a voluntary transfer on terms agreeable to him *ex ante*. Only under a property rule would he be. This distinguishes our view from the alternative according to which both property and liability rules afford the entitled party a liberty to secure *ex ante* agreement. In the alternative view, the difference between liability and property rules, therefore, is to be understood entirely in terms of the liberties each affords nonentitled parties. Under property rules the nonentitled party is not at liberty to impose a transfer on terms other than those agreeable to the entitled party, whereas under a liability rule he is at liberty to impose transfers provided he compensates *ex post*.

19 This last point is important because it demonstrates that legitimate claims (and liberties) may exist even where a party has no prior entitlement. *A* may have no right to pollute, for example, but if *B*'s right that *A* not pollute is given content only by a liability rule, *A* is at liberty to pollute under certain conditions. Because he is at liberty to pollute, he has a claim against *B*, who ironically is the entitled party, that he (*B*) not interfere with his (*A*'s) forcing a transfer (of pollution for dollars) upon him.

20 We might choose a liability rule rather than a property rule if we thought that *B* was likely to underestimate his damages significantly. This is not intended to suggest that the liability rule is the only alternative. We might choose to set the terms of transfer by an inalienability rule and a liability rule. The inalienability rule forecloses alienation, and a liability rule gives rise to claims for damages.

21 Joel Feinberg, "Voluntary Euthanasia and the Inalienable Right to Life," *Philosophy and Public Affairs* 7 (1978): 93.

22 Judith Jarvis Thomson, "Rights and Compensation," *Nous* 14 (1980): 3.

23 Jules L. Coleman, "Moral Theories of Torts: Their Scope and Limits" (pts. 1–2), *Law and Philosophy* 1 (1982): 371; 2 (1983): 5.

24 The debate does not end here (even if we wish it did). All I can claim to have shown is that one can specify the content of a right in such a way that compensation exhausts the relevant claims. This means that one cannot defend the Infringement Thesis by appealing to the essential nature

of rights and by arguing that the meaning of a right is such that it entails
compensation for its violation. But this may just shift debate back to the
foundational level. For the claim may then be that no rights should ever
be for compensation only. If the point of having institutions is to do
justice, then that cannot be done by giving content to rights in terms of
claims to *ex post* relief and to no more.

25   On the economic side of the debate see Richard Posner, "A Theory
of Negligence," *Journal of Legal Studies* 1 (1972): 29; Steven Shavell, *Economic Analysis of Accident Law* (1987). On the corrective justice side see
R. Epstein, "A Theory of Strict Liability," *Journal of Legal Studies* 2 (1973):
151; George Fletcher, "Fairness and Utility in Tort Theory," *Harvard
Law Review* 85 (1972): 537. Some of the most interesting work on corrective justice currently being done is by Ernest Weinrib, "Toward a
Moral Theory of Negligence Law," *Law and Philosophy* 2 (1983): 37.

26   Vincent v. Lake Erie Trans. Co., 109 Minn. 456, 124 N.W. 221
(1910).

27   Spano v. Perini Corp., 25 N.Y.2d 11, 250 N.E.2d 31, 302 N.W.S.2d
527 (1969).

28   For a contrasting view, see Coleman, "Economics and the Law."

29   See Richard Posner, *The Economics of Justice* (1982), pp. 231–407.

30   See Jules L. Coleman, "The Normative Basis of Economic Analysis:
A Critical Review of Richard Posner's *The Economics of Justice*" (book
review), *Stanford Law Review* 34 (1982): 1105, 1117–31.

31   It is important to distinguish between two claims: that rights are just
guarantees of utility, and that the rights we have, whatever rights are,
can be justified on utilitarian grounds. The first claim is an analytic one
about the meaning of rights. The second is a normative one about their
foundations. Someone can hold both, of course. But someone who asserts the normative claim need not be committed to the analytic one. We
are here discussing the economic analysis of rights, not their economic
foundation.

32   The conclusion of the argument in this section is analogous to that
in the previous one. We cannot claim to have demonstrated the inadequacy of economic analysis by showing that in our legal system liability
rules do not always serve a legitimating function. What we have demonstrated, quite convincingly (we hope), is that it is not analytically necessary that liability rules play a legitimating role and that to the extent to
which they do not play such a role in our legal system, economic analysis
cannot explain current tort law.

33   See Posner, *Economic Analysis of Law*, pp. 201–22.

34   See Klevorick, "Economic Analysis of Crime," p. 289.

35   It is no response to this objection, moreover, to argue that the criminal law is necessary to enforce injunctions. It may well be. Indeed, we
have conceded as much. Still, it is one thing to allege that a criminal law
is necessary to enforce the institutions that enforce property and liability
rules, i.e., injunctions and compensatory awards; it is quite another to
say that the criminal law is necessary to prevent someone from convert-

ing property to liability rules. Injunctions may suffice to enforce the property–liability rule distinction. At best, the criminal law may be necessary to render injunctions and compensatory awards adequately effective. But here the criminal law plays no role peculiar to an economic analysis; rather it plays an enforcement role countenanced by every theory of law.

36 Economic analyses do not speak with one mind when it comes to the criminal law. There are at least two ways of thinking about the criminal law that are, broadly speaking, economic. In the line of argument we have been discussing in this section, the criminal law is represented as either parasitic upon other enforcement institutions or in the background, supporting the transaction structure as a whole. At the very least, the criminal law is of a different order of enforcement than are, say, torts. Whenever economists discuss the criminal law outside of the context of giving an economic explanation of the need for it, however, they treat the criminal law as if it were on a par with torts. In those contexts, the question often is whether to enforce public norms publicly (via the criminal law) or privately (through torts). The question is never whether a criminal statute is established in order to prevent conversion of a property rule to a liability rule. Instead, it is invariably of the following sort: Given an enforcement budget, how much ought to be allocated to public enforcement and how much to private? Putting the matter this way reveals a very different conception of the relationship between criminal and other branches of the law than that which emerges within the economic explanation of the criminal category.

We should note as well that both forms of economic analysis of the criminal law attend inadequately to the fact that the conditions which must be satisfied before the criminal sanction can legitimately be imposed are more demanding than those necessary for civil liability. The scope of potential excusing conditions and severe restrictions on the scope of strict liability in the criminal law – at least compared with the expansive scope of strict liability in torts – suggests a difference in the normative dimensions of criminal and civil law inadequately comprehended by either of the ways in which economic analysis thinks about the relationship between criminal and civil law.

3. EFFICIENCY, AUCTION AND EXCHANGE

1 R. Posner, "A Theory of Negligence," *Journal of Legal Studies* 1 (1972): 29.
2 I. Ehrlich, "The Deterrent Effects of Criminal Law Enforcement," *Journal of Legal Studies* 1 (1972): 259.
3 G. Calabresi, *The Costs of Accidents: A Legal and Economic Analysis* (1970).
4 Even this list of efficiency notions is incomplete. Yet another efficiency standard has been advanced, such that an efficient distribution of resources is wealth optimizing (Posner, "Utilitarianism, Economics, and

Legal Theory," *Journal of Legal Studies* 8 [1979]: 103). Moreover, the notion of allocative efficiency, which is here employed in externality problems only, has a wider and ambiguous usage in broader microeconomic contexts. Posner's novel conception of efficiency is discussed in J. L. Coleman, "Efficiency, Utility, and Wealth Maximization," Chapter 4 in this volume.

5 The theorem is developed in R. Coase, "The Problem of Social Cost," *Journal of Law and Economics* 3 (1960): 1.

6 Commentators often assert that the Coase theorem requires that parties to the negotiations have perfect knowledge. This assumption trivializes the theorem and is stronger than necessary. One need assume only that the relevant parties have substantial relevant information. Additional pertinent information is revealed once actual negotiations are under way.

7 Bids are free from income effects when they do not reflect relative wealth. The consequences of income effects on efforts to employ the Coase theorem as a basis for assigning entitlements are discussed summarily in sec. 3.

8 For a graphic demonstration of this point, see sec. 4, in which Coasian and Pigouvian approaches to externalities are contrasted.

9 P. French, "The Extended Coase Theorem and Long Run Equilibrium," *Economic Inquiry* 17 (1979): 254.

10 Ibid.

11 R. Nozick, *Anarchy, State and Utopia* (1974).

12 Nozick would be rightly suspicious of any effort to transpose his distinction in this manner unless it were made clear that he rejects the entirety of the economic approach to law. That is because the economic approach justifies intervening in free market exchanges if the exchanges are inefficient. Nozick, of course, would reject economic "interventionism" as a violation of autonomy and as an illegitimate extension of the state's coercive powers. Moreover, the distinction he draws between patterned and historical principles is employed for the sole purpose of providing criteria by which the legitimacy of current right claims may be assessed. There is no deep analogy between his arguments and the economic ones. Still, the distinction he draws is an important one which is useful in analyzing different aspects of the Paretian efficiency notions.

13 G. Fletcher, "Law and Economics" (unpublished typescript).

14 Ibid.

15 See generally Coleman, Chapter 4 below.

16 Some readers of previous drafts of this essay, including Fletcher, have questioned whether assigning entitlements could ever be considered Pareto superior. These skeptics could mean one of two things: Either the allocations that result from assigning entitlements are never in fact Pareto superior or it is conceptually impossible to determine if they are. In the first case, the claim is that the proposition "assigning entitlements to *x* is Pareto superior to the case in which no entitlements exist" is always false; in the second case, the claim is that the proposition is meaningless. Both of these claims are, I think, mistaken. The view that the relevant proposition is always false assumes that Pareto comparisons are at least mean-ingful. It would then be an empirical question whether in fact a particular assignment of entitlements was Pareto superior. And it is hard to imag-ine why, in the absence of empirical data pertinent to each case, one would confidently assert that the assignment could never be Pareto su-perior.

The more interesting claim is that it is conceptually impossible to com-pare an assignment of entitlements to a previous allocation. There are two arguments one might advance to support this claim, both of which are ultimately unconvincing. First, one could argue that as a matter of fact there never is a distribution of resources in which entitlements are not assigned. So the state never assigns entitlements; it merely either recognizes or reorganizes them. This claim is false. Moreover, it does not undermine the Pareto comparison. Alternatively, one could argue that assigning entitlements does not itself reallocate resources; it merely entitles people to act in certain ways. For example, if the rancher has one cow at t and then is assigned the right to another cow at t_2, the distri-bution of resources need not change as long as the rancher chooses not to raise a second cow. So the distribution of resources need not be af-fected by the assignment of entitlements only. But this argument misses the point. Entitlements are themselves resources; in addition, the Pareto comparisons are made between welfare levels of persons. So the rancher is better off, even if he does not ranch the second cow, merely because he now has the right to.

17   The arguments in this section summarize points developed in greater detail in Chapter 4.

18   The distinction between externalities and external effects is widely misunderstood even in elementary economics texts, e.g., W. Nicholson, *Intermediate Microeconomics and Its Application* (1975).

19   R. Epstein, "A Theory of Strict Liability," *Journal of Legal Studies* 2 (1973): 151.

20   But cf. A. M. Polinsky, "Notes on the Symmetry of Taxes and Subsidies in Pollution Control," *Canadian Journal of Economics* 12 (1979): 75 (compared with a tax, subsidies may be asymmetric and inefficient in both the long and short run).

21   The liability rule–property rule distinction is traced to the important paper by G. Calabresi and D. Melamed, "Property Rules, Liability Rules, and Inalienability: One View of the Cathedral," *Harvard Law Review* 85 (1972): 1089.

22   Economists are more often concerned with the question of how en-titlements are to be protected once assigned than with the question of how they are to be assigned. See generally A. M. Polinsky, "Controlling Externalities and Protecting Entitlements: Property Rights, Liability Rule, and Tax Subsidy Approaches," *Journal of Legal Studies* 8 (1972): 1.

23   R. Posner, *Economic Analysis of Law* (1972).

24   There are Pareto-optimal distributions that cannot be represented in an Edgeworth box. Such distributions are the optimal resolutions of externality problems. The reason why they cannot be so represented is discussed later in this section.

25 I use the term "auction rule" advisedly. Posner's rule does not actually involve an auction. Instead, his is a rule that assigns entitlements *as if* they were being auctioned.

26 Whether the result of an assignment along Posner's lines is Pareto optimal will depend on exactly what entitlement is being assigned. The result will be Pareto optimal, of course, only if the entitlement is to the optimal amount of, for example, pollution or smoke. But then the problem is: How can we determine the optimal level of pollution or smoke? This information problem is compounded by income effects. Both are discussed in J. L. Coleman and W. Holahan, "Mimicking Markets and Auctioning Entitlements" (unpublished essay).

4. EFFICIENCY, UTILITY AND WEALTH MAXIMIZATION

1 This is the second in a series of essays on the economic analysis of the law. The first was "Efficiency, Exchange, and Auction: Philosophic Aspects of the Economic Approach to Law," *California Law Review* 68 (1980): 221.

2 See D. Lyons, "Utility as a Possible Ground of Rights," *Nous* 14 (1980): 17.

3 R. Posner, "Utilitarianism, Economics, and Legal Theory," *Journal of Legal Studies* 8 (1979): 103.

4 Ibid. pp. 111–19.

5 Ibid. p. 103.

6 For a discussion of productive efficiency see Coleman, "Efficiency, Exchange, and Auction," pp. 223–31.

7 See G. Calabresi and P. Bobbitt, *Tragic Choices* (1978), pp. 85–6.

8 For further discussion of this point see L. Bebchuk, "The Pursuit of a Bigger Pie: Can Everyone Expect a Bigger Slice?" *Hofstra Law Review* 8 (1980): 671, 691–4.

9 See generally A. Sen, *Collective Choice and Social Welfare* (1970).

10 See sec. 5 below.

11 It is Pareto superior to only some because some movements to optimality occur as a result of Kaldor–Hicks moves. See below.

12 T. Scitovsky, "A Note on Welfare Propositions in Economics," *Review of Economic Studies* 9 (1941): 77.

13 See K. Arrow, *Social Choice and Individual Values* (2d ed., 1963), pp. 38–45.

14 See Figure 4.3.

15 Posner, "Utilitarianism, Economics, and Legal Theory," p. 119. Posner defines wealth in its relationship to the system of wealth maximization as follows: "the value in dollars or dollar equivalents . . . of everything in society. It is measured by what people are willing to pay for something or, if they already own it, what they demand in money to give it up. The only kind of preference that counts in a system of wealth maximization is thus one that is backed up by money – in other words, that is registered in a market" (ibid.).

Instead of imploring individuals to act to promote utility, the system of wealth maximization requires them to act to increase social wealth – defined as the dollar equivalents of everything in society, including producer and consumer surplus.

16 This fact alone should shed some doubt on the claim that Paretianism is rooted in utilitarianism, since it is perfectly possible to employ the Pareto standards to compare social states in terms of their wealth rather than their utilities.

17 See R. Coase, "The Problem of Social Cost," *Journal of Law and Economics* 3 (1960): 1, 2–8.

18 A related point is developed by Lewis Kornhauser, who argues that wealth maximization encourages monopolization. See "A Guide to the Perplexed Claims of Efficiency in the Law," *Hofstra Law Review* 8 (1980): 591, 596–7 and n. 9.

19 Coleman, "Efficiency, Exchange, and Auction," pp. 237–47.

20 Posner, "The Ethical and Political Basis of the Efficiency Norm in Common Law Adjudication," *Hofstra Law Review* 8 (1980): 487, 491.

21 See J. Rawls, *A Theory of Justice* (1971), pp. 3–53.

22 Posner, "Ethical and Political Basis of the Efficiency Norm," pp. 494–7.

23 Ibid. p. 487 (footnote omitted).

24 Posner specifically refers to rights as instruments in the pursuit of wealth ("Utilitarianism, Economics, and Legal Theory," p. 127).

25 Many of these criticisms of wealth maximization involve the consequentialist nature of moral reasoning and the instrumentalist conception of rights involved in it. To that extent, they may be directed against utilitarianism as well. It does not follow, however, that wealth maximization is no less attractive than utilitarianism – though, of course, Posner's claim is that it is *more* attractive.

First, though Posner claims that wealth maximization is a complete moral theory, whereas, because of its boundary problems, utilitarianism is not, wealth maximization cannot, whereas utilitarianism can, provide a guide to action in the absence of prices. Presumably, some acts are right and others wrong, even in the absence of scarcity. Second, whether the elimination of scarcity is a good thing on utilitarian grounds is a contingent matter depending on the effect on the well-being of the populace of eliminating scarcity. On wealth-maximizing grounds, the elimination of scarcity eliminates prices and therefore wealth, and for that reason is necessarily a bad thing. Third, though on both utilitarian and wealth-maximizing grounds rights will be mere instruments in the pursuit of some conception of efficiency, the utilitarian theory can provide the basis for an initial distribution of them; the system of wealth maximization cannot.

According to wealth maximization, preference calculations undertaken by civil authority in the course of deciding among alternative legislative proposals are restricted to the preferences of those with money. In contrast, utilitarianism is committed to taking into account the preferences of all those who have an interest in some piece of legislation. Indeed, one source of utilitarianism's appeal is that it treats people as equals in the sense that each person's preferences count for one and no more than one before the utilitarian calculus. This practice of considering preferences equally is one way in which utilitarianism may be said to treat people as equals. Because wealth maximization fails to count everyone's preferences equally – indeed, it fails to take everyone's preferences into account – it is incompatible with the principle of equal consideration of interests. To that extent, wealth maximization fails to satisfy even this minimal conception of treatment as an equal. It is hard to imagine therefore that rational individuals, from a position of equality, would choose a system in which their interests were taken seriously only to the extent to which their preferences could be registered in a market.

My guess is that Posner is not particularly interested in the principle of equal consideration of interests or with treating persons as equals; but he should be. If civil authority is concerned with individuals' preferences, it is because legislation affects the welfare of those individuals; and part of what it means to be concerned with the welfare of individuals is to be concerned with the effects of legislation on the frustration or satisfaction of their preferences. But to take seriously only the preferences of those with money – and to do so only to the extent to which their preferences are expressed monetarily – is in effect to hold that in spite of the fact that the legislation will affect either adversely or favorably the interests of others, the fact that they are unable to express their interests monetarily excuses the government for failing to countenance them. Yet it is a person's capacity for satisfaction and frustration – not his or her wealth – that imposes the duty upon civil authority to take into account the effect of legislation upon him.

Obviously, Posner has an implicit moral theory concerning why the interests of some but not others should be countenanced, but because his principle will conflict with the principle of equal consideration, it will be *prima facie* an unattractive one to which the system of wealth maximization will be committed.

26 Posner, "Ethical and Political Basis of the Efficiency Norm," pp. 488–97.

27 Ibid. pp. 489–90.

28 Ibid. p. 490.

29 This is because wealth maximization relies on prices. See sec. 2 above.

30 See sec. 2.2.

31 Posner, "Ethical and Political Basis of the Efficiency Norm," pp. 488–9.

32 Ibid. pp. 492–6.

33 See sec. 3.2.3 above.

34 Posner, "Ethical and Political Basis of the Efficiency Norm," pp. 491–2 (emphasis added).

35 See ibid. pp. 492–7.
36 Ibid. p. 492.
37 Ibid.
38 Ibid. pp. 493–5.
39 See ibid. pp. 493–7.
40 See ibid.
41 Consider the following example. Suppose that, having accepted a teaching position at the University of Chicago, you are deciding whether to live in Evanston, where house prices are high but where the crime rate is relatively low, or in Hyde Park, where the crime rate is higher but the house prices, though high, are low compared with those in Evanston. Knowing this, suppose you decide to purchase a house in Hyde Park. The difference you pocket between the prices for comparable housing in Evanston and Hyde Park constitutes a kind of *ex ante* compensation. Suppose now that your house is burglarized. Is it at all plausible to say that you had given your consent to the burglary by accepting *ex ante* compensation in the form of a reduced housing price? Could the burglar introduce your consent as a defense in court? Hardly.

This example illustrates not only the mistake in thinking that compensation – either *ex post* or *ex ante* – is equivalent to consent; it demonstrates as well that knowledge of a risk does not always amount to either explicit or implicit waiver of a right or, in other words, to an assumption of risk.

42 Posner, "Ethical and Political Basis of the Efficiency Norm," p. 490.
43 See generally R. Nozick, *Anarchy, State, and Utopia* (1974); R. Epstein, "Nuisance Law: Corrective Justice and Its Utilitarian Constraints," *Journal of Legal Studies* 8 (1979): 49.
44 See generally Nozick, *Anarchy, State, and Utopia.*
45 Posner does not impose the constraint of uncertainty, whereas Rawls and others do. However, it is the power of Rawls's argument that he can derive or purport to derive principles of justice from an agreement involving people who do not know their current or future station in life. Why Posner leaves this constraint out is a mystery. His doing so weakens his argument significantly.
46 The argument stands or falls on the risk aversion of individuals, who are supposed to make the relevant choice under uncertainty, and whether Posner is committed to any principle of equal respect that would give to each a veto over the choices of others. If each person has a veto, the most risk-averse will demand a more conservative strategy than that associated with the Kaldor–Hicks test. The argument against Kaldor–Hicks is going to follow the lines of Rawls's argument against individuals in the initial position choosing the principle of utility. See Rawls, *Theory of Justice,* pp. 167–83.
47 See sec. 3.1. See also R. Dworkin, "Is Wealth a Value?" *Journal of Legal Studies* 9 (1980): 191, 194–7.
48 See J. Feinberg, "Legal Paternalism," *Canadian Journal of Philosophy* 1 (1971): 105, 110–12.

49 It may turn out to be neither.

50 See Coleman, "Efficiency, Exchange, and Auction," p. 239.

51 See ibid. pp. 242–6.

52 See Posner, "Utilitarianism, Economics, and Legal Theory," p. 120.

53 See Coleman, "Efficiency, Exchange, and Auction," pp. 237–42.

54 The libertarian is not opposed to all intervention. He restricts the justification of intervention to those cases involving one person's harming another. The proponent of economic efficiency, however, endorses intervention wherever conduct is inefficient, even if it is otherwise unharmful.

55 Coleman, "Efficiency, Exchange, and Auction," pp. 242–6.

56 But, as I have already argued, accepting compensation *ex post* need not constitute consent.

57 Interestingly enough, Nicholas Kaldor (of the Kaldor–Hicks test) early on conceived of the Pareto-superior test as rooted in the principle of consent. In discussing a reference to the employment of the Kaldor–Hicks principle, Kaldor notes, "This principle, as the reader will observe, simply amounts to saying that there is no interpersonal comparison of satisfactions involved in judging any policy designed to increase the sum total of wealth just *because any such policy could be carried out in a way as to secure unanimous consent*" ("Welfare Propositions of Economics and Interpersonal Comparisons of Utility," *Economic Journal* 49 [1939]: 549, 551 n. 1 [emphasis added]).

Kaldor was here defending his "hypothetical compensation principle" by arguing that *were* compensation actually paid, a Kaldor–Hicks move would be a Pareto-superior one, one which would be justified because – as a Pareto-superior one – it would be consented to.

58 Kaldor's argument is inadequate in its own terms, since one cannot extend the consent argument from Pareto superiority to Kaldor–Hicks, simply because Pareto superiority is *not* Kaldor–Hicks. To say that people *would* consent to a Pareto-superior move is not to say that they in fact consent to a Kaldor–Hicks move just because it *could* be a Pareto-superior move. In fact it is not; and because it is not, there is no reason to think people would consent to it in virtue of its potential to be something other than it is. If a move is Pareto superior, that does not mean it has been consented to; remember the traffic accident case. We could always *define* Pareto superiority in a way that obviated this problem: S_1 is Pareto superior to S if and only if everyone prefers S_1 to S. In that case, a move that is Pareto superior is consented to, since in order for it to be Pareto superior everyone must prefer it. However, the connection between Pareto superiority and consent is then *analytic* or conceptual. The fact that one state of affairs is Pareto superior to another state of affairs could not then constitute a *reason* for consenting to the move, since the claim that it is Pareto superior would mean by definition that it had been consented to.

59 See also Coleman, "Efficiency, Exchange, and Auction," pp. 247–9.

60 See Figure 4.1 and subsequent discussion of it.
61 J. Brown and W. Holahan, "Taxes and Legal Rules for the Control of Externalities When There Are Strategic Responses," *Journal of Legal Studies* 9 (1980): 165.
62 See e.g., A. M. Polinsky, "Private Versus Public Enforcement of Fines," *Journal of Legal Studies* 9 (1980): 105, and "Probabilistic Compensation Criteria," *Quarterly Journal of Economics* 86 (1972): 407; S. Shavell, "Strict Liability versus Negligence," *Journal of Legal Studies* 9 (1980): 1, and "Accidents, Liability, and Insurance," Harvard Institute for Economic Research Discussion Paper No. 685 (June 1979).
63 P. Samuelson, *Foundations of Economic Analysis* (1947), pp. 219–30.
64 After all, we could wonder why we should be concerned about which liability rules are efficient. There must be a policy reason behind interests; and as long as there is, the question of the normative roots of efficiency will be with us. Still, there is a difference between saying: If you want to promote utility or wealth, then these are the rules you should adopt; and saying: Because these rules would promote utility or wealth in the abstract, we should adopt them.
65 See R. Dworkin, *Taking Rights Seriously* (1977), pp. 35–6.
66 United States v. Carroll Towing Co., 159 F.2d 169, 173, (2d Cir. 1947) (the so-called Hand Formula).
67 For a fuller discussion see Coleman, review of Dworkin, *Taking Rights Seriously, California Law Review* 66 (1978): 885.

5. THE FOUNDATIONS OF CONSTITUTIONAL ECONOMICS

1 I do not mean to suggest by this distinction that there are no other nonteleological or deontic modes of justification. In this chapter I discuss only these two modes of justification because I want to show how they have been confused by advocates of various forms of economic analyses.

6. CRIMES, KICKERS AND TRANSACTION STRUCTURES

1 Alvin Klevorick, "The Economic Analysis of Crime," in *Criminal Justice: Nomos XXVII,* ed. J. Roland Pennock and John W. Chapman (1985), p. 289.
2 Risk-neutral actors are concerned only with expected outcomes and are indifferent among outcomes with the same expected value, regardless of the likelihood of the outcome's occurrence.
3 Guido Calabresi and Douglas Melamed, "Property Rules, Liability Rules, and Inalienability: One View of the Cathedral," *Harvard Law Review* 85 (1972): 1089.
4 One reason I have always been troubled by the Calabresi–Melamed approach is that if a right is secured by a property rule, then when one negotiates successfully with the right bearer for it there is no sense in which the bargainer acts *contrary* to the right bearer's entitlement; whereas under a liability rule the action is contrary to the right bearer's entitle-

ment, period, and it makes no matter that the intruder renders compensation *ex post*.

It strikes me as simply confused to see liability rules as entitling injurers to purchase at their will "parts" of (another very peculiar notion) the rights of others. It is hard to conceive of an individual as having a freedom that consists of nothing other than his acting contrary to the rights of others. Normally we should think of such action as *prima facie* wrong and in need of justification. The root of the problem is that advocates of the Calabresi–Melamed dichotomy ask the notion of a liability rule to do too much work, much of it internally inconsistent: How can we conceive of a liability rule as a protector of one's rights to the security of one's holding and at the same time as a vehicle that enables others to act contrary to the duties those rights are presumed to entail?

5 Ronald Coase, "The Problem of Social Cost," *Journal of Law and Economics* 3 (1960): 1.

6 Klevorick, "Economic Analysis of Crime," p. 295.

7 Ibid.

8 In other words, the very idea of turning an inalienability rule into a liability rule may be incoherent. Inalienability rules are aimed at restricting the freedom of those who have rights, not those whose conduct interferes with rights. So there is a sense in which it is impossible for an offender to act contrary to an inalienability rule; only one whose rights are protected by an inalienability rule can do that, by, for example, trading one's rights – that is, by trying to turn an inalienability rule into a property rule.

7. THE MORALITY OF STRICT TORT LIABILITY

1 The term "fault" takes on different shades of meaning, depending upon the legal context in which it is used. For example, the liability of an intentional or reckless tortfeasor is determined differently from that of a negligent tortfeasor. The term here is used to mean limited determinations of fault in the context of accidents resulting from negligent conduct. Any such fault imputation can be viewed as consisting of two components, one relating to the act and its relationship to an appropriate standard of behavior, and the other relating to the purported responsibility of the actor for the alleged defect in his action (Jules L. Coleman, "On the Moral Argument for the Fault System," *Journal of Philosophy* 71 (1974): 473 [hereinafter cited as Coleman, "Fault System"]).

For a general and helpful discussion of what here is called the fault principle see J. Feinberg, "Sua Culpa," *Doing and Deserving* (1970), p. 187. A similar position is taken in R. Keeton, *Legal Cause in the Law of Torts* (1963), which unfortunately is no longer in print. Guido Calabresi recently has put forth a different view. See *Concerning Cause* (to be published by Indiana University Press) and "Concerning Cause and the Law of Torts: An Essay for Harry Kalven, Jr.," *University of Chicago Law Review* 43 (1975): 69.

2 Ives v. South Buffalo Ry., 201 N.Y. 271, 94 N.E. 431 (1911).

3 In *Ives,* the Court of Appeals of New York castigated a 1909 New York Workmen's compensation law as "plainly revolutionary" and "totally at variance with the common-law theory of the employer's liability" (ibid. pp. 285, 288; 94 N.E., pp. 436, 347). The court went on to hold the law void as a "taking of property without due process of law" (ibid. p. 317; 94 N.E., p. 448) which violated both the federal and state constitutions. In justifying its decision, the court stressed that strict liability was a creature virtually totally unknown to the common law: "When our Constitutions were adopted, it was the law of the land that no man who was without fault or negligence could be held liable in damages for injuries sustained by another. That is still the law, except as to the employers enumerated in the new statute" (ibid. p. 293; 94 N.E., p. 439).

That the court overstated this point is plain upon consideration of the historical roots of the concept of strict liability. Apparently the early common law of tort liability focused primarily on the undeserved damage suffered by victims rather than on the fault or negligence of injurers. Although it was never universally true that one acted at his peril and was responsible for any and all harm resulting from his actions, liability commonly was imposed without regard to the moral guilt or innocence of the injurer. The common law gradually evolved toward recognition of "fault" as a basis of liability, but it was not until the close of the nineteenth century that this tendency reached the peak epitomized by the *Ives* decision. See W. Prosser, *Handbook of the Law of Torts* (4th ed., 1971), sec. 4, p. 75. Even in this period, however, the concept of strict liability was by no means a dead issue. See, e.g., Rylands v. Fletcher, [1968] L.R. 3 H.L. 330.

4 O. W. Holmes, *The Common Law* (1963), pp. 76–7.

5 A general theory of initial injurer liability has been defended by Richard Epstein. See "A Theory of Strict Liability," *Journal of Legal Studies* 2 (1973): 151. Epstein's analysis draws heavily on a prior exhaustive treatment of conceptual and practical aspects of legal liability in tort and others areas of the law in H. L. A. Hart and A. M. Honoré, *Causation in the Law* (1959).

6 See Prosser, *Handbook,* pp. 75–81, 98.

7 Holmes, *Common Law,* pp. 76–7.

8 The term "liability rule" is most closely associated with a recent article discussing various theories available to protect "entitlements," i.e., to decide which side should prevail whenever the interests of two or more people conflict (Guido Calabresi and Douglas Melamed, "Property Rules, Liability Rules, and Inalienability: One View of the Cathedral," *Harvard Law Review* 85 [1972]: 1089). The authors argue that a distribution of initial entitlements to holdings can be protected in one of three ways. An entitlement can be protected by a property rule so that the entitlement can be transferred to another by a sale at an agreed price. It is often too costly or inconvenient, and occasionally impossible, to contract for transfer of entitlements at mutually acceptable prices, however. Therefore, it may be desirable to protect entitlements by means of a liability rule that enables one to effect the partial or complete transfer of an entitlement at an objectively set price. For example, suppose that X operates a polluting feedlot and that Y is a homeowner in the neighboring residential community. After consulting criteria of economic efficiency and wealth distribution, we might decide that Y ought to be entitled to be free from unnecessary pollution generated by X's feedlot. To give effect to our decision to protect Y's interest, we award him the requisite initial entitlement. Should X's feedlot pollute Y's airspace in violation of Y's protected interest, we then should require X to compensate him. In other words, we make X's conduct tortious and hold him liable in damages to Y so that he can pollute only at the price of rendering compensation to Y. The damages X is required to pay Y are set objectively, usually by a court of law. In this way, liability rules protect entitlements. Of course, an entitlement can be protected by both property and liability rules.

When an entitlement is protected by what Calabresi and Melamed call an inalienability rule, the holder of it is denied the right or freedom to negotiate its sale. For example, the right to freedom from indentured servitude is one that we might want to protect by an inalienability rule forbidding the sale of one's freedom. The right to exercise one's franchise might be another such entitlement (ibid. pp. 1105–15).

The importance of the Calabresi–Melamed analysis is that, on the one hand, it details the diversity of protective devices for securing entitlements while, on the other, it suggests a fundamental relationship between the foundations of tort and property law. The need to provide legal rules to effect transfers of entitlements also suggests the role of a legal system in overcoming what economists call market failures (ibid. pp. 1109–10 and n. 39). Of additional conceptual interest to philosophers in the Calabresi–Melamed scheme is the role of the criminal law primarily as a means for securing the integrity of the market and private law (property, tort, contract) approach to protecting and transferring entitlements (ibid. pp. 1124–7).

For further discussion of Calabresi's position and its consequences in political theory see G. Calabresi, "Torts – The Law of the Mixed Society" (unpublished manuscript on file at the Yale Law School library). For a general criticism of the Calabresi–Melamed analysis see note 54.

9   For a detailed discussion of the limits of retributive theories of torts see Coleman, "Fault System."

10   For a general discussion of the relationship between compensatory claims and tort law see Coleman, "Justice and the Argument for No-Fault," *Social Theory and Practice* 3 (1974): 161 (hereinafter cited as Coleman, "Justice"); James Nickel, "Justice in Compensation," *William and Mary Law Review* 18 (1976): 389.

11   The "risk-spreading" analysis of tort law is well presented in the writings of Fleming James. See, e.g., "Accident Liability Reconsidered:

The Impact of Liability Insurance," *Yale Law Journal* 57 (1948): 549. The general argument is canvassed and analyzed carefully in G. Calabresi, *The Costs of Accidents: A Legal and Economic Analysis* (1970), pp. 37–67.

12 The cost-minimization theory of torts, namely that the primary goal of tort law is to allocate losses as incentives to minimize the sum of the costs of accidents and the costs of avoiding them, has been given its most thorough treatment in the works of lawyers trained in economics. The essential essays include Guido Calabresi and Jon Hirschoff, "Toward a Test for Strict Liability in Torts," *Yale Law Journal* 71 (1972): 1055; Richard Posner, "Strict Liability: A Comment," *Journal of Legal Studies* 2 (1973): 205; Posner, "A Theory of Negligence," *Journal of Legal Studies* 1 (1972): 29. Although Posner and Calabresi agree that cost avoidance (or efficiency in the economic sense) is the fundamental goal of tort law, they differ with respect to whether such a result is best fostered by a system of strict liability. Calabresi appears optimistic that a strict liability system is more likely than a negligence system to minimize the sum of accident costs and accident avoidance costs (Calabresi and Hirschoff, p. 1084). Posner, on the other hand, has concluded that economic theory provides no basis for preferring strict liability to negligence ("Strict Liability," p. 221).

For an essential introduction to the economic model of law see Ronald Coase, "The Problem of Social Cost," *Journal of Law and Economics* 3 (1960): 1, and Richard Posner, *The Economic Analysis of Law* (1972). A. Mitchell Polinsky has written an exemplary review of Posner's book and of the foundations of the economic analysis of legal rules generally ("Economic Analysis as a Potentially Defective Product: A Buyer's Guide to Posner's *Economic Analysis of Law*," *Harvard Law Review* 87 [1974]). For another useful review of both the book and the general methodology, see C. Edwin Baker, "The Ideology of the Economic Analysis of Law," *Philosophy and Public Affairs* 5 (1975): 3.

13 Calabresi and Hirschoff, p. 1084.

14 See Coleman, "Fault System," and "Justice."

15 See Coleman, "Fault System," pp. 475–83.

16 See Coleman, "Justice," p. 173.

17 See ibid. pp. 176–8.

18 I do not mean to suggest that the fault system is not the best compromise, but to argue only that justice in tort liability does not require the fault criterion. For an argument that fault is the best compromise see Walter Blum and Harry Kalven, "The Empty Cabinet of Dr. Calabresi: Auto Accidents and General Deterrence," *University of Chicago Law Review* 34 (1967): 239.

19 See Coleman, "Fault System," pp. 484–6.

20 This view, or at least one similar to it, was considered and rejected in *Wagon Mound I. Overseas Tankship (U.K.) Ltd. v. Morts Dock & Eng'r. Co.* ([1961] A.C. 388 [P.C.]). The court held that a shipowner was not liable for damage to a wharf that resulted when oil spilled from the ship ignited and burned, and stressed that such damage was not a foreseeable consequence of the lack of care that resulted in the spillage. "There can be no liability until the damage has been done. It is not the act but the consequences upon which tortious liability is founded. Just as . . . there is no such thing as negligence in the air, so there is no such thing as liability in the air" (ibid., p. 425).

21   See notes 1–2 above and the accompanying text.

22   See Prosser, *Handbook,* p. 65.

23   Although it was a viable concept in older common law, imputed contributory negligence is all but nonexistent in modern tort law. Today it survives principally as an adjunct to "automobile consent" statutes in those states where courts have interpreted such statutes as mandating the imputation of a driver's contributory negligence to an automobile owner, thus barring his action for damages.

24   See e.g., Brown v. San Francisco Ball Club, 99 Cal. App. 2d 484, 222 P.2d 19 (1950); Hunn v. Windsor Hotel Co., 119 W. Va. 215, 193 S.E. 57 (1937).

25   See e.g., Palsgraf v. Long Island R.R., 248 N.Y. 339, 162 N.E. 99 (1928); Green-Wheeler Shoe Co. v. Chicago, R.I. & P. Ry., 130 Iowa 123, 106 N.W. 498 (1906); In re Polemis, [1921] 33 K.B. 560 (C.A.). Given that the injurer is at fault and that his fault is a cause of the victim's injury, the question in such cases is whether it is sufficiently proximate to entitle the victim to recovery.

Hart and Honoré have attempted to construct a coherent analysis of the concept of legal cause in torts and elsewhere. Their general analysis involves two steps. First, in order for liability to be imposed, a minimal causal relation must exist between the defendant's conduct and the alleged harm. Once the minimal condition has been established, the next step is to determine if any conditions exist that would defeat or negate the attribution of legal responsibility based on the first-step causal inquiry. Their paradigm of a negating condition is the intervening voluntary action of a third party. In the absence of such conditions, liability is justly imposed. See *Causation in the Law,* pp. 126–30. Compare their analysis with Joel Feinberg, "Causing Voluntary Actions," *Doing and Deserving* (1970), p. 152, and with Calabresi, "Concerning Cause and the Law of Torts," p. 69.

26   The common-law distinction among licensees, invitees and trespassers provides perhaps the best example of cases in which the right to recovery for accidental injury has been determined by the status of the victim rather than by the culpability of the defendant. In general terms, a landowner has been held to a duty of ordinary care in maintaining his property in a safe condition when injury has occurred to an invitee. A less stringent standard of care has been applied when the victim was a licensee, and the landowner has been held to owe virtually no duty of care to a trespasser.

The approach to tort law exemplified by these distinctions is one that analyzes fault in terms of a failure to discharge a duty of care, and incorporates in doctrinal terms the duty owed to various categories of victims.

Recent cases have made significant inroads into the doctrinal invitee–licensee–trespasser trichotomy. Courts that have rejected the common-law categories generally have done so when they have been presented with the issue in an invitee–licensee context. See e.g., Keimarec v. Compagnie Générale Transatlantique, 358 U.S. 625 (1959); Smith v. Arbaugh's Restaurant, Inc. 469 F.2d 97 (D.C.C. (1972); Rowland v. Christian, 69 Cal. 2d 108, 443 P.2d 561, 70 Cal. Rptr. 97 (1968).

27 The common-law rule barring personal tort actions between spouses still is followed in many jurisdictions. However, there is a growing trend toward outright rejection of spousal immunity and a concomitant allowance of an action by either spouse for personal torts, negligent or intentional, committed by the other. The common-law parental immunity from personal tort actions by children remains more prevalent than spousal immunity, but in many jurisdictions it too has been eroded by exception or abrogated outright.

28 The common-law tort immunity of charitable organizations and enterprises has been abrogated in a majority of jurisdictions and has been limited in one way or another in almost all others.

29 A large portion of the field of law governing employer liability for injuries to employees has been preempted by workmen's compensation acts, which have been enacted in all states. These acts impose a form of strict liability in that the employer, aided by a stem of compulsory liability insurance, is made liable for injuries arising out of his business, irrespective of whether accidents are caused by his own negligence, his employees' or no one's.

30 Strict liability generally is imposed when a defendant damages another by a thing or activity that is unduly dangerous and inappropriate to the place it is maintained. This rule was derived from the famous English case of Rylands v. Fletcher ([1868] L.R. 3 H.L. 330), in which defendants were held strictly liable when water from their reservoir escaped through abandoned coalmining shafts and flooded an adjoining mine. American courts have applied the rule in a variety of contexts. See e.g., Exner v. Sherman Power Constr. Co., 54 F.2d 510 (2d Cir. 1931) (quantity of explosives stored in city); Britton v. Harrison Constr. Co., 87 F. Supp. 405 (W.D. Va. 1950) (blasting); Green v. Gen. Petroleum Corp., 205 Cal. 328, 270 P. 952 (1928) (drilling oil well in residential area).

31 Liability for nuisance may be based on any of three types of conduct encroaching upon the interests of another: an intentional encroachment, a negligent one or one resulting from conduct that is abnormally dangerous and out of place in its surroundings. It is to this last type of conduct that strict liability applies. See, e.g., Whittemore v. Baxter Laundry Co., 181 Mich. 564, 148 N.W. 427 (1914) (quantity of gasoline stored near plaintiff's residence); Rider v. Clarkson, 77 N.J. Eq. 469, 78 A. 676 (1910) (vicious dog).

32 The development of products liability law has involved an interplay of three conceptual bases of liability: negligence, warranty and strict lia-

bility. Strict liability is now applied in this area by some two-thirds of the courts.

33   See e.g., Calabresi and Hirschoff; Epstein, "A Theory of Strict Liability"; Posner, "Strict Liability."

34   There are at least two kinds of cases in which liability need not require a causal connection between the conduct of the party held strictly liable and the harm: (1) liability on the model of workmen's compensation statutes and (2) liability for results (not actions). Liability for results is most prevalent in criminal law, in which criminal penalties have been imposed despite the prosecutor's failure to prove criminal intent, most frequently when statutes impose sanctions for offenses against public health or safety (see Morissette v. United States, 342 U.S. 246, 256–60 [1952]; United States v. Dotterweich, 320 U.S. 277, 281 [1942]), and including, recently, violations of environmental protection laws (see State v. Arizona Mines Supply Co., 107 Ariz. 199, 484 P.2d 619 [1971]).

35   See H. L. A. Hart, "Prolegomenon to the principles of Punishment," *Punishment and Responsibility* (1968), pp. 1, 13–14.

36   H. L. A. Hart, "Legal Responsibility and Excuses," *Punishment and Responsibility* (1968), pp. 28, 39.

37   Although liability without fault, in the sense of liability in the absence of culpability or responsibility, presents interesting philosophic issues, adequate analysis of the role of excuses in a theory of tort liability ought to be discussed within the context of a general appraisal of the objective even when liability is imposed on the basis of fault, the fault required need not be a moral one. Thus, a defendant may be at fault even if his failure to exercise due care is not his doing – if he has an excuse – provided the reasonable man could have exercised proper care and foresight. This is a lesson to be derived from the landmark case of *Vaughan v. Menlove* (132 Eng. Rep. 490 [C.P. 1837]), in which the court made its classic statement on the objectivity of the standard to be applied in determining negligence: "Instead, therefore, of saying that the liability for negligence should be coextensive with the judgment of each individual, which would be as variable as the length of the foot of each individual, we ought rather to adhere to the rule which requires in all cases a regard to caution such as a man of ordinary prudence would observe" (ibid. p. 493). See also J. L. Coleman, "Fault, Defeasibility and Blame" (Dec. 6, 1976; unpublished typescript in the University of Wisconsin–Milwaukee library). Consequently, the standards of both fault and strict liability may impose the obligation of recompense in the absence of moral responsibility. For that reason a discussion of the alleged injustice of strict liability for excusable conduct is best left for an overall appraisal of the role of responsibility as a condition of tort liability. Ultimately, the issue boils down to a jurisprudential one: Is tort liability fundamentally a problem in the theory of responsibility or in the economic theory of loss allocation or both?

38   See notes 22–8 above and the accompanying text.

39   See note 7 and the accompanying text.

40 See notes 21–31 and the accompanying text.

41 A plaintiff's mere lack of ordinary care is generally not enough to constitute the degree of contributory fault required to bar his recovery in a strict liability case. But if the plaintiff voluntarily and unreasonably has exposed himself to a known danger, he will be deemed to have been contributorily negligent, or to have assumed the risk. See, e.g., Hughey v. Fergus County, 98 Mont. 89, 37 P.2d 1035 (1934) (entering field with bull); Worth v. Dunn, 98 Conn. 51, 118 A. 467 (1922) (plaintiff's conduct increased danger from blasting).

42 The general role of workmen's compensation laws is that misconduct of the employee, whether negligent or willful, is immaterial, because the basic test for recovery is whether the injury is related to the employment, not whether one part or the other was responsible. Exceptions to the rule exist in those jurisdictions whose statutes provide for "willful misconduct," or some similar terminology, as a defense and in those whose statutes provide for more narrow grounds of defense, such as "willful violation of a safety regulation." The most common type of statute provides for no such affirmative defenses based on employee misconduct in the course of employment.

43 Generally the seller is entitled to expect normal uses of his product and is not liable when it is put to abnormal uses. See, e.g., Zesch v. Abrasive Co., 354 Mo. 1147, 193 S.W.2d 581 (1946) (grinding wheel used improperly); Dubbs v. Zak Bros. Co., 38 Ohio App. 299, 175 N.E. 626 (1931) (shoes intentionally worn two sizes too small).

There is a subtle but important distinction between the contributory fault and victim misuse defenses from liability, though both require establishing a defect in a victim's conduct. One can imagine an emergency in which it would be reasonable (i.e., not faulty) for a person to drive a power lawnmower down a busy street and through a dangerous intersection. For example, suppose one's car fails to start after a guest at one's house is suddenly stricken by a heart attack and must be taken to a hospital a mile or so away. Clearly it may be a misuse, and certainly an unforeseeable use, of the mower to employ it in this fashion. Should an inherent defect in the mower cause an accident resulting in injury to the operator of the mower, his stricken passenger or some other third party, the mower company, normally liable under products liability law, could escape liability, not because the injury was caused by the driver's fault, but because it resulted from product misuse.

44 As with strict liability generally (see note 41), mere lack of ordinary care is insufficient to constitute contributory fault to bar a plaintiff's recovery in a products liability case. Thus, that plaintiff has failed to discover the danger in a product is not a viable defense to strict liability, (see, e.g., Brockett v. Harrell Bros., 206 Va. 457, 143 S.E.2d 897 [1965] [failure to discover shot in ham]); nor that he has failed to take precautions against its existence, (see, e.g., Dagley v. Armstrong Rubber Co., 344 F.2d 245 [7th Cir. 1965] [negligent driving on defective tire]). However, when the plaintiff voluntarily and unreasonably encounters a known

Notes to pages 175–6

danger, he will be barred from recovery on a contributory negligence or assumption-of-risk theory. See, e.g., Youtz v. Thompson Tire Co., 46 Cal. App. 2d 672, 116 P.2d 636 (1941) (negligent driving on tire known to be defective); Gutelius v. General Elec. Co., 37 Cal. App. 2d 455, 99 P.2d 682 (1940) (washing machine used after discovery of dangerous defect).

45 This would be true, for example, if a state "dog bite" statute provided for owner liability for all injuries caused by his dog unless the person injured was committing trespass or a tort. See e.g., Nelson v. Hansen, 10 Wis. 2d 107, 102 N.W.2d 251 (1960); Ingeneri v. Kluya, 129 Conn. 208, 27 A.2d 124 (1942). Similarly, no plaintiff-related defense will succeed in a jurisdiction whose workmen's compensation statute provides for no defenses based on employee misconduct. See note 42.

46 Guido Calabresi, "Optimal Deterrence and Accidents: To Fleming James, Jr.," *Yale Law Journal* 84 (1975): 656.

47 See note 7 and the accompanying text.

48 According to the prevailing wisdom of neo-classical welfare economics, efficiency is the primary standard for evaluating an allocation of resources. An allocation of resources is maximally efficient when it is Pareto optimal. To say that resources are allocated in a Pareto-optimal fashion is to claim that any further voluntary (costless) transfer (contract or sale) of resources will make someone better off only by making at least one other person worse off. So a Pareto-optimal distribution exists when no one can be made better off without making someone else worse off, judged by each individual's standard of welfare or satisfaction.

The distinction between Pareto optimality (maximal economic efficiency) and both Pareto superiority and maximal product output must be kept clear. An allocation scheme is Pareto superior to an alternative if and only if in the Pareto-superior distribution no one conceives of himself as worse off and at least one person conceives of himself as better off. A distribution of goods may be Pareto superior without being Pareto optimal. Interestingly, it does not follow from a policy-making standpoint that a Pareto-optimal allocation is preferable to a Pareto-superior one.

The weaker policy-making implications of Pareto optimality have been largely ignored by lawyers and ought to be examined closely by philosophers concerned with the foundations of institutional rule making. Imagine a two-person universe and an all-purpose resource, manna. Suppose that the manna is distributed so that A receives all of it. Any redistribution of the resources (without compensatory provisions) would make A worse off. Thus, this apparently unfair allocation scheme is Pareto optimal. Although there seem to be good reasons for adopting a Pareto-superior distribution scheme to an alternative rule because, by hypothesis, it makes no one worse off and at least one person better off, the same cannot be said always of a Pareto-optimal distribution. A Pareto-optimal distribution need not maximize output. A Pareto-optimal resource distribution may involve transforming all the manna into five pairs of shoes that are then awarded to *A*. If it turns out that *A*'s welfare is maximized by owning five pairs of shoes, then any other resource use and allocation would make him worse off than he is now.

This would be true even if the manna could have been transformed into large quantities of books, works of art, food, shelter and the like. It is important for philosophers venturing into the economic analysis of legal rules to recognize the limited role of Pareto optimality in policy making. For a useful and altogether readable discussion of these basic concepts, see B. Ackerman, *Economic Foundations of Property Law* (1975).

49 Holmes, *Common Law*, p. 77.

50 Arguments based on the condemnatory or attitudinal aspects of punishment have been advanced to shed doubt on the moral propriety of strict criminal liability as a general theory of criminal responsibility. For a discussion of these arguments and their limits, see Joel Feinberg, "The Expressive Function of Punishment," *Doing and Deserving* (1970), p. 95.

For reasons I shall suggest (see notes 1–64 and the accompanying text), arguments based on the expressive elements in tort liability or compensation do not weigh nearly so heavily against strict tort liability. My arguments do not hold (nor should they) when tort liability involves so-called punitive damages.

51 See note 16 and the accompanying text.

52 Feinberg, "Expressive Function of Punishment," p. 115.

53 The Fifth Amendment to the Constitution provides: "nor shall private property be taken for public use, without just compensation." This section of the amendment has come to be called the takings clause. It is a well of philosophically interesting problems. First, its implementation requires a model for determining if a taking of property is a taking in the constitutional sense, i.e., one that requires compensation. Such a formula is needed if consistent answers are to be given to the practical questions that arise under the clause. For example, are condemnation of property and consequent transfer of title necessary ingredients in the takings formula? Are zoning changes and consequent limitations of owner prerogatives remediable under the clause? Next, the takings clause requires formulation of a workable distinction between private and public uses without begging the entire question. Third, it demands a well-formulated theory of fittingness or appropriateness in compensation. Ultimately, the entire takings question leads one to an independent analysis of the concepts of property and ownership.

One recent approach to understanding tort liability analogizes polluting one's neighbor to a taking of his property by diminishing its value sufficiently to require compensation. Whether compensation is owed to someone, in this case the neighboring resident, is not at issue. The issue is how the compensation rendered is conceived. The advantage of the takings analogy is that it subsumes compensation in tort law under a property law model. Specifically, compensation rendered by injurers to their victims in certain tort cases is based on the model of eminent domain. Thus conceived, compensation in torts does not center on expressions of regret, shame or apology; it requires no element of culpability. Instead, compensation is a cost one must accept in order to pollute or in some sense use the property rights initially conferred upon another.

The takings analogy is of questionable validity. At the least, in order for it to hold, the injurer (tortfeasor) must be an agent of the state or must satisfy the state action requirement in some other way. After all, the Fifth Amendment enumerates limitations or restrictions on state, not private, action. The analogy would be less questionable, for example, were the polluter a public utility. Nevertheless, the takings analogy sometimes is employed to explain holdings in a variety of tort cases. For example, in Vincent v. Lake Erie Transp. Co. (109 Minn. 456, 124 N.W. 221 [1910]), the court employed takings-analogy reasoning to hold the owner of a steamship that was moored to a dock during a storm liable for damages to the dock. Although the master of the steamship had "exercised good judgment and prudent seamanship," (ibid. p. 458; 124 N.W., p. 221) in keeping the vessel fast to the dock, the court found liability because "those in charge of the vessel deliberately . . . held her in such a position that the damage to the dock resulted, and, having thus preserved the ship at the expense of the dock, . . . her owners are responsible to the dock owners to the extent of the injury inflicted" (ibid. p. 459; 124 N.W., p. 222). Compare this reasoning with that of the court in Holmes v. Mather (L.R. 10 Ex. 261 [1875]), in which the court decided that the owner of a horse was not liable when the animal, startled by a barking dog, ran out of control and injured the plaintiff. In reaching this holding the court relied upon its finding that the defendant had committed no wrongful act and therefore could not be held liable. The basic factual situation was similar to that in *Vincent,* yet the holding was opposite.

The literature on the takings question itself is sparse but improving. For useful overviews see F. Bosselman, D. Callies and J. Banta, *The Taking Issue* (1973), and Bruce Ackerman, *Private Property and the Constitution* (1979).

54   The view that tort liability has a right-purchasing component is suggested by the takings analogy. A general analysis of tort liability presented along these lines can be attributed to Calabresi and Malamed (see note 8). Calabresi and I part company at this point. It is a necessary consequence of his notion of a liability rule that compensation in torts be regarded as a vehicle for purchasing partial or entire entitlements from those upon whom they have been conferred initially. For example, even if X is initially entitled to security from Y's harmful conduct, Y may become entitled *de facto* to harm X at that price by compensating X for his losses. Thus, compensation is merely the price Y must pay to purchase the entitlement from X. Moreover, X has no say in determining the price Y is to pay, a say that he would have were his right protected by a property rule buttressed by an appropriate criminal prohibition against theft.

Ironically, Calabresi and other legal theorists inclined to economic analysis have fostered an unfortunate analogy between tort and criminal liability. By conceiving of compensation primarily as an operating cost of harmful conduct, they have suggested an analogy with the criminal-law conception of punishment or incarceration as the cost of harmful conduct. Thus the rational, utilitarian offender is given the option of complying with a set of rules (criminal law), complying with an allocation of entitlements to security (tort law), or violating the norms or purchasing the entitlement at a price. Through this analogy, therefore, both criminal law and tort law are seen as pricing systems setting the requisite "costs" should one choose the latter option. This seems altogether misleading. Neither tort nor criminal law is primarily cost setting in its goals. The criminal law establishes standards of conduct that one ought to follow; it is not a pricing system for violations of that code of conduct. But that does not mean tort law is also primarily concerned with setting standards of conduct. Although establishing standards of responsible behavior is one function of tort law, its primary goal is to provide a vehicle for protecting victims from unjustifiable or wrongfully absorbed losses. Thus, compensation is a vehicle for protecting or securing entitlements by annulling or rectifying losses that result from their violation. Compensation, at least when fault is involved, is an instrument for reinforcing one's entitlement; it is not a vehicle for transferring it.

55 This is not to suggest that imposing liability on the polluter is the *only* way to ensure that the prices of his goods adequately reflect the impact of their production on resources; nor is compensation through liability rules required to ensure that the neighbors are freed from the costs of internalizing the effects of pollution. For example, one might try to tax the polluter and pass the revenue to the affected parties. This could prove quite unsatisfactory, however, where the polluter is a monopoly. See James Buchanan, "External Diseconomics, Corrective Taxes, and Market Structure," *American Economic Review* 59 (1969): 175.

56 See note 48.

57 See notes 3–4 and the accompanying text.

58 279 U.S. 639 (1929).

59 Sec. 1 states in pertinent part: "No state shall . . . deprive any person of life, liberty, or property, without due process of law."

Although the Court noted that legislation creating evidentiary presumptions is valid "if there is a rational connection between what is proved and what is to be inferred," the Court found the Georgia statute violative of the due process clause because it created "a presumption that is arbitrary or that operates to deny a fair opportunity to repel it" (279 U.S., p. 642).

60 Commenting upon the construction given to the statute by the Georgia court, the Court wrote: "Upon the mere fact of collision and resulting death, the statute is held to raise *a presumption that defendant and its employees were negligent* in each of the particulars alleged, and that every act or omission in plaintiff's specifications of negligence was the proximate cause of death; and it makes defendant liable unless it showed due care in respect of every matter alleged against it" (279 U.S., p. 641; emphasis added).

61 Ibid. p. 640.

62 165 U.S. 1 (1897).

63 Ibid. p. 2. In holding the statute to be valid under the due process clause, the Court considered the competing interests of the railroad and property owners, and concluded: "To require the utmost care and diligence of the railroad corporations in taking precautions against the escape of fire from their engines might not afford sufficient protection to the owners of property in the neighborhood of the railroads. When both parties are equally faultless, the legislature may properly consider it to be just that the duty of insuring private property against loss or injury caused by the use of dangerous instruments should rest upon the railroad company, which employs the instruments and creates the peril for its own profit. . . . *The statute is not a penal one, imposing punishment for a violation of law, but it is purely remedial, making the party, doing a lawful act for its own profit, liable in damages* to the innocent party injured thereby" (ibid. pp. 26–7; emphasis added).

64 Ives v. South Buffalo Ry., 201 N.Y. 271, 94 N.E. 431. See note 3.

65 As a general theory of loss allocation, absolute *victim* liability maintains that losses ought to be internalized by victims. In terms familiar to economists, absolute victim liability requires potential victims to be self-insurers or to purchase first-party insurance policies. Because of the availability of insurance, we really are deciding in many areas of tort law upon whom the burden of securing insurance ought to fall.

66 See note 42.

67 Feinberg, "Sua Culpa," pp. 217–21.

68 Fault-free loss bearing is justified when it is agreed to by contractual arrangement. Certainly no one has seriously argued that it is unjust for insurance companies to offer indemnification policies. If there is a counterargument, it is not based on the view that it is unfair to the insurance company to impose the burden on it. After all, the company contractually agreed to bear it. Instead, it arguably undermines the restorative and character-building elements of tort law to allow persons to indemnify themselves against the costs of injuries their fault causes others to suffer.

More to the point, the "contract" justification for absolute tort liability is at the core of products liability holdings. Specifically, in products liability it often is hard to identify whether it is the tort theory of absolute liability or the contract doctrine of implied warranty that supports compensation. In fact, the development of the absolute liability rule in products liability has its roots in contract analysis. See e.g., Henningsen v. Bloomfield Motors, Inc., 32 N.J. 358, 161 A.2d 69 (1960); Baxter v. Ford Motor Co., 168 Wash. 456, 12 P.2d 409 (1932); Winterbottom v. Wright, 10 M. & W. 109, 152 Eng. Rep. 402 (1842).

In part because of contractual origins of the tort doctrine of absolute products liability and the tort character of the contract doctrine of promissory estoppel, some recent scholarship has focused on the viability of the tort–contract dichotomy. The most impressive of these works is Grant Gilmore's excellent book *The Death of Contract* (1974).

69 This argument holds whether one conceives of the concept of fault in tort law as primarily moral or primarily economic. If one conceives of the fault concept as a quasi-moral one, as I do, that an injurer is at fault may constitute a good reason for his bearing the costs of accidents caused by his fault. As I have argued earlier here (see notes 15–17 and the accompanying text) and elsewhere, (see "Fault System," pp. 488–90; "Justice," pp. 173–8), that an injurer is at fault is a good reason for conferring on the victims of his fault a right to recompense. By itself, however, his fault does not imply that he ought to discharge the corresponding obligation to provide recompense.

On the other hand, if, as Posner and Calabresi contend (see note 12), fault is infected by cost-avoidance implications, pursuit of economic efficiency could well justify having those at fault bear the costs of accidents for which they are responsible. Neither specification of the tort concept of fault succeeds in justifying any particular allocation of accident costs in the absence of fault.

8. CORRECTIVE JUSTICE AND WRONGFUL GAIN

1 Richard Posner, "The Concept of Corrective Justice in Recent Theories of Tort Law" *Journal of Legal Studies* 10 (1981): 187.

2 Jules L. Coleman, "On the Moral Argument for the Fault System," *Journal of Philosophy* 71 (1974): 473, and "Justice and the Argument for No-Fault," *Social Theory and Practice* 3 (1974): 161.

3 Jules L. Coleman, "The Morality of Strict Tort Liability," Chapter 7 in this volume.

4 Jules L. Coleman, "Mental Abnormality, Personal Responsibility and Tort Liability," in *Mental Illness: Law and Public Policy,* ed. Baruch A. Brody and H. Tristram Englehardt, Jr. (1980), p. 107.

5 The question of whether my analysis is intended to be normative or positive often comes up in connection with my insistence upon this distinction – a distinction which appears to play little role in existing tort practice. An honest answer is that my analysis is intended to be both normative and positive. It is normative in the sense that were I a legislator charged with the task of doing justice in the allocation of accident costs, I should be concerned first with identifying the relevant principles of justice and then with inquiring whether the current tort system or some alternative to it would best be able to meet the demands of justice. I do not argue that the principle of corrective justice explains everything that goes on in torts, and to this extent my position is more modest than those of other proponents of corrective justice accounts of tort law. Proponents of the economic analysis of torts, in particular my friends Richard Posner and William Landes, have asked me why it is that I adhere to an account of torts that by my own admission explains only certain elements of the law, especially when there exists an alternative analysis – the economic one – that explains nearly all of tort law. This is a fair question that merits at least some response in the context of a reply to an essay by a major proponent of the economic analysis. First, I take as a starting point the commonsense view that in resolving disputes judges try to do justice – not economics – though they may fail to do either or both very well. Given the ordinary person's view that in resolving controversial disputes judges attempt to do justice, I have tried to get a handle on exactly what sort of justice they do by developing an analysis of corrective justice that seems to make sense of a fair amount of what they do. Second, in response to the claim that economics makes sense out of more of what judges in torts do, my response is that it does not make better sense of it. The economic theory of adjudication is incompatible with any defensible analysis of judicial competence or authority. For it ascribes to judges the role of fixing rights and duties in particular disputes in order to serve the social goal of efficiency, when a proper theory of adjudication would (in my view anyway) restrict judicial authority to resolving disputes in terms of the respective claims litigants have against one another. Finally, the efficiency analysis of torts cannot explain why it is that judges impose the costs of harms on either of the litigants to the dispute. The efficient outcome might be secured by imposing the costs on some third party who, though not party to the disputes, may be the cheapest cost avoider. Economics, in other words, cannot explain the most basic feature of tort law, namely the implicit decision to allocate losses as between respective litigants.

6 In my previous work I did not use the terms "wrongful gain" and "wrongful loss." Instead, I talked about unwarranted, undeserved or unjustified losses and gains. I am using "wrongful" here as a catchphrase to cover all such compensable losses and rectifiable gains.

7 I owe the reader an account of how it is that justifiable or right conduct can sometimes create wrongful or compensable losses. That is, if what A does to B is justifiable or legitimate, why should we say that the losses B might suffer as a consequence are "wrongful" ones, or why should we feel that A has a duty to make good B's losses? I have suggested that the basic concept may be that of a "taking," which only shifts the burden to an analysis of which loss impositions are takings in the sense that requires compensation. I do not have a fully worked-out analysis of a "taking," but I did not want the reader to think that I had not realized the importance of developing one.

8 Joel Feinberg, "Voluntary Euthanasia and the Right to Life," *Philosophy and Public Affairs* 7 (1978): 93.

9 For a different view, see Posner, "Concept of Corrective Justice," p. 198 and n. 44.

10 There are means other than a tort system for rectifying wrongful gains and losses, for example, general insurance pools of the sort I have discussed elsewhere (See "On the Moral Argument for the Fault System"). With respect to the matter of modes of rectification, I want to draw attention to a serious error in Posner's article. After noting the distinction between grounds and modes of rectification, Posner claims that there is nothing in Aristotle's view that would prohibit him from endorsing a system of penal sanctions as the best means of rectifying both wrongful losses and gains. Surely this is confused, since punishing an offender does not by itself annul his gain, and even if punishment deters future wrongs, reducing the incidence of wrongful gains is logically distinct from rectifying the gains and losses wrongs occasion.

11   Questions concerning the appropriate extent of rectification arise in determining damages and in explaining the principle of comparative negligence.

12   I have discussed and rejected the defense of fault liability in "On the Moral Argument for the Fault System."

13   One obvious problem with this line of defense is that it assumes a particular mode of rectifying the innocent victim's wrongful loss, namely by conferring upon him a claim right to recompense. Such a claim right logically imposes a duty on someone – usually the injurer. Assuming a system of correlative rights and duties, that is, a tort system, begs the justificatory question, namely: Why choose this rather than some other mode of rectification?

14   This line of argument is intended to be a catchall for the wide variety of economic analyses of fault liability. Whatever their differences, these accounts all believe that fault is a criterion of economic efficiency and that liability is imposed on the basis of fault to reduce inefficient costs.

15   10 Minn, 456, 124 N.W. 221 (1910).

16   When I presented a version of this paper at the University of Chicago Law School, Richard Posner expressed a powerful objection to my account which I want to share and discuss here. The objection relies on contrasting two cases. In the first case, Jones wrongfully injures Smith for no reason other than to have Smith suffer a loss. Jones secures no gain through his misconduct; indeed, he may have arranged things to preclude the very possibility of his securing any gain other than the satisfaction he will derive from Smith's suffering. In the second case, in order to save valuable property (and perhaps life), Jones is compelled by good sense to harm Smith in some nontrivial but not terribly disastrous way. Suppose now that the second case falls within the takings analogy that I have suggested can be employed to explain aspects of strict tort liability. If that is the case, Jones is obligated to compensate Smith in the second case, though he acted reasonably – even admirably. This obligation to render compensation is, in my view, apparently a matter of corrective justice. In the first case, however, Jones has no such obligation – since he did not gain in virtue of his mischief – though his conduct is hardly admirable, or even defensible. It (apparently) turns out that, in my view, right conduct may not free one from liability, but wrongful conduct can. Surely this is counterintuitive. The objection misses its mark, however. First, it is not my view that there are no grounds upon which to impose an obligation to repair in the first case. The fact that Jones intentionally injured Smith for no good reason may itself be reason enough for imposing Smith's loss upon him. But this response is inadequate, for Posner will argue that the real problem is not that we cannot develop some other reason for holding Jones liable in the first case; the problem is that my theory of corrective justice is unable to generate such an obligation. What's worse, corrective justice not only fails to impose an obligation where doing so is appropriate; it imposes one where doing so is inappropriate – in the second case. If this is the objection, then the problem with it is that it misunderstands my view. For my view need not impose an obligation in either case; that will depend on the mode of rectification. In the first case, there simply is no wrongful gain which it is the concern of corrective justice to rectify. There is, however, a wrongful loss. In this sort of case the appropriate mode of rectification may well be to impose the victim's loss on his injurer – though it is my view that the principle of corrective justice does not require that we do so. In the second case, there is once again a wrongful loss. But is there a wrongful gain as well? I am not sure. In Feinberg's example there is a gain that the mountain climber secures in virtue of his destroying the cabin owner's furniture and emptying his shelves: He stays alive. Does justice require that we annul *that* advantage – that we kill him? I do not think so. In *Vincent v. Lake Erie,* the ship and its goods were saved because the captain secured the boat to the dock, thereby causing the dock to suffer damage during the subsequent storm. Does justice require the shipowner to eliminate his gain in virtue of such conduct? I doubt it. So I am not clear that there is a wrongful gain in all such cases, though there is a gain that would not have occurred but for the loss others have suffered. (In some cases of nonwrongful conduct there can be wrongful gain or advantage which should as a matter of justice be annulled. Suppose unwittingly I wrongly step in front of you while we are queuing up for the theater. As it turns out, by stepping in front I get in and you do not. Justice does require that both my gain and your loss be rectified in some manner – probably by my getting out of and your getting into the theater.) When we have a wrongful loss but no wrongful gain, as we very well might in the second case, my view does not necessarily impose the victim's loss on the injurer. Indeed, even if we had both wrongful gain and loss in a case involving nonwrongful conduct, it still would not follow that on my view the "injurer" would be obligated to his victim. Once again, that would depend on the chosen mode of rectification. In my view, there would be a gain and a loss to be rectified, but that would be the only way in which the first and second cases would differ. Whether there would be an obligation to repair imposed on the injurer in either, both or neither of the cases is, I emphasize, another matter.

17   Richard Epstein's views seem to have changed somewhat. See the discussion in the text at notes 20–4.

18 George Fletcher, "Fairness and Utility in Tort Theory," *Harvard Law Review* 85 (1972): 537.
19 3 Bing. (N.C.) 468, 132 Eng. Rep. 490 (1837).
20 Richard Epstein, "A Theory of Strict Liability," *Journal of Legal Studies* 2 (1973): 151.
21 See my "Mental Abnormality, Personal Responsibility and Tort Liability."
22 Richard Epstein, "Nuisance Law: Corrective Justice and Its Utilitarian Constraints," *Journal of Legal Studies* 8 (1979): 49.
23 See Jules L. Coleman, "Moral Theories of Torts: Their Scope and Limits," *Law and Philosophy* 1 (1982): 371; 2 (1983): 5.
24 I raise doubts about the plausibility of nonreciprocity of risk as a standard of liability in "Justice and Reciprocity in Tort Theory," *University of Western Ontario Law Review* 14 (1975): 105.
25 Posner, "Concept of Corrective Justice," p. 197.
26 Ibid. p. 198.
27 Ibid. p. 198.
28 See my "Justice and the Argument for No-Fault."

9. JUSTICE IN SETTLEMENTS

1 See In re Agent Orange Product Liability Litigation, 597 F.Supp. 740 (E.D.N.Y. 1984); and In re Agent Orange Product Liability Litigation, 611 F.Supp. 1396 (E.D.N.Y. 1985).
2 The history of the Agent Orange case is chronicled in detail in Peter H. Schuck, *Agent Orange on Trial: Mass Toxic Disasters in the Courts* (1987). See also Schuck, "The role of Judges in Settling Cases: The Agent Orange Example," Working Paper 36, Program in Civil Liability, Yale Law School (September 1985).
3 Even Abraham Lincoln favored settlements. He addressed the following remarks to a group of young attorneys: "Discourage litigation. Persuade your neighbors to compromise whenever you can. Point out to them how the nominal winner is often a real loser – in fees, expenses and waste of time. As a peacemaker, the lawyer has a superior opportunity for good. There will still be business enough" (quoted in an editorial by Gary T. Johnson, *Chicago Tribune,* August 9, 1985; the source for Lincoln's remarks is *Fragment: Notes from a Law Lecture,* July 1, 1850).
4 See, for example, Derek Bok, "A Flawed System," *Harvard Magazine,* May–June 1983; Warren E. Burger, "Isn't There a Better Way?" *American Bar Association Journal* 68 (1982): 274, and "Agenda for 2000 A.D. – A Need for Systematic Anticipation," *F.R.D.* 70 (1976): 93; Richard A. Epstein, "Settlement and Litigation: Of Vices Individual and Institutional," *University of Chicago Law School Record* 30 (Spring 1984): 2.
5 "In order to produce a climate in which counsel may explore the possibility of early settlement, the judge should ask the views of counsel

on the possibility of settlement at the first principal pretrial conference.
. . . Settlement should always be encouraged" (*Manual for Complex Litigation,* sec. 1.21).

6 "In any action, the court may in its discretion direct the attorneys for the parties and any unrepresented parties to appear before it for a conference or conferences before trial for such purposes as . . . facilitating the settlement of the case" (*Federal Rules of Civil Procedure,* rule 16 [a] [5]).

7 Owen Fiss, "Against Settlement," *Yale Law Journal* 93 (1984): 1074. For the text of the proposed amendment to Rule 68, see Committee on Rules of Practice and Procedure of the Judicial Conference of the United States, "Preliminary Draft of Proposed Amendments to the Federal Rules of Civil Procedure," *F.R.D.* 98 (1983): 361.

8 See e.g., Burger, "Isn't There a Better Way?" pp. 275ff.

9 "The resolution of controversies and uncertainties by means of compromise and settlement is generally faster and less expensive than litigation; it results in a saving of time for the parties, the lawyers, and the courts, and it is thus advantageous to judicial administration, and, in turn, to government as a whole. Moreover, the use of compromise and settlement is conducive to amicable and peaceful relations between the parties to a controversy" (*American Jurisprudence,* 2d ed., 1985 supplement, sec. 5 ["Compromise and Settlement"], p. 15A).

10 Fiss, "Against Settlement." See also the response to Fiss by Andrew W. McThemia and Thomas L. Shaffer, "For Reconciliation," *Yale Law Journal* 94 (1985): 1660, and Fiss's rejoinder, "Out of Eden," ibid. p. 1669. Federal District Court Judge Jack Weinstein also grapples with one of Fiss's arguments in *In re Agent Orange Product Liability* Litigation, p. 760.

11 Fiss, "Against Settlement," p. 1075.

12 We thank David Schlecker of the law firm of Anderson, Russell, Kill & Olick for giving us the benefit of his experience in litigating and settling personal injury lawsuits.

13 The judge may do so *sua sponte* or at the request of counsel for either party.

14 Although the word "price" calls the idea of money to mind, defendants often agree to provide services in lieu of, or in addition to, cash. In-kind relief is especially likely to be offered or requested in cases alleging civil rights violations. For example, in *Women's Committee for Equal Employment Opportunity v. National Broadcasting Co.* (76 F.R.D. 173 [S.D.N.Y. 1977]), a case brought under Title VII of the Civil Rights Act of 1964, the defendant agreed to revamp its policies concerning the employment and promotion of women and to award back pay. When in-kind relief is agreed to, the parties ask the judge to enter a consent decree in which their rights and obligations are spelled out in detail.

15 Judges use a variety of tactics to bring parties together. In the Agent Orange case, for example, Judge Weinstein appointed a special master for settlement, told counsel how he was likely to decide close issues, arbitrated disputes, set limits on the settlement price and required counsel to attend a marathon bargaining session immediately before the trial was to begin. See Schuck, *Agent Orange on Trial*.

16 See Richard A. Posner, *Economic Analysis of Law* (2d ed., 1977), pp. 434–41.

17 See e.g., Beecher v. Able, 575 F.2d 1010 (2d Cir. 1978), a securities fraud case in which the parties disagreed over their rights to an unused portion of a settlement fund.

18 A "claim need not be valid or well founded to support a compromise, and as long as there has been good faith, the courts will not inquire into the merits of a claim or the actual rights of the parties. . . . The courts will not inquire into the validity of a claim which was compromised in good faith" ("Compromise and Settlement," sec. 17). See also Fiss, "Against Settlement," p. 1082.

19 "Compromise and Settlement," sec. 16.

20 The grounds for invalidating a compromise or settlement are illegality, fraud, duress, undue influence and mistake. See ibid. secs. 27–34.

21 Fiss, "Against Settlement," p. 1086.

22 Epstein writes, "Early in teaching I received this advice from a shrewd and experienced lawyer. 'You can tell the sign of a good deal – everyone leaves the room happy. You can also tell the sign of a good settlement – everyone leaves the room unhappy' " ("Settlement and Litigation," p. 3).

23 We thank Leo Katz of the law firm of Mayer, Brown & Platt for suggesting this formulation of the matter. See also Fiss, "Against Settlement," pp. 1085–7.

24 Since settlements may occur at any time prior to final judgment, the amount of information available to parties who settle may also vary considerably. For example, there may be more reason to think that a plaintiff who settles to avoid an appeal after winning at trial is entitled to compensation than there is to think that a plaintiff who settles before trial is so entitled, because more information may be available about the former's claim than about the latter's. Even so, since many cases settle before trial, and since additional resources could be invested in gathering and processing information whenever a case settles, it is plausible that we could promote compensatory justice more fully by trying every complaint to finality. Moreover, settlements and trials differ procedurally in relevant ways. For example, trials, but not settlements, are held in public, are conducted in accordance with rules of evidence, involve the formal presentation and argument of issues of law and fact, are subject to appeal and are often decided by judges who rationalize their rulings in written opinions. If, as we have assumed, these procedures tend to increase the reliability of trials as means of discerning the validity of claims, our confidence that claims that are vindicated at trial are in fact valid may greatly exceed our confidence that people who settle deserve the payments they receive.

25 See Anthony Kronman, "Paternalism and the Law of Contracts,"

Yale Law Journal 92 (1983): 763, for a discussion of nondisclaimable rights. See Joel Feinberg, "Legal Paternalism," *Canadian Journal of Philosophy* 1 (1971): 105, for a discussion of related philosophical issues.

26 Kronman, "Paternalism and the Law of Contracts," pp. 770–4.

27 See Fiss, "Against Settlement," pp. 1076–8.

28 See "The Availability of Excess Damages for Wrongful Refusal to Honor First Party Insurance Claims – An Emerging Trend" (note), *Fordham Law Review* 45 (1976): 164.

29 See, e.g., In re Cuisinart Food Processor Antitrust Litigation, 1983–2 *Trade Cases* (CCH), p. 69, 472 (D. Conn. 1983), in which the damages alleged ranged from $32 to $75 per class member and the class contained in excess of 1.5 million members, so that Cuisinart's total possible liability after trebling was between $144 million and $337.5 million. See also Phillips Petroleum Co. v. Shutts, 105 S. Ct. 2965 (1985), a suit for failure to pay royalties on oil leases, in which claims averaged $100 per member for a class of 28,100 people. The use of the class action device to threaten defendants with extraordinary litigation expenses and liabilities prompted one author to write of the "in terrorem" effect of class antitrust actions, and to describe them as "legalized blackmail" (Handler, "The Shift from Substantive to Procedural Innovations in Antitrust Suits – The Twenty-Third Annual Antitrust Review," *Columbia Law Review* 71 [1971]:9).

30 See Jules L. Coleman, "Liberalism, Unfair Advantage, and the Volunteer Armed Forces," in *Conscripts and Volunteers: Military Requirements, Social Justice, and the All-Volunteer Force,* ed. Robert K. Fullinwider (1983). It is worth noting that power imbalances may obtain at trials, too. Wealthy parties may be able to hire better lawyers and to maneuver more freely than poor ones. However, trial procedures are designed to reduce the impact of such imbalances in ways that settlement procedures are not. For example, a trial judge can ask questions, suggest motions and take other steps to ensure that a proceeding is fair, and the appeals process provides a measure of security that obvious imbalances will be redressed.

31 Globus v. Law Research Service, Inc., 287 F.Supp 188 (S.D.N.Y. 1968); affirmed in part and reversed in part, 418 F.2d 1276 (2d Cir. 1969); *certiorari* denied, 397 U.S. 913 (1970).

32 278 F.Supp., p. 199.

33 418 F.2d, p. 1288.

34 For discussions of indemnification, see Dale A. Oesterle, "Limits on a Corporation's Protection of Its Directors and Officers from Personal Liability," *Wisconsin Law Review* 1983 (1983): 513; Joseph W. Bishop, Jr., "New Problems in Indemnifying and Insuring Directors: Protection against Liability under the Federal Securities Laws," *Duke Law Journal* 1972 (1972): 1153, and "Sitting Ducks and Decoy Ducks: New Trends in the Indemnification of Corporate Directors and Officers," *Yale Law Journal* 77 (1968): 1078.

35 In the opinion affirming *Globus* the Court of Appeals noted that the Securities and Exchange Commission "has announced its view that indemnification of directors, officers and controlling persons for liabilities arising under" the securities laws is against public policy. See 418 F.2d, p. 1288.

36 For example, had Law Research and Blair & Co. settled *Globus, Blair & Co.* would have been entitled to an indemnity per the underwriting agreement. See e.g., Cambridge Fund. Inc. v. Abella, 501 F. Supp. 598, 618 (S.D.N.Y. 1980) (distinguishing *Globus* on the ground that "unlike the situation [*Globus,* here] there has been no adjudication of willfulness – only the entry of a consent order with such findings").

37 Indeed, in view of the size of the judgment after the first appeal – approximately $32,500 – it is startling that they continued to press their claims at all.

38 It is worth noting that after losing on the indemnification issue, Blair & Co. sued Law Research for contribution – allocation of responsibility for a judgment among defendants each of whom is liable for it in its entirety – and won (Globus, Inc. v. Law Research Service, Inc., 318 F. Supp. 955 [S.D.N.Y. 1970]; affirmed sub nom Globus v. Law Research Service, Inc., 442 F.2d 1346 [2nd Cir.]; *certiorari denied sub nom* Law Research Service, Inc. v. Blair & Co., 404 U.S. 941 [1971]). Even so, since indemnification and contribution are distinct claims, settlement of the indemnification issue would have been against public policy. It would have further reduced Blair & Co.'s liability.

39 Throughout this section we have assumed that the policy of preventing people from insulating themselves from the legal consequences of securities fraud is correct. This assumption is questionable; that is, it is possible that *Globus* was wrongly decided and that indemnification agreements are unobjectionable. An argument to this effect could be made on the ground that issuers who can monitor underwriters efficiently should be permitted to offer insurance as a means of enticing underwriters to handle their securities. Even if *Globus* was wrongly decided, however, the analytical point that people may use settlement agreements to accomplish ends they are legally forbidden to achieve by means of contracts would remain intact. Only the example we have used would be impeached. In other words, the general point that settlements may undermine sound public policy goals would survive a showing that the policy of forbidding indemnification in securities fraud cases is unwarranted. It is the general point, not the example suggested by *Globus,* to which we are committed.

40 This is the case, for example, when judges perform their Tunney Act duty to determine that a proposed settlement of a government antitrust suit is in the public interest (15 U.S.C. sec. 16 [e] [1980]). It is also the case when judges perform their duty to assess the fairness, reasonableness and adequacy of proposed settlements to class actions. See below, note 74.

41 It must be noted that settlement agreements contrary to public policy could be negotiated even if all complaints were tried. Parties would simply need to conspire with each other to achieve this result. Our suggestion is only that the frequency of such agreements may decline as the rate of trials increases. We thank Don Regan for helping us clarify this point.

42 This paragraph draws heavily on examples and arguments discussed by Owen Fiss. In addition to "Against Settlement," we direct the reader to the following articles by Fiss: "The Supreme Court 1978 Term – Forward: The Forms of Justice," *Harvard Law Review* 93 (1978): 1; "The Social and Political Foundations of Adjudication," *Law and Human Behavior* 6 (1982); and "Objectivity and Interpretation," *Stanford Law Review* 34 (1982). To avoid misleading the reader, we should also note that trials can affect the interests of nonparties in much the same way that settlements can. However, third parties can sometimes intervene in trials in ways that they cannot intervene in settlements, as when a dispute is resolved before a complaint is filed.

43 Fiss, "Against Settlement," pp. 1078–82.

44 Ibid. p. 1085.

45 It is estimated that public funds were used to support the federal courts (excluding the Supreme Court) in the following amounts in 1985: judges' salaries, $74,540,000; salaries of supporting personnel, $370,228,000; fees of jurors and commissioners, $42,000,000; expenses of operation and maintenance of the courts, $101,500,000; space and facilities, $140,000,000; court security, $25,500,000 (*1984 Annual Report of the Director of the Administrative Office of the U.S. Courts* [1985] pp. 78–80). Although these fixed costs apply to both civil and criminal matters, the former far outnumber the latter. In 1984, 261,485 civil cases and only 36,845 criminal cases were filed in the U.S. District Courts (ibid. pp. 4–6).

46 This may come as a surprise to readers who think that litigation costs are already prohibitively high.

47 See Posner, *Economic Analysis of Law,* pp. 400–1, 419–27.

48 For a discussion of the conditions under which it may be fair to require people to defray the costs of public goods they consume see Richard J. Arneson, "The Principle of Fairness and Free-Rider Problems," *Ethics* 92 (1982): 616.

49 Class action settlements are an exception to this rule. And of course we realize that precedents concerning the enforcement of settlements arise from settled cases. However, even these precedents emerge only because claims concerning settlements are taken to trial.

50 Even Richard Posner, a proponent of settlements, writes that "if the function of the legal system were solely to settle disputes, it would be appropriate to impose the entire costs of the system on the disputants" (*Economic Analysis of Law,* p. 401).

51 "The settlement rate is an important determinant of the direct costs of resolving legal disputes. Beyond a certain point, however, a further increase in the settlement rate would increase the total costs of dispute resolution by reducing the production of precedents below the optimal level" (ibid. p. 434).

52 Ibid. p. 422.

53 Ibid.

54 See Epstein, "Settlement and Litigation," for a discussion of the trend away from "bright line" rules.

55 The number of civil cases filed annually increased by more than 100 percent between 1977 and 1984 (*1984 Annual Report . . . U.S. Courts,* p. 4).

56 See Geoffrey P. Miller, "An Economic Analysis of Rule 68," *Journal of Legal Studies* 15 (1986): 93, and George L. Priest, "Regulating the Content and Volume of Litigation: An Economic Analysis," *Supreme Court Economic Review* 1 (1982): 163.

57 "A tort settlement, conceptually and in practice, is intended to compensate an individual for injuries to his or her person" (In re Agent Orange Product Liability Litigation, 611 F.Supp., pp. 1424–5).

58 Classes can be both plaintiffs and defendants. In this essay, however, we shall be concerned only with plaintiff classes.

59 Class members are not permitted to exclude themselves when, to all intents and purposes, the trial of a class action would be dispositive of their interests. For example, the trial of a school desegregation class action would adjudicate the rights of all minority students, even those who wished to exempt themselves from the lawsuit.

60 A rational person will refuse to sue on a claim when the opportunity cost of a lawsuit exceeds its expected return (the payoff given that the lawsuit may be won, lost or settled times the probability of each outcome).

61 Phillips Petroleum Co. v. Shutts, p. 2974.

62 See In re Cuisinart Food Processor Antitrust Litigation and In re Corrugated Container Antitrust Litigation, 643 F.2d 195 (5th Cir. 1981).

63 See Ohio Public Interest Campaign v. Fisher Foods, 546 F. Supp. 1 (N.D. Ohio 1982).

64 See 611 F. Supp., p. 1411.

65 In In re Corrugated Container Antitrust Litigation, p. 220, for example, Judge Tjoflat wrote, "It is *self-evident* that [a] distribution should be weighed heavily in favor of plaintiffs whose claims" are most likely to succeed at trial (emphasis added).

66 "Whether or not the defendants have formally admitted some responsibility for defects in their products and for possible injuries to some plaintiffs, the public can justifiably assume, for perhaps the first time, that there is some merit to the claims of those exposed to Agent Orange that they are suffering because of their war and post-war experiences" (In re Agent Orange Product Liability Litigation, 597 F. Supp., p. 749).

67 "All the settlements release the claims of all class members for the entire eighteen-year period of the alleged conspiracy. Thus it is appropriate that some compensation be given for purchases made in the pre–statute of limitations period" (In re Corrugated Container Antitrust Litigation, 1981–1 *Trade Cases* [CCH], p. 64, 114 [S.D. Tex. 1981], pp. 76, 717; affirmed, 659 F.2d 1329 [5th Cir. 1981]).

68 "Where it is not economically feasible to obtain relief within the

traditional framework of a multiplicity of small individual suits for damages, aggrieved persons may be without any effective redress unless they
may employ the class action device" (Deposit Guaranty National Bank
v. Roper, 445 U.S. 339 [1980]). See also State of West Virginia v. Chas.
Pfizer & Co., 440 F.2d 1090 (2nd Cir. 1970).

69 See Schuck, *Agent Orange on Trial.*

70 Stephen Sugarman, "Doing Away with Tort Law," *California Law
Review* 73 (1985): 598.

71 Preliminary results of a twenty-year study of people who worked
with Agent Orange suggest that it neither decreased the subjects' longev-
ity nor caused their deaths (*Miami Herald,* December 28, 1985, p. 7A).

72 Except when the parties explicitly recognize their validity, as discussed further below. See the text immediately preceding and accompanying notes 18–22.

73 See the text accompanying notes 18–22.

74 Cotton v. Hinton, 559 F.2d 1330 (5th Cir. 1977). Settlements of
class actions must be approved by judges, because Rule 23, which empowers plaintiffs to bring class actions, also provides that a "class action
shall not be dismissed or compromised without the approval of the court"
(*Federal Rules of Civil Procedure,* rule 23 [e]).

75 See above, sec. 2.3, and the text following note 81.

76 Several cases attest to the facts that class counsel may attempt to buy
off named plaintiffs and that named plaintiffs may be receptive to such
overtures. See, e.g., Plummer v. Chemical Bank, 91 F.R.D. 434
(S.D.N.Y. 1981) (disapproving a proposed settlement in which named
plaintiffs were to receive "substantially more benefits" than other members of the class); and Holmes v. Continental Can Co., 706 F.2d 1144
(11th Cir. 1983) (reversing and remanding lower court decision approving settlement under which the eight named plaintiffs would have received half of the settlement fund).

77 For an excellent discussion of the effect of attorneys' fees on settlement rates see Geoffrey P. Miller, "Agency Problems in Settlement"
(unpublished typescript, University of Chicago, 1986).

78 In re Corrugated Container Antitrust Litigation, p. 219 (quoting In
re Equity Funding Corp. of America Securities Litigation, 603 F.2d 1465
[9th Cir. 1979]).

79 "Compromise and Settlement," sec. 4.

80 In re Folding Carton Antitrust Litigation, 744 F.2d 1258. Judge Flaum
was confused because he failed to see the effect adjudication has on class
members' legal rights. He cited *Boeing Co. V. Van Gemert,* (444 U.S. 482
[1980]), one of the few class actions ever to be won at trial, for the
proposition that class members are the equitable owners of settlement
funds. When a class wins at trial, its members acquire rights to compensation. It is therefore true that they are entitled to payments. However,
when a class action settles, the validity of members' claims is never proved.
Consequently, class members may not be the equitable owners of shares
in a settlement fund and *Boeing* is off point.

81 "If the spouses and children of the veterans were completely without any colorable legal claims against [the] defendants, it would [be] an abuse of the court's discretion to allow them to share in the settlement fund" (In re Agent Orange Product Liability Litigation, 611 F. Supp., p. 1411 [quoting In re Chicken Antitrust Litigation American Poultry, 669 F.2d 238 (5th Cir. 1982)]).

82 It is consistent with the view that the right to sue, or the power to exercise that right, transfers from class members to a class on certification (rather than at settlement) that individual class members cannot sue on claims on which a class action is already pending, although people who have opted out of a class may do so. Moreover, since class members retain the right to settle with a defendant individually at any time during the pendency of a class action, the most appropriate reading of the law seems to be that, by remaining in a class, members grant the class the nonexclusive authority to exercise their right to settle. That is, they empower a class to settle on their behalf if they do not do so themselves.

83 *Newberg on Class Actions* (1985), sec. 10.05.

84 See Judge J. Joseph Smith's opinion in *State of West Virginia v. Chas. Pfizer & Co.,* (440 F.2d 1091).

85 North Carolina v. Chas. Pfizer & Co., 69 N.Y. Civ. Ct. 839 (S.D.N.Y. 1970).

86 The sample replies are quoted in *Newberg on Class Actions,* sec. 8.39, where it is suggested that they "typify the misunderstanding attendant such notice."

87 See references in note 1; see also Schuck, *Agent Orange on Trial.*

88 Colson v. Hilton Hotels, Inc., 59 F.R.D. 324 (ND Ill. 1972).

89 See note 63.

90 Grossman v. Playboy Clubs Int'l, Inc., Civil No. 882939 (L.A. Super. Ct. 1970).

91 This case is discussed in Handler, "The Shift from Substantive to Procedural Innovations in Antitrust Suits," p. 10.

92 Phemister v. Harcourt Brace Jovanovich, No. 77C39, slip opinion (N.D. Ill. Sept. 14, 1984). We thank Victor Freedman of the law firm of Fried, Frank, Harris, Shriver and Jacobson for bringing this case to our attention and for discussing many of the arguments in this essay with us.

93 We assume for now that extinguishing the right to sue imposes a wrongful loss on class members. We dispute this assumption below.

94 We shall use the phrases "expected value of a claim at trial" and "size and strength of a claim" interchangeably.

95 See, e.g., A. Mitchell Polinsky, *An Introduction to Law and Economics* (1983), p. 29; and Jeffrie Murphy and Jules L. Coleman, *The Philosophy of Law: An Introduction to Jurisprudence* (1984), p. 243.

96 See Charles Silver, "Using Class Action Settlement Funds Justly and Wisely" (unpublished typescript, University of Texas Law School library, 1986), for a discussion of other reasons that could be given in support of the practice of dividing settlement funds among class members.

97   28 U.S.C. 2042.

98   Richard Epstein has raised the concern that the proposal to escheat settlement funds to the federal government would blur the distinction between public civil proceedings and private class actions. Under this proposal, defendants who settle private class actions would pay money into public coffers, just as they do when they lose or settle public proceedings. But, Epstein's objection continues, if what we want to see is the payment of money into public coffers, what role remains for private class actions? In other words, by denying class members settlement payments, have we not obviated the need for class actions altogether?

If it were true that the escheat option would blur the distinction between private and public lawsuits, it would be a real question whether a private form of action should be available. It would not follow, however, that merely because the categories of public action and private action were merged, private class actions would cease to serve any purpose. It might be reasonable to make both public and private proceedings available, for example because the plaintiffs' bar is better than the government at monitoring some kinds of illegal activities. Thus, even if it would be appropriate to conceptualize class actions as public proceedings in the event that settlement funds were not divided among class members, it could still be reasonable to empower private citizens to bring class actions.

More to the point, the distinction between private and public actions would remain even if class members were denied settlement payments. After all, class actions can and occasionally do go to trial, and when classes prevail at trial their members acquire rights to damage payments. Since class actions can go to trial, a difference between class actions and public proceedings would remain even if the practice of dividing settlement funds among class members were abolished. The difference would be that class actions could sometimes result in civil recoveries, whereas public proceedings can result in only fines and penalties.

Further, it is in any event wrong to think of payments made in settlement of civil suits as fines. As was mentioned, when class actions settle, ordinarily no finding of guilt, liability or wrongdoing is made. By contrast, a fine is paid after a public proceeding only when a defendant is adjudged guilty of an offense. The difference between fines and settlement payments is important both morally and legally. From a moral point of view, settlement payments carry none of the opprobrium associated with fines and penalties, because they do not indicate that a norm of behavior has been violated. From a legal point of view, a settlement payment is a good-faith attempt to buy peace of mind, not an admission of guilt, and the obligation to make a settlement payment arises under a contract, not under public law.

The only possible reason to lump settlement payments together with fines and penalties is that the former have the same effect as the latter on defendants' behavior. From a defendant's point of view, it may make little difference whether money passes into public coffers or into the hands of individual defendants. The economic result is the same, because in both cases a cost is associated with an activity as a result of a lawsuit. For the same reason that penalties and fines may deter people from violating any securities laws, the prospect of having to make a settlement payment may deter a manufacturer from producing a new and potentially defective product line.

It seems likely that defendants view settlement payments like fines and adjust their behavior to minimize both. This is not, however, a good reason to put fines and settlement payments in the same category. On the contrary, it is a reason to keep the two kinds of payment distinct. When the prospect of a fine dissuades a person from violating the law, a form of behavior is deterred which, according to prevailing social policy, ought to be deterred. However, when the prospect of a settlement payment causes a person to refrain from an activity, there is less reason to be happy with the result, because the behavior that is deterred may, in light of social policy, be desirable. For example, suppose we want to encourage manufacturers to market innovative products that increase social welfare while at the same time we empower people who are injured by defective products to sue for compensation and to settle when they like. If the prospect of having to make settlement payments deters manufacturers from marketing products that are sound, fewer new products will be made available to the public than is desirable under this policy. Thus, if settlement payments have the same effect as fines on people's behavior, there is added reason to be concerned about the level of settlement activity in our society.

10. MARKET CONTRACTARIANISM

1 This essay is drawn from work that will appear in a forthcoming book entitled *The Market Paradigm* (unpublished manuscript). The book is an account of what happens when welfare economics and public choice meet political and legal theory. It is an effort to explore the extent to which welfare-economic and rational choice models can account for political institutions, including constitutions, courts and legislatures, and the extent to which markets themselves presuppose such institutional arrangements.
2 There is a difference between maximizing the satisfaction of one's preferences and maximizing one's welfare, well-being or utility. The Pareto criteria can be expressed in terms of all four. For ease of exposition, I shall write mostly in terms of preference satisfaction, because nothing in the argument I advance depends on the differences, and because it is common in welfare economics to treat these interchangeably – though in many contexts doing so is a mistake.
3 Work by "catastrophe," "chaos" or "disequilibrium" theorists has raised doubts about whether even the first theorem of welfare economics obtains. Their view is that the core is empty. The seminal piece is J. Ostroy, "The No-Surplus Condition as a Characteristic of Perfectly

Competitive Equilibrium," *Journal of Economic Theory* 22 (1980): 138. The absence of a core in the voting context has been demonstrated by both Norman Schofield and Richard McKelvey. Both prove that simple majority voting rules create cycles under conditions that almost always obtain. See Schofield, "Instability of Simple Dynamic Games," *Review of Economic Studies* 45 (1978): 575; and McKelvey, "General Conditions for Global Intransitivities in Formal Voting models," *Econometrica* 47 (1979): 1085. Both papers are extremely technical. The general view, expressed best by Schofield, is that both politics and economics are chaotic – marginalism is out, and anything can happen.

4 Within limits. There is a tension between claims (2) and (3). If one advances a Nozickian account, then there exists no way of moving the economy along the frontier that does not create injustice. So an economy can secure both (1) and (2) only by restricting or constraining the competitive mechanism somewhat, i.e., by violating (3). Alternatively, we might consider simply redistributing property rights *ex ante* to satisfy (1), (2) and in a weaker sense (3). This approach follows naturally from what Sen refers to as the Converse Theorem of Welfare Economics, which is roughly: For any point on the frontier, there exists an initial allocation of property rights capable of securing it as a unique outcome of the competitive mechanism. Following the dictates of the Converse theorem may be no less troublesome to a "noninterventionist" than would be *ex post* redistribution, however. See A. Sen, "The Moral Standing of the Market," *Social Philosophy and Policy* 2 (1984): 1.

5 For a more complete discussion see below, sec. 3.4.2.

6 It is worth distinguishing between two notions of equilibrium: Nashian and dominant. The prisoners' dilemma is a dominant equilibrium. That means that in equilibrium no agent will alter his strategy no matter what anyone else does, because his current play constitutes the best he can do no matter what others do. In Nashian equilibrium, an agent might change his play if others do, but he is unwilling to change his play alone. The difference is important. In several approaches to solving the public goods prisoners' dilemma, it turns out that honestly revealing one's preferences for public goods will not be a dominant strategy. Only a weaker, Nashian equilibrium emerges, for example, under a Groves–Ledyard incentive-compatible mechanism.

7 Russell Hardin, "Collective Action as an Agreeable *n*-Prisoner's Dilemma," *Behavioral Science* 16 (1971): 472.

8 The seminal piece is R. Coase, "The Problem of Social Cost," *Journal of Law and Economics* 3 (1960): 1.

9 This highlights the importance of demand revelation mechanisms. All such mechanisms seek to induce individuals to reveal information, making honesty be in each individual's rational self-interest. Bargaining in the absence of such incentives will be swamped by strategic behavior.

10 G. Calabresi and A. Melamed, "Property Rules, Liability Rules, and Inalienability: One View of the Cathedral," *Harvard Law Review* 85 (1972): 1089.

11 It is doubtful that there can be indefinitely increasing economies of scale. Consequently, the argument works only for groups of certain sizes.

12 My claim is not that for each person in the state of nature the rational strategy is to engage in both attack and defense strategies. Instead, my claim is the weaker one: Given the assumptions of the argument, for those who engage in both attack and defense the expected payoff for doing so is $H-(p+a)$ for each. Others in the state of nature may seek membership in the coalition that provides protection on other grounds.

13 My original interest in this project grew out of my work in law-and-economics. Advocates of the economic approach to law typically claim that the law should seek to promote both efficiency and wealth distribution, but they give no foundation for that claim. The market contractarian account of rational political association provides the missing foundation.

14 The following argument was much influenced by several discussions with James Buchanan.

15 Here is one argument for constitutional constraints on budgets that goes in the opposite direction from the standard one. Usually those who advance the cause of a constitutional amendment want to limit spending to collected revenues. The argument here is to restrict collected revenues so they do not exceed the sum of provision and administrative costs necessary to provide optimal levels of public goods.

16 Jules L. Coleman, "Economics and the Law: A Critical Review of the Foundations of the Economic Approach to Law," *Ethics* 94 (1984): 664–7.

17 D. Gauthier, *Morals by Agreement* (1986).

18 For a contrasting view see ibid.

19 Alternatively, one could argue that the outcome is efficient because it has secured everyone's consent, whether or not it is efficient in the standard economic sense. This is Buchanan's view. For a discussion of its motivations and its problems, see below, Chapter 11, "Unanimity."

20 The claim here is that even a fair bargain is subject to rent-seeking efforts. That is because self-interested actors abide by fair bargains only if they view the fairness of the bargain as working to their advantage.

21 Even then it is not clear that the fairness of the point of departure suffices to stabilize bargains. Indeed, I want to go so far as to say that bargaining – even from a fair status quo point – will yield stable outcomes only if the parties already have a sense of fairness or a commitment to the ideal of fairness. It is a further question whether commitment to the ideal of fairness or to being bound to one's bargains can itself be grounded on the rational self-interest of bargainers.

22 A. Feldman, *Social Choice and Welfare Economics* (1980).

11. UNANIMITY

1 For a fuller discussion of demand–revelation mechanisms see the special supplement to *Public Choice,* 29, 2 (Spring 1977).

2 K. Wicksell, "A New Principle of Just Taxation," *Finanztheoretische Untersuchungen* (1896).

3 E. Lindahl, "Just Taxation – A Positive Solution," in *Classics in the Theory of Public Finance,* ed. R. Musgrave and A. T. Peacock (1967), p. 168.

4 D. Mueller, *Public Choice* (1979), p. 39.

5 The lens defines the range of Pareto-improving tax packages.

6 Cf. J. Buchanan, *The Limits of Liberty: Between Anarchy and Leviathan* (1975).

7 B. Barry, "Review of *The Limits of Liberty: Between Anarchy and Leviathan,*" *Theory and Decision* 12 (1980): 95, 96.

8 J. L. Coleman, "The Foundations of Constitutional Economics," Chapter 5 in this volume.

9 See P. A. Samuelson, "The Pure Theory of Public Expenditure," *Review of Economic Statistics* 36 (1954): 386.

10 The inefficiency of majority rule is neatly discussed in Mueller, *Public Choice,* pp. 31–47.

11 I have a conjecture that I argue for in *The Market Paradigm* (manuscript in progress), and it is as follows: All institutional mechanisms for solving the public goods problems – from Wicksell–Lindahl taxes to Groves–Ledyard incentive-compatible mechanisms – are subject to problems precisely analogous to those that arise in the private provision of public goods. Therefore, they also tend to solve the public goods problem under the same conditions the private market does, i.e., iteration or honest preference revelation.

12 Because of the incentives for strategic behavior in the collective choice and cooperative contexts, economists have been driven to develop demand-revealing mechanisms that seek to solve the problem of demand revelation noncooperatively. An example of a noncooperative, demand-revelation mechanism is the second-bid auction. In a second-bid auction, the high bidder wins but pays a price determined by the second highest bid. Therefore, he has no incentive to behave strategically. His best strategy is to reveal his true preference.

13 The problem is that the unanimity rule gives a special standing to the status quo. To see this, consider two allocations, R_1 and R_2. First, let R_1 be the status quo. Now unless everyone agrees to R_2, R_1 obtains. Suppose, however, we treat R_2 as the status quo. Now unless everyone agrees to R_1, R_2 obtains. If R_1 is in fact the status quo, it obtains if not everyone agrees to R_2, even though, from another perspective – the vantage point of persons at $R_2 - R_1$ is not itself efficient. The only justification for giving R_1 a privileged status is the belief that it somehow emerged from a series of Pareto improvements. In general I see no reason to hold such a belief.

14 This is just the question of whether rational bargaining also provides a theory of "moral bargaining": whether, in my terms, market contractarianism can also yield a version of "moral contractarianism." I take this issue up in the final section of *The Market Paradigm*.

15 Buchanan, *Limits of Liberty*, pp. 78, 82–3.

16 Consider a simple illustration of cycling, when a rule of simple majority is used for redistributive purposes only. Suppose *A, B* and *C* are to split $10,000 among them. *A* and *B* form a winning coalition to omit *C* and split the $10,000 as follows: $7,000 to *A* (it was his idea), $3,000 to *B*. Now *C* offers *B* a different split, say $6,000 to *C*, $4,000 to *B*. *B* accepts, and *B* and *C* are a winning coalition. Now *A* is left out, so he offers *B* or *C* a split favorable to either, and so it goes.

17 See Marquis de Condorcet, *Essai sur l'application de l'analyse à la probabilité des décisions rendues à la pluraliste des voix* (Paris, 1785).

18 Michael Trebilcock has pointed out to me that this objection may not be a fair one in the context of developing a market theory of collective choice in which we assume individuals act to advance the satisfaction of their interests.

19 See J. L. Coleman, "The Unsteady Foundations of Liberal Democracy" (unpublished typescript).

12. DEMOCRACY AND SOCIAL CHOICE

1 Douglas Rae, "Decision-Rules and Individual Values in Constitutional Choice," *American Political Science Review* 63 (March 1969): 40–56 (emphasis added).

2 For a further discussion see J. L. Coleman, "Competition and Cooperation," *Ethics* 97 (1987): 76.

3 William Riker, *Liberalism against Populism: A Confrontation between the Theory of Democracy and the Theory of Social Choice* (San Francisco: W. H. Freeman & Co., 1982).

4 Ibid. p. 5.

5 Ibid.

6 Ibid.

7 Ibid. p. 7 (emphasis added).

8 Ibid.

9 Ibid.

10 Ibid. p. 8.

11 Marquis de Condorcet, *Essai sur l'application de l'analyse à la probabilité des décisions rendues à la pluralité des voix* (Paris, 1785).

12 Kenneth Arrow, *Social Choice and Individual Values* (New Haven, Conn.: Yale University Press, 1963).

13 Richard McKelvey, "Intransitivities in Multidimensional Voting Models and Some Implications for Agenda Control," *Journal of Economic Theory* 12 (June 1976): 472–82; Norman Schofield, "Instability of Simple Dynamics Games," *Review of Economic Studies* 45 (October 1978): 575–94.

14 In a Borda count, each individual voter assigns points to choices; for example, five points to the first choice, four to the second and so on. The points for each are summed, and the winner is the choice with the highest point total.

15   Under the "Bentham rule," each person assigns cardinal values to his choices; e.g., ten for the first choice, but only five for the second if he prefers the first twice as much as the second. Then the total for each choice is found by adding up the points each individual has assigned to it. The winner is the choice with the highest total. In Borda counting, each voter must use the same scaling, that is, award the same number of points to his first, second and third choices. Different voters, under the Bentham rule, can assign different values to similarly ordered choices.

16   In "Nashian" voting, the cardinal utilities assigned by each voter are multiplied rather than summed. Again, the winner is the choice with the highest total.

17   In Condorcet voting, there is a winner if and only if it defeats all other choices when paired against them individually.

18   Riker, *Liberalism against Populism*, p. 37.

19   Ibid. p. 36.

20   James Madison, *The Federalist Papers*, no. 52 (New York: Mentor Books, 1961), p. 327.

21   Riker, *Liberalism against Populism*, pp. 181–200.

22   For a further discussion see sec. 4 and notes 28–32, below.

23   Kenneth O. May, "A Set of Necessary and Sufficient Conditions for Simple Majority Decision," *Econometrica* 20 (October 1952): 680–4.

24   A rule is monotone whenever, in moving from one preference configuration to another, if one choice becomes more attractive relative to the other choices for some individual, it does not move down in the social judgment. Strong monotonicity requires, in addition, that, if two choices are tied in the social decision and one choice "moves up" relative to the others, the tie is broken in favor of that choice.

25   Roughly the same remarks are in order in regard to the anonymity condition. While anonymity may seem, on its face, to express the requirement that voters be treated equally, it is, in fact, much stronger than this. By requiring that every pair of voters be interchangeable, anonymity rules out a variety of procedures that accord everyone the same influence over the collective choice but which are not anonymous. An example of such a rule would be a "representative" procedure in which, for a proposal to prevail, it must receive a majority vote in each of the majority of districts.

26   Riker, *Liberalism against Populism*, p. 244.

27   Ibid. p. 245.

28   Gerald Kramer, "A Dynamical Model of Political Equilibrium," *Journal of Economic Theory* 16 (1977): 310–44.

29   John Ferejohn, Richard McKelvey and Edward Packel, "Limiting Distributions for Continuous State Markov Voting Models," *Social Choice and Welfare* 1 (1984): 45–68.

30   Nicholas Miller, "A New Solution Set for Tournaments and Majority Voting," *American Journal of Political Science* 24 (1980): 68–69.

31   Kenneth Shepsle and Barry Weingast, "Uncovered Sets and Sophis-

ticated Voting Outcomes with Implications for Agenda Institutions," *American Journal of Political Science* 28 (1984): 49–74.
32 Richard McKelvey, *Covering Dominance, and Institution-Free Properties of Social Choice,* Social Science Working Paper No. 494 (Pasadena: California Institute of Technology, 1983).

13. MORALITY AND THE THEORY OF RATIONAL CHOICE

1 David Gauthier, *Morals by Agreement* (1986).
2 Russell Hardin, "Collective Action as an Agreeable *n*-Prisoner's Dilemma," *Behavioral Science* 16 (1971): 472–81, and *Collective Action* (1982).
3 John Rawls, *A Theory of Justice* (1972).
4 Gauthier, *Morals by Agreement,* pp. 174–7.
5 See James Buchanan, *The Limits of Liberty* (1975).
6 Gauthier, *Morals by Agreement,* p. 197.
7 Ibid. p. 178.
8 Ibid. p. 195.
9 Ibid.
10 Ibid. p. 225 (emphasis added).
11 Ibid. p. 178.
12 Ibid. p. 226.
13 Ibid. pp. 226–7.
14 Ibid. p. 226.